The Coming of Christianity
to Anglo-Saxon England

The Coming of Christianity to Anglo-Saxon England

Henry Mayr-Harting

*Fellow of St. Peter's
College, Oxford*

B. T. Batsford, London

To my colleagues and pupils (1960–68),
School of History, University of Liverpool

First published 1972
© Henry Mayr-Harting 1972

Reprinted 1977

Printed in Great Britain by
J. W. Arrowsmith Ltd., Bristol
for the publishers B. T. Batsford Ltd,
4 Fitzhardinge Street, London W1H 0AH

ISBN 0 7134 1030 2

Contents

List of Illustrations

ACKNOWLEDGEMENTS

I would like to thank the following for the help they have given with the illustrations: Mr P. C. D. Brown for help with the objects in the Ashmolean Museum, Oxford (Figs. 3 and 4); Dr T. H. Henry for Fig. 7; the Reverend Canon R. Lemmon, Rector of Hexham, and Mr Alan Wiper for Fig. 10; the Rector of Stonyhurst College for Fig. 12; Thames and Hudson Ltd., and Verlag Aurel Bongers for permission to use the illustration of the Saqqara wall-painting from Klaus Wessel's *Coptic Art*; Society of Antiquaries for Fig. 9; the Dean and Chapter of Durham Cathedral for Fig. 2; the British Museum for Fig. 13; Royal Commission on Historical Monuments for Fig. 6; Oifig nÓibreacha Poiblí for Fig. 8; the Mansell Collection for Fig. 5; the Walters Art Gallery, Baltimore, Maryland, USA for Fig. 17; the Institute of Archaeology, Oxford for Fig. 1, and Trinity College, Dublin for Fig. 15.

H. M-H.

ANGLO-SAXON ENGLAND IN THE EARLY CHRISTIAN PERIOD

STRATHCLYDE

R. Clyde

R. Forth

Abercorn

BERNICIA

R. Tweed

LINDISFARNE ISLAND

Melrose

Bamburgh

NORTHUMBRIA

RHEGED

R. Tyne

Hexham

R. Wear

Jarrow

Whithorn

Solway Firth

Wearmouth

R. Tees

Hartlepool

Gilling

DEIRA

Whitby

Lastingham

Ripon

R. Ribble

York

R. Ouse

N

R. Mersey

LINDSEY

R. Humber

Lincoln

The Wash

WELSH KINGDOMS

R. Dee

MERCIA

R. Trent

Lichfield

Leicester

Crowland

Elmham

EAST ANGLIA

R. Severn

Oundle

Brixworth

R. Ouse

Worcester

Dunwich

Sutton Hoo

R. Teifi

Hereford

R. Wye

St. David's

Wing

R. Blackwater

Llantwit Major

Dorchester

ESSEX

Barking

Bradwell

Malmesbury

London

Bristol Channel

Bradford-on-Avon

WESSEX

R. Thames

Rochester

Canterbury

KENT

Sherborne

Winchester

Selsey

SUSSEX

DUMNONIA

R. Tamar

Golant

0   50
Miles

~ARTHUR BANKS~

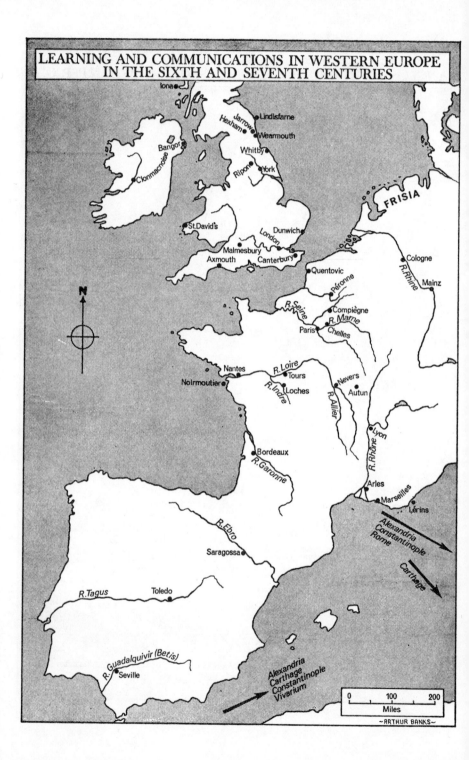

LEARNING AND COMMUNICATIONS IN WESTERN EUROPE IN THE SIXTH AND SEVENTH CENTURIES

Preface

It may be that a prospective reader of this book, glancing through its contents, will notice that the sub-section of one of the chapters is entitled 'Some Social Institutions'; and he may say to himself, especially if he reflects that some of the most fruitful recent advances in Anglo-Saxon studies have come in the field of social understanding, 'Here is the nub of the matter, and this poor innocent of an author affects to brush it off in one third of his last chapter!' Now it is certainly true that no book on the subject of this one can be written without constant awareness of and reference to early Anglo-Saxon society. Gone are the days when English Christianity in this period could be conceived as a kind of nodule of perpetual churchmanship, occupied by a mild Mr. Harding (Bede) or an aggressive and authoritarian Archdeacon Grantly (Wilfrid), and floating, as it were, in a social vacuum. The paradox of monasticism itself in these centuries—and the role of monks in the English conversion was a dominant one from the start—was that it fostered on the one hand an intense pre-occupation with the withdrawal from the world and personal salvation of the individual, and on the other hand a vivid social consciousness and desire to conquer or reconquer the whole of human society for Christ. It is impossible to cite any Christian scholar or ascetic in early Anglo-Saxon history who thought it necessary or even right to wash his hands of his fellow men in order to devote himself to God.

And yet the central theme of the book is not exactly how Christianity was absorbed into Anglo-Saxon society, although aspects of this question are considered. It is rather how Christianity itself was fashioned in this island, how churchmen prepared themselves, by prayer and study and travel, as well as by social awareness, to christianize their world, and how they conceived their task. If I were to say that in this way alone could a book with my title be written I should deny one of my main arguments in it—the possibility of achieving the same end by many different means. This is simply the book which I myself felt best able to write. But it is perhaps also that which requires the least distension of the sources as they survive. There is indeed much material for so distant a time which sheds light on society and its impregnation with Christianity—archaeological finds like the Sutton Hoo ship burial, the laws and charters of early kings, the great poem *Beowulf*, etc. There is, however, much more—the histories and saints' lives, the prayers, the scholarly writings, the surviving remains of church or monastic buildings, illuminated books, and ornaments—which sheds light primarily on those who spread the Gospel rather than on those to whom it was spread.

I have tried above all, therefore, to show the way in which traditions of great variety and richness came together to create early Anglo-Saxon Christianity. In the second part this has been attempted through a series of studies dealing with various aspects of the Christian achievement in the period from c.650 to c.750. In the first part it has taken the form chiefly of trying to give equal imaginative weight to the Roman and Irish missionaries, and of trying to put the element of conflict into some perspective. It is too easy to think of Iona or Lindisfarne as if they were the camps of primeval Protestants, staunchly opposing the already familiar characteristics of Roman Catholicism to be seen at Canterbury or Ripon. The path to historical understanding does not lie along these lines. I am aware, indeed, that the whole Roman-Irish dualism, which my treatment of the conversion of the Anglo-Saxon kingdoms seems to imply, is an oversimplification. When we consider figures like Birinus, Fursey, Agilbert and others, it would appear that the Anglo-Saxons were the object of much private missionary enterprise in the seventh century and that their conversion was by no means a matter only for those sent or summoned officially from Rome or Iona. And it is beyond question that the influence of Gaulish Christianity was stronger, at least in the conversion of Wessex and East Anglia. But our knowledge of all this is somewhat shadowy. However much can be said about Gaulish and other influences after about 650, in the first phase of Anglo-Saxon Christianity our attention is necessarily focused on the primary creative forces of the Roman and Irish traditions.

In the church of the seventh and eighth centuries the papacy exercised a certain degree of authority and influence which was on the increase. For this very reason we have to be on our guard against seeing Church History in this period as the inexorable falling on Western Europe of the dull-grey, blanket-cloud of Rome-centred uniformity. First of all, it is easy to confuse what Rome gave with what she received. There was much in the way of worship and devotion, monastic custom, and ideas, which was being developed outside Rome (some of it amongst the Anglo-Saxons) at this time, and which later came to be considered as characteristic of the Roman communion. Localism, in the best sense, was still alive and vigorous. And secondly, to the extent that there was a development towards Romanism, it is particularly important to discern the workings of the Church on principles of much greater diversity earlier, to see the way in which the coming together of many different traditions was a source of inspiration, and to understand how little any movement towards uniformity seemed inevitable.

It will be clear from the foregoing that I have not attempted to supe sede the general accounts of the English conversion contained in such books on the Anglo-Saxon Church as those by Professor Margaret Deanesly and the Revd. C. J. Godfrey. On the contrary, I have relied on the excellence of their accounts in order to recommend the reader to them and so to absolve myself from telling the story again in detail.

For the help which I have received from individual scholars, I have acknowledged my debt at the head of the notes to the relevant chapters or sections. To Professor C. N. L. Brooke I owe the proposal that I should write this book and much subsequent encouragement; Mr Samuel Carr has made several helpful comments. My wife has made several acute suggestions in the interest of logic and clarity.

Much of the work for this book was done in the School of History at Liverpool University. The setting was by no means an unsuitable one: almost under the shadow of the Roman Catholic cathedral which was being built, commanding a fine view of the magnificent and mysterious tower of the Anglican cathedral, and within sight of rows of back-to-back houses until they were demolished to make way for the University's Arts Library. What I benefitted from above all, however, was not the setting, but the School of History itself, and the ideally congenial and stimulating atmosphere created both by colleagues and pupils. More recently I have had the advantage of discussion with pupils in St. Peter's College, and with the members of history societies in some other Oxford colleges, where I have talked on aspects of this book.

I am indebted to the skill and patience of several typists, particularly Miss Lily Dear and Miss Janet Robson.

The proofs have been read by Mr. Patrick Wormald, through whose *industria*, to use a favourite word of Bede, the whole level of the book has been raised. Nobody could have been more acute in saving me from mistakes and misprints, more generous with his learning in suggesting improvements, and more stimulating and constructive in discussing the alterations needed. Had I shown him the book at an earlier stage much more could have been corrected and improved, and he is certainly not responsible for any errors which remain.

PREFACE TO THE SECOND EDITION

I have taken the opportunity of a new edition to correct some errors and to remedy some infelicities, several of them kindly pointed out by friends and reviewers, and also to effect some small improvements, as they seemed to me. It would have been desirable to make some more extensive revisions had they not fallen outside the scope of what was at present possible. On this page in the first edition a list was given of scholarly works published in 1970 or 1971, too late for me to use fully or at all. I should have benefited in a general way from all these works, and from others which have been published since, but one at least would still cause me to rewrite specific passages, namely James Campbell, 'The first century of Christianity in England,' *Ampleforth Journal* 76 (1971), pp. 12–29. I have received much stimulus and illumination in recent years from the writings and conversation of Dr Kathleen Hughes whose early death is a heavy loss to friends and scholars.

I have to thank Mr Paul J. Sorrell of Corpus Christi College, Cambridge, for finding the source of Aldhelm's fig-eating hermit (see p. 208) in Jerome's *Vita Pauli* c. 6 (P.L. 23, col. 21). As he says, this does not undermine the arguments based on *bubalus* and *tragelaphus*, but it does render some of my text and note 55 on pp. 312–13 obsolete.

Part I

KINGS AND CONVERSION, 597-664

1 The Pagan Kingdoms

THE PAGAN KINGS

The Romans might write poetry about the sea, but they did not themselves much care to be on it;[1] that is why the Saxons, entirely without fear in their boats, were a source of peculiar terror and wonderment to them. Every oarsman in the Saxon crew, said a fifth-century Gallo-Roman aristocrat, looked like a pirate captain. They were masters of the surprise attack, but if anticipated they slipped away; shipwreck was to them a form of training rather than a source of terror; they were entirely at home amidst the hazards of rough seas and jagged coasts, gladly enduring such things in the hope of taking their prey unawares.[2] Sidonius Apollinaris wrote these impressions in the heyday of the Saxons' raids on the shores of Britain and Gaul from their North European homeland.

Saxons were settled in this island by the Romans at least as early as the fourth century. They were confederate soldiers, brought in to cope with the growing threat of the Picts from the North or the sea-raids of their fellow barbarians from the Continent who were on the move in search of lands. When not at war these confederates were farmers, and so they were settled in lands just outside the fortified towns of eastern Britain such as York or Caistor in Norfolk, or just off the Roman roads which linked the towns. Even after the withdrawal of Roman forces and the official Roman political presence in 410, Romano-British tribal rulers kept going with this help for nearly half a century. But the help got out of hand, the Saxons revolted, and the second half of the fifth century saw a period of uncontrollable settlement by the confederates and their continental brethren, which penetrated to the heart of the island and which finally wiped out the cultural and political life of Roman Britain.[3]

The movements of these peoples can be traced with the help of archaeology, and above all by the excavation of their cemeteries. If they were cremated there are their pottery cremation urns; if they were inhumed (for we are here in the long period of transition from cremation to inhumation amongst the Germanic peoples) there are personal objects buried with them for use during the life of the grave in which they still believed. Men might be buried with their weapons, women (or even men) with their brooches. Both cremation pots and brooches can be dated to within a half-century by their stylistic features. In the process of settlement which we can study by these and other means one point stands out above all others—the importance of rivers in determining the pattern and in providing the essential means of communication which knit settlements together. The Thames, the Trent, the Humber, the rivers of East Anglia, it is with these that some of the great areas of primary Saxon habitation are associated. That is not surprising if one considers that many of these people, whether they were ultimately continental Saxons or Angles or Jutes, had come immediately from the seaboard of Frisia, that boats were their normal means of movement, and that in an island consisting mainly of forests and swamps the Roman roads and the rivers were the only effective lines of communication.

If archaeology shows that the fifth century was a period of uncontrolled settlement by masses of Anglo-Saxons, who must have been mainly peasant farmers, the surviving literary traditions show that this was also a booming period for warrior adventurers. We learn, for instance, that Hengest and Horsa were invited to the aid of the British ruler, Vortigern, and after they had come to Kent in three ships in 449, they turned on their hosts and defeated them in battle. This Hengest is very likely the Jute who figures in an ancient Germanic saga which relates how he fought (as a mercenary) under a Dane called Hnaef; how Hnaef had been killed in battle against the Frisian, Finn; how Hengest had sworn to live at peace with Finn; and how, in Hengest's ensuing personal conflict between keeping his oath and desiring to avenge his dead lord, vengeance had in the end carried the day. If this identification is correct, Kent had in Hengest one of the great mercenaries and exiles of the Migration Period.[4] We also learn that Aelle arrived on the coast of Sussex with three ships in 477;

and that in 495 Cerdic and Cynric sailed up Southampton Water with five ships, landed, and defeated the British.

The ships in these cases would have been something like that of the fourth century, found in a bog at Nydam in South Jutland; open ships carrying perhaps 30 to 40 men. Thus we are dealing with nothing like mass and concerted invasions, but with quite small and unconnected parties of adventurers, with warrior leaders surrounded by their companions or *comitatus*. There must have been many bands like theirs in these unsettled times, holding their own amongst hostile British rulers, but the names of Hengest and Cerdic and a few others were preserved in literature because it was to these remote and legendary figures that the rulers of the later Anglo-Saxon kingdoms traced their dynasties. Nothing would have marked them out in the fifth century from others like them. The memory of these others, however, survives not at all, or at best in ancient place-names like Hastings (Hastingas = the followers of Hasta).

Around 500 the British rulers of the West of the island to some extent recovered their grasp of the situation, and not only held back the westward advance of the Anglo-Saxons, but apparently even regained something of their political control over Saxon-settled areas. This situation lasted until between 550 and 570, when once again the Saxon chieftains began to make headway. After that British political power was pushed gradually but inexorably westwards, although there is no question of a whole-sale wiping out or emigration of the local British (or, in other words, Celtic) population. And around 600 the historical kingdoms of the Anglo-Saxons, as we see them in Bede's *Ecclesiastical History of the English People* (the chief literary source for early Anglo-Saxon history, completed in 731), began to take shape.

In the South were the kingdoms of Kent, the South Saxons (Sussex), the East Saxons (Essex), the West Saxons (Wessex); in the Midlands were the kingdoms of Mercia, the Middle Angles (roughly Leicestershire), the East Angles, Lindsey (roughly Lincolnshire), and to the West the kingdom of the people called the Hwicce (roughly Worcestershire and Gloucestershire); to the North of the Humber was Northumbria. In 600 Northumbrian power was confined to the east of the Pennines and the Cheviots, and between the Humber and the Tweed. In the course of the following century it was to be pushed westwards and northwards, so that the British kingdom of the Gododdin around the Forth fell to the Angles and left that river as the effective boundary between the Angles and the Picts in the east, while the British kingdom of Rheged in present-day North-West England and South-West Scotland also fell to them, leaving the British kingdom of Strathclyde South of the Clyde in the West. There were really two Northumbrian kingdoms originating from distinct settlements and with distinct dynasties—Bernicia in the north and Deira in the south, with a kind of ill-defined borderland consisting roughly of the modern County Durham between them. Sometimes the two were ruled together by a representative of one line or the other, sometimes they were held separately. The picture is still more complicated and fragmented. There were smaller kingdoms like that of the Isle of Wight, but the very existence of the smaller kingdoms was itself a matter of fluctuation. In course of time all the kingdoms tended to become submerged in Northumbria, Mercia and Wessex, while ultimately the Wessex dynasty became the leaders of Englishmen in the time of Alfred.

The area of many of these early kingdoms was defined by strongly marked geographical features. Between Kent and Sussex stretched the densely forested Weald. The Hwicce were divided on their East side from the West Saxons by a ridge of forest land, the memory of which is still preserved in three North-West Oxfordshire place-names—Ascot, Milton and Shipton, all of them 'under-Wychwood.' The estuary of the Humber, originally a highway into the island uniting the settlements on both sides of it, became with its marshes a political boundary of great significance.[5] And between the Middle Angles and the East Angles stretched the swamps described by the biographer of the hermit, Guthlac, in the eighth century:[6]

> There is in the midland district of Britain a most dismal fen of immense size, which begins at the banks of the river Granta not far from the camp which is called Cambridge and stretches from the south as far north as the sea (i.e. the Wash). It is a very long tract, now consisting of marshes, now of bogs, sometimes of black waters overhung by fog, sometimes studded with wooded islands and traversed by the windings of tortuous streams.

It was through these trackless bogs that a local man call Tatwine took Guthlac to the island of Crowland in a small boat.

Geographical limitation of a kingdom, however, is not the same thing as a specific boundary. These early kingdoms should not be thought of as if they were territorial states with boundaries precisely drawn. They were more in the nature of confederations of tribes, confederations tending to be located in certain areas, which often bore a relation to the tribal divisions of Celtic Britain. After all, Anglo-Saxon peoples were often densely settled in an area before those who were ultimately to be their rulers arrived on the scene. There were Anglo-Saxon settlers in the Thames Valley in the fifth century, but not until the 570's did Ceawlin, the grandson of Cerdic, sweep these people into the orbit of his power. The *Wuffingas* of East Anglia were possibly Geats who came from Sweden and established themselves in South-East Suffolk around the estuary of the river Deben only in the mid-sixth century. It was perhaps they who brought over the Swedish weapons which were to be buried as ancient heirlooms in the Sutton Hoo ship burial in the following century.[7] From this region they established their supremacy over much earlier settlements in the rest of East Anglia. Doubtless this kind of thing had happened on a smaller scale previously; that is why we may say that the kingdoms were confederations of smaller peoples who had already established tribal identities of their own, born in part through kinship, in part through war. It was to happen on a larger scale with the *Bretwaldas*, to whom we shall come shortly.

What was the essential nature of the kingship held by these early kings? In a famous sentence of his *Germania* (98 A.D.) Tacitus says that kings were chosen for their noble blood, war-leaders for their prowess (*reges ex nobilitate, duces ex virtute sumunt.*) That was not to say, of course, that a king could not also be a *dux* or war-leader. *Nobilitas*, which meant chiefly tracing one's ancestry back to the god Woden, was not incompatible with *virtus*, which meant having a strong right arm, a good sword, and a body of young companions (a *comitatus*) who would think it a disgrace to survive their leader on the battlefield. Woden himself was a war god. Now the Hengests and Cerdics of the Migration Period were pre-eminently war-leaders, *duces ex virtute*. But having established their power in this island in circumstances which left memories very faded about who was and who was not descended from Woden, it was not long before appropriate genealogies were constructed for them. Only from the eighth century do genealogies survive in writing which trace the dynasties of the English kings back to their founders, and further back through lists of mythical but picturesque names to Woden's various sons. Yet at the time that these genealogies were finally written down it is clear, not least from the archaic forms of personal names which they contained, that their tradition was already an ancient one.[8]

As we can see it now, therefore, the pagan kingship of the Anglo-Saxons was not something based purely or even mainly on magic and ceremonial, but it combined *nobilitas*, the mystique of descent from the gods, with *virtus*, success in war.

Among the kingdoms there was always a tendency for certain kings to gain a position of ascendancy and to establish varying degrees of power or influence over other kings and kingdoms. When Bede recorded the death of King Ethelbert of Kent, who had received Augustine and his monks from Rome, he said that Ethelbert was the third of the English kings who had the superiority of all the southern provinces which are divided from the northern by the river Humber, and he then listed the seven kings whom he considered to have held a similar position— Aelle of Sussex, Ceawlin of Wessex, Ethelbert of Kent, Redwald of East Anglia, Edwin, Oswald and Oswy of Northumbria.[9] This list perhaps flattered the power of some kings and ignored that of others, but for our purposes the important point is the fact of such an ascendancy. Much later, in Alfred's reign, the Anglo-Saxon Chronicle copied this list from Bede and called the seven kings *bretwaldas*, or rulers of Britain.[10]

Behind the power of a *bretwalda* was the memory of the political unity of Britain under the Romans.[11] When King Edwin of Northumbria, early in the seventh century, wanted to express the power of his rule, it was to a type of Roman legionary banner called *tufa* that he resorted, and this was carried about before him. The power itself was based primarily on personality and supremacy in war.

Supremacy in war meant, amongst other things, being able to attract the best warriors. This was partly a question of the personal reputation of kings for military prowess. But there were other considerations as well. One of these was the availability of luxury goods by which a warrior aristocracy might be distinguished from lesser men. It is no accident that two of the earliest *bretwaldaships*, those of Ethelbert of Kent, and Redwald of the East Angles (late sixth and early seventh century), are

associated with kingdoms whose position made contacts with the
Continent easy. Archaeology teaches us much about these *bret-
waldships*. The sophisticated products of the Frankish glass factory
at Faversham and the superb gold and garnet jewellery of Kent
around 600 are not irrelevant to Ethelbert's dominion[12] (Fig. 4); nor
are the Merovingian gold coins and the Byzantine silver in the
Sutton Hoo ship burial irrelevant to that of Redwald.[13]

To attract warriors a *bretwalda* had to show generosity, not
perhaps on the same idealized scale, but in the same way as King
Hrothgar, in the poem, had shown it to Beowulf, who had come
with his companions to rid Hrothgar's kingdom of the monster,
Grendel:[14]

> Hrothgar gave Beowulf an embroidered banner of gold, a helmet
> and a corselet, in reward for his victory. Multitudes saw the
> jewel-studded sword of honour presented to the hero. Beowulf
> drank a ceremonial cup in the banqueting-hall, for the gifts
> were so costly that in accepting them he need feel no shame
> before the fighting-men. Few men have presented four such
> treasures of gold over a banqueting-table with so much good
> will. Round the top of the helmet a projecting rim bound with
> wire guarded the head in such a way that no sword, however
> sharp and tough, might cripple the wearer when he joined battle
> with his enemies. In addition, Hrothgar ordered eight horses
> with golden bridles to be led under the courtyard and inside the
> hall. Upon one was a saddle cunningly inlaid with jewels.
> This was the king's war saddle, which Hrothgar used when he
> went out to battle—and that famous leader never failed to be
> in the van where the dead fell thickest. The king of the Danes
> now delivered the horses and weapons into the keeping of
> Beowulf, and told him to use them well. Thus the renowned
> prince, guardian of the soldier's treasure, repaid Beowulf for
> his combat with Grendel in horses and gold, with a generosity
> of which every honest man must approve.

In this passage, in the bright gold and shining jewels and the
mention of Hrothgar's personal bravery, we catch something of
the atmosphere of the Heroic Age in which the *bretwaldas* fought
for and won their power and wealth.

The prospect of plunder was another great attraction to
warriors. If a victorious army got no further than the battlefield
its plunder might yet be considerable—the jewelled swords, the

belts with golden buckles and the other military accoutrements of its opponents, the kind of things we know they would have had from lesser burials than that of Sutton Hoo. To the monastic biographer of the Mercian prince Guthlac it was a mark of special virtue that Guthlac always restored a third part of the plunder which he took; to his companions it was no doubt a rather odd eccentricity in an otherwise manly leader.[15] If a king wanted to reward his companions in war, who were his aristocracy, he could give them lands, but that would often be something for quite late in their careers. And as land could not normally be held securely in the family and left by will from one generation to the next until the eighth century, there was no presumption that a young man would succeed to his father's lands. He would as likely become one of a king's retainers, would live and feast in the king's hall and would sleep there when 'the benches were cleared away and pillows and bedding were spread upon the floor'.[16] It is clear that in the seventh century there must have been many such young nobles who had no lands. If the king wanted to keep the support of these men in particular and attract more of their kind to himself, the prospect of plunder through war was essential. Sigbert, king of the East Saxons, was murdered by his kinsmen, and when they were asked why they had done it, they had no better answer than that they were incensed 'because he was too apt to spare his enemies and forgive the wrongs they had done him'.[17] Barbarian society imposed a positive duty of revenge on all men; but in addition the thing a king could not afford to do, if he wanted to fulfil his warriors' expectations of rewards, was to forgive his enemies; it was a fatal virtue.

Over and above these things the success of a *bretwaldaship* depended, in the long term, on the continuous availability of estates with which a king could reward his retainers. Control of this kind was itself a reflection of the successful acquisition and maintenance of power, but it was also something more. This is not the place to enter at length into the institutions of early English land tenure, but, briefly, it can be dimly perceived that the alienation of estates from royal control, and the granting of exemptions from royal dues and services especially to monasteries, were causes of serious weakness to the Northumbrian kingdom probably from the late seventh century. When dominion passed to the Mercian kings in the eighth century there are signs that the learning of this lesson was one of their sources of strength.[18]

The early *bretwaldas* are misty figures, but occasionally they loom up in the pages of Bede, and we catch momentary glimpses of their political and military power over other kingdoms. Let us look for a moment at Redwald, king of the East Angles, in action. Redwald was the fourth king in Bede's list, the man who laid the foundations of East Anglian power, and perhaps the man whose memorial was the Sutton Hoo ship burial. Here Redwald is seen at war; but more than that, he is seen actually establishing in position another king who was himself later to rank as a *bretwalda*, namely Edwin of Northumbria. The action occurs around 616. Edwin belonged to the royal line of Deira, the southern of the Northumbrian kingdoms, and had been driven into exile by Ethelfrith of Bernicia. He had wandered about until he came finally to Redwald, who promised him help. Ethelfrith then bribed Redwald to kill Edwin or surrender him: [19]

But when Redwald had privately acquainted the queen with his intention, she dissuaded him from it, declaring it was unworthy of so great a king to sell his good friend in such distress for gold, and to sacrifice his honour, which is more valuable than all other ornaments, for the lucre of money. In short the king did as he was advised, and not only refused to deliver up the banished man to his enemy's messengers, but assisted him to recover his kingdom. For as soon as the ambassadors were returned home, he raised a mighty army to make war on Ethelfrith; who meeting him with much inferior forces (for Redwald had not given him time to gather all his power), was slain on the borders of the kingdom of the Mercians, on the east bank of the river that is called Idle.... Thus Edwin, pursuant to the oracle he had received, not only escaped the danger from the king, his enemy, but, by his death, succeeded him in the glory of the kingdom.

Redwald's queen was clearly a forceful woman, one of the many in seventh-century England.

The problem of the conversion of the Anglo-Saxon peoples to Christianity is in the first instance the problem of converting the kings and their immediate followers, and the position of the *bretwaldas* is here of the greatest importance. That is why we have dwelt on it for a few pages. Before coming to the conversion of the Anglo-Saxons, however, we must consider the paganism which

Christianity sought to replace; the surviving British population, some of whom must have been Christians; Bede's *Ecclesiastical History* as our main source of knowledge for the conversion; and Pope Gregory the Great, who sent from Rome the first missionaries to the Anglo-Saxons.

PAGANISM

In his great work on chronology, the *De Temporum Ratione* (725) Bede has a passage in which he explains the Anglo-Saxon names for the months of the year.[20] Not all of them had a specifically pagan significance. May, for instance, was called *Thrilmilchi* because in that month cows were milked three times a day, and August was called *Weodmonath* because that was the month in which weeds were most abundant. But the names of four, at least, signified pagan festivals. March (*Hredmonath*), and April (*Eosturmonath*) were the months in which the festivals of the goddesses Hretha and Eostre were celebrated. February (*Solmonath*) was the month of cakes, which were offered to the gods; and November (*Blodmonath*) was the month in which cattle were sacrificed.

Suspect though some of Bede's etymology may be, and allusive as some of the information is, it is nonetheless likely that this passage is a first-class record of the festal aspects of English paganism of which it treats; it is possible that Bede's father and almost certain that his grandfather could remember the heyday of Northumbrian heathenism. And yet Bede did not feel that all was well with what he had written. He did not entirely like the look of it, and was moved to add, 'Thanks be to you, O Jesus, who have turned us away from these vanities and granted that we should offer sacrifices of praise to yourself.' Here lies the clue to our greatest difficulty in trying to penetrate into the heart of Anglo-Saxon paganism. The Christian writers to whom we are entirely indebted for our knowledge of Anglo-Saxon England did not think it seemly to preserve a systematic record of the pagan religion; no useful or edifying purpose could be achieved by the tale of 'these vanities'. Such knowledge of the subject as we have, therefore, must be pieced together from fragmentary and varied sources.

Bede himself tells us hardly anything about the subject in his *Ecclesiastical History*. One of the few informative passages is the account of Coifi, the chief pagan priest of Northumbria under

Edwin, desecrating the temple at Goodmanham near York after he had decided to become a Christian.[21] This incident followed immediately the discussion by Edwin and his counsellors about whether they should accept Christianity, in which Coifi's contribution (according to Bede) was to observe that in spite of his having always served the old gods faithfully they had done him little good. First, Coifi mounted a stallion and took a spear, although it was not lawful for priests to bear arms or to ride anything but a mare. Next he rode to the temple and (to the astonishment of the bystanders who thought he had gone mad) hurled his spear into it. Finally he ordered his colleagues to set it alight, with all its enclosures. From this narrative, therefore, we can conclude that there was an established professional priesthood, governed by its own rules of conduct, and that there were temples of wood (as most buildings in the Northumbria of that time would have been), which were substantial enough centres of worship to have their own enclosures.

Fortunately, we do not have to rely only on the crumbs from the literary table for our knowledge of Old English paganism. In the first place, we have the archaeological finds of Anglo-Saxon cemeteries, which shed light on burial customs during the fifth and sixth centuries.[22] This was a period when either cremation or inhumation might be practised, for the trend towards inhumation was going on all over the Germanic world in these centuries, and inhumation in itself implied, of course, no acceptance of Christianity. Within pagan society the choice of rite was probably a matter for the kindred group as a whole. Between those who cremated and those who inhumed there was a general feeling of tolerance, as is evidenced by the use of the same cemeteries for both kinds of burial, and by the fact that in some cases the same potters made both cremation urns and small accessory vessels for inhumation. After all, there was a more fundamental issue, over which the devotees of both rites were in agreement, namely belief in an after-life of the grave. True there was some divergence of emphasis about what equipment men, that is males, might need in this after-life; thus inhumed bodies tend to be provided with spears, shields and even swords, while the kindred of the cremated perhaps allowed their minds to dwell more on toilet requisites like combs or tweezers. But that *something* would be needed nobody had any doubt.

The distribution of cremation cemeteries in the upper Thames

Valley has been studied by Joan Kirk, who noted that these (for
instance the cemeteries at Abingdon or Brighthampton) were all
practically at the water's side. She made the arresting suggestion
that cremation, a magnificent but skilled and dying art, could
only be performed at certain centres near cemeteries, and that if
the river were not actually in some way connected with the rite,
at least these centres would naturally be placed on the river so that
bodies might be easily transported to them by water.[23]

By far the most important single source for paganism is the
place-names of the early Anglo-Saxons.[24] To this day some 40 or
50 place-names with indubitably pagan associations survive,
mainly in the central Midlands and the south or south-east of
England. None of them can be later than the mid-seventh century
at the latest, and considering the efforts which Christian churchmen might have been expected to make to eliminate all traces of
paganism, they represent a remarkable tally. Some are simply
names for the sites of heathen worship. Harrow in Middlesex is
derived from the Anglo-Saxon word *hearh*, meaning a sanctuary,
or at this time a hill-sanctuary. This dominating hill was indeed a
superb site for a place of worship. But something less would do in
an emergency, as on the occasion when St. Wilfrid was ship-
wrecked on the coast of Sussex, and a South Saxon priest came
down to the beach and stood on a mound in an attempt to
paralyse the saint with incantations.[25] The element *leah* in a
place-name means a grove, or a sacred place in the woods, and the
element *weoh* means an idol or shrine or temple. The two are
found together in Weoley (Worcestershire), shrine in the grove.
There is a particularly interesting knot of pagan place-names in the
south-west of Surrey, which includes Peper Harow (Pippa's
hearh), Thursley (grove of the god Thunor or Thor), Willey (the
same as Weoley) and Tuesley (grove of the god Tiw). It may be
that the survival of this little group of names depended on the
fact that Surrey, wavering between the hegemony of Wessex
and of Kent during the seventh century, was a region of political
instability not early suited to the activities of missionaries. But it
would be unwise to push this argument too far in view of the
survival of heathen place-names well within the orbit of missionary
centres.

Certain place-names suggest that some places of pagan worship
may have been owned by individuals. In Peper Harow or Pippa's
hearh, for instance, Pippa is an archaic personal name. Patchway,

north-east of Brighton in Stanmer Park, means the *weoh* of a man named Paeccel, and there is a now unidentifiable Surrey site called *Cusan weoh*. Other ancient names suggest sanctuaries of forgotten tribes. The original name of Harrow in Middlesex was *Gumeninga hearh*, the sanctuary of the otherwise unrecorded Gumeningas; while a late seventh-century grant of King Caedwalla of Wessex refers to a site near Farnham in Surrey, which was called *Besinga hearh*, the sanctuary of the Besingas. In these old tribal names we catch a glimpse of the tribes which were later swept into the confederations which formed the early Anglo-Saxon kingdoms.

The place-name elements *weoh* and *hearh*—and it is practically certain that these refer uniformly to Anglo-Saxon rather than to Romano-British temples—are never combined with the name of an individual god. This is probably because such sanctuaries would have contained images or altars of a number of gods. They would have been like that pantheon of Redwald, king of the East Angles, about which Bede speaks; this was a temple with altars to various gods in which Redwald ecumenically added one to Christ. But the names of individual gods do occur quite often in place-names, in particular three gods who have given their names to days of our week, Tiw, Woden and Thor. Thor occurs mainly in connection with groves, and Woden, by this time the chief of the Germanic gods and the one from whom kings most often traced their descent, tends to be associated with mounds and earthworks, as in Wednesbury (Staffordshire) or Wandsdike in Wessex.

The gods of the ancient Germans occupied a celestial region called Asgard.[26] Woden was the god of war, the promoter of strife. It was he who had caused nine thralls, peacefully mowing in a meadow, to fight over a fine whetstone which he carried in his belt, and to slash each other's heads with their scythes. One of his halls was Valhalla, in which he received brave warriors who had fallen in battle on earth, feasted them nightly, and would lead them out, a picked band, in the last fight of the gods against the giants. It was the great work of the gods to fight the giants, the forces of evil. Woden was also the god of poetry, for in the disguise of one of the thralls whose death he had caused, he slept three nights with the daughter of the giant Suttung, and he was able to make off with the 'precious mead' of poetry which the giant guarded. The warfare against the giants which Woden pursued with resource and trickery, Thor pursued by more direct and frontal means. He simply threw his hammer at their skulls. It may be that Thor's symbol, the swastika, originated as a device of hammers. Thor was also the god of thunder. There were two bases for this, the one being that the hammer acted as thunderbolt, and the other that the god rode through the sky in a chariot drawn by two goats, and the rumble of the chariot as it passed, the *thunorrad*, created the noise of thunder. In fact he was a sky god of whom it was said, 'he rules the air which controls the thunder and lightning, the winds and the showers, the fair weather and the fruits of the earth.' It followed naturally then that he was a fertility god, whence, perhaps, his special connection with groves. Tiw stands out as a less clear figure than either of these other two, but his worship as a war god was certainly of great age amongst the Germanic peoples.

Just as all the Germanic peoples had issued ultimately from Scandinavia, so they shared a common stock of mythology with the Scandinavians. In its written form this mythology comes to us from the tenth to the thirteenth centuries, but its existence was much older than that, and there is every reason to believe that it was already highly developed amongst the Anglo-Saxons in their pagan days. The action of the pagan priest Coifi in flinging his spear into the temple, for instance, is a small but highly significant pointer to the cult of Woden and the knowledge of his mythology at that time. The rite of flinging a spear over the enemy and invoking the name of Woden (or Odinn) is one well attested in Scandinavian saga, and it was said that Woden himself had first caused war amongst the gods by flinging his spear into their host.[27] Again, a seventh-century Kentish buckle of gilt-bronze, found recently at Finglesham, bears a figure of a warrior, naked but for his helmet and belt, which may well be a cult symbol of Woden. The beaked crests of this warrior's helmet represent eagles and in each hand he holds a spear. Eagle and spear were both Woden-symbols; while Woden's special champions, trusting to the god's protection, sometimes disdained armour and fought naked (Fig. 1).

As god of poetry Woden was also lord of the runes, the magic letters by which evil could be repelled. In one Old English charm, the Nine Herbs Charm, we see an example of Woden's power in this field. Having recited the power of nine herbs in turn, the charm continues:[28]

These nine have power against nine poisons.
A worm came crawling, it killed nothing.
For Woden took nine glory-twigs,
He smote then the adder that it flew apart into nine parts.

Against the attacks of the Evil One, Woden himself comes to the assistance of the herbs. His nine glory-twigs are twigs each with the rune of the initial letter of a plant on it.

The evidence of mythological knowledge in the case of Thor's cult is much clearer than it is in Woden's. Many cremation pots of the early Anglo-Saxons have the swastika sign marked on them, and in some the swastikas seems to be confronted with serpents or dragons in a decorative design. This is a clear reference to the greatest of all Thor's struggles, that with the World Serpent which lay coiled round the earth.[29] Two things made Thor pre-eminently a god of funerals and of the dead. One was his bringing to life of his goats and his hallowing them with the hammer after he had sacrificed them; the other was that his association with fire through thunder and lightning marked him out as the special protector of a cremating people.

The ancient name of an Essex half-hundred, Thurstable (Thunres Stapol, or Thor's pillar) takes us deep into another side of Thor's cult.[30] Thor had a particularly close association with oak trees, very likely because the sight of an oak struck by lightning was such a dramatic one. Thus he became the god of men's homes, protecting them because their pillars, particularly the 'high pillars' which stood on either side of the seat of honour in aristocratic halls, were made of his oaks. There are many stories in Icelandic and Scandinavian sagas of men taking their high pillars with them when they left their homes, so that they would be guided by the god to where they should live in the future. Thor's pillar in Essex was thus a kind of 'high pillar', probably believed to support the sky, and so also the world.

It cannot be ruled out that the paganism of the ancient Britons shows through some of the Anglo-Saxon survivals. There had been a period around the first century A.D. when contact between the Germanic and Celtic peoples on the Continent was close; and when we see place-names like Ravenshead, Boarshead and Heronshead, which look like cult centres marked by the symbol of a sacred animal, or even by its sacrifice, we are dealing with animals as sacred amongst the Celtic Britons as amongst the

Anglo-Saxons.[31] Furthermore, it cannot be assumed, as we shall see, that the British countryside was totally christianized in the fifth century. A particular instance of the general problem is Tysoe in South Warwickshire. This is Tiw's *hoh* or hill-spur, and it is known that on the hill above the settlement was an ancient red horse, red by reason of the earth's colour, the outline of which was scoured annually at least into the seventeenth century. Now in the Celtic world horses were associated with the cults of war-gods and red was a colour associated with death. Red horses, there-fore, were an omen of disaster.[32] It is possible to suppose that here we have a British cult-symbol, a protection against enemies approaching across the South Warwickshire plain, and that the Anglo-Saxons, always sensitive to the earlier religious associations of sites, installed in this place the worship of their own war god Tiw.

Behind the official worship of paganism was a whole world of superstitious lore, mainly of a medical character, which came to be embodied in the eleventh-century manuscripts of leech knowledge, charms, and wort cunning. It lasted because it was thought by educated men to be useful and detachable from its pagan religious context. By the time it was written down this material was heavily overlaid with medical and plant knowledge derived from the late classical writers on medicine, possibly with some recent elements of Scandinavian paganism, and certainly with a great deal of Christian theology and prayer, without which it would have been unacceptable in the monastic libraries which housed the manuscripts.[33] In fact there is still much scope for study of the various layers of the superstructure. But what is quite clear is that amidst all the elaborate information about the magical and medicinal properties of lichens and herbs, the rituals of mixing and spitting, the formulae of curses and incantations—much of which is just the stuff of superstition in many societies—amidst all this it is possible to penetrate to an ancient core of material directly related to Anglo-Saxon paganism. It is, for instance, not to be wondered at that a month was named from the offerings of cakes to the gods when we read that the remedy for piles was the roots of greater burdock made into a hot cake.[34] Elsewhere we may read what had to be done if a horse was 'elf-shot'. The Teutons and Celts shared a belief that disease was caused by elves who fired shafts at the sufferer. In Christian times human beings came to be attacked by devils; thus for a man 'possessed by a devil' there was prescribed a mixture of holy water and ale into which bishopwort, water agrimony and other plants had been stirred.[35] But elves were allowed to be continuing their activities in the animal kingdom. The following, then, were the instructions for an elf-shot horse:[36] 'Take that knife of which the handle is made from the fallow horn of an ox, and let there be three brass nails on it ... and write these words on the horn of the knife, *Benedicite omnia opera domini dominum*.' The words of the psalm but thinly disguise the fact that this was once a cure which depended on magic runes; it was Woden's sphere.

We know enough of Anglo-Saxon paganism to see that while it was rich and highly developed in content and mythology, it was basically simple in purpose. Its purpose, of course, was to make supernatural provision for the whole gamut of social needs. For the warrior aristocracy there was Woden to preside over their activities on the battlefield and in the hall. In the hall they would listen to heroic sagas recited in the poetry which he had won from the giants; and after their death he would be another lord to them, entertaining them in another hall. For all men there was Thor to hold up their houses, to clear their forests, to provide freedom from storm and fair winds for their sea journeys, and to watch over them when they were laid to rest. For the high points of the agricultural year there was a host of lesser deities who welcomed their sacrifices. While the whole company of gods was continuously engaged in combating for them the forces of evil represented by so many giants and monsters. It would be the crudest mistake, then, to imagine that the pagan religion was no more than a picturesque adornment of life, to be cast off at the first moment that the Anglo-Saxons were presented with a *real* religion in Christianity.

The question is sometimes put why the Anglo-Saxons were converted to Christianity so quickly. The truth is that they were not converted at all quickly. In spite of there being good political and cultural reasons for the conversion of kings to Christianity, in spite of an extraordinary galaxy of able and saintly missionaries, it took nearly 90 years to convert just the kings and the greater part of their aristocracy, not to speak of the country-side which was a question of centuries. In the course of that near-90 years hardly a court was converted which did not suffer at least one subsequent relapse into paganism before being recon-verted. The old religious instincts died hard. Years after the conversion of the Mercian court to Christianity, a Mercian earl, confronted with the strange phenomenon of a prisoner's chains falling off him, could ask if he had *litteras solutorias* on his person.[37] He believed him to have some object in his pocket carved with magic runes. It was constantly incumbent on the Christian saints to show that they were in all essentials the equals of Thor's priests. The wooden post against which Aidan was leaning when he died came to be venerated for its miraculous properties.[38] Aidan's pillar succeeded Thor's. And Cuthbert was called on to cope with real and illusory fires, which broke out in the villages where he was preaching and which dogged his progress.[39] The threat of Thor's displeasure lay close to the surface of his listeners' consciousness. All in all, the struggle between Christianity and paganism was not like an evening's game of *Kriegspiel;* it was the genuine engagement of two life principles.

BRITONS

It is natural to ask whether the Christianity of Roman Britain survived to be in any way an advantageous background to the missionaries working later among the Anglo-Saxons.

The features of Roman life which disappeared, with some exceptions, from Britain in the fifth century were the towns and the villas.[40] The towns had already been suffering from an exodus of population in the fourth century and in some cases from the disregard of their citizens for defensive measures in the early fifth, before the Saxons, who were farmers rather than city dwellers, dealt them the *coup de grâce*. During the first half of the fifth century the initiative in government and defence had been less in the hands of the towns than in those of British tribal kings like Vortigern. There is, of course, evidence for the occupation of some Roman towns in the period of Saxon settlements, doubtless by Saxon squatters; Bede uses the word *civitas* to describe such places. But the essentials of Roman town life and institutions were gone. Latin would have vanished with them, for that was the language of law and government, of army and large-scale trade. The Romanized Britons of the rural villas, who had probably been bilingual in Latin and British (i.e. a Celtic language), would very likely have reverted to speaking British in the first half of the fifth century until they, too, were submerged by the barbarian tide;[41] and there is every indication that they were submerged, notwithstanding occasional evidence of continuity from a Roman villa to a Saxon estate.[42]

The passing of Roman town and villa did not mean the wholesale extermination or mass emigration of the native British population. No historian now believes that anything of the sort can have happened. And here we are speaking not of those Britons in the British kingdoms remaining in the north and west of the island, with whom the Anglo-Saxons were continuously rubbing shoulders as their own kingdoms expanded, but of the Britons left within areas of Anglo-Saxon political power. In some parts of the country there is reason to believe that Britons continued to form a particularly high proportion of the population; in Kent, for instance, this is suggested by the survival of Romano-British administrative centres, craftsmen and place-names, and in early Northumbria by the relative sparsity of Anglo-Saxon settlement.[43] It would be the case *a fortiori* in those regions like the Pennines and westwards, or the parts of Somerset, Dorset and Devon, which came under Anglo-Saxon domination only in the course of the seventh century. But everywhere many must have survived and been absorbed into the Saxon system of agriculture and society, albeit in numerous instances as slaves. Intermarriage must have been quite normal to judge by British personal names found at all levels of Anglo-Saxon society from Caedwalla, king of Wessex, to Caedmon, cowherd of Whitby Abbey. The fewness of surviving British place-names or of British words in the Anglo-Saxon language has sometimes been taken as evidence of British extermination. But the best interpretation of the philological evidence is that the Britons learned the Anglo-Saxon language very thoroughly, with its sound system and vocabulary; that such place-names as they did give to English had their sounds adapted to fit Anglo-Saxon tongues; and that in the period in which these Britons must have been bilingual they did not confuse the two languages, as is seen from the rarity of British words in Anglo-Saxon. In other words, the Anglo-Saxons, besides being lords and masters, presented their not unusual aspect as poor linguists, and the burden of linguistic adaptation fell on the British.[44] Everything in fact suggests that what makes the British hard to detect in Anglo-Saxon society is their gradual loss of racial identity.

With regard to the survival of Christianity, however, the survival of the British population is of little significance in the

B

credit column compared with the fall of Roman institutions in
the debit. For it was precisely in the towns and the prosperous
villas of Roman Britain that the real strength of Christianity
seems to have lain.[45] Leaving aside the army, the kinds of
evidence which we have for Christianity in Roman times—and it
does not amount to that much—is the attendance of bishops from
British cities at church councils in Gaul and Italy; the martyrdom
of St. Alban at Verulamium; the Christian word-wheel from the
plaster of a Cirencester house; the upper room of Lullingstone
villa in Kent with its large Chi-Rho monogram and its wall-
paintings of well-dressed persons in the attitude of prayer
(*orantes*); and above all the superb mosaic floor of the villa of
Hinton St. Mary in Dorset, and its roundel showing the bust of a
young man, clean shaven with penetrating eyes, having pome-
granates (symbols of immortality) on either side of him and the
Chi-Rho monogram behind his head—almost certainly a representation of Christ. Again, the vigorous theological debate in
Britain which centred on the doctrines of Pelagius in the early
decades of the fifth century, was conducted by the very upper-
class of urban society who, whatever the state of their fortifications
were to suffer their doom in the next generation.[46] We know
that Germanus of Auxerre, who came from Gaul to combat the
Pelagian heresy in Britain, debated with the citizens of
Verulamium. Verulamium sank without trace under the Saxon
advance. When the Franks invaded Gaul they were met at
almost all the cities by formidable Gallo-Roman bishops who
were in effective control and eased their cities into the new
régime. There was nothing comparable to greet the Anglo-
Saxons. Only in Kent did Roman town life survive in any sort of
shape, and even in Canterbury Augustine found the churches in
ruins when he arrived there. He had to be transported to the
River Severn in order to make contact with the official leaders of
the British Church.

All this is not to say that there were no Christians whatever left
among the British population at large. There certainly must have
been. There are 20 English place-names which have the form *eccles*,
from the British *egles* meaning a church; such, for instance, are
Eccles in Kent, Eccles in Norfolk and Egglescliffe in County
Durham. Most of these places are on or near Roman roads, and
although not all of them lie in parts of the country early brought
under Saxon control, every instance must mean that the Saxons

noted the existence of a British church and called a place after
it.[47] Very likely there were at least the remnants of recognizably
British Christian communities living here and there amongst the
Anglo-Saxons. It has been aptly said that as Aidan walked over the
vast tracts of Northumbria, there must have been those to whom
he came as a remembrancer rather than a missionary.[48]

But that is as far as we can go. It would be easy to exaggerate
the likely number of Britons who were Christians. There had been
a pagan revival in fourth-century Britain, and the evidence of
pagan cult objects from the late Roman period is substantial.[49]
Such British Christians as there were would lack the organization
and probably, from a certain point in time, the social identity to
make much impact on the process of converting the Anglo-Saxons.
Indeed one may well ask in what sense people for the most part
quite uneducated would remain Christians if they were lacking
regular pastoral ministry and organization. As Mrs. Chadwick has
said of the break-up of British institutions—and nobody would
accuse her of overstating the case for this break-up—'a Church
cannot survive and thrive long without wealth and patronage
based on current political power.'[50] Even if it could be shown that
British Christians were at all numerous within the Anglo-Saxon
kingdoms, they would more likely have been an obstacle than a
help to the conversion of Anglo-Saxon kings and their nobles.
Why should the latter have emulated in religion their underlings
and, in many cases, their recent enemies in battle?

Besides the question of the Britons living under Anglo-Saxon
rule, there is the question of the British kingdoms remaining in the
north and west of the island. What of the progress of Christianity
in these kingdoms during the period of Saxon invasion and
settlement and before the arrival of St. Augustine at Canterbury
in 597? This is where the distinction between the Lowland Zone
of Britain, with which the present book is mainly concerned, and
the Highland Zone comes in. Sir Cyril Fox made this distinction
familiar in his *The Personality of Britain* (1932) (where he
included in his definition of the Highland Zone the Pennines
and the Peak District of Derbyshire, whereas we confine ourselves
here more narrowly to what is roughly present-day Scotland, Wales
and Devon and Cornwall). He pointed out that the Lowland Zone
was an easy prey to invaders and so to the imposition of new
cultures, and that while it was suffering such incursions, the
Highland Zone might be able (as the archaeology of its pre-

history testifies) to preserve its cultural unity on an older basis
and to engage in quite independent activity.[51] This is the real clue
to the history of British Christianity in the fifth and six centuries,
and to that of Ireland as well, by reason of the historic role of the
Irish Sea as a great Celtic lake.

Nowhere is the nature of Highland religious continuity with
Roman Britain to be seen more clearly than in the *De Excidio
Britanniae* (The Devastation of Britain) written by the Welshman
Gildas around 540.[52] Like the Gaulish monk Salvian a hundred
years earlier, Gildas wrote a moral treatise to explain how and
why God had allowed the barbarian ravages. But more than that,
he was writing during the period when the British had to some
extent recovered their hold over the situation and a generation had
grown up which could not remember the times of war and
desolation when 'the savage tongue' had all but licked the western
ocean. It was essential that this generation should not be allowed
to forget these things, the more so as it was a wicked generation,
loose in morals and worldly in ambitions, heading straight (as no
man with the slightest pretensions to prophecy could doubt) for
another dose of divine retribution. The real trouble lay in
tyrannical kings and in the secular-minded bishops and priests
who were their stooges. Not that there appeared too much that
could be said specifically about these people—although Gildas had
some observations of great historical interest. But there were
many and long passages from the Old Testament to show what
might happen to unworthy kings and priests, and these Gildas
poured with ardour and rhetoric into his pages, showing a
special predilection for the prophet Jeremiah.

Gildas's book conveys an impression of conservatism in church
life and organization, first by his Latin, which though no longer in
touch with the spoken language of everyday life is still the old,
correct, school Latin; second, by continuity in the orders of
bishops, priests and deacons, and in diocesan administration, albeit
that in the absence of city life the dioceses are now associated
with the tribal kingships; and third, by the suggestion of continuing contacts with Gaul in Gildas's reproof of those who go abroad
to seek fancy consecrations to the episcopate.[53]

It is now becoming clear that North Britain, also, was developing
in the fifth and sixth centuries an ecclesiastical organization
similar to that of Wales. From the archaeological study of
cemeteries and early memorial stones as well as from the frag-

ments of surviving literature, it seems that the best way to understand the evidence is to posit the existence of territorial bishoprics
corresponding to tribal divisions. In the fifth century Carlisle and
Whithorn were apparently the centres of dioceses, and from the
sixth century there is also evidence of dioceses for the people called
the Gododdin around the Forth and Fife, and for those of Strathclyde and of the valley of the Tweed.[54] This continuity of diocesan
organization is worth stressing since it used sometimes to be
assumed that the so-called Celtic Church was always purely
monastic in character.

Not less worth stressing are the contacts with Gaul, since this
was much more than a question of mere continuity. While
lowland Britain was subjected to continental invasion from the
east, its Atlantic seaways became channels of activity through
which Gaul pumped life-blood into the British Church. The general
importance of contacts between West Britain and Gaul can be
seen from the excavated farmstead of Dinas Powys near the
Bristol Channel in Glamorgan. Here were found examples of red
pottery bowls and wine jars imported from the Mediterranean
lands into West Britain during the fifth and sixth centuries, and
quantities of glassware—claw beakers and cone-shaped beakers,
bearing 'only a cousinly relationship' to the Frankish glass found
in Kent, but probably imported by sea from somewhere in Gaul.
From the inscriptions on the earliest memorial stones of Wales,
we can see that alongside the Irish influence, there is much of
Romano-Gaulish epigraphy; some of the stones would appear
actually to commemorate Gaulish Christians. The great majority
of them stand or stood significantly near to the coast. Mr. Leslie
Alcock has written of how these stones reveal a synthesis of
Celtic and Mediterranean culture in sixth-century Wales. Concerning the stone commemorating Vortipor, tyrant of the Demetians
in South-West Wales (of whom Gildas said that he was from
the bottom to the top stained with murders and adulteries), Mr.
Alcock writes![55]

Here is the epitaph of an Irishman, who has become so
naturalized in Wales that his name is given in the British as
well as the Irish form. He appears as a *tyrannus*, a local strong
man thrown up by the Celtic political revival on the departure
of the Romans; yet he claims to be *protector*, a member of the
imperial bodyguard, and this title, hereditary in his family,

invested his rule with some aura of Roman authority. His monument is a rough, undressed pillar, a typical pagan standing stone, and even its inscription, VOTECORIGAS, could well mark a pagan memorial of purely Irish derivation. But the Christian context and Mediterranean inspiration are not in doubt, for the main face of the stone bears a ring-cross and the inscription— characteristically North African—MEMORIA VOTEPORIGIS PROTICTORIS.

Gaul probably gave a great impetus to the monastic movement which developed in the British church during the sixth century. The Gaulish monastic movement had in effect begun with St. Martin of Tours in imperial times and had developed quickly under the Frankish kingdoms of the sixth century. Gildas came to be known as a wise counsellor on the monastic life. Although there is no more than a trace of monasticism in his *De Excidio Britanniae*,[56] Gildas's dissatisfaction with the bishops and clergy, too occupied as they were with their worldly position and too closely identified with the politics of the tribal kingdoms, gives us a valuable clue to what would constitute one of the chief attractions of monasticism and the flight from the world in the following generation.

Very little reliable knowledge of the founding fathers of Welsh monasticism now exists. There are indeed plenty of saints' lives but these come mainly from the eleventh and twelfth centuries or later, and justification for monastic territorial pretensions or sheer pious fantasy are their uppermost elements. More can be learnt from the dedications of churches and chapels and their locations, as Professor E. Bowen has shown.[57] Where the actual church or chapel is gone, these dedications may still leave their mark in a place-name formed of *llan* (i.e. an enclosure) and the saint's name. There is evidence of over 600 churches or chapels in Wales dedicated to Welsh saints. Now this kind of evidence is not without its dangers, as Professor Bowen himself was the first to explain. Dedications might have nothing to do with the activity of a saint and his disciples but only with his subsequent reputation. St. David, for instance, became the patron of a diocese whose cathedral church might have been very anxious to extend its influence by having churches dedicated to St. David, or even by rededicating churches which had initially been under the patronage of another saint.

When all is said and done, however, certain points do seem clear, if we adopt a geographical approach to this evidence of dedications. They can shed light on the intense activity of spiritual renewal and internal missionizing which seized the British Church during the sixth century.

First, something can be seen of the character and influence of 'the mother churches', the great training centres of monks. One of the earliest of these was the monastry of St. Illtud at Llanilltud Fawr, or Llantwit Major. Illtud is mentioned in the life of St. Samson of Dol, which has a seventh-century core, as giving in his monastery a classic type of Roman education based on grammar and rhetoric. The excavation of the site of Llantwit has revealed that it was only a few hundred yards from a Roman villa, one of whose mosaic pavements has been found. And whatever the dates of particular dedications to St. Illtud, their general location in the highly Romanized coastal region of South Glamorgan is a clear indication of the likely character of his monasticism. It may well be right to see him, as some have done, as the type of the humane Roman country gentleman, like Paulinus of Nola, who turned their own houses into monasteries. With the dedications to St. David there is a particular danger, as we mentioned, of reading too much into them. But it is surely permissible to see the initial influence of David radiating from Mynyw (Menevia), the present St. David's in North-West Pembrokeshire. This influence moved eastwards along what was left of the Roman roads and their extensions and also by sea to Cornwall and Brittany—for the Pembrokeshire peninsula was a hub of communications in the Western Seas. This is the story told by dedications to St. David, and without prejudice to the question of their date, they would be nonsense without the original centre of influence. The sphere of St. David, then, was, that of South-West Wales which lay beyond the region of Roman villas, and some colour is given by this fact, as well as by a letter on the monastic life attributed to Gildas, to the idea that David was the leader of a kind of 'puritan revival within the Celtic Church'—David 'the water-drinker'.[58]

Second, the dedications of North Wales provide, among other things, some ecclesiastical background for the close association between North Britain and Wales, to which literary sources testify. Thus, for instance, an early annal speaks of the migration

of a northern chieftain called Cunedda to North Wales, and his
descendants are commemorated in church dedications.

Third, we see the way in which the monastic movement
embraced the whole Celtic thalassocracy on the Atlantic seaboard
—Brittany, Cornwall, Wales, Ireland (to which we return in a
later chapter), and very likely North Britain, as well. For instance,
there is a group of dedications within quite a short distance of
each other around the estuary of the River Teifi (which divides
Pembrokeshire and Carmarthenshire) to the Welsh saints
Carannog, Gwbert, Pedrog, Briog and Meugan. The same group
occurs on or near the coast in mid-Cornwall and in North
Brittany.[59] Whether these dedications represent the travels and
foundations of these saints in a common missionary and monastic
enterprise, or whether they merely show the general contacts
which caused one region to honour another's saints, is a moot
point. Canon G. H. Doble showed, in his fine studies of *The
Saints of Cornwall*, that many Breton saints were represented in
Cornish dedications, of whom there can be no supposition that
they had all worked in Cornwall. Nonetheless the first possibility
is not to be ruled out. If we read Gregory of Tours' *Lives of the
Fathers*, it is clear that monastic founders in fifth- and sixth-century
Gaul, at least, did travel extensively, did work in association with
each other, and did found churches or monasteries which came to
bear their names. The brothers Lupicinus and Romanus founded
two monasteries in the Jura mountains within ten miles of each
other, to cater for the followers whom they attracted to their
original hermitage. One monastery came to be called Saint-Lupicin,
the other Romainmotier.[60] Lupicinus and Romanus were not
travellers, whose foundations were far apart from each other, but
others, like Brachio, were.[61] Such men put us in mind of Saint
Samson of Dol, who was educated in Wales under Illtud, passed
through Cornwall (where his name is associated with Golant
church, superbly situated above the River Fowey), and finally
spent the most important part of his working life in Brittany.

Many of the Celtic saints did not at all set out to be pastors or
missionaries; they preferred to be hermits, living on stormy head-
lands, or on off-shore islands, or in deep and forested valleys.
Professor Bowen has shown that the settlements of Celtic saints
were on the average much lower than the ordinary areas of
habitation in dark-age Wales. Of their low-lying settlements he has
made the striking observation that, 'such clearings on alluvial fans

or on river terraces in valley bottoms, each with its tiny church and a few wattle and daub buildings, may well have appeared from above as an island, or *ynys*, in a tree-filled loch.'[62] The most resolutely withdrawn hermits, however, often attracted numerous followers by their way of life, and found it impossible to set their face against these seekers of true spirituality. The monasteries of the Gaulish saint, Patroculus, for instance, were such thriving concerns that he established for himself a refuge and oratory (which came to be named after him) in the high woods eight miles away from one of them.[63] The actions of Patroculus may help us to interpret another feature of Celtic church dedications, namely the cases of a saint who has an inland church and a coastal chapel dedicated to him (e.g. St. Trillo, with Llandrillo near Corwen and Llandrillo on the Denbighshire coast).[64] The coastal dedication could be a saint's hermitage and retreat from the involvements of administering a monastery.

The mentions of Gregory of Tours and of the monastic founders in Gaul in the fifth and sixth centuries bring us back to our earlier point about Gaulish contacts. How much, as between the Gaulish and the Welsh saints, was direct influence, and how much was no more than analogy? This is a question which hardly admits of a confident answer. But if we think of the contacts suggested by archaeology, the prehistoric importance of the route from the Loire basin to West Britain, and the known importance of Brittany within the Celtic Church (which brings us actually to the lower Loire) the likelihood is that direct influence played its part.

The British Church was hardly one of the great formative influences on Anglo-Saxon Christianity, and the Welsh part of it contributed particularly little. But even in a book which sets out to deal with the Anglo-Saxons, that is mainly with the Lowland Zone of Britain, it would be particularly lacking in perspective to treat the Highland Zone as if there were nothing to be said about it, to forget that it had a great Christian tradition before the Anglo-Saxons knew of Christ, and to ignore the Church with which Augustine of Canterbury failed to come to terms.

2 Bede's *Ecclesiastical History*

Much the greatest part of what we know about the conversion of the Anglo-Saxons and their Christianity up to 664 comes from Bede's *Ecclesiastical History of the English People*, completed in the year 731 when its author was 58. It is a work written in excellent Latin. Bede was born in 672 or 673 and at the age of seven was given to Abbot Benedict Biscop to be educated in his monastery at Wearmouth (Co. Durham). Biscop was a Northumbrian nobleman, or gesith, who had founded this monastery in 674 and founded its sister-monastery, Jarrow, a few miles away on the Tyne in 681. Bede was a local boy and he was to spend his life (he died in 735) as a monk of Jarrow.[1] The story was told of how in the monastery's earliest days an epidemic carried off everyone who understood the services except Abbot Ceolfrid and a young boy—who might have been Bede—and how for a time the abbot being determined that morale should not be allowed to slump, the two of them struggled by themselves through the whole divine office, singing the antiphons and all.[2]

To Bede the real world was to a considerable extent the world of books. We know of one journey which he made to Lindisfarne and of another to York, both in the last 15 years of his life. Otherwise he would appear to have stayed in Jarrow and made himself the most learned man in Europe on the strength of the fine library which Biscop assembled for his two monasteries. Most of his time was occupied expounding to his pupils in the monastery —there is much of the schoolmaster in Bede's works—and writing about the books of the Bible. He also wrote works on grammar (necessary for pupils who had to learn Latin as a working language), saints' lives and treatises on chronology. It was from this background of study and with these interests that he came, late in his life, to write his *Ecclesiastical History*.[3] He never became an abbot, let alone a bishop; he remained just an ordinary monk and priest. Untravelled, and anything but a man of affairs, Bede conveys an impression almost of idyllic times, even though he was writing of a period of turbulence and violent deaths. All this is quite unlike another famous history of the early Middle Ages, namely Gregory of Tours' *History of the Franks*, which was written in the 590's and was known to Bede. Gregory of Tours was a Gaulish bishop. He knew what thugs the Merovingian kings could be, and even if he might applaud their *strenuitas* as he called it, he had experienced that a bishop could be involved in a dangerous game trying to preserve public order and protect his flock. Bede, too, approved of *strenuitas* in kings, but he had no idea what it was like to be on the receiving end of it.

Yet Bede was not a mere desiccated academic. It was no part of a monk's business to thrust his own personality to the fore in his writings, which would have contravened the spirit of humility, but in such glimpses as we obtain, we discern the current of a strongly emotional nature flowing just beneath the surface of Anglo-Saxon good sense. There are his outbursts against those who had accused him of heresy in the presence of Bishop Wilfrid—'I am grieved enough, as angry as is lawful, and more angry than I am accustomed to be';[4] there are the emotional excitements and upheavals connected with Abbot Ceolfrid's departure for Rome, after which Bede was glad to return to scrutinizing the marvels of Holy Scripture with all his attention;[5] and there is the account by a fellow monk of his last days, where it is recalled how on the feast of the Ascension before his death, when he was singing the antiphon 'O King of Glory, Lord of Might' and came to the words 'leave us not comfortless', he burst into tears.[6]

This side of Bede's nature gives its own force to the *Ecclesiastical History*, both in its method of exposition and in its general aims. One could hardly call Bede supreme in character depiction, although extraordinary sidelights do occasionally flash on to a personality, but when it comes to a sense of situation and power to evoke a moving image Bede is certainly the master. For instance, he gives a detailed account of the visions of Fursey, an Irish saint who lived among the East Angles in the 630's. He describes how Fursey saw the fires which would consume the world, how a tortured soul was thrown at him and burnt him, and how finally he received some good advice from an angel. All this was of great interest to men in the early Middle Ages, to judge by the manuscript circulation of the *Life of Fursey*, from which book Bede

had his information. But at the end of it there comes the personal
Bedan touch—one Latin sentence which brings Fursey suddenly to
life and leaves an indelible impression:[7]

> An aged brother is still living in our monastery who is wont to
> relate that a most truthful and pious man told him that he had
> seen Fursey himself in the kingdom of the East Angles and
> had heard these visions from his own mouth. He added that
> though it was during a time of severe winter weather and a
> hard frost and though Fursey sat wearing only a thin garment
> when he told his story, yet he sweated as though it were the
> middle of summer, because of the great terror and joy which
> his recollections aroused.

The *Ecclesiastical History* is like one of the great dark-age
brooches; it combines a certain grandeur and sweep of overall
design with the utmost delicacy of detail. It is made up of five
books and the divisions between them are singularly apt. The
ending of the second book is more than apt; it is profoundly
dramatic. After the clashes between Augustine and the British
bishops, the conversions and relapses of the southern kingdoms,
the laborious efforts to convert King Edwin, and the final
disaster of Edwin's defeat and death and Paulinus's flight from
Northumbria, a great calm comes over the last lines. They concern
James, the deacon, who remained in Northumbria, baptizing,
rescuing prey from the old enemy of mankind, teaching the
faithful the Roman custom of singing, in which he was out-
standingly skilful, until 'being old and full of days, he went the
way of his forefathers'. Historians sometimes wonder why Bede
says almost nothing more about James the deacon, although he
lived for over 30 years after Paulinus's flight. May it not be that
here he finished a stirring book of movement and cataclysm
with the picture of this peace-loving and musical old man, and the
effect would be ruined if the deacon appeared on the stage again
next minute performing the humdrum activities of his middle age?

What were the general aims of Bede's book? First of all Bede
wanted to write about the way in which the order and unity of
the English Church had been achieved. Order meant the organization of dioceses and this is one theme which Bede followed
through the book, being careful like Eusebius of Caesarea in his
famous *Ecclesiastical History* to show the succession of bishops
in most dioceses. To Bede, however, order meant chiefly Roman

order. He admired the Irish missionaries, but he lived in a monastery which had derived its services from the archchanter of St. Peter's and much of its library from Rome, or at least from Italy. He recognized that the power of binding and loosing had been given to all the apostles, but he believed that to Peter had been given a special power:[8]

> To all the Church of the elect authority of binding and loosing is given. But then blessed Peter, who confessed Christ with a true faith and was attached to him with a true love, received in a special way the keys of the kingdom of heaven and the primacy of judicial power, so that all believers throughout the world might understand that those who separate themselves from the unity of his faith and society cannot be absolved from the chains of sin, nor enter the door of the heavenly kingdom.

Here is one reason why Bede felt so strongly about those who adhered to their own traditions rather than to the authority of the pope in their calculation of the date of Easter. What more wanton disruption of the unity of the Church and its discipline could be imagined? The triumph of order and unity based on papal authority, the triumph of the Roman Easter, forms one of the principal themes of Bede's book. In the closing chapters he describes how the Picts were won round and the last Irish resistance was broken down. At the end only the Britons remain beyond hope.

Another important aim of Bede was to present moral examples. This is how he himself puts it in his preface:[9]

> If History relates good things of good men, the attentive hearer is excited to imitate that which is good; or if it mentions evil things of wicked persons, nevertheless the religious and pious hearer or reader, shunning that which is hurtful and perverse, is the more earnestly excited to perform those things which he knows to be good and worthy of God.

On the whole Bede thought it was safer not to say too much about wicked persons. Still less did he think it worth mentioning evil things about those whom he thought good; his history was marked throughout by the utmost discretion. There were, after all, plenty of good examples of good men whom Bede could present to his public—plenty, that is, provided one did not look for them too close to the present day; for there had been a Golden Age of saints in the English Church (as Bede thought) which had lamentably passed away by the time he wrote, and so there was to him very little point in saying much about the immediately previous 20 or 30 years. But in an earlier age there were splendid examples of kings whom he could present to the laymen, who would listen to his work perhaps in a vernacular translation. The book itself was dedicated to King Ceolwulf of Northumbria, and much of it 'was intended to show how the needs of kings could best be fulfilled and where their true interests lay'.[10] Mr. J. Campbell writes of Bede's treatment of St. Oswald, for example, as 'an excellent instance of how Christianity could be represented to suit the needs and feelings of the rulers of England. If the Church deprived the kings of Northumbria of the gods whom they had regarded as their ancestors it soon provided their dynasty with a royal saint, a hero of exactly the kind most appreciated by the Anglo-Saxons, a great and famous man who met disaster nobly.' Not less notable were the examples of monks and ideal pastors for the clergy in Bede's audience. There was, for instance, Aidan, whose life Bede considered to be so far removed from the sloth of his own time. Of him Mr. Campbell writes, 'it is noticeable how much he (Bede) stresses those aspects of Aidan's conduct which defied the customs of Anglo-Saxon society which had so powerful and inevitable an effect upon the Church, in particular entertainment and gift exchange'.

To present moral examples implies a standard of moral judgement. Bede's standard was strongly influenced by Gildas, and before him by Orosius, the Spanish historian and pupil of Augustine of Hippo. Orosius had tried to show Rome as a 'chosen nation' progressing towards unity with Christ's Church. This had brought its appropriate earthly rewards, for God punished sin and rewarded goodness in the course of History. Bede, too, tried to show how good Christian kings brought peace and prosperity. He also took his cue from Orosius in another way, as had several of the great historians of barbarian peoples before him. He saw the pattern of his people's history as 'a national history of salvation organized around the triumph of Christianity and its beneficent effects, and relayed in the typifying personages of Christian social heroes'. His reading of Gildas helped Bede to focus his 'conception of a nation's destiny under God' and of the relation between salvation and prosperity on the one hand and sin and disaster on the other.[11]

Behind all this lay Bede's sense of the movement of History towards the end of this world and the everlasting life of the next. He was an enthusiastic adherent to the doctrine, current in his day, of the Six Ages of the World. History, it was thought, fell naturally into six phases, beginning in turn with the Creation, the Flood, Abraham, David, the Babylonian captivity and the Incarnation of Christ. Thus the world was then in its last age, the end might come at any time, and although the time could not be exactly calculated, there were indeed many signs that it was actually approaching. According to Bede there was a seventh age, running concurrently with these six, 'in which the souls of the just rested from their labours of this life in a place marred by no sadness.'[12] This age had been inaugurated with the martyrdom of Abel. When all these ages were over and the souls of the just had received their bodies again, the age of eternal happiness would begin. This would be the eighth age. Nothing of this is directly introduced into the *Ecclesiastical History*, but it is vitally important because it explains the sense of purpose and the passion with which Bede wrote. This doctrine of the ages recurs constantly in his scriptural writings, and at these points his text is often gripped with a sudden intensity. Commenting on the Circumcision of Christ, for instance, in his work on Luke, he writes of the special significance of this ceremony's being on the eighth day after the Incarnation:[13]

For we ourselves, after the six ages of this world and the seventh which is going on concurrently in another life for souls in their sabbath, will rise as if in the eighth age truly circumcised. We shall be free of all stain of carnal concupiscence, of all the corruptions among which luxury reigns supreme; our impurity will be truly done away with.

The *Ecclesiastical History* reads so fluently and seems such a finely woven fabric, that we have to remind ourselves how patchy and uneven were the sources on which Bede was forced to rely.[14] For the main body of his work he must have sent round to various monasteries and episcopal sees for information. Knowledge of the past did not float in the air. Besides a few bald annals and some saints' lives much of the knowledge about the Anglo-Saxon past was strictly localized in the particular courts and ecclesiastical institutions which had a specific interest in preserving it. The response of these institutions to Bede was very varied.

Some sent in a barrage of miracle stories about the saints whose cults they fostered; others like Canterbury sent in batches of official documents. On some matters he had spoken with eye-witnesses, but for parts of the country he might have a contact with no more than one monastery, a kind of oasis of information. For the church in the East Saxon kingdom in the later seventh century Barking Abbey was such an oasis. The history of the nuns of Barking is not, of course, the history of the East Saxon church, but simply the greatest part of what Bede knew about it in a certain period. The saints about whom Bede writes were not necessarily the only great figures in the English conversion, but simply those about whom he had accessible information because they were venerated at monasteries with whom he had contacts. Added to these difficulties were those which Bede encountered through the muddled state of chronology and the various systems of dating in operation in his time. In order to produce a chronological account of the English Church 'he had to correlate dates given according to the regnal years of the kings of different kingdoms with one another and with dates from ecclesiastical sources expressed in imperial or consular years or in terms of the position of the year in a nineteen-year cycle, the indiction'.[15]

Not surprisingly, then, Bede was unable to avoid the occasional mistake or confusion, and apart from his omissions dictated by discretion, he was forced to leave many gaps in his story. Yet it is rather worth emphasizing the positive side of his achievement, that out of all this medley he was able to construct a coherent and roughly chronological narrative of the progress of the conversion which surveyed together contemporaneous developments in the separate kingdoms. Sometimes he had a book on some particular saint in front of him; he used Eddius's *Life of Wilfrid* and his own book on Cuthbert. It would have been easy for a writer with less sense of proportion to have decanted an abundance of attractive material from these into the *Ecclesiastical History*. Bede resisted the temptation.

Bede's long experience as a scholar, particularly in the fields of biblical commentary and chronology, admirably equipped him to cope with the difficulties of his sources in writing his history. He was very used to the critical comparison of texts. He wrote, for instance, two commentaries on the Acts of the Apostles, the first not long after 709 and the second not long before 731. The second is by far the maturer work of scholarship, and Bede was by that time using a Bible which gave side by side the Greek Septuagint text and the Old Latin version. The manuscript which he used still survives. With the help of the Greek, in which he became increasingly proficient during the course of his scholarly work, he was able to make much better sense than he had previously made of many passages in the Acts.[16] Again, he knew what it meant to test generalizations by the use of observable evidence. In his *De Temporum Ratione* he quoted a certain author on the differing times of high tide up different rivers; he went on to say that it was known that high tide occurred at different times on various parts of the British coast and that those who lived to the north of himself always had the tide earlier than those who lived to the south.[17]

For many readers of today the chief obstacle to complete sympathy and *rapport* with Bede is his delight in miracles—visions, cures, heavenly lights and many other things besides.[18] Bede had written about the abbots of his own monastery, probably for his own monastery, and had related no miracle in the course of this work. That the miraculous element in the *Ecclesiastical History* reflects the intended wider circulation of the book can be seen in two different ways. First of all the pagan gods had been officially abolished and it was up to Christianity to show that this could be done without loss of the old benefits, that Christian medicine could work as well as pagan magic, that the earth where King Oswald had shed his blood or the chips of wood from the post against which Aidan had leaned were just as efficacious in drinking water as all the things which pagans dropped into it. Second, Bede had most of his miracle stories from the monks and nuns with whom he had friendly contact and these miracles were often told in connection with saints whose memories were revered or whose shrines were fostered at the particular religious houses, saints who immensely enhanced the prestige of a house and whose presence and power was felt with great immediacy. The *Ecclesiastical History* would have been sent round when it was finished to be read out in these monasteries, and their members would no doubt feel gratified to hear their own contributions incorporated into a work of so important and majestic a general theme. Bede of course believed in these miracles himself; at the same time he thought, following no doubt St Paul and also Pope Gregory the Great's sermon on the Epiphany where Gregory explains why an angel had announced Christ's birth to the shepherds while a star had guided the gentiles, that some people needed *signa* (as he often called miracles) more than others.[18a]

But this is by no means the whole story. If one looks at the groups of miracles which Bede told about a particular saint, one sometimes sees a very interesting thing; some of the stories will come from the monastery where the saint was specially revered, but one will perhaps come from a personal friend of Bede who had nothing to do with that monastery. Thus there are three miracles about Aidan. Two of them probably came from Whitby, where the wife and daughter of King Oswy of Northumbria had in turn been abbess, but a third, about how some holy oil given by Aidan to certain sailors had calmed a stormy sea, was told to Bede by a monk of his own monastery, who had it from Abbot Utta of Gateshead, a close neighbour to Jarrow on the Tyne.[19] Again, of the miracles attributed to King Oswald, some obviously came to Bede from Bardney Abbey, which had Oswald's body, or from Partney nearby, but one came from Bishop Acca of Hexham.[20] It concerned the cure of an Irish scholar who had drunk water into which had been dropped a chip from the stake on which the pagans had fixed Oswald's head after his death. Utta and Acca were both reputable persons in high office and the latter, at least, was a notable scholar. In other words, Bede did not rely simply on the miracles which were sent in, but also included in his book miraculous narratives which were the product of conversation in his own highly educated circle.

What, then, was the interest of miracles to educated men? First of all, we assume that a material relation of cause and effect is the most satisfactory and valid explanation for anything, whereas the intellectual climate of Bede's age was not at all favourable to such an assumption. This was not merely because physical laws were less well grasped. It was rather because people were deliberately trained to see the spiritual significance which lay behind any occurrence or literal statement. Such, for instance, was the aim of biblical scholarship which accounts for most of what Bede himself wrote. Jerusalem was more than a city; the word was intended to convey the pure soul, or even heaven itself. When cause and effect were not plain, therefore, there was little interest to establish what these were on a purely material basis. In many cases it is clear, and was clear to Bede, that a natural explanation could not be ruled out, that for instance storms might come and go very quickly of their own accord at sea and without the help of prophecy and holy oil, but it was the element of prayer and prophecy which was of interest in these events. This was not necessarily credulity so much as a focus of attention completely different from our own.

It was in fact the moral aspect of miracles which was primarily important to Bede. In his life of Saint Cuthbert he speaks of the way in which the creatures of the air and sea, indeed the air and sea themselves, obeyed him. Man had lost his dominion over the creation which had been made subject to him, but it was possible for individuals to recover it by obeying the commands of God.[21] It was as if a principle of obedience would operate consistently from top to bottom of the scale of creation. Miracles were indicative of moral worth and spiritual advancement, and moreover their value as stories was enhanced according to the degree in which Bede's informants themselves possessed these qualities. The function of Bede's miracles in the *Ecclesiastical History*, particularly those clusters of miracles which he told of certain holy men, was to highlight the figures of importance in the English conversion, to mark out clearly those whom his history presented as the pre-eminent examples to be followed by his readers or listeners. And it is right always to bear in mind the question of function when considering miracles in Bede. There is an analogy here with after-dinner speeches in our own day. If any such speeches survive in written form for posterity, it may come to seem rather odd if not almost unintelligible that these should be just a tissue of jokes and anecdotes, and yet we know that it makes all the difference whether there is a genuine structure and even a serious purpose to these anecdotes, or whether they are simply irrelevant to occasion, to theme and to each other. On this criterion Bede's miracles emerge if not completely vindicated, when one thinks, for instance, of the occasional miracle taken from the pages of earlier saints' lives which he had before him, certainly with a high claim to respect. He had no preference for miraculous narratives in which the facts themselves were fanciful or improbable, as some did, nor can many such narratives be found of which the moral purpose is other than immediately apparent.

It can be seen, therefore, that Bede's attitude to miracles was complex and is not to be comprised in any single formula. Generally Bede was at pains to show with names and credentials the high value of his testimony. Occasionally, however, he appears to make his own observations, and nowhere more attractively or with more of what Professor Knowles calls the 'deceptive appearance of naiveté' than in his very first chapter.[22] This is a geographical survey of Britain and Ireland. He has been describing Ireland and begins (as Englishmen often do when writing of other countries) with an encomium of its weather. Then he continues:[23]

> No reptile is found there nor could a serpent survive; for although serpents have often been brought from Britain, as soon as the ship approaches land they are affected by the scent of the air and quickly perish. In fact almost everything that the island produces is efficacious against poison. For instance, we have seen how, in the case of people suffering from snake-bite, the leaves of manuscripts from Ireland were scraped, and the scrapings put in water and given to the sufferer to drink. These scrapings at once absorbed the whole violence of the spreading poison and assuaged the swelling.

The appearance of naiveté here is very deceptive indeed. First of all Bede takes his cue from Isidore of Seville's *Etymologies* which was the standard encyclopaedia of knowledge available in his day. Under *Ireland* Isidore observed that this island had no snakes, few birds and no bees. He then went on to say, in a passage which must have been well known to many of Bede's audience, that if dust or pebbles from Ireland were sprinkled in a bee-hive, the swarms deserted their honey-combs.[24] Bede's passage is evidently a witty parody of this sort of nonsense. Moreover, it must have been well known to Bede and to many of his audience that in the opinion of some people (like Aldhelm) too many Anglo-Saxons had been going off to study in Ireland, and that, admirable as the best Irish scholarship was, the Irish were filling rather too many leaves of parchment with learning, not all of it entirely free from pedantry or wild fantasy. Bede himself had had occasion, in his own commentaries on the Bible, to correct certain excesses of their scriptural exegesis.[25] What better use, then, for some of these leaves, than that they should be applied to snake-bites?

The whole of this passage seems to imply, on Bede's part, that there will be more serious stuff in the way of miracles later, but meanwhile the reader need not feel, already in the first chapter, that his author is a dull dog.

3 The Gregorian Mission

GREGORY THE GREAT

Pope Gregory I (590-604), who sent the first missionaries to the Anglo-Saxons, is one of the greatest popes in History. It is hard to name another occupant of the see of Peter who was at once so great as a ruler and so sensitive to the spiritual possibilities of his position. The historian of the papacy, Erich Caspar, said of him, 'it is right to call not Gregory but Gelasius the greatest pope between Leo the Great and Nicholas I, but if one asks about the greatest Christian then the palm is due to Gregory before all popes'.[1] Gregory was born in Rome of a patrician family about the year 540. In 573 he became Prefect of the City, which meant that he was responsible for its finances, public buildings and food supply. The following year, however, he espoused the monastic life, founded six monasteries on his family estates in Sicily, turned his own family home on the Coelian Hill into the monastery of St. Andrew, and became an ordinary monk in it. After four years of seclusion and contemplation, which he regarded as the happiest years of his life, Pope Benedict I made him a deacon in 578 and put him in charge of the charitable administration in one of the districts of Rome. Shortly afterwards he was sent by Pope Pelagius II to be papal ambassador, or *apocrisiarius*, at the imperial court of Constantinople. While there he came into conflict with the patriarch Eutychius, about whether the saints would rise with their real bodies, in a dispute of such violence that it left both participants fit only for bed. Gregory lived in a world in which East and West, for all their contacts, were drifting apart intellectually and culturally. While in Constantinople he never learned Greek, and as pope he refused to answer a correspondent in Constantinople because, although a Latin, she had written to him in Greek. He professed not to understand how the patrician

lady Rusticiana could be so enamoured of Constantinople and so
forgetful of Rome.[2] And now that Arianism was losing its hold in
the West he could only regard the Eastern Church as the prime
nursery of heretics. Gregory hated heretics. They were like the
hot wind from the South; they made as if to comfort the Church
but did not understand her sorrow; they were precipitated day by
day into further extremes (and Gregory hated extremes); they
gave the appearance of humility while preaching proud doctrines;
they began with soft words and ended in the bitterest invectives;
they talked too much.[3] In 585 he was glad to return home where
he became abbot of his own monastery and so remained until he
was elected pope, much against his will, in 590.

Gregory was not well served by biographers. The *Liber
Pontificalis* contains only a brief and unenthusiastic notice about
him; the earliest life of the pope was written at Whitby interestingly enough, but is very thin; and not until the ninth century did
he find a Roman biographer in John the deacon. There is, however,
ample compensation in his own writings and above all in the
superb series of about 850 letters which survive from his pontificate in the papal registers. These are certainly not all the letters
written by Gregory as pope, but they must be the great majority.[4]
The qualities which these letters pre-eminently reveal are
versatility, balance and humaneness. Here are letters expounding
passages of scripture and giving directives on complicated points
of law. One moment the pope will be discussing an episcopal
election at Syracuse with a good knowledge of local personnel,[5]
the next he will be advising the bishop of Ravenna how to treat
his sickness and warning him particularly against sudden outbursts of anger.[6] He was very anxious to show himself a protector
of monasteries. Several letters are written to restrain local bishops
from interfering in their affairs,[7] one reproves a bishop for
excommunicating an old and sick abbot even if he had done
wrong,[8] and there is an order to the papal rector in Corsica to sail
round the island and prospect for a suitable coastal site for a
monastery.[9]

In general it was not easy for Gregory to sustain the authority
of the papacy throughout the Church. Over the churches of Italy
and Sicily he exercised control with relative ease, but the more
distant provinces were another matter. In Dalmatia he failed to
secure the election of his favoured candidate to the metropolitan
see of Salona (the modern Split in Yugoslavia), and his attempts

to bring the rival candidate to Rome to confess his simony showed the weakness of his hold over most of the other bishops in this province.[10] In North Africa he had the greatest difficulties to make bishops or local officials comply with his orders, while his one firm supporter amongst the Numidian episcopate complained to the pope of his growing unpopularity because he was receiving so many papal letters.[11] The most serious challenge to the papacy in this period, however, came from the patriarchs of Constantinople with their refusal to drop the style 'universal bishop' which had been adopted at the Synod of Constantinople in 588. Gregory's reaction to this style was characteristically subtle. He did not allow the papal primacy to go completely by the board, but his most petrine statements were diplomatically reserved for the ears of the emperor and empress at Constantinople, whom he hoped would put pressure on the patriarch.[12] To the patriarch, John, he contented himself with saying that if anyone should have such a style it was the bishop of Rome, but in reality nobody should. He emphasized to him what would nowadays be called the collegiality of all the bishops: 'are not all the bishops together clouds, who both rain in the words of preaching, and glitter in the light of good works?'[13] The unity of the Church, he pleaded, should be preserved not by the assumption of proud titles but by the bonds of brotherly love. Always this theme was to the fore with Gregory. If he had occasion to correct a bishop he preferred to slip in an allusion to his authority but to enlarge on the duty of Christians to correct each other as brothers. If he himself were in need of correction, he declared, he would be glad that any man should administer it to him.[14] It was the theme of brotherhood which Gregory stressed in his letters about the Constantinopolitan style to the other patriarchs of the East. To Eulogius of Alexandria he wrote an extraordinarily neat letter, which looked as if it would be a downright assertion of papal authority and suddenly, by a twist, turned out not to be:[15]

For, as it is clear to all that the blessed evangelist Mark was sent by the holy apostle Peter, his master, to Alexandria, so we are bound together in the unity of this master and his disciple, so that I seem to preside over the see of the disciple because of the master, and you over the see of the master because of the disciple.

Gregory himself gloried in the style 'servant of the servants of

God' (*servus servorum dei*), with its reference to St. Mark's Gospel, 'whosoever will be the first among you shall be the servant of all.' It was a paradoxical style, therefore, because it embodied a claim to be 'first', to be primate, but the method of this claim, arising out of the developing monastic piety of the sixth century, can only be called the method of monastic humility.[16] Gregory's reaction to the whole problem of papal authority owed a lot to his monastic experience and inclinations. So also did his writings. These writings were for the most part composed while he was pope and are an astonishing testimony to the energy of a man caught up in affairs, yet caught up in such a way that he still had time to think about and ability to focus on his fundamental aims. Nothing shows this more clearly than his *Pastoral Care*, or *Regula Pastoralis*, which describes not only the moral and pastoral obligations of a bishop's office, but also what sort of a man a bishop should be and how he should preserve within himself humility and a love of contemplation. This same concern is seen in the long and rambling commentary on the Book of Job. Another side of Gregory's monasticism shows itself in the *Dialogues* (so called because it is cast in the form of a dialogue between himself and Peter the deacon), or *Miracles of the Italian Fathers*, which the book is really about. Here Gregory, the patriotic Roman, wanted to show that the asceticism of the East had taken root in Italy.[17] Like the Irish, Gregory was spiritual heir to the hermits and monasteries of Syria and Egypt. The life of St. Benedict, which occupies the second book, conveys through the stories and miracles of St. Benedict, a pattern of life for the monk. Some have thought that the preoccupation by an educated man with miracles shows a sad decline in the intellectual level of the upper classes and they point also to Gregory's express suspicion of grammatical studies to show that in his day Classical Antiquity was giving way to the Middle Ages. Be that as it may, the positive aspect of the *Dialogues* is its evidence of the revolutionary impact of ascetic monasticism on society and even of its power to knit social classes together.[18] Gregory's missionary zeal, which issued in the English mission conducted by monks, sprang from this monasticism, from his knowledge that St. Benedict had converted pagans, and from his general emphasis that monastic contemplation should bear fruit in action. It sprang also from his record of service to the city.

Gregory's chief problem as pope was the struggle for the survival of Rome itself. For more than two centuries Rome had

not been the centre of Western imperial government and since
476 there had been no Western Emperor at all. In Gregory's time
the Exarch of Ravenna was the representative of imperial government in Italy. Had it not been for the popes who kept alive its
traditions and gave it government and ecclesiastical importance,
Rome might have become an insignificant place. The city was
subject to two major threats in the 590's—from its own economic
problems and from the Lombards. With regard to economic
problems, the surroundings of Rome had in the course of
centuries become increasingly marshy and infertile and were by
this time quite incapable of supplying a large population with
food; Rome was subject to chronic shortage of wheat. Moreover,
it was slum- and plague-ridden. In the year before Gregory became
pope the Tiber had flooded and there had followed a terrible
plague; during the litanies of penance with which Gregory
inaugurated his pontificate and which lasted an hour it was said
that 80 people fell dead.[19] With regard to the Lombards, they had
descended into Italy in 568 and quickly conquered much of it;
the Romans were in constant fear of attack from them. Gregory
ended his Homilies on Ezechiel because he could not go on in the
midst of this danger:[20]

> On all sides we are surrounded by swords, on all sides we go
> in imminent fear of death. Some men return to us with their
> hands cut off, others have been captured or killed. I am forced
> now to hold my tongue from expounding because my soul is
> weary of this life. None should ask me to persevere in holy
> eloquence because my harp is turned to mourning and my organ
> to the voice of tears.

In fact as Gregory considered the general state of things one
conclusion pressed itself ineluctably on him—the end of the
world must be drawing near. Only this could explain the over-
throw of cities, the destruction of churches, the sickness
everywhere, the general smiting.

There might be good grounds for ceasing to expound the
prophet Ezechiel (in sermons which stress the fruits of the active
life), but there were none for sitting back and doing nothing.
Gregory set about the task of feeding Rome with energy and
resource. John the deacon had seen in the *scrinium* of the Lateran
Palace a register from Gregory's time containing lists of poor
persons and widows in Rome, giving their names and ages and
the rations of corn, wine, cheese, oil and cooked foods regularly

distributed to each.[21] Such activity demanded the systematic exploitation of the papal patrimony, the estates which emperors from Constantine onwards, and others, had given to the popes. The most important of these estates were in the rich corn-growing lands of Sicily; Sicily was the chief supplier of corn to Rome. Here, for instance, is a part of a letter from Gregory to Peter the subdeacon, rector of the papal patrimony in Sicily, ordering him to send the usual corn from the patrimony immediately and to buy up extra for transmission to Rome the following February:[22]

Get together from those outside the patrimony corn of this year's growth to the value of 50 pounds of gold, and lay it up in Sicily in places where it will not rot so that we may send as many ships as we can to convey this corn to us in February. But in case we delay to send ships, provide some yourself and, with the help of the Lord, transmit this corn to us in February, except for the corn which we expect to have sent to us now, according to custom, in the months of September or October. Your experience should so proceed, therefore, that without annoyance to any tenant of the Church, (the justice of his administration towards his own tenants was a constant concern of Gregory) the corn may be collected, since there has been here such a scanty crop that, unless by God's help corn is collected from Sicily, there is a serious prospect of famine.

Efficiency was a primary object with Gregory; he had no patience with incompetence in temporal administration. Of an order of his to this same Peter the subdeacon he once wrote, 'you have so consigned the matter to oblivion that it might have been something said to you by the least of your slaves. But now let even Your Negligence—I cannot say Your Experience—be eager to get this done.'[23] And to a bishop of Cagliari he wrote 'we have found that Your Charity needs the written word for the augmentation of your firmness.'[24]

It was over his policy towards the Lombards that Gregory came into conflict with the Eastern Emperor. Although the emperor had his court at Constantinople the whole of Italy fell under his political shadow. The Emperor Maurice did not wish to see the Lombards wipe out the effects of Justinian's hard-won reconquest of Italy from the Ostrogoths, and he had a policy of supporting the Franks against them. Whereas Gregory, besieged in Rome, forced to see Romans taken captive and treated like dogs, unable to count on active assistance from the Ravenna government, and spending money like a kind of unofficial imperial treasurer in Rome (as he himself complained) in order to buy the Lombards off, was much more inclined to come to terms with them. And so he did. The emperor called him a fool, and he replied that he was indeed a fool; only a fool would have suffered so long among the swords of the Lombards.[25] There was, however, another consideration about the Lombards which Gregory hinted at in a letter to his *apocrisiarius* in Constantinople. He said in this letter that if he had been willing to concern himself with the death of Lombards they would have no king nor dukes nor counts but would be divided in utter confusion. The Lombards were a scourge; but perhaps because Gregory was as impressed with the paganism amongst them as with the Arianism of their priests (judging from his *Dialogues*), he saw in them a potential field of pastoral activity.[26]

This brief sketch will perhaps serve to show the mainspring of spiritual and pastoral motivation from which Gregory's dispatching of the Anglo-Saxon mission proceeded. It shows also the remarkable alertness, generosity and farsightedness needed to send this mission; many a pope in Gregory's situation might have thought that he had done well enough to weather the crises nearer home.

THE ENGLISH MISSION

The first biography of Gregory the Great, written at Whitby probably between 704 and 714, has a well-known version of how he originally became interested in converting the Anglo-Saxons:[27]

There is a story told by the faithful that, before he became pope, there came to Rome certain people of our nation, fair-skinned and light-haired. When he heard of their arrival he was eager to see them; being prompted by a fortunate intuition, being puzzled by their new and unusual appearance, and above all, being inspired by God, he received them and asked what race they belonged to. (Now some say they were beautiful boys, while others say that they were curly-haired, handsome youths.) They answered, 'the people we belong to are called Angles.' 'Angels of God,' he replied. Then he asked further, 'what is the

name of the king of that people?' They said, 'Aelli,' whereupon
he said, 'Alleluia, God's praise must be heard there.' Then he
asked the name of their own tribe, to which they answered,
'Deire,' and he replied, 'They shall flee from the wrath of God
(*de ira dei*) to the faith.'

The story continues how at Gregory's urgent request his
predecessor, Pope Benedict, allowed him to set out for England,
but the Roman crowd were greatly perturbed by this and as the
pope went along the road to St. Peter's they shouted in chorus,
'you have offended Peter, you have destroyed Rome, you have sent
Gregory away.' And so Gregory was recalled.

Now as it stands it is easy to pick holes in the credibility of this
story.[28] Pope Benedict was not Gregory's predecessor; he was his
predecessor but one. It is very unlikely that Gregory would have
wanted to undertake a journey to Britain in Benedict's time, just
when he had found the peace of the cloister. And the Roman
crowd, so worried about his going to England, seem to have had
nothing to say about his subsequent dispatch to Constantinople.
Yet this anonymous author was in quite a good position to have
access to genuine Roman traditions. The abbess of Whitby in his
(or her) time was Aelffled, the daughter of Eanfled. Eanfled had
herself lived at Whitby for some years, and she had been brought
up in Kent, having been taken there from Northumbria by
Paulinus, one of the missionaries from Rome. Aeffled herself was
a friend of St. Wilfrid who knew Rome well. In fact that author
had one piece of knowledge about Gregory which Bede lacked
and which was both Roman and correct. He knew that Gregory's
mother was called Sylvia, and John the deacon later saw a named
portrait of this lady in Gregory's monastery on the Coelian Hill.

It has been shown convincingly by Dom Suso Brechter that this
story does very probably contain a kernel of historical truth in
it.[29] First, there is nothing unlikely about Deiran slaves being in
Rome around, say, 590. We have only to think of the wars
between Anglo-Saxon kingdoms in general and between Bernicia
and Deira in particular about this time, of the fact that war
captives were often sold into slavery, and of the known slave
traffic between Britain and Gaul and between Gaul and Italy. Our
patriotic Deiran author does not actually say that these boys were
slaves, but that is probably what they were. Second, we know
that Gregory was interested in Anglo-Saxon slaves, because in

September 595 he wrote to his administrator or rector in Gaul and ordered him to buy English boys of 17 and 18 years who could be educated in monasteries, and his letter clearly envisages that they would be brought to Rome for this purpose.[30] There is nothing in this letter alone to show whether the Anglo-Saxon boys so bought (if they were bought) originally inspired Gregory's interest in the conversion of this people, or whether it reflected an interest already there. But the latter is perhaps suggested, third, by other evidence, and in particular a letter of Gregory to the bishop of Autun in 599, in which he says he had long thought of a preaching mission to the Anglo-Saxons.[31] It is at least likely, therefore, that Gregory's interest in preaching the Gospel to the Anglo-Saxons was aroused by his encountering pagan slaves of that race in Rome either before or during his pontificate.

All this is not to say that Gregory had no other motives for sending the English Mission, though nothing very convincing has been put forward. It used to be thought that he was anxious to convert the Anglo-Saxons before the British church, with its irregular customs and tenuous links with Rome, tried to do so. But Gregory knew practically nothing about the British church and in any case the Anglo-Saxons had been safe enough from them for a century and a half. Still less plausible is the notion that Gregory would just have been becoming aware of the Irishman, Columbanus, who was establishing his monasteries in Burgundy, and would feel the danger that such men, with their eccentric methods of calculating Easter and their ambiguous attitude to papal authority, might get their hands on the Anglo-Saxons. There is, however, no evidence that Gregory had heard of Columbanus before he sent the English Mission. The view is held that the mission was of importance to Gregory as signifying an extension of papal ecclesiastical and jurisdictional influence. It is maintained that Gregory pounced on the style 'universal bishop', used by the patriarch of Constantinople, because this was incompatible with the extension of the pope's jurisdiction in the West.[32] But since, as we have seen, Gregory's correspondence did not emphasize the jurisdictional but the moral aspect of this issue, the supposed relation of it to the English mission must be considered very hypothetical. Finally, it is sometimes argued that Gregory hoped for the reform of the Frankish church in Gaul, whose worldliness and simony disturbed him, and that this might be achieved by the links that would be created between the Anglo-

Saxon and Gaulish churches. That Gregory wanted to foster links between the two churches is undeniable.[33] The letters written to Frankish kings and bishops asking them to protect and help his missionaries is evidence of that; so is his advice to Augustine, which was adopted, that he should take Frankish interpreters with him to Kent. Whether he had any more specific or far-reaching scheme is doubtful. Gregory's letter to the Bishop of Arles, advising him to listen to any correction which Augustine might suggest while with him, could be taken to show that Augustine was intended to be an instrument of reform in the Frankish Church. But the Rule of St. Benedict recommended an abbot to consider prudently any criticisms made in charity by a monk who visited his monastery,[34] and Gregory's idea was perhaps no more than this, that God might speak through an outsider.

However large or small the English mission figured in his general scheme of things, it seems clear that Gregory's motive in sending it was primarily a pastoral one. He wanted the English to have the benefit of the Gospel.

There are perhaps three reasons why Gregory should have picked specifically on the Anglo-Saxons as the object of his missionary interest. First, Britain had been a province of the Roman Empire, and the idea of the Roman Empire was the dominant factor in Gregory's conception of geography. The Anglo-Saxons were the only obvious case of a pagan people within the empire. Gregory's mission was an act of some originality. The Roman church had not often sent missionaries to preach to pagan peoples before, although missionary enterprises not under the auspices of Rome, like St. Patrick's, were common. But those peoples who came into the Roman empire, like the Franks, were quickly converted to Roman Christianity, unless they had been won for Arian Christianity first.[35] Thus, original as the mission was in one sense, the fact that it was to a lost province of the empire placed it in another sense within a previous pattern. Secondly, the Anglo-Saxons were still honest-to-goodness heathens; they were not, as the Visigoths had been and the Lombards still were, Arian heretics. The possibility that the Anglo-Saxons might be tainted by Arianism, if nothing were done about them, is likely to have worried Gregory far more than their being tainted by Irishmen. Arianism was the bogey which he knew. And thirdly, he probably had an idea that Ethelbert's *bretwaldaship* had created a condition of political stability in which such a mission would be viable.

Gregory would certainly have little enough knowledge about this island on the fringes of his world; a few old geographies and a little hearsay might have accounted for most of it. But as Ethelbert was married to a Frankish Christian princess (Bertha, daughter of King Charibert), as Kent of which Ethelbert was king had important trading and other contacts with Gaul, particularly south of the Loire,[36] and as Gregory also had contacts with Gaul, he clearly could have had an impression of Ethelbert's position.

Why did Gregory choose Augustine to head his mission? For those to whom Augustine appears as an unintelligent coward and bigot it is naturally a puzzle why so shrewd a man as Gregory should have sent him. We shall have occasion in the next chapter to see whether Augustine was quite the unimpressive figure which is usually depicted; there is, however, another point here, which has been brought out by Miss Deanesly.[37] There were indeed plenty of able clergy in Rome on whom Gregory's choice might have fallen, but perhaps they would not exactly have leapt at the opportunity to come to this island, ridden as it was with fogs, swamps, forests and kings with unpronounceable names. On the other hand, Augustine was a monk. He was the prefect of Gregory's own monastery, with responsibility for its discipline and the supervision of its estates. His companions on the journey were likewise monks. They were all bound to Gregory by the vow of obedience; and to Augustine, especially when he was appointed their abbot. Moreover, there were by now many precedents, both in the East and in the West, for the use of monks as missionaries, near to their monasteries and far away from them.[38]

We can follow the route taken through Gaul during 596–97 by Augustine and his companions with the help of Gregory's surviving letters of recommendation to the bishops whose sees lay on their journey. They came to Marseilles, probably by sea, and then went up the Rhône, through Vienne, and across, by way of Autun, to the Loire and Tours.[39] Tours was by no means on the direct line from the Rhône to Kent, but the missionaries could pray there at the famous shrine of the missionary bishop, Martin; they would probably find it easiest to take a boat from Tours to Kent because of the close trading and political links between the two; they might for the same reason ensure for themselves a warmer welcome in Kent coming directly from this city; it might have been here that Augustine secured his interpreters. There could have been many good reasons for visiting

Tours. King Ethelbert met the party on the island of Thanet—in the open air for fear that indoors they might get the better of him with their magical arts. Augustine preached effectively, and the king, though not willing to abandon his own religion there and then, gave them a place in Canterbury and complete liberty to preach their religion.[40] In the following year, July 598, Gregory wrote to the Patriarch Eulogius of Alexandria. He had already had news of his mission to the English, a people 'placed in the corner of the world and until this time worshipping sticks and stones.' Augustine had been so resplendent with miracles that he seemed to imitate the powers of the apostles; and on his first Christmas Day amongst them it was said that over 10,000 of these people had been baptized.[41] In due course Augustine sent Laurentius, the priest, and Peter, the monk, to Rome and in the summer of 601 Gregory sent a second mission, headed by Mellitus, to join Augustine. With these he sent some answers to questions of church discipline which Augustine had put to him, and various books, sacred vessels, vestments and relics.

It is worth considering briefly the nature of the establishment founded by Augustine at Canterbury. Was it a monastery, with ascetic and contemplative monks, living a communal life according to a monastic rule? Or was it a cathedral church, staffed by clergy who were essentially administrators, engaged in pastoral work, and perhaps even living in private quarters on their own stipends? In Rome at this time the distinction was a perfectly clear one. Monks lived a contemplative life in monasteries, while the secular clergy were responsible for organizing the finances, the pastoral work and the celebration of mass in the city's basilicas. Gregory the Great insisted that the duties of each way of life were so onerous that nobody should combine the two; nobody in the daily service of the church should be bound by the restraint of the monastic life. But in Canterbury, and in the early Anglo-Saxon church in general, the distinction was not nearly so clear. Augustine himself was a monk, and Gregory advised him that, as he had been instructed in the monastic rule, he should not live apart from his clergy. Gregory also envisaged, however, that Augustine would be taking in Anglo-Saxon boys and training them for the ministry, and that some of these, while remaining in the service of the church in minor orders, might wish to marry, receive stipends and live in separate houses. In fact, it was probably envisaged that the cathedral church would become in the

The Finglesham Buckle, seventh century, Kent (see pp. 26 and 64)

2. St. Cuthbert's Cross, probably seventh century, Northumbria (see p. 163)

3. The Ixworth (Stanton) Cross, seventh century, East Anglia (see p. 65)

4. The Sarre Brooch, seventh century, Kent (see p. 19)

5. Santa Sabina, Rome, fifth century (see p. 168)

6. St. Peter's, Bradwell-on-Sea, Essex, seventh century (see p. 101)

future a corporation of secular clergy, of the kind common in city and country churches on the Continent. And so Augustine also founded the church of SS. Peter and Paul, just outside the city, as a specifically monastic centre. The actual development of the cathedral church in the two centuries after Augustine's time, however, is a matter of conjecture.[42]

It is necessary to say that we are ignorant about much of importance in the Gregorian mission to Kent. We do not know what liturgical books, if any, were brought by Augustine or Mellitus, as we shall see in a later chapter. We know that Augustine was only an abbot in 596 and that he was a bishop by 598. He was presumably consecrated bishop in Gaul, but when and where we do not know. Autun, Lyon and Arles have all been put forward as possibilities. We cannot even be certain from when he thought of himself as having a permanent see at Canterbury. Perhaps most important of all, we cannot be certain when King Ethelbert was baptized. Bede drew the conclusion that he was amongst the earliest converts in 597. There is, however, reason to believe that Bede knew very little about the Gregorian mission except what he could learn from those of Gregory's letters with which the priest Nothelm had supplied him. And none of Gregory's letters show clearly whether Ethelbert was a Christian or not even in 601. All that is certain is that he was baptized before his death in 616.[43]

There were, of course, some good reasons why Ethelbert should want to be a Christian. Quite apart from spiritual considerations about which we have no evidence, it was worth having the notice of the pope and being drawn closer to the civilized and wealthy axis of Mediterranean life. More particularly—and this was the point to impress an old warrior *bretwalda*—the Christian God seemed to serve his adherents well in battle. Ethelbert had been married 30 years to a Frankish queen and could not be ignorant of the handsome dividends which the great Merovingian, Clovis, and his successors had reaped from their Christianity and Catholicism. It may well be asked why he had not allowed his wife to convert him earlier. The answer seems to lie in the implication of political dependence on the Franks which such a step might raise. The indications are, as Dr. Wallace-Hadrill has recently suggested, that Ethelbert was ready by 597 to think of accepting Christianity from Rome, where he had not been ready to accept it from the Franks earlier.[44] On the other hand, there

were also good reasons why he should pause before being converted, or why if he were converted, he should be tolerant
towards those who remained loyal to the old religion. The chief
reason was the strength of the attachment to paganism in Kent
and in the other kingdoms of which Ethelbert was overlord. As
Sir Frank Stenton remarked, 'five undoubted places of heathen
worship can still be identified within a radius of 12 miles from
Augustine's church of Canterbury;' and at least one Kentish
warrior was wearing a buckle, adorned with a symbol of Woden's
cult, half a century later[45] (Fig. 1). In the kingdom of the East Saxons,
Ethelbert's nephew, Sabert, was sufficiently under his thumb to
accept Christianity when his uncle did, and Ethelbert himself
established a bishop's church in this kingdom at London, but this
was actually within view of the commanding pagan sanctuary of
Harrow-on-the-Hill.

The strength of Anglo-Saxon paganism impressed itself on
Gregory's mind, though not without a struggle. When the party
headed by Mellitus left Rome late in June 601, they took with
them orders from the pope that pagan temples and idols were to
be systematically destroyed. But a month later Gregory sent
another letter after Mellitus on his journey. He had been thinking
for a long time about the matter of the English, and he did not
after all think their temples should be destroyed; they should be
sprinkled with holy water and used for Christian worship. Moreover, on the great feasts of the Church they should be allowed to
slaughter cattle and have feasts as they had formerly done; people
with such obdurate minds had to be allowed to reach the
highest peaks by gradual steps rather than by sudden leaps.[46]

Nothing shows more clearly the nature of the calculated risk
which Ethelbert had to take in becoming a Christian than the
fact that his own son, Eadbald, and the three sons of King Sabert
remained pagans. In each kingdom, that is to say, a court party
formed which was opposed to Christianity. After Ethelbert's death
Eadbald led a pagan reaction in Kent, (albeit a short-lived one
before he was converted), and the same thing happened amongst
the East Saxons after Sabert's death in 616 or 617.[47] Sabert's
sons teased Mellitus, who was bishop of London. When they saw
him distributing communion they demanded to be given a little
piece of the white bread, surely a small enough request, and when
he refused they drove him out of the kingdom.

The position of the bretwaldas was of great importance in

bringing about the conversion of lesser kings. Not only were they anxious to propagate their newly acquired faith, but they were also nervous lest their failure to carry their under-kings should result in the under-kings' seeing where they might get with the old gods in rebellion. They were rightly nervous. The decision to accept or reject Christianity was bound to have a political aspect where kings were concerned. This is clearly seen in the case of Redwald, king of the East Angles, who was converted to Christianity while he was visiting Ethelbert in Kent:[48]

> But (says Bede) returning home he was seduced by his wife and certain perverse teachers; he turned away from the sincerity of faith, and his last state was worse than his first. Thus in the manner of the ancient Samaritans he seemed to serve both Christ and the gods whom he served before; in one and the same temple he had an altar for the sacrifice of Christ and another for the victims of demons.

Redwald was the only East Anglian king who ever became a *bretwalda*, and moreover he seems to have achieved this position before Ethelbert's death in 616. When Ethelbert died he had been king for 56 years and his powers may have been failing before the end. It is now thought by several scholars, on the basis of the coin dates, that the Sutton Hoo ship burial may be Redwald's memorial.[49] Even if it were later, the power expressed by it was the creation of Redwald; and it may have been he, who returning from Ethelbert's court a convert to Christianity, brought with him the pair of Byzantine silver spoons with the words PAULOS and SAULOS inscribed on them, which were laid amongst the treasure and had evidently been a baptismal present to a convert. Had the Sutton Hoo ship burial never been discovered, the prosperity of South-East Suffolk, where the centre of East Anglian royal power lay in the first half of the seventh century, would nonetheless have been evident from the archaeological finds of imported glass in other places.[50]

Now the political significance of Redwald's conversion and relapse must be clear. When he was converted he was still an under-king of Ethelbert; when he relapsed he was shaking off the overlordship of Kent and emerging as a *bretwalda* himself. Not that he rejected Christ. Many gods could be worshipped in his temple, many could be invoked on the battlefield. But the point was that as Ethelbert was a Christian there was room for Redwald to try something else in order to achieve his independence of him. This was perhaps what Redwald's ambitious, formidable and perceptive wife had appreciated.

We have already seen how Redwald secured for Edwin of Deira, son of Aelle, the kingdom of Northumbria, around 616. Edwin was then a pagan, but some time afterwards he married a Christian princess of Kent, Ethelburga, and she went north accompanied by Paulinus, one of the Roman monks whom Gregory had sent to England with Mellitus in 601. When Edwin married Ethelburga and the question of his own conversion was raised he promised to think about it, but it proved to be a Herculean labour to bring him finally to the point of baptism. The story is told in Bede.[51] Every stop was pulled out—letters and gifts from the pope, prophecies by Paulinus, a brilliant victory over the West Saxons (again the test in battle was a vital one); and the upshot of it all was that Edwin was moved—not to anything rash, for no one would have called Edwin a rash man—was moved to discuss the matter with his counsellors. What was the cause of this 'somewhat inexplicable procrastination', as it has recently been called?[52] Of course, Edwin may have held back largely on account of his spiritual and intellectual difficulties, but again we cannot discuss the matter in these terms for lack of evidence. But a careful study of Bede's *Ecclesiastical History* enables us to see political factors in his hesitation and conversion.

The whole question is made more interesting and easier to understand if Dr. D. P. Kirby is right in his recent suggestion, which seems convincingly argued, that Paulinus went north with Ethelburga not in 625 but as early as 619. Bede gave 625 as the date, but what he had was the date of Paulinus's episcopal consecration as bishop of York, and the assumption that Paulinus was consecrated at the beginning of his mission is not necessarily valid.[53] As Edwin was baptized in 628, Dr. Kirby's date would mean that he procrastinated not just for three years but for nine.

The obvious difficulty for Edwin was Redwald and East Anglia. While Redwald lived, conversion was all but impossible for Edwin; and even after his death (probably 624/625) East Anglia may still have been strong for a while under his son Eorpwald, a weaker man. It was not that Redwald was particularly intolerant of Christianity; he himself, after all, had an altar for Christ. But when his own *bretwaldaship* had depended on his shaking off the overlordship and the Christianity of Ethelbert of Kent, he might be expected to show much less tolerance towards a protégé of his who accepted Christianity precisely from Kent and the Kentish court.[54] What Edwin had to wait for, then, was a change in the balance of power between his own kingdom and that of the East Angles. He was to become a very powerful king, a *bretwalda* in fact, but for a long time he had to keep looking back over his shoulder at Redwald. By 628 when he became a Christian he was able to disregard the pagan power of East Anglia.[55] All the same, the first thing he did after his own baptism is most revealing; it was to turn round and secure the baptism of Eorpwald.[56] He made sure to set the tune for the East Anglian king to play.

What little we know of the efforts of Paulinus in all this suggests that he was a man of some subtlety and perception. The story was told that while Edwin was an exile at Redwald's court in 616, and while it looked for a black moment as if he were going to be handed over to his Bernician enemies, he had been sitting outside at dead of night brooding over his misfortunes, when a stranger suddenly approached him. The stranger foretold that 'a certain man' would persuade Redwald to deliver him from his troubles, establish him in his kingdom, and later would give him advice for his life and salvation. Edwin promised to submit to the counsel of such a man. Thereupon the stranger laid his hand on Edwin's head, admonished him to remember what had passed between them when that sign should be given him again, and vanished as quickly as he had appeared. And now, years later, as he sat alone brooding again—as usual one might almost say—Paulinus came upon him, laid his hand on his head, and asked whether he knew that sign.[57]

This was a decisive incident in the aeneid of the awestruck king towards Christianity, and what it shows is that Paulinus had put his finger on the East Anglian difficulty, on Edwin's fear of the power which Redwald had created. Bede had at second hand the reminiscences of an old man whom Paulinus had baptized in the River Trent not far from Lincoln and who remembered his tall figure and slight stoop, his black hair, his ascetic face and slender, acquiline nose.[58] Here was evidently a man of considerable presence, not to say psychological power. Whatever lay behind the vision at Redwald's court, Paulinus was using his gifts now in order to play upon something in Edwin's spiritual experience or in the workings of his mind and to point a moral which was perfectly clear. Not Redwald of East Anglia but a higher agency had saved him and set him up in his kingdom, and he, Paulinus, was now the representative of that higher agency.

In the last years of Edwin's reign the power of Penda, the pagan king of Mercia, developed, and in 633 he and the British king Cadwalla in alliance defeated and killed Edwin at the battle of Heathfield. Paulinus fled back to Kent with the queen and her young daughter, Eanfled, and only James the deacon was left in Northumbria. The momentum of the Roman mission was spent. The see of Canterbury passed into the hands of worthy men but men without apparent stature; the initiative came to be with the Irish monks whom Oswald, when he reunited Northumbria, summoned from Iona. But Kent remained a foothold of Roman Christianity in England, nor was the memory or indeed the presence of the Roman Church ever obliterated from Northumbria. The achievements of Gregory's mission, therefore, were of decisive importance in the history of English Christianity.[59]

4 The Roman Missionaries

One of the major puzzles of Bede's *Ecclesiastical History* is that when one puts it down after reading the first three books one realizes that though Bede was a supporter of the Roman Church order it is the Irish missionaries who have made the overwhelming impact on the imagination. The pages about the Romans, who should have been his heroes, rather limp along, while the pages about the Irish or Irish-trained monks, whose church order and calculation of the date of Easter left much to be desired, are full of life and attractive information. There is nothing about Augustine at once so outstanding and so vivid as the famous story of how King Oswin of Deira gave a splendid horse to Aidan, and of how, after Aidan had given it away to the first beggar whom he met, a highly charged scene of mutual reproof and reconciliation occurred between the two men. The pages on the Romans, like their subject, seem dignified and official rather than warm.

The first point which we have to appreciate is Bede's difficulty over information about the Romans. It was not just that he could have spoken to people who knew Aidan, which he could hardly do for Augustine or even Paulinus, for Bede relied mainly on traditions preserved by one religious community or another, and traditions could have been preserved at Canterbury as well as anywhere. His informant at Canterbury was Abbot Albinus. 'He carefully ascertained,' says Bede, 'from written records or from the old traditions, all that the disciples of St. Gregory had done in the kingdom of Kent or in the neighbouring kingdoms. He passed on to me whatever seemed worth remembering through Nothelm, a godly priest of the church in London, either in writing or by word of mouth.'[1] Nothelm had also brought back from the Lateran archives at Rome copies of papal letters which he passed on to Bede. Now when we ask what Abbot Albinus thought 'worth remembering', the answer is that while he regarded anything which looked like an official document almost with veneration his notions of interest were otherwise severely circumscribed. Not for him these fanciful extravaganza about horses!

It is here that we come upon the effect of the Roman virtue of *gravitas*. A religious man must be grave. The highest praise which Gregory the Great could bestow on any man, as his letters constantly show, was to call him a man of gravity; this was the virtue which, above all virtues, recommended someone to the episcopate in his view.[2] The Rule of St. Benedict gives a fairly good idea of what is meant by gravity. When the bell goes for the night office, it says, the monks are to rise without delay and hasten to forestall one another to the work of God, but in such a way that there is no unseemly bouncing about; everything is to be done with self-restraint and gravity. The intoning of psalms or antiphons in church shall not be entrusted to any and every person, but only to those who can edify, since everything should be done with humility, reverence and gravity. Particularly illuminating is the passage where it is said that when a monk speaks he is to do so gently and without laughter, humbly and with gravity, in a few sensible words, for 'a wise man is known by the fewness of his words'.[3] To a Roman, excessive talk was the height of 'levity'. In his *Morals on Job*, Gregory wrote against precipitate talk, unrestrained talk, and the talkativeness of heretics, and he devoted a long passage to the evils of the indiscriminate talk of Eliphaz the Themanite when he sat with Job.[4] All this has an important bearing on Bede's Canterbury sources. Where gravity is cultivated as a primary virtue, where exterior deportment, calm dignity and restraint in words and actions count for so much, there will be an ethos unfavourable to the spontaneous exhibitions of personality and to the retailing of such stories as circulated about Fursey or Aidan. It is hard to conceive of Augustine involved in emotional scenes and weeping at dinner with Ethelbert, and equally hard to think that the grave monks or clerics of Canterbury, with their legal wisdom and their few words, would be passing round such stories. The atmosphere of Augustine's school at Canterbury, where he was training Kentish and other Anglo-Saxon boys for the ministry, must have resembled that of Dr. Arnold's classes at Rugby and 'the startling earnestness with which the doctor would check in a moment the slightest approach to levity'.[5]

So Bede had no revealing anecdotes about Augustine from

Canterbury. Augustine's meetings with the British bishops are the subject of the only narrative of any substance about him. Pope Gregory had laid down that the British bishops, about whom he knew very little, should be subject to Augustine, and with this end in view Augustine arranged a conference with them on the borders of their own territory somewhere near the River Severn, in order to attempt to secure their co-operation in his mission. The British ecclesiastical leaders, however, doubtless thinking of the great traditions of their church, saw no reason to give up their own customs where they differed from those of the Romans, nor to subordinate themselves to missionaries who came under the auspices of their Anglo-Saxon enemies from a Rome which long ago had abandoned them to the tender mercies of those very enemies. From the start Augustine was suspect. But when he healed a blind man whom the British had been unable to heal, an Englishman oddly enough, they agreed to consult with their people about giving up their old customs (their calculation of the date of Easter in particular, according to Bede). Those who were to go to the second council went first to seek advice from a wise hermit. Ought they to abandon their traditions at the preaching of Augustine? They asked. The hermit answered : [6]

> 'If he is a man of God, follow him.' They replied, 'But how can we tell?' He answered, 'The Lord said : take my yoke upon you and learn of me, for I am meek and lowly of heart. If this Augustine is meek and lowly of heart, it is to be supposed that he himself bears the yoke of Christ and is offering it to you to bear; but if he is harsh and proud, it follows that he is not from God and we have no need to regard his words.' Once more they said, 'But how can we know even this?' He said, 'Contrive that he and his followers arrive first at the meeting place and, if he rises on your approach, you will know that he is a servant of Christ and will listen to him obediently; but if he despises you and is not willing to rise in your presence, even though your numbers are greater, you should despise him in return.'

Bede's whole purpose in reciting this lengthy story about the British bishops was to show how stiff-necked they were when confronted with the Roman order and the right way of calculating Easter. Yet he must have been sensitive enough to realize that he had now brought every reader or listener to the point of feeling that any man in Augustine's position, even one with right on his side in calculating the date of Easter, was bound to stand up. Unfortunately, Augustine remained seated. And from his chair he proceeded to lay down his terms for co-operation, employing a rather high and mighty tone. The British contradicted everything he said, but it was no part of Augustine's philosophy merely to shrug his shoulders and take the view that against stupidity the gods themselves wage war in vain. He promised divine vengeance, and it came, as Bede records not without glee, when Ethelfrith of Northumbria slaughtered the British some years later at the battle of Chester. Mrs. Chadwick suggested that Bede had this saga (as she calls it) from some monastery in Mercia, on the British border and violently anti-British.[7] Actually, for all the strictures on the British in the rest of the story, the passage about their consultation with the hermit and their second meeting with Augustine are seen so much through British eyes—that is how Augustine himself is seen—that that part may originally have come from the British themselves and have been woven into the story elsewhere. But we need not go into this question. Our point is that the story as a whole came to Bede from someone who was very anxious to show how pig-headed the British were, but had not the slightest brief to save Augustine's face. It was no Canterbury tradition. Here is the kind of difficulty which Bede had with his information. He had but one extended narrative about Augustine and it forces us to see him through the eyes of his enemies or at least of those who were indifferent to him.

Augustine clearly had little idea of the great tradition which made the British Church resent his approaches. His attitude was perhaps similar to what it would have been if, as the prefect of Gregory's monastery in Rome, he had gone out to deal with some truculent tenants on one of the monastic estates. Had he also, perhaps, Gregory's *Pastoral Care* in mind: the passages about how a pastor, even though he should always keep a sense of his own lowliness and should show the loving-kindness of a mother, was not to be so humble as to prevent his showing the sternness of a father;[8] how Peter had refused to accept the veneration of Cornelius but had shown more authority when he struck down Ananias and Saphira;[9] particularly, how the pastor's reproof was to be very severe when the fault was not recognized by the one committing it?[10] Was he perhaps thinking of Gregory's comment on Job's curse, that it was right for holy men to deliver a curse if this were done not from the malice of revenge but from strictness of justice?[11] There is no attempt here to offer an excuse for Augustine. Gregory himself insisted that the true pastor had always to judge which approach was the right one with particular people in particular cases. Whether the loving-kindness of a mother or the sternness of a father were appropriate was a matter of discretion; and it could be argued that Augustine had not judged very nicely in these circumstances. What this does lead on to, however, is the close relation between the behaviour of the Roman missionaries and the ideals of Gregory the Great.

One question greatly exercised Gregory. He had held public office in Rome but had given it up to become a monk. Gregory had fled from the world and had sought a life of contemplation, only to find himself snatched from the quiet of his cloister by the force of circumstances, and swept onto the papal throne. An administrator once again: what could he do? His first letters and writings after he became pope are full of this problem, and full of attempts to rationalize about it. It was certainly wrong to covet office and glory in its exercise, he wrote in the *Pastoral Care*; was it not in just such a way that the king of Babylon had glowed in the achievement of building his city? Yet to refuse office out of a desire for the contemplative life was surely inexcusable obstinacy.[12] Fortunately, as Gregory pondered over his situation he perceived that it was not hopeless. Contemplation could be practised within the life of action. Indeed, it was necessary that it should be so. It was essential that men who performed 'outward works' should be always returning to the fire of contemplation in order to revive the flame of their holy zeal, to glow again from the touch of heavenly brightness; otherwise, good as their outward works were, they might freeze amidst them. To freeze amidst one's outward works—that was the effective metaphor which Gregory used in his *Morals on Job* to describe a way of life without prayer and contemplation.[13] When we look at Augustine, we see very much the man of affairs, organizing bishops' sees, framing questions on law and administration to put to the pope, persuading and helping Ethelbert to draw up in writing a code of laws, collecting liturgical information, making arrangements for the protection of church property, and conferring with British churchmen. Whatever one might find to censure in Augustine's conduct of those meetings with the British, it is impossible to mistake the air of a man intent on doing a brisk and efficient piece of business. One should not, however, forget the way of life which

Augustine and his companions led in their house at Canterbury; a life, as Bede reports baldly, characterized by frequent prayer, watching and fasting. Many found faith and were baptized through their admiration of the simplicity of it all.[14] One of Gregory the Great's most important contributions to the history of Christian thought lay in his advancement of the ideas about reconciling the active and contemplative lives. On this point Augustine had imbibed the lessons of his master.

So, it appears, he had upon another—the right attitude to miracles. A few years after Gregory had become pope he wrote the *Dialogues*, which tells of the lives and miracles of recent and contemporary Italian saints. One of the main lessons which Gregory wished to convey in this work, particularly in its first chapters, was that miracles were all very well, but what really mattered were a man's virtues. Nobody could work miracles unless these were preceded by virtues; the point of several of Gregory's stories was to show how the virtue was the necessary precondition for the working of the miracle. It was because his heart was touched by his sympathy for the mother, because he was a man of such exquisite charity, that Libertinus, prior of Fondi, was prevailed upon to restore the dead son to life; it was because he was a man of such chastity that it was given to Equitius of Valeria to calm the hysterical nun. And when Peter had heard about the miracles of Constantius, the sacristan, he asked to hear about his humility, and Gregory praised him. It was right to look among a man's virtues to discover his true self; the miracles which he performed were more often a temptation to his spirit; Constantius was great in his miracles but greater in his humility. A temptation to the spirit—the holy hermit of Mount Argentarius would never afterwards visit the scene of his miracle for fear of the earthly honour which it might secure him.[15] Gregory's attitude was to have a deep influence on those who wrote later about miracles. He gave expression to it once again in a letter to Augustine which is not evidence of Augustine's arrogance but of Gregory's strong feeling that he must awaken him to spiritual dangers. He had heard that through Augustine God was working great miracles among the English. That was matter for rejoicing because by outward miracles the English were drawn to inner grace. But it was also matter for fear, fear lest Augustine's own mind should be puffed up. Let him remember that when the disciples returned with joy after preaching and said to their heavenly master, 'Lord in thy name even the devils are subject to us,' they were immediately told, 'Do not rejoice on this account, but rather rejoice that your names are written in heaven':[16]

It remains, therefore, most dear brother, (the pope went on), that amidst those outward deeds which you perform through the Lord's power, you should always judge your inner self with strictness, and clearly understand both what you are yourself, and how great is the grace shown to that people for whose conversion you have received the gift of working miracles.

Perhaps it was because of the pope's admonition that Augustine should not glory in them that no record of any of his miracles survived—except that one which he was 'compelled by absolute necessity' to work in order to prove his case against the British.[17]

Nothing has had the effect of detracting from the reputation of the Roman missionaries more than their habit of deserting when things went badly for them. There was Paulinus's flight from Northumbria after Edwin's death and there was the drama of Mellitus, Laurentius and Justus (c.616). Mellitus, as we saw, was forced out of his see of London by a pagan reaction. He came into Kent (where there had also been a pagan reaction under Ethelbert's son, Eadbald) to consult with his colleagues, Laurentius, who had succeeded Augustine at Canterbury, and Justus of Rochester. They all agreed 'that it was better for them to return to their own country, where they might serve God in freedom, than to continue without any advantage among those barbarians, who had rebelled against the faith'. Mellitus and Justus crossed to Gaul and Laurentius was about to follow them, in fact he was spending his last night with his bed laid out in the church of SS. Peter and Paul and had fallen asleep after many prayers and tears to God for the state of the Church, when, in the dead of night, the prince of the apostles appeared to him, and scourged him, and rebuked him for deserting his flock. 'Have you,' he said, 'forgotten my example? For the sake of the little ones whom Christ entrusted to me as a token of his love, I endured chains, blows, imprisonment and every affliction. Finally I suffered death, even the death of the cross at the hands of infidels and enemies of Christ that I might at the last be crowned with him.' If Laurentius had forgotten, he was a very different man after this reminder. The scars left by St. Peter's stripes made scarcely less impression on Eadbald when he saw them; he was baptized and he recalled Mellitus and Justus.[18] If it could be said in justification of the Roman missionaries that their business was with kings and courts, that without royal support they were impotent, that, in addition, at least in 616 the pope was not particularly favourable to the general policies of Pope Gregory or particularly interested to support the English mission,[19] that to hold their ground in these circumstances would have been an exhibition of pointless courage and mere bravado—*nemo ad inutile tenetur*; yet did not the reproof of St. Peter, with his reminder to Laurentius of his own martyrdom, show where their duty lay?

To this one can only say that though St. Peter may have formed such a view of matters in heaven, his great successor on earth had earlier elaborated a quite different opinion. For Gregory the Great had a discussion of the very principle at issue in his *Dialogues*, and it is scarcely conceivable that any of the Roman missionaries should have been ignorant of it. He was speaking of how St. Benedict had left a monastery of which he was abbot after the monks, tiring of his monastic discipline, had tried to poison him. At this point Peter the deacon asked Gregory whether it was right for him to forsake the community once he had taken it under his care. The prudent pope, in answer to his high-principled deacon, said he thought it was right. 'In this matter,' he maintained, 'we cannot afford to overlook the attitude of the saints. When they find their work producing no results in one place, they move on to another where it can do some good.' Nobody could have accused St. Paul of fearing death, but he had escaped from Damascus. 'When he saw how little he was accomplishing there and with what great toil,' Gregory concluded, 'he saved himself for more fruitful labours elsewhere.'[20] It is hard to think that in the anxious consultation between Laurentius, Mellitus and Justus there was no talk of Benedict or of Paul at Damascus, and hard to think that those examples did not reverberate through the mind of Paulinus when he finally left Northumbria.

Mellitus, at least, was not lacking in courage, as we know from something Bede tells us of him. He succeeded Laurentius as archbishop of Canterbury, and on one occasion a fire broke out in the city of Canterbury as a result of some carelessness, and every effort against it seemed in vain; it raged on, rapidly destroying the city. Now an event of this nature was a crucial test to the missionaries; it was this kind of thing, and its effects on people's lives, which swayed them to accept or lapse from the Christian faith. Although Mellitus was ill, therefore, (suffering from gout, according to Bede) he had himself carried to the church of the Four Crowned Martyrs, where the fire was worst, and there, standing before it, he raised his hands in prayer. Immediately the wind changed and the fire stopped.[21] It would be a strange thing if Mellitus did not think of Marcellinus, bishop of Ancona, on this occasion. For in Gregory the Great's *Dialogues* there is an exactly similar story about him and his cathedral city, even down to the details that the fire was the result of carelessness and that Marcellinus suffered from gout.[22] Bede certainly knew the story but Mellitus presumably knew it too. Once again, therefore, the Roman missionaries had turned to the great pope for inspiration.

It will by now be obvious that if we are to make any sense of the few things which we know about these men who have been too little understood we must look to the man who sent them. They were for the most part his monks; they had probably heard his discourses and had the inestimable benefit of conversation with him; they must have had his books. His ideals were their ideals; everything suggests that they strove with all their might to live by them. And they could hardly have chosen a finer model.

5 Ireland

Unlike the British Churches, the Irish Church had a direct and profound influence on Anglo-Saxon Christianity. Irish Christianity in the seventh century was predominantly monastic, but it had not always been so. St. Patrick was a Roman Briton and he established in Ireland the sort of church organization normal in the Roman Empire, namely one based on bishops and dioceses, although there were certainly ways in which he adapted this organization to the tribal pattern of Irish society. In the mid-sixth century this episcopal organization was still the norm. But the period between about 540 and 615 was the great age of the monastic founders like Finnian of Clonard, Ciaran of Clonmacnoise, Comgall of Bangor and above all Columba, a member of the family of O'Neill, later high kings of Ireland, who sailed off to found his monastery on the island of Iona. The monasteries founded by these men became, in several cases, the heads of important confederations of monasteries (or monastic *paruchiae*), which became attached to or were founded from them.[1]

These founders, where we have anything approaching reliable knowledge about them, are seen as personalities of great power and contrasting colours. Columba, for instance, was a man of gentleness, who could not bear to think of his abbot at Durrow, one of the Ionan monasteries, forcing his monks outside for heavy labour in the rough weather, and who on the last day of his life forbade the attendant to drive off the white cart-horse which came and wept into his lap as he sat resting from weariness. But Columba was not, and could not afford to be soft-centred; a man in his position was expected to exercise some of the powers of the old druids. When he went among the Picts he had to compete with pagan magicians, purifying polluted wells and raising boys from the dead. At home he had to protect the property of his monastery by excommunicating men who attacked it. He had to be able to curse—in the flesh or (what was rarely less effective with these saints and very necessary for the subsequent protection and prosperity of their monasteries) from the grave. The Irish developed quite a ceremonial for cursing, but they had not always time to wait on ceremony. In the hagiographies that were written later, the curses of the Irish saints positively proliferate, until, as Plummer said, 'it seems to be regarded as extraordinary self-restraint if a saint does not use his maledictory powers on the slightest provocation'.[2] In those later *Lives*, written by men with fertile imaginations, they become whimsical in much else besides, hanging their cloaks over sunbeams and sailing across oceans on stone altars.[3]

The general character of Irish monasticism was derived ultimately from the monasteries of Egypt. The deserts of Egypt became a great retreat for hermits both when Christians were fleeing from persecution and after the persecutions when they fled from the decadence of late imperial city life and from a Church increasingly losing its pristine purity and becoming involved in worldly society. During the fourth century many of these hermits were organizing themselves into communities, often communities of men who had been attracted by the reputation of one particular hermit to live near him as his followers. The degree and type of organization varied very much from one place to another. St. Pachomius, who had been a soldier in the imperial army, had thousands of monks under him, divided into monasteries in which there were large cells like barracks housing some 40 monks each; the monks lived under a rule which contained detailed stipulations about times of prayer and instruction, times and quantities of food, and hours of sleep. Even here, however, Pachomius only professed to lay down minimum standards of asceticism and left it open to individuals to lead lives of greater austerity. But he regarded the community life as a satisfactory, indeed ideal, lifelong vocation, whereas at other monasteries it was regarded as merely the training for a more hermit-like existence.[4] In fact many communities retained strong traces of their origins—semi-eremitical monasteries, one might call them. The monks would live in separate cells of their own, cells in natural caves or built by themselves of stones or baked mud according to the locality, and they might join together for worship in the church or churches only at the night office of Saturday

to Sunday.[5] For the rest they prayed in a common act at certain
hours, each in his own cell, and otherwise weaved mats or rope
out of palm trees or made linen, meditating the while on
Scripture or reciting the psalms by heart. The Greek monks in
these communities might be learned, but the Copts would for the
most part not be, and much stress was laid on the memory. We
read of one monk who had an excellent knowledge of scripture
without ever having learnt to read, and of another who was said
to know by heart the Old and New Testaments and some six
million lines of Origen and other writers.[6]

Most Egyptian monks would probably have lived together in
communities under the rule of a single elder; but for those living
rather in loose-knit congregations of hermits, authority might be
exercised very informally, being less vested in the rule of an abbot
than in the experience of senior monks.[7] These preserved the
traditions of monastic observance, guided novices in their
spiritual development (sometimes by taking them in to their own
cells), helped them to understand the nature of prayer, and exposed
for them their weaknesses upon which the devil could play with
great technical versatility and deftness. Aspiring hermits were
remarkably free to wander from one community to another. The
most famous and experienced monks spent a good part of their
time seeing a succession of visitors, some of whom were genuine
seekers after the spiritual life, perhaps from distant countries,
while others were blatantly inquisitive tourists.[8] The courtesy and
even warmth with which complete strangers were received by
these men is a mark of their acute social consciousness, and of the
value which, lovers of solitude as they were, they placed on
Christian charity. In those monasteries which placed a higher
value on eremitic than on conventual life, the connection of some
of the hermits with the community was loose and their cells
distant in the extreme. One would carry the bucket of water,
which was to last him the week, five miles back to his cell after
the Sunday office,[9] another had to divide his bread into seven
portions for each day of the week, in order to remind himself
when he must return to church.[10] It was their high degree of
spiritual advancement which was thought to make this kind of
withdrawal possible to such men. Indeed the distractions of
company, the daily routine of a community, were so many
obstacles to their wrapt communion with God. And if the devil
should attack them—though there would come a time when such

attacks were the most unusual of despairing sallies on his part—
they were armed to meet him in single combat.

The life was austere, though it is not easy to give an idea of the
norm amongst so great a variety of monastic customs. Sleep might
run to four or five hours and that would be cut on the Saturday
night vigil. Food might consist of bread and water and perhaps
some fruit or vegetables, which would not be taken before late in
the day on Wednesdays and Fridays, the fast days. The practice
of asceticism, however, was largely a matter for the individual.
Although one finds little in Egypt to rival the ascetic feats of the
Syrian hermits, one must not call the Matterhorn a hillock just
because it is not Mount Everest. The hermits of Egypt considered
that *too* little food had an enervating effect on the life of prayer; it
was advisable to eat every day. But when Abbot Serenus enter-
tained John Cassian and his friend to dinner they ate table salt and
three olives each, and five grains of parched vetches, two prunes
and a fig. The amount of oil which Abbot Serenus took was hardly
enough to pass down his food, and he took it not so much for
its gastronomic value as to avoid the pride in abstaining from it.[11]
Macarius of Alexandria also believed that a man needed one meal
every day. There was a period in his life when he would break
up his biscuits and put them in a narrow-necked jar, and his
daily meal would consist of so much as he could extract with
one grasp of the hand. This Macarius was the hermit to whose cell
a hyena came with her cub in her mouth and gave the cub to him.
He saw that it was blind and with prayers and groans and spitting
cured it and gave it back to its mother. The next day the mother
returned with a sheep skin for him.[12] The love of animals was,
for the Irish, in part the spiritual inheritance of the Egyptian
desert.

Within the enclosure of an Irish monastery there would be,
rather in the way of an Egyptian community, many separate
buildings. There would be one or more churches, a refectory, guest-
house and workshops, and the huts which served as the cells for
the monks, perhaps in most cases two or three monks to a cell.
It was in such a hut that Columba sat on the day before he died
copying out the psalter.[13] On the West coast of Ireland, where
there were few trees, monasteries would be constructed in stone
from the beginning and some of these still survive. Generally,
however, the buildings would all be of wood or wattle, which is
why, until quite recently, most of the early monasteries were

thought to have disappeared without trace. But in 1969 a remarkable air survey of Ireland was published. A whole new world has been revealed by this survey in a country, which, because so much of it has remained undisturbed by urban and industrial development, lends itself peculiarly well to this kind of X-ray treatment. And amongst other things the sites of many early Irish monasteries have been discovered on account of the great circular embankments of earth by which they were originally enclosed. Some of these now remain only as very low banks, some are merely marked by a ring of hedges and ditches, some are no more than crop marks. Such features cannot be made out from the ground, but they are visible from an aeroplane in the late evening sunshine, though even in these conditions they are sometimes only just discernible.[14]

The organization of Irish monasteries, firmly centred on the rule of an abbot, was much tighter than in Egypt; survival would have been impossible if it had not been. Irish monks valued learning in a way which was foreign to most Egyptian monasteries. One could multiply the differences. But besides the lay-out of the monasteries there was a trace of Egypt in the special length and importance of the Saturday night vigil,[15] and in the attitude to food. The Irish were austere about food, although of course customs varied from one monastery to another, but they did not favour excessive austerity and it needed more to support life in Ireland than in Egypt. The monks of Iona consumed fish, as well as bread and milk. Nevertheless there were extremists in this matter also. The monks of St. Fintan of Cloneenaugh, a sixth-century abbot, lived on nothing but herbs and water, and in a later age they were praised for doing so. They had realized, said the eighth invocation of a *Litany of the Pilgrim Saints* (c. 800), that there was no abiding citizenship on this earth.[16] Fintan's contemporaries, however, were not sure that man's citizenship attached him to this earth by quite so slender a thread, and according to a later tradition, a group of neighbouring abbots visited him in a delegation in order to remonstrate with him. But he, forewarned of their visit by an angel, had a meal prepared as monastic hospitality demanded, after which the abbots were in no mood to make their criticisms before they departed. The next day Cloneenaugh went back on to herbs and water.[17]

It is essential always to be conscious that generalizations about one confederation of Irish monasteries are not necessarily valid for another. Their ethos may vary enormously and always bear the stamp of the founder and the traditions of spirituality and monastic observance associated with him. For the spirit of Ionan monasticism Adamnan's account of Columba's last day is the supreme testimony—the weeping horse, the copying of the psalter in the hut, Columba's running into the dark church as soon as the signal was given for the night office, the great light which shone for a moment in the church as he sank before the altar and then faded as others came, and the look of joy which spread over his face when he saw the angels who were to carry him to heaven.[18] It all happened in 597, the very year that Augustine landed in Kent. When Adamnan, Abbot of Iona, wrote about Columba a century after the saint's death, he was obviously drawing here on traditions which had been kept alive among the community. The bare rock, he tells us, formed Columba's bed, and for his pillow he used a stone which was still to be seen in Adamnan's own day. That stone pillow represented the characteristic type of austerity practised by the Egyptian monks.[19] On one occasion Columba retired to a wilder island near Iona and shut himself up there in a hut for three days without eating or drinking a thing. But at night an extraordinary light was seen escaping through the key-hole and the chinks in the door, and then it was that everything in Holy Scripture was made clear as the day 'to the eyes of his most pure heart'.[20] These great floods of light were the outward manifestation of the exquisite spiritual experiences which came to those who lead this life of physical hardship. The tenderness of these experiences was the other side of the matter.

Eastern monasticism was the source of inspiration for the monastic movements of the West, and if we ask how this inspiration actually reached Ireland, by what channels it was conveyed, the answer must lie primarily in Gaul. There were many direct links between Gaul and the Eastern Mediterranean in the fifth and sixth centuries. The monastic movement in Britain has sometimes been seen as the immediate influence on Ireland, but though the contacts between British and Irish clergy were numerous, it seems more likely that both in Britain and Ireland monasticism was developing simultaneously—in the course of the sixth century —under the same external, Gaulish stimulus. One of the first exponents of Eastern monasticism in Gaul was St. Martin, bishop of Tours, who founded a semi-eremitical monastery just outside his cathedral city in the late fourth century. The way of life of this unkempt and unprepossessing Pannonian was very different from the grand manner of the aristocratic Gallo-Roman bishops of his day. St. Martin himself, buried at Tours, became venerated as a saint, and Sulpicius Severus's attractive biography of him made an enormous impact. By itself, however, Martin's monasticism was too similar to monasteries in the East of which he could have had experience, was too lacking in organization, to attract a numerous following in Gaul. It was too much a loose association of solitaries. The really important figures in Gaulish monasticism were Honoratus, who founded the island monastery of Lérins off the French riviera, and John Cassian, abbot of St. Victor of Marseilles.

Cassian wrote his *Institutes* and his *Conferences* about 425. In his earlier days he had travelled among the communities of Egypt and discussed their customs with senior monks. The *Institutes* was his guide to their way of life for the benefit of Gaulish monasteries; the *Conferences* were — not exactly his conversations with the elders, for that was rather their literary form; there were 24 of them, precisely the number of elders in the Apocalypse — but they drew upon his conversations and experiences for the purpose of presenting his own spiritual and monastic teaching in a systematic exposition.[21] He and Honoratus, therefore, interpreted Eastern monasticism to the Gauls, but they also effected two adaptations which made it viable and gave it its distinctive character in the West. First, their monasteries were centres of learning. Several of the most significant scholars, theologians and occupants of episcopal sees in fifth-century Gaul had earlier been monks of Lérins. Second, they emphasized the cohesion and community aspect of monasteries, and above all, and in all circumstances, the rule of the abbot. In this way they made monasticism accessible to greater numbers; by about 475, over a century after Martin's arrival in Gaul, there were 62 known monasteries, whereas by 600 there were 215 as well as many more which cannot now be identified by name.[22]

The monasteries of Ireland clearly exhibited these Gaulish adaptations. It is not impossible, but perhaps unlikely, that Lérins and Marseilles were the chief direct influence on Irish monasticism. There seems little or no evidence of contacts, and if anything the indications are that Cassian was not much read amongst the Irish,[23] although he certainly gives insights into a tradition to which the Irish also had access. The likelihood is that the direct source of influence was the monasticism of the Loire basin. We have already spoken in an earlier chapter of Gregory of Tours' *Lives of the Fathers* (c.590). Gregory wanted here, as often in his literary activity, to glorify St. Martin whose shrine was in his own cathedral church. St. Martin's glory and that of Tours itself were closely interwined in his outlook.[24] He describes in this book the work of certain fifth- and sixth-century monastic founders. Some of them had a special devotion to St. Martin; many of them were active near the Loire or its tributaries on which Tours was the most important city. The monasteries of Brachio were at Vensat in the Auvergne near the river Allier and at Tours itself,[25] those of Patroculus were near the Allier,[26] and Ursus founded a monastery at Loches on the river Indre where he constructed a mill for his monks.[27] Nothing shows the importance of the Loire and its tributaries as a system of communications in the sixth century more clearly than the way in which the inspiration of St. Martin moved up and down it and the way in which it meant so much in Gregory of Tours' own knowledge. But the inspiration of Martin in all this was one on which the monasticism of Lérins and Marseilles had acted strongly.[28]

Now it is clear that in the early seventh century, and probably earlier, there was a flourishing intercourse between the region of the Loire and Ireland. The Gaulish sailors, whom Adamnan seems to suggest came regularly to Iona,[29] might have come from anywhere; but more particularly, when Columbanus was to be deported from Gaul in 610 and sailed up the Loire from Nevers, it was assumed as a matter of course than an Irish boat would be found for him at Nantes—and so it was.[30] Again, St. Philibert, abbot of Noirmoutier, a coastal island near the mouth of the Loire, was said to have prophesied that ships would come to his monastery with opportune supplies—and so they did, Irish ships bringing food and shoes.[31] Shoes were the great export of the Irish (with their cattle breeding and their tradition of craftsmen) at this period, shoes finely made from a single piece of leather.[32] The poorest hermits in Ireland itself counted it no luxury to possess a pair of leather shoes.[33] The chief commodities which the Irish took back from the Loire (and from the Garonne) were wine and oil. That seems to be the lesson of the fine red Mediterranean pottery ware of the sixth century which archaeologists have found at Bordeaux, Nantes and

Clonmacnoise, amongst other places.[34] And this in turn gives colour to a late and otherwise unreliable story about Gaulish wine merchants arriving at Clonmacnoise in the time of its founder St. Ciaran.[35] It may be that the Irish ascetics drank wine with as little compunction as those of Egypt are known to have done,[36] and that Fintan of Cloneenaugh was considered worthy of note, like St. David, precisely because he was a water-drinker. One commodity of greater importance than wine was also imported from the Loire region to Ireland, namely Sulpicius Severus's writings on St. Martin. It has been shown that these had a great vogue amongst the Irish.[37]

To make a suggestion about the external influence on the develoment of monasticisim in Ireland is not to explain the attractions of monasticism to the Irish, attractions so great that although the system of tribal bishops and dioceses probably continued alongside monasteries at least in many parts of Ireland, the monasteries became in the seventh century the more effective force in church life as a whole. The fact that Ireland was a rural country entirely lacking towns may have had something to do with this. Episcopacy flourishes where there are towns for episcopal sees; monasteries might have seemed more suitable ecclesiastical centres for a tribal society. Dr. Kathleen Hughes has recently offered a helpful explanation along two further lines.[38] The first has to do with the sacrosanctity of family property, an important feature of Old Irish law and society. Aristocratic families could found monasteries and their members could retain certain rights in them, the abbot founder could be a member of the family and his successors in the abbacy would be his family heirs. The tribal bishops of the sixth century, on the other hand, had been very much for excluding the interest of lay families from church property. Her second point is that the monastic confederations, the chief abbot of which was in an analogous position to the tribal over-king, could be widely scattered. Monks who travelled, monasteries founded by them in distant lands, were all part of the confede-ration. Thus monasticism was the perfect flexible institution to accommodate the Irish love for wandering.

As monasteries became more important than dioceses, abbots became more important than bishops. Bishops remained necessary at the least to administer the sacraments of orders and con-firmation, but it was thought that they should be chosen not so much for their capacity to rule as for their spiritual excellence,

and they could show their spiritual excellence in no better way
than by living in humility, subject to the commands of an abbot.
The Irish drew heavily on an Egyptian tradition—or one could call
it a monastic tradition—of the bishop's office, to which Martin
of Tours had belonged. The nature of this tradition was that holy
orders and episcopal consecration were among the weapons with
which the devil attacked the humility of religious men. Cassian
wrote of how an elder in the desert of Scete had gone to visit the
cell of one of the brethren and when he reached the door he heard
muttering inside. Now it was quite common for monks to recite
psalms while they worked, but as the elder listened it became clear
to him that this was something more serious. The brother was
imagining himself to be a deacon, delivering a stirring sermon to
the people, and when that was over, giving out the dismissal of
the catechumens as the deacon did.[39] If the mere thought of
the diaconate could so drag a man down into the slime of vainglory, what might the episcopate do? It was a thought that so
worried the ascetics that one of them, on being offered a
bishopric, had been known to cut off his left ear in the hope that
the mutilation would disqualify him.[40] Generally, however, it
was thought wrong to persist in refusing office; it was closing
one's eyes to the declared will of God. The best a monk could do
if offered a bishopric was to accept, to change his way of life as
little as possible, to preserve his humility by constant self-
reminders of his lowliness, and to seek out frequent opportunities
for being slighted. Bishop Archbius of Panephysis lived his
life in solitude and used to declare that 'he had not been
summoned to his office as fit for it, but complained that he had
been expelled from the monastic system as unworthy, because
though he had spent 37 years in it, he had never been able to
arrive at the purity which so high a profession demands'.[41] Still,
however many disclaimers a man might make on his own account,
he could not always stop others from respecting him. Respect
could become so intolerable, even to those who were not bishops,
that the only solution seemed to lie in disguise and flight, the
course taken by Abbot Pinufius, presbyter of a large Egyptian
monastery. He fled, and while his monks scoured the country for
him, he put on secular dress and gained admittance to another
monastery far away—as the assistant gardener.[42]

Now let us see what happened one day at Iona in Columba's
time:[43]

At another time there came to the saint a stranger who humbly kept himself out of sight as much as he could, so that none knew that he was a bishop. But yet that could not remain hidden from the saint. For on the next Lord's day, when he was bidden by the saint to prepare, according to custom, the body of Christ, he called the saint to assist him so that they should as two presbyters together break the Lord's bread. [It was the custom in Ireland for bishops to celebrate mass alone, but for other priests to concelebrate.] Thereupon the saint, going to the altar, suddenly looked upon his face, and thus addressed him: 'Christ bless you, brother; break this bread alone, according to the episcopal rite. Now we know you are a bishop: why until now have you tried to conceal yourself, so that the reverence due to you was not paid by us?'

This story reveals, of course, that by the time Adamnan was writing, a century after Columba's death, things were changing. Adamnan was bringing something Roman into the Irish idea of a bishop, trying to show with the authority of the saint himself that the bishop's position was one of respect.[44] The English bishops of the later seventh century who were trained in the Irish tradition also showed themselves more aware of the Roman values. But what was Adamnan—and Columba if the story is true—struggling against? Against the notions of humility, concealment and self-deprecation which had been part of the Irish concept of the episcopal office.

One of the most striking characteristics of the Irish was their sensitivity to nature. A ninth-century manuscript of Cassiodorus on the Psalms, written by a scribe who had been using a dip candle all winter, has a note in the margin which reads: 'Pleasant is the glint of the sun to-day upon these margins, because it flickers so.' The Irish scribes were great writers in the margin. Into the margin they poured all their personal observations. It was the outlet for their exuberant natures, which such disciplined works as Cassiodorus on the Psalms scarcely satisfied.[45] There was, moreover, much greater reason to wonder at the forces of nature once it became plain that to do so was not merely to satisfy the romantic inclination of man, but was also to discern with unmistakable clarity the ways of God. This was how it seemed to Chad, the bishop of the Mercians, an Englishman, but trained in the Irish tradition at Lindisfarne:[46]

If it happened that there blew a strong gust of wind when he was reading or doing any other thing, he immediately called upon God for mercy, and begged it might be extended to all mankind. If the wind grew stronger, he closed his book, and prostrating himself on the ground, prayed still more earnestly. But, if it proved a violent storm of wind or rain, or else that the earth and air were filled with thunder and lightning, he would repair to the church and devote himself to prayers and repeating of psalms till the weather became calm.

When Chad's followers asked him why he behaved like this he spoke to them of how 'the Lord thundered in the heavens, and the Highest gave forth his voice. Yea, he sent out his arrows and scattered them; and he sent out lightnings and discomfited them'. It was the purpose of God, he said, to remind men of that dreadful hour when the heavens and earth would be aflame and He would come to judge the living and the dead. From time to time He raised His hand through the trembling sky as if to strike, but did not yet allow it to fall. Those were the moments when we should search our hearts and consciences.

The Irish were not merely responsive to nature in general; they loved their own country in particular. So Comgall of Bangor and his monks were overwhelmed by the beauty of the swans which swam in Lough Foyle;[47] so it came about that many of the Irish historic traditions or legends were associated with places, particularly with high places. History in early Ireland was to a great extent the poetic explanation of the features of the Irish landscape. It was an embarrassing moment, indeed a professional setback, for the poet, Eochu, when he could not explain, on being challenged, who had set in place six mighty pillar stones.[48] Thus to leave his country, to cut himself off irrevocably from friends, relatives, places which he loved—a man could do no more than that to resign his own will to the will of God; that was martyrdom as surely as was the kind in which the martyr's blood actually flowed for Christ; that was the peculiar martyrdom of pilgrimage.

Pilgrimage (*peregrinatio*) was the single-minded search for God on this earth. The hermit might, in the language of the Irish, lead a life of pilgrimage in his cell. In fact such a life was preferable to pilgrimage in the body, unless pilgrimage in the body was undertaken for the one and only motive which could justify it— the removal of every earthly tie in order to be free for God. But if that was why a man left his country, he was in a long tradition of Christian perfection. Pilgrimage was one of the great driving forces in Irish Christianity. Some put to sea without knowing or caring where they were going, like the three Irishmen in 891 (a late example), about whose unpractical voyage the *Anglo-Saxon Chronicle* writes:[49]

> And three Scots came to King Alfred in a boat without any oars from Ireland, which they had left secretly, because they wished for the love of God to be in foreign lands, they cared not where. The boat in which they travelled was made of two and a half hides, and they took with them enough food for seven days. And after seven days they came to land in Cornwall, and went immediately to King Alfred. Their names were as follows: Dubslane, Macbethu, and Maclinmum.

Others had somewhat more specific objectives. There was a widespread feeling that somewhere in the middle of the ocean—nobody quite knew where—there was an island of paradise where the land was fertile and full of flowers, where the brilliance of Christ's light shone perpetually. And men embarked upon enormous voyages to find it. They put out into the Atlantic in tiny crafts, they were attacked by monsters, they landed on islands with astonishing singing birds, they even celebrated Easter on the backs of great whales. In these legends of later days they found their island, penetrable only through a dense cloud.[50] But there is no evidence from the sixth or seventh centuries that those who without doubt made these voyages had such good fortune, although it was thought that Cormac might have had, were it not for the monk who joined the expedition without his abbot's permission and so incurred the wrath of God.[51]

The perfect island might elude them, but the Irish had many islands off their own coast, and on these, monks chose to live out remote lives. The most remarkable of all the island sanctuaries was Skellig Michael, a pyramid of rock, some 700 feet high, seven miles out into the Atlantic off the South-West coast of Ireland. There, on a 600-feet precipice can still be seen the six stone bee-hive cells and the oratory of a small monastery. The cells are built with stone cupboards and paving, and are to this day well drained, 'weatherproof and snug'. This is the description of the recent air survey of Ireland:[52]

The monks built their cells within a series of enclosing terrace-walls on the steep eastern sides of the rock, some 600 feet above the sea. There are six dry-stone clochán of corbelled work, a Gallarus-type oratory, and a later church ('St. Michael's Church'). At the higher end of the shelf is a second, smaller oratory, and in the saddle between the two parts of the island is an enclosure which may have been the cemetery. In many places there are walled-in ledges forming small artificial terraces of earth which were used for the cultivation of herbs and vegetables.

These little ledges remind us of the small fertile patch in which St. Anthony, the greatest and one of the earliest of all Egyptian hermits, cultivated grain. And the site as a whole reminds us of the attitude of Anthony to his hermitage on the Inner Mountain; of how, stark and horrific as it was, he loved the place. Here, then, the monks lived in 'pilgrimage', looking out across the sea.

Around 800, a litany of Pilgrim Saints was composed in Ireland, probably in the monastery of Lismore. Although the meaning and allusions of many of its invocations are now lost upon us, we can still feel in some of them the sense of spiritual exaltation which surrounded the whole idea of pilgrimage. Such is the mysterious invocation which runs, 'Three thousand anchorites who assembled with Mumu for one quest with Bishop Ibar, to whom the angels brought the great feast which St. Brigit made to Jesus in her heart.'[58] People who lived in a world of that kind were never far from the angels; they experienced constantly their ministrations. And the spirit of the archangel Michael hovered with singular appropriateness over his high rock in the Atlantic Ocean.

It is often said that the Irish were motivated in their pilgrimages by missionary zeal. But we have to understand what is meant by missionary work in this context. If it meant that holy men who settle in some remote place to lead a life of prayer and asceticism will attract followers, or even that they are concerned to revitalize the whole of Christian society through this way of life, then the Irish were missionaries. But if it is meant that they deliberately set out to preach to, convert and minister to pagans, this is truer of some than of others. The founding of the monastery of Iona was, of course, an example of pilgrimage. Columba had left his own country to live on this island, and from it he went to convert King Brude of the Picts. Was that not a piece of missionary work, and by the community which later sent missionaries to England?

It certainly was, but the circumstances were perhaps exceptional. Iona was just off King Brude's coast and if his monks were to remain there in security, King Brude had to be converted to Christianity.

The Irishman who is often regarded as the missionary *par excellence* is St. Columbanus. Columbanus was a monk under Comgall at Bangor and about 590 he went to Gaul where his monastic life was profoundly influential in the spread of monasticism. His motive for leaving Ireland, however, is made quite clear by his biographer. He began to desire pilgrimage, being mindful of the Lord's command to Abraham, 'Go forth out of thy country and from thy kindred, and out of thy father's house, and come into the land which I shall show thee.'[54]

Now the Frankish kings in Gaul were Christians and Columbanus considered it important to have their support. The first thing, however, which he asked King Theuderic to do for him was not to find him pagans to convert or even churches to reform, but a wilderness for himself and his monks to live in. And so the King settled him in the wastes of Burgundy at Annegray. The Rule and Penitential of Columbanus, which survive, as well as the biography of Jonas written in the first generation after the saint's death, suggest that Columbanus's régime was unusually severe amongst those of Irish monasteries.[55] His penances were strict, although some of his orders may reflect economic constraints. Whereas Columba spared his monks outdoor labour in rough weather, Columbanus sent his monks out to bring in the harvest during a storm and those who obeyed his commands were kept miraculously dry; and the monk, Gall, relying on greater expertise in fishing than that of his abbot, went to a river other than the one to which he had been ordered and caught no fish.[56] Columbanus himself frequently retired some miles from Annegray, to lead an even more solitary life in a hollow of rock from which he had expelled a bear.[57] Not that he was generally on bad terms with bears. Later, when he was living as a solitary near Bregenz, he came to a most amicable agreement with a bear about their respective share of the blackberries.[58] In all this way of life there was little that could be called missionary in the ordinary sense.[59]

There was indeed a moment when Columbanus conceived during his time near Bregenz a genuine missionary project to go and preach to a tribe of pagan Slavs. But then he had a most significant experience in which the Irish strain was quick to re-assert itself. An angel appeared to him, drew the world as a circle and showed him that the whole of it was a wilderness in which he could continue to pursue his spiritual labours. From this he understood that he was not to take on himself the conversion of that people and he remained where he was.[60] The monks of Iona, in their turn came to Northumbria not because they wanted to satisfy a natural urge for undertaking missionary work, but because King Oswald, when he obtained the Northumbrian king-ship and reunited Deira and Bernicia under himself in 634, asked for them and the abbot of Iona responded to his appeal. It was an issue of obedience.

6 The Irish Missionaries

Oswald, as a Bernician and son of Ethelfrith, had lived in exile amongst the Irish during Edwin's reign, and had been converted by them to Christianity. Political exile was a powerful factor in royal conversions. When, on becoming king (635) he applied to the monastery of Iona, as was natural for him to do, for a bishop to further the Christian faith in his kingdom, he was first of all sent a man who could make no headway with the English. They thought him rigid and he found them uncouth. So he returned to Iona, and Aidan, who was considered to have more discretion, was sent instead.[1] Bede wanted primarily to present Aidan (with his love of peace, lack of avarice and concern for the poor) as an example to the clergy of his own day (see p. 44), but in order to do this he had to be particularly careful to dissociate himself from Aidan's Easter observance. He himself had once before been accused of heresy for his chronological teachings and had been greatly upset by it (see p. 41). Hence, by a rhetorical device, he turned his point inside out, expressing first his distaste for the Irishman's Easter, and then implying that he wrote of his good qualities only because, for the truthful historian (*verax historicus*), it was unavoidable.[2] In fact Aidan commanded universal respect in Northumbria, and was esteemed by such men as the Gaulish Felix in East Anglia and the Roman Honorius at Canterbury. While he lived nobody was willing to hold his observance of Easter against him.[3]

Aidan established a monastery and a base for his activities on the island of Lindisfarne, off the Northumberland coast near the royal castle of Bamburgh. At low tide this island is linked to the mainland by a causeway. Lindisfarne superseded Canterbury as the effective ecclesiastical centre of England for 30 years because of the calibre of its monks and the Northumbrian *bretwaldaship*

7. (*above*) Lastingham Abbey, Yorkshire. The present church is eleventh century onwards (see p. 102)

8. (*left*) The Kilfountain Stone, Co. Kerry, Ireland, sixth to seventh century (see p. 110)

9. (*right*) Bronze ornament for bookbinding, Whitby, eighth century (see p. 150)

10. The Hexham Chalice, eighth century (see p. 244)

which lay behind it. Bede explains the constitution of Lindisfarne in his *Life of St. Cuthbert* (721). He says that Aidan, who was its first bishop, was a monk and lived according to the monastic rule. From his time onwards the bishops of Lindisfarne had exercised their episcopal functions, while the abbots, whom they themselves appointed, had ruled the monastery.[4] Although he chose his own abbot, therefore, in all other respects Aidan was in the position which was thought correct for an Irish bishop—of a monk subject to monastic vows and the rule of an abbot. Whether Aidan would actually have thought of himself as bishop of Lindisfarne may be doubted. It was natural for Bede to think in these terms for he had grown up amidst a system of dioceses based on sees. There had been a bishop of Lindisfarne since he was a small boy, and since Archbishop Theodore organized the diocese of Northumbria in 678–79. But Aidan was a wandering missionary bishop (an *episcopus vagans*) and Lindisfarne was merely his monastic centre; he would have thought of himself simply as bishop of the Northumbrians.

Aidan was no bishop in the grand style. Bede says of him:[5]

He neither sought after nor cared for worldly possessions but he rejoiced to hand over at once, to any poor man he met, the gifts which he had received from kings or rich men of the world. He used to travel everywhere, in town and country, not on horseback but on foot, unless compelled by urgent necessity to do otherwise, in order that, as he walked along, whenever he saw people whether rich or poor, he might at once approach them and, if they were unbelievers, invite them to accept the mystery of faith; or if they were believers, that he might strengthen them in the faith, urging them by word and deed to practise almsgiving and good works.

In this matter of horseback Aidan was adamant. Bede has a famous story, the chief purpose of which was to illustrate the humility of Oswin, king of Deira for a while after Oswald's death until he was killed by Oswy of Bernicia. Oswin, he says, was a tall, good-looking man with pleasing manners, an open nature and a generous heart:[6]

He had given Bishop Aidan an excellent horse so that, though he was normally accustomed to walk, he could ride if he had to cross a river or if any other urgent necessity compelled him.

A short time afterwards Aidan was met by a beggar who asked him for alms. He at once alighted and offered the horse with all its royal trappings to the beggar; for he was extremely compassionate, a friend of the poor and a real father to the wretched. The king was told of this and, happening to meet the bishop as they were going in to dinner, he said, 'My lord bishop, why did you want to give a beggar the royal horse intended for you? Have we not many less valuable horses or other things which would have been good enough to give to the poor, without letting the beggar have the horse which I had specially chosen for your own use? The bishop at once replied, 'O King, what are you saying? Surely this son of a mare is not dearer to you than that son of God?' After these words they went in to dine. The bishop sat down in his own place, and the king, who had just come in from hunting, stood warming himself by the fire with his thegns. Suddenly he remembered the bishop's words; at once he took off his sword, gave it to a thegn, and then hastening to where the bishop sat, threw himself at his feet and asked his pardon. 'Never from henceforth,' he said, 'will I speak of this again nor will I form any opinion as to what money of mine or how much of it you should give to the sons of God.' When the bishop saw this he was greatly alarmed; he got up immediately and raised the king to his feet, declaring that he would be perfectly satisfied if only the king would banish his sorrow and sit down to the feast. The king, in accordance with the bishop's entreaties and commands, recovered his spirits, but the bishop on the other hand, grew sadder and sadder and at last began to shed tears. Thereupon a priest asked him in his native tongue, which the king and his thegns did not understand, why he was weeping, and Aidan answered, 'I know that the king will not live long; for I never before saw a humble king. Therefore I think that he will very soon be snatched from this life; for this nation does not deserve to have such a ruler.'

Not every bishop reared in the Irish tradition eschewed horseback; but those of Aidan's pupils like the humble Chad, who specially revered his memory, made a point of going about preaching on foot 'after the manner of the apostles'.[7] There was an issue of convenience here. To be on foot made it easier to talk with those whom the preacher met, and to talk on the level rather than *de haut en bas*. But there was also an issue of principle which could be clearly seen in the life of Martin of Tours. The whole point of Martin's life as bishop of Tours, or at least the whole point as presented by Sulpicius Severus, was that it should be a standing indictment of the pomp and grandeur with which many of the Gaulish bishops in the fourth and fifth centuries lived. Riding a horse was a mark of social standing.[8] Martin might ride a donkey—he had been riding a donkey, dressed in ragged old clothes, when some soldiers, not dreaming that he was a bishop, mobbed him.[9] But he would never ride a horse. Indeed the mere keeping of horses was to him a sign of the worst vainglory. After the monk Brictio had been induced to do such a thing, Martin actually saw the demons who were egging him on, two of them perched on a high rock.[10]

The bishops of the Irish tradition looked to Martin's life for inspiration in many ways. Aidan would often retreat from his pastoral labours to pray in the solitude of one of the Farne islands, some miles out in the North Sea from Lindisfarne.[11] Columba and Columbanus both had solitary retreats away from their monasteries. Chad, whose see amongst the Mercians was at Lichfield, built himself a place not far from his church to which he would retire to read and pray as often as possible, and it was there that he heard the wonderful song of rejoicing sung by those who were calling him from this world.[12] In the same way, Martin, 'who kept up the position of a bishop but not so as to lay aside the virtues of a monk', had established a monastery for himself about two miles outside Tours:[13]

> This spot was so secret and retired that he enjoyed in it the solitude of a hermit. For, on one side it was surrounded by a precipitous rock of a lofty mountain, while the river Loire had shut in the rest of the plain by a bay extending back for a little distance; and the place could be approached only by one, and that a very narrow, passage. Here, then, he possessed a cell constructed of wood. Many also of the brethren had, in the same manner, fashioned retreats for themselves, but most of them had formed these out of the rock of the overhanging mountain, hollowed into caves.

A first glance at the pages of Bede and one might think Aidan was really something of a courtier. Although Bede tells us that Aidan hardly ever ate with the king,[14] the next thing we learn is

Aidan's sitting at dinner with King Oswald when the king ordered the dainties which were set before him to be given to the poor, and likewise the silver dish, which was to be cut into pieces and distributed among them.[15] And then a little further on we see Aidan with King Oswin—again at dinner—when the scene about the horse occurred. It appears that, in spite of Aidan's being an infrequent diner at court, most of what Bede knew about him, apart from the miracles, had happened at dinner with the king. Bede might have relished a story or two about his preaching in the wilds of Northumbria, but he could not play the door-to-door sociologist; he was a monk, more or less tied to his monastery, and he had to wait for what information came in to him there. His sources of information on Aidan were obviously court sources.[16] Naturally, therefore, Aidan looks more of a courtier than he was. The truth is, Aidan was in an awkward dilemma. Missionary work could not succeed without the support of the king. It was Oswald who acted as Aidan's interpreter to his nobles,[17] it was the king's country seats which he used as bases for his preaching expeditions;[18] above all, it was royal approval and the freedom to move in court circles which gave him his contacts with the aristocracy, and such contacts were essential for his work. However remote Farne Island might have been, the island of Lindisfarne itself was nearly opposite King Oswald's main stronghold of Bamburgh on the coast, and it was, and still is, easy to reach the mainland on foot at low tide. As Miss Rosalind Hill has pointed out, Lindisfarne also has a good harbour.[19] Aidan well realized that he had to take some part in the life of the court. But at what cost? Were there not opportunities for the devil here, and worldly scenes which it would be unbecoming for a man of God even to witness? We know enough about Anglo-Saxon royal banquets to see that not infrequently 'the revels ran high and the troops became flushed with wine.'[20] Aidan was bound to ask himself whether the luxuries, the brilliance, the fast living at court were compatible with his calling as a monk and a man of prayer. Somehow he had to try and strike a balance; that was his problem. His answer, on the occasions when he was invited to eat with the king—and perhaps here he remembered St. Martin's reluctance to dine with the emperor[21]—was to go 'with one or two clerks, and having taken a small repast, make haste to be gone with them, either to read or write'.[22]

Aidan died in 651, leaning against an external wooden post of a church on a Northumbrian royal estate.[23] He had been a bishop for 16 years.

AFTER AIDAN

The spread of Christianity from Northumbria to other Anglo-Saxon kingdoms during the reigns of Oswald (635–43) and his brother Oswy (643–71) was an important function of their *bretwaldaship*. This *bretwaldaship* was none too secure until the death of Penda, the pagan king of the Mercians, at the battle of Winwaed in 656. Penda engaged in constant raids on Northumbria, sometimes far into its territory; we learn quite incidentally from one of Bede's miracle narratives about Aidan that on one occasion he had attacked the castle of Bamburgh in the north of Northumberland.[24] The peculiar power of Penda derived from his firm alliance with the Christian British kings of Gwynned, which left him free (in fact made him stronger) to concentrate on his Northumbrian front. This alliance may help to explain the Northumbrian hatred of Welsh Christians so clearly displayed by Bede. Oswald was killed in battle against Penda and Oswy tried every means of buying him off before entrusting the issue to battle in a last desperate gesture of survival. After his victory, Oswy, who had vowed in the event of success to give 12 estates (*XII possessiones*) to the founding of monasteries gave 12 little estates (*XII possessiunculis*), as Bede specifically calls them on the next page, one for the founding of Hartlepool.[25] Of all the Northumbrian *bretwaldas* Oswy was the one towards whom Bede was most cool. The triumph at the river Winwaed, however, was crucial to the survival of Northumbria as any sort of power, and Oswy's defeat might have had adverse and widespread repercussions for the progress of Christianity. For already before this battle, Northumbria had been decisive or instrumental in the establishment of Christianity in several kingdoms, by direct influence and by marriage alliances. Oswald had stood godfather to King Cynegils of Wessex when he was baptized around 635 by St. Birinus.[26] Oswy persuaded Sigbert of the East Saxons, a frequent visitor to his court, to become a Christian; this kingdom was thus recovered for Christianity after a relapse into paganism lasting nearly 40 years.[27] About the same time he insisted that Peada should become a Christian when the latter sought his daughter Alchfled, in marriage. Peada was the son of Penda and by leave of his father ruled the Middle Angles, a people settled in what was roughly modern Leicestershire.[28]

These successes were followed up by the dispatch of missionaries, and it was here that Lindisfarne proved its importance as a training centre both for Irishmen and for the English boys who had joined Aidan. Not that all the Irish monks at work in English kingdoms had come from Lindisfarne. Malmesbury in Wessex had an Irish abbot who played a most significant role in Anglo-Saxon Christian education; and Fursey, who during the 630's established a monastery amongst the East Angles in the disused Roman coastal fort of Burgh Castle near Yarmouth had nothing to do with Lindisfarne. Fursey was an Irishman leading a life of pilgrimage and was, like many in his position, drawn into the preaching the Gospel.[29]

The most interesting of the Lindisfarne missionaries in the 20 years after Aidan's death was the Anglo-Saxon Cedd, one of four brothers who were all priests. Cedd was withdrawn from the Middle Angles and sent by Finan, Aidan's successor, to the East Saxons after Sigbert's conversion. His mission there occupied the period when Oswy's power and the influence of Lindisfarne were at their zenith after Winwaed. Mellitus had been answerable to Augustine of Canterbury, but it was to Finan of Lindisfarne that Cedd reported back on the success of his mission.[30] The bishopric of Cedd was essentially tribal. The Roman missionaries had established their sees in such Roman towns as had survived at least as places of habitation; *civitates*, Bede called them. They were bishops of London, or Rochester or Canterbury. Paulinus had established his see at York, where there was some kind of continuity from Roman times. Birinus, whose origins are unknown but who was consecrated by Asterius, bishop of Milan, established a see at the *civitas* of Dorchester-on-Thames, where there are equally signs of continuity between Roman and Saxon times.[31] Cedd established no see amongst the East Saxons in this sense; he was not bishop of a place but simply bishop of the East Saxons. He certainly established two monastic centres, one of them in the disused coastal fort at Bradwell-on-Sea, a kind of site which had been favoured both by Irish and Gaulish ascetics, but neither of these was an episcopal see. This was similar to the way in which Lindisfarne itself had been founded as a monastic centre, for a bishop who was a monk, rather than as a seat of episcopal government. The adaptation of episcopal organization to the tribal and largely non-urban character of Anglo-Saxon society was one which the Romans could not effect; but the Irish were well qualified to do so, and it was in substance perpetuated by Theodore, archbishop of Canterbury.

In some ways, however, Cedd may mark the beginning of a synthesis between Irish and Roman attitudes to the bishop's office, which we shall see later and more clearly in the most famous of all Lindisfarne monks, namely Cuthbert. In this connection Bede has a story surrounding the death of King Sigbert. The king had accepted hospitality from one of his gesiths who had been excommunicated for matrimonial irregularities:[32]

> As he came away the bishop met him. The king was overcome with fear on seeing him, dismounted from his horse, and fell at his feet to ask pardon for his fault. The bishop likewise dismounted, for he also had been sitting on a horse. In anger he touched the prostrate king with the staff which he held in his hand and gave pronouncement with pontifical authority: 'I say to you,' he said 'that because you were unwilling to hold yourself aloof from the house of that lost and damned man, you will meet your death in that very house.'

The solemn curse with the lowering of the pastoral staff is something found in early Ireland.[33] But the horse, as we have seen, was no part of the accoutrements of Aidan's episcopate (unless Cedd regarded himself as 'compelled by urgent necessity' to rush to the house where the king was feasting in order to curse him). It was a means of sustaining episcopal dignity of which the Romans would certainly have approved.

Cedd's church at Bradwell-on-Sea was like the early Italian-style churches of Kent in its general plan—nave separated from chancel and apse by a triple arch, and side chapels or *porticus*. The church itself was built out of the Roman stones of the fort. In architecture, therefore, one might call it Roman; but its site in a remote and deserted fort harks back to the sites of certain early Irish monasteries.[34] (Fig. 6).

The most Irish thing known about Cedd is his association with Ethelwald, son of Oswald, in the foundation of Lastingham monastery. Cedd himself chose the site in the North Yorkshire moors, 'amongst steep and remote hills, which seemed rather to contain the dens of robbers and the lairs of wild beasts than the habitations of men'.[35] Now Miss Rosalind Hill has rightly pointed out that Lastingham in fact lay near a Roman road; it was not that remote.[36] Bede, therefore, who understood the Irish mentality well, was not thinking of the geographical situation of the place so much as its visual aspect, and from that point of view his description was accurate, as anyone can see who goes there and tries to eliminate the nicely cultivated modern village from his mind's eye. (Fig. 7). It was the awesome and remote *feel* of a place which the Irish (and the Egyptians) loved. The chosen site had to be purged of its 'pristine shame and filth', and so Cedd, according to the customs of those from whom he had received the monastic life, i.e. at Lindisfarne, entered upon a mammoth fast there. Every day except Sunday throughout the 40 days of one Lent he consumed nothing until evening, and then only a small quantity of bread, one hen's egg, and a little milk mixed with water. When ten of the 40 days remained he was summoned by the king, and his brother Cynibill completed the fast in his stead. After that he established the monastic customs of Lindisfarne in the monastery. The 'shame and filth' which had to be removed were those of the demons who inhabited it. These remote sites, like those in the Egyptian deserts, were the domain of devils, who could be driven away only by the most strenuous exertions on the part of religious men.[37] And that these exertions should occupy the 40 days of Lent was a clear reference to Christ's sojourn in the wilderness, which had such a powerful influence on early monastic asceticism.

Cedd died of the great plague in 664 while he was visiting Lastingham, soon after the fateful Synod of Whitby in which he had acted as interpreter, with great alertness so it was said.[38] Bede often touched on that most crucial of missionary problems— language. The Irish-speaking Aidan seems to have come to grips with Anglo-Saxon, the Frankish Agilbert failed to do so, with clear consequences in each case. Bede held that the pride of Babel had caused a dispersal of tongues and that the humility of the Church had again enabled each man to understand St. Peter at the first Pentecost; and more, that the Church in heaven would experience a unity of tongues (*adunatio linguarum*) as all men praised God in harmony of mind and voice.[38a] To Bede, Cedd must have represented at Whitby the humility and harmony of the Church, because in him was achieved there the *adunatio linguarum*.

7 The Synod of Whitby

The Synod of Whitby (664) is one of the most celebrated of ecclesiastical gatherings in the history of the English church, on account of the distinction of those present, on account of the direct confrontation between adherents of the Irish and Roman traditions, and on account of Bede's dramatic description of the proceedings which ended with King Oswy giving his decision (with a smile, so Eddius says) for Rome.

The chief issue of debate was the calculation of the date of Easter.[1] There were two major problems here. First, the date of the Jewish passover was the fourteenth day of the first lunar month of the Jewish year, Nisan, and the early Christians had originally celebrated Christ's Resurrection on that day. But it came to be considered that Easter ought to be on a Sunday and that the Jewish feast ought to be avoided. The Council of Nicea in 325 condemned as heretics all who celebrated Easter on Nisan 14 regardless of whether that day were a Sunday or not. These heretics were known as Quartodecimans. Easter, the Council insisted, must be celebrated on a Sunday. But the fathers of Nicea left an ambiguity. Was Easter to be celebrated on Nisan 14 if that day fell on a Sunday? Or was the Jewish festival to be avoided by Christians *at all costs* so that Easter was to be celebrated on the Sunday within Nisan 15–21, which meant that if Nisan 14 were a Sunday, Easter was celebrated on Nisan 21? The Roman church adopted the latter solution, which was probably what the fathers of Nicea intended, and celebrated within Nisan 15–21. But the Irish monks from Iona and those who followed them celebrated within Nisan 14 and 20, basing themselves on Anatolius, Bishop of Laodicea, who wrote before the Council of Nicea. They were not Quartodecimans, but whenever Nisan 14 fell on a Sunday they celebrated Easter a week earlier than the Roman church.

The second problem arose from the need to have cycles of years. Easter was based on lunar months and on the occurrence of the vernal equinox, before which it might not be celebrated. The correlating of this system to the solar year and the Roman calendar meant that into a cycle of so many years a certain number of lunar months had to be intercalated. This was a rich source of confusion in the Church. The computists of Alexandria, who were the professionals in this line, produced Easter tables using 19-year cycles; the process culminated around 525 in the tables of Dionysius Exiguus. But in the mid-fifth century Victorius of Aquitaine, in an effort to construct an almost perpetual Easter table which would take into account every-thing and prevent all further controversy, had produced a 532-year cycle (19 x 28). Like those of the Alexandrians this was based on a 19-year cycle, but Victorius misunderstood the Alexandrian cal-culations of the vernal equinox and so his tables, which were adopted by the Roman church, created a divergence from the Alexandrian tables. The Irish differed from both in that they used not a 19-year cycle but an older 84-year one derived from a tract wrongly attributed to Anatolius.

At first sight it may appear astonishing that practical Englishmen should have become steamed up in these seemingly academic pedantries. But they were not really pedantries at all; on the contrary they were genuinely momentous issues. What did the unity of Christians mean if they could not even agree about the date on which their main festival should be celebrated? In fact some of the great divisions in the history of the Church had expressed themselves precisely in the date of Easter. This had been the focus of broader conflicts—in the early days of the Church between Judaists and anti-Semites, in the days of Pope Leo I between rival patriarchs, and more recently in the days of Columbanus between Gaulish bishops and Irish ascetics. And then, apart from the emotions which the date of Easter drew like a magnet to itself, it was the most obvious instance of the problem of calculating time and fitting these calculations to astronomical realities. We have seen that before Easter could be celebrated it was necessary to establish the vernal equinoxes, the relation of lunar months to calendar years and of lunar to solar data. The whole lengthy dispute about the dating of Easter represents a struggle by man to orientate himself in time, no less significant than his struggle of the present day to orientate himself in space. And if it was natural in the circumstances of that age for much of the controversy to take the form of the citation of earlier authorities, the wonder is how much of it did not.

We have to ask now what was the nature of the feelings aroused by this problem in Anglo-Saxon England. What caused the Synod of Whitby to take place? First of all, it is impossible to represent it as the climax of a long cumulation of controversy and of conflict between the Romans and the so-called Celts. There had, of course, been Augustine's dispute with the British bishops, if Bede was right to say that Easter had played a part in it; but that was a quite separate problem from the relations between the Romans and the Irish. Nothing more is heard of it after Augustine's time. A few years after Augustine met the British bishops, the Roman bishops Laurentius, Mellitus and Justus did, it is true, write a letter to the Irish shaking their sad heads to discover that the Irish were as bad as the British in observing customs contrary to those of the universal church. This letter, however, seems to have been received in a not unfriendly spirit, for it is the most likely source from which the compiler of an early Irish missal had the names of these three bishops which he inserted into the canon of the mass where the souls of the dead are commemorated.[2] There is no other evidence of friction between adherents of the Roman and Ionan Easters until the three years or so before the Synod. Aidan was held in universal esteem by everyone, including Honorius, archbishop of Canterbury. The one person actually named as taking issue with Finan, Aidan's successor, was another Irishman called Ronan, who provoked the bishop to a violent temper, which was apparently not difficult.[3] Only in the time of Colman, a third Iona monk who became bishop of the Northumbrians in 661, did the storm break.

One of the causes of trouble of which Bede speaks was the situation at the Northumbrian court. About 643 King Oswy married Eanfled, daughter of Edwin, whom after her father's death Paulinus had taken to Kent where she was brought up. In Kent she had naturally grown up with the Roman observance of Easter. She continued to keep it in Northumbria with the result that sometimes, while the king was celebrating Easter according to the customs of Iona (i.e. on Nisan 14), the queen and her followers were still fasting and celebrating Palm Sunday. Now it was certainly no laughing matter when this kind of thing happened to the ceremonial of the chief Christian festival at the court of the Northumbrian *bretwalda*, and this situation must clearly have been used to precipitate the synod. But it is easy to exaggerate its significance. Divergences in the dates of Easter had occurred on several occasions in the 20 years before the synod, and if Oswy (who would generally be feasting while his wife was still fasting) had felt very strongly about it, he could have settled the matter earlier. Moreover we know what a royal hall or a *villa regalis* of this time would have been like for one has been excavated at Yeavering in Northumberland.[4] Apart from several relatively small halls on the site, perhaps for noble retainers, there were four large ones built of wood and each nearly 100 feet long. When a case of this kind arose, therefore, even if king and queen were both at the same royal hall which was not necessary, it need have occasioned nothing unseemly or farcical.

The men who lived in the generation before the Synod of Whitby were not so sensitive to the 'basic conflict' between Romans and Celts as modern historians have sometimes been. The foundation of a monastery at Gilling in Deira is an instance. Eanfled persuaded Oswy to grant the land for this monastery soon after 651 in reparation for his crime in killing Oswin of Deira, her relation.[5] Whatever kind of monastic rule was followed at Gilling, its monks were probably observing the Roman Easter before 664.[6] And yet when the first abbot, Trumhere, a relation both of Oswin and Queen Eanfled, was chosen to be bishop of the Mercians, he accepted consecration without demur from the Irish who, we are told, had educated him.[7] His successor in the abbacy, Tunbert, resigned after a while in order to devote himself to prayer and scriptural study in Ireland.[8] It is not easy to say whether we would call Gilling a Roman or a Celtic institution; and contemporaries felt no need to label it in these terms. To them, if anything, it was a Deiran monastery, very much a family affair of the Deiran royal dynasty, set up at the insistence of Eanfled, daughter of Edwin of Deira, to compound the injustice of the Bernician dynasty towards that of Deira. Its foundation was in effect an act of compensation in a blood-feud; and like many barbarian women, Eanfled felt as much loyalty to her family as to her husband. So often in this period, political or religious actions were motivated primarily by feeling for the kindred. In spite of her Roman Easter, Eanfled was not the least troubled by Trumhere's Irish background; what mattered was that he was her relation and Oswin's.

The chief cause of the trouble which led to the Synod of Whitby was the person of King Alfrith. Alfrith was Oswy's son and held a sub-kingdom which might have been the whole of Deira or it might have been something more restricted within it.[9] He had originally been an adherent of the Ionan Easter like his father, as is suggested by his originally giving his monastery at Ripon to Lindisfarne monks of this tradition. But around 660 he came into contact with Wilfrid.

Wilfrid was born probably in 633 of a Northumbrian aristocratic family. At the age of 14 he had gone to Lindisfarne as the servant of a paralysed nobleman, who had retired to become a monk there. He remained at Lindisfarne for four years in Aidan's time, loved by all and, though not a monk, seeking to live the full monastic life 'with a loving heart'.[10] Happy as he was there, however, he began to realize that Lindisfarne was not exactly the centre of European religious life. Having spent a year in Kent, he set out for Rome (653), but on his way to Rome he struck up a friendship with Annemundus, bishop of Lyon, which was to be one of the important influences in his life. He stayed in Lyon for a while, where the bishop offered him his niece in marriage and a province (bonam partem Galliarum) to administer, but Wilfrid was not to be deflected from his goal. In Rome he struck up another friendship with Boniface the archdeacon, and learned from him about much, including the Roman Easter. On his return, however, he spent three years at Lyon with Annemundus, and there, according to his biographer Eddius, 'he learned much from learned teachers.' He returned to Britain and was introduced by his friend King Coenwalh of Wessex to King Alfrith. The latter was quickly impressed with Wilfrid's adroitness in conversation, a gift which he possessed to such a degree that Alfrith felt almost as if an angel were addressing him.[11] Alfrith, whose gifts lay rather in propagating other people's ideas with frenetic energy than in conceiving any of his own, turned the Lindisfarne monks out of Ripon, gave the monastery to Wilfrid, and had him ordained priest.

There seems little doubt that Alfrith took the initiative in getting everyone to Whitby, including his father Oswy, whose view seems to have been roughly that what was good enough for him in his younger days was good enough for him now, although what anyone else chose to do was no great concern of his.[12] Obsessive religiosity was the last weakness which anyone could impute to him. And this is not the impression obtained just from Bede; it is Eddius who reveals that he spoke at the Synod of Whitby *subridens* i.e. with a smile.[13] The established figures of the Northumbrian church at the synod—Colman of Lindisfarne, Cedd, Hilda of Whitby—were all on the Celtic side. The Roman side had to be packed, packed first of all with people who wouldn't have dreamt of stirring up the debate themselves, like the chaplain who had come from Kent with Eanfled, or the peaceful and now elderly James the deacon; and secondly with outsiders like Agilbert, the Frankish bishop of the West Saxons, and his priest Agatho, who were friends of Alfrith and Wilfrid. Nothing shows more clearly than the composition of the Roman party at Whitby what hard work was needed to make a debate of it.[14]

It is not at all likely that Alfrith was moved in all this solely by love of the truth about the date of Easter. The Synod of Whitby was very much a Northumbrian affair and it reflected the traditional rivalry of Bernicia and Deira and of their kings to rule all the Northumbrians. It may be surmised that Alfrith saw in it an opportunity to bring political pressure to bear and weaken the influence of his father in Bernicia; to change Colman for another bishop of Northumbria who would, as an adherent of the Roman Easter, be in closer association with himself than with his father. If this was his hope, however, it was thwarted by Oswy's politically expedient change of sides and his decision for Rome at the synod. There was good reason for the smile. After that, only open rebellion was left to Alfrith, and here is the probable explanation of why we hear almost nothing more of him.[15]

The debate at the Synod of Whitby was in one sense an artificial one, in that it had been stirred up by Alfrith out of very little real trouble, at least trouble of a purely ecclesiastical nature; but in another sense it was a genuine debate, in that apart from the political issues involved, it brought an important if latent ecclesiastical issue into the open, which was doubtless the chief concern of Wilfrid himself. This issue was the extent to which the customs of great monastic founders like Columba could be allowed free play against the doctrine and discipline of the Roman Church. At the actual gathering Colman was called upon to justify his custom and based himself first on John the Apostle. Whereupon Wilfrid, speaking for the Roman party with confidence, knowledge and irony, pointed out that much water had flowed under the bridge since John was compelled to celebrate Easter on the fourteenth day of the month to avoid giving scandal to the Jews, and in any case Colman did not really follow John, because the latter had celebrated on the fourteenth day regardless of whether it was a Sunday. If Colman actually followed John he would now be a Quartodeciman heretic. Next, Colman based himself on Anatolius and Columba. It was Columba who really mattered to him. Could it be believed that this man, whose sanctity and virtue were attested by so many miracles, whose life and customs had been an inspiration to so many holy men after him, had taught or done anything contrary to Holy Scripture? Wilfrid immediately demonstrated that Anatolius used a 19-year cycle unlike Colman, and when he calculated the fourteenth day he considered that by evening it was the fifteenth, so Colman was no true follower of Anatolius. As to Columba, he was no doubt a holy man and did as much as his 'rustic simplicity' would allow, but Colman had had the advantage of coming into contact with more educated influences and would certainly sin by trying to insulate himself from them. There he was, one of a small number of men on a remote island in a corner of the world, and was he to be setting up 'that Columba of yours' (*ille Columba vester*) against the prince of the apostles, to whom the Lord had said, 'Thou art Peter, and upon this rock I will build my church'?

Reported speech was often invented for dramatic effect by medieval chroniclers, but if Bede made all this up it was certainly done with a sense of Wilfrid's character and an obvious understanding of the nub of the problem to which this last passage brings us. The monks at the Ionan confederation would not abandon the customs of the Columba. The same problem had occurred in Ireland over 30 years earlier. A synod met in Southern Ireland, at Magh Lene in 631 to consider the question of Easter, and the bishops and abbots who were assembled there sent a delegation to Rome in order to seek guidance, as a result of which the Southern Irish went over to the Roman Easter in 633. They were not the first among the Irish to do so, for in the first decade of the century, not long after the departure of Columbanus, the monastery of Bangor in Northern Ireland had gone Roman under Abbot Sillan; and it was probably there that the tract with Alexandrian matter (*Epistola Cyrilli*) was forged in the name of the famous computist, Cyril, with reference to the Easter of 607.[16] At the time of the change in 633 a Southern Irish abbot, Cummian, wrote a letter to Abbot Seghene of Iona trying to convert him to the Roman Easter. If Rome were wrong and Alexandria were wrong, and Gaul were wrong, and only Iona and the tip of Ireland were right, then (argued Cummian) something very peculiar must have happened. At Magh Lene at least, he said, it looked as if there would be unanimity in the acceptance of the Roman Easter, but this hope had been dashed by some 'whited wall, pretending to observe the traditions of his elders.' He trusted that the Lord would strike him down in whatever way he saw fit.[17] The monks of Iona, however, were unmoved; as Cummian seemed to know, they too preferred the traditions of their elders. Columba was as great a ruler from the grave as any of the Irish monastic founders. He protected Iona from its depredators, objects connected with his life were carefully preserved, when there was a drought on the monastic lands books which he had written were carried over them. Late in the seventh century Adamnan, abbot of Iona, was converted to the Roman Easter, but he could not bring round his own monks. It was not until 716 that the Englishman, Egbert, converted them. Veneration for Columba, then, explains why in 664 Colman and every other Irishman at Lindisfarne felt obliged to leave Northumbria.

There stands at Kilfountain, in the fields of County Kerry, Ireland, a stone slab of the late sixth or early seventh century, carved with an encircled cross, some primitive but characteristic curvilinear ornament, and the name FINTEN written vertically. Such slabs often stood next to an oratory and have survived where the oratory (as in this case) is a ruin or has vanished altogether. They are thought to mark the tomb of the first hermit or perhaps the saintly founder of a small monastery.[18] Their memorials in stone have lasted, eloquent symbols of the kind of feelings towards Columba, the saintly founder, which inspired the Irish side at the Synod of Whitby. (Fig. 8).

Colman's departure was not effected in a spirit of shaking the dust off his feet, nor did it signal any kind of anti-Irish reaction in Northumbria. His successor in the bishopric, Tuda, accepted the Roman Easter, but he had been educated among the Southern Irish. The abbacy of Lindisfarne went to Eata, who now accepted the Roman Easter, but was one of the English boys who had been trained by Aidan. His appointment was made as the result of a request by Colman to Oswy. It shows Oswy's continuing respect for his bishop and Colman's magnanimity in understanding a different reaction to the decision of the synod from his own. Bede himself chose the moment of Colman's departure to give an encomium on the purity of the monastic life at Lindisfarne during this bishop's time, and thereby to present another example of his undying admiration for the Irish tradition, whatever its failings over Easter.

Colman is not reported to have specifically denied the authority of the papacy at Whitby, but as the question did not present itself to him primarily as one of acceptance or rejection of the petrine office, we may imagine that his attitude towards it was somewhat ambiguous. The letters of Columbanus (of an earlier date) to various popes about the date of Easter are a good example of the kind of ambiguity which could exist.[19] Columbanus accepted the primacy of the pope and his authority in doctrinal matters in the way that any other Catholic of the same period would have done. But nobody thought that a pope might indulge in the unrestrained preaching of heresy. Columbanus's first letter, to Gregory the Great, adopted a very independent tone for all its recognition of papal authority, and suggested that as Anatolius, whom he himself followed, had won the approval of no less a person than Jerome, Gregory might be guilty of heresy if he brought into question Jerome's authority. In other words he writes as though the matter might be one of doctrine. In the next letter, however, written during a vacancy, to whoever was to become pope, his tune was rather different. He was seeking papal support against the Frankish bishops who were molesting him on this matter and was wondering why the Irish could not be left in peace to practice their own customs if these were not contrary to the Faith. Here, in contrast to the earlier letter, he seems to make the whole question less one of doctrine than one of custom and discipline in which there was no overriding obligation for particular churches to conform with Rome or with one another. This, perhaps was nearer to Colman's view, as against the browbeating implications of Wilfrid that the matter was one of Faith.

So far as Bede was concerned, with his great interest in, and strong feelings about, computistical matters, whether one called the date of Easter a matter of faith or a matter of discipline (he himself seems to have preferred the latter), conformity to the Roman usage in this point was essential to the order and unity of the Church. Amongst the Anglo-Saxons the debate flared up suddenly and quickly and died out as quickly after 664 with the triumph of Rome. It is very doubtful, then, whether Bede made such a long and emphatic story out of the Synod of Whitby purely because he thought it so important in the Anglo-Saxon context. It is permissible to wonder whether the Irish context in which he also saw it did not seem to him just as important if not more so. Bede was a lover of Ireland and took a great interest in its intellectual activity, as did the English scholars of his time who went to Ireland in droves to study.[20] Bede himself had many books from Ireland. The manuscript of computistical texts and tables which he used still survives; this does not represent the whole of the computistical literature known to him by any means, but is a kind of file containing letters, extracts, short treatises and tables. Bede was the most learned man of his day in this subject, and we can see that the basis of his collection of material was Irish.[21] He knew all about the tract attributed wrongly to Anatolius from which the Irish had their 84-year cycle. He could well have known Cummian's letter to Seghene of Iona. In fact if he made up any of Wilfrid's speech at Whitby when he wrote the *Ecclesiastical History*, that letter was the sort of thing he could have had in front of him. He would be too sensitive an artist just to copy out chunks of the letter and give it as Wilfrid's speech; he certainly did not do that. But he might have used it or something like it as a 'reminder' of what Wilfrid said. Almost every one of Wilfrid's points can be found in some form in Cummian's letter.[22] Bede certainly followed the long Irish Easter controversy very carefully.

He was particularly interested in the part which the Englishman, Egbert, had played in winning round the Irish. Now a chapter about Egbert follows immediately on Bede's account of the Synod of Whitby and Colman's withdrawal. It describes how in that very year, Egbert, a young man in his twenties, had recovered from an all but fatal illness, and vowed—here the Irish influence comes out—that for the sake of God he would live in a strange place so as never to return to the island of Britain where he was born, that he would say the whole psalter daily, and that every week he would fast for a whole day and night. He lived as a priest among the Picts and the Irish, in great humility, meekness and simplicity until he was ninety.[23] What is more, soon after the Synod of Whitby a monastery of English monks was founded at Mayo and became a centre of the Roman observance in the north of Ireland. It was possibly founded by Egbert and very likely used as a base for his activity in proselytizing for the Roman Easter. Bede certainly had connections with this monastery.[24] And almost the last thing in the *Ecclesiastical History* is the chapter on how Egbert, already high in his seventies in 716, won round the monks of Iona by his way of life and his qualities as a teacher.[25] That was the crowning moment of Bede's book, that was the end of those labours which had begun in the year of the Synod of Whitby; the story of the synod showed clearly how much such labours were needed.

Part II

CHRISTIAN ACHIEVEMENT
c.650 – c.750

8 Background:
Politics and Communications

At the time of the Synod of Whitby the main political issue facing the Anglo-Saxons must have seemed to be whether or not the king of the Northumbrians would maintain and strengthen his rule over the Southern English. As Mr. Hunter Blair has said, the question at stake in the battles both at the river Idle in 616, when Redwald fought Ethelfrith, and at the Winwaed in 656, was whether a king of the Northern English or of the Southern English was to have *imperium*.[1] Two things, however, checked the power of Northumbria, although neither rendered it insignificant. The first was the rise of Mercia. Only three years after the battle of the Winwaed, a Christian party of the Mercian court, a party whose actions are described by Bede almost in terms of Mercian patriotism, established the youthful and Christian son of Penda, Wulfhere, as their king, and turned Oswy out of Mercia itself. This rebellion had already been presaged two years earlier in the murder of Peada, Oswy's creature in South Mercia (i.e. as sub-king of the Middle Angles).[2] By the early 670s Wulfhere had established his control over Lindsey, which had previously been under Northumbrian hegemony; even earlier in 667 it was he who sent Bishop Jaruman among the East Saxons to bring this people back to Christianity after another relapse during the great plague of 664; and the moving of the West Saxon see from Dorchester-on-Thames to Winchester seems to be connected with his pressure on the Thames Valley.[3] It is significant that the next important synod of the English Church after Whitby was held in 672 at Hertford, by then within Mercian dominion. In Lindsey, at least, the issue was in some doubt as between Northumbrian and Mercian rule in the 670s until the battle at the river Trent between Ethelred, king of the Mercians, and Egfrith, king of the Northumbrians, in 679. Egfrith's defeat at this battle was the final blow to Northumbrian hopes of domination over the English south of the Humber.

The second check to Northumbrian power came from the Picts in the North. By the mid-seventh century the Bernicians had been firmly established in the Tweed basin. By 680 the foundation of the Anglian bishopric at Abercorn and the imprisonment of Wilfrid by King Egfrith in Dunbar suggest that the whole of what had been British territory south of the Forth was firmly in Northumbrian hands, and the Northumbrian kings were establishing overlordship of the Picts further North. This overlordship was effectively stopped by the defeat of Egfrith at the hands of the Picts at *Nechtansmere* in 685. The Northumbrians continued in defensive wars against the Picts, not without success, in order to hold the line of the Forth. Early in the eighth century under the Pictish king, Nechtan IV, friendlier relations were established and Bede's abbot, Ceolfrid, acted as adviser to him in his ecclesiastical affairs, sending him architects as well as a long letter about the date of Easter.[4]

The general pattern of Anglo-Saxon politics which emerges in the late seventh century is one dominated by Northumbria, Mercia and Wessex. The power of the other kingdoms was tending increasingly to become absorbed into these three, but between the three was established for a while something like a state of equilibrium. Between 680 and 730 no king was known as *bretwalda* or had a claim to be considered one. The Northumbrians were being reduced in size. The Mercians had to cope with the development of Welsh hostility around 700 or somewhat earlier and this perhaps checked their rise until the overlordship which their King Ethelbald (716–57) achieved in the last two-thirds of his reign. The chronicle of West Saxon history in this period is filled with the continuing and successful process of conquest and settlement against the British under their kings Centwine (676–85) and Ine (688–722) which absorbed their energies and took them westwards to the Tamar.

We have said nothing in the first part of this book about the work of British missionaries amongst the Anglo-Saxons, because although it has recently been suggested that there may have been such missionaries in Northumbria, there seems no good evidence for it.[5] It is undoubtedly the case, however, that Bede minimized the benefit to the Anglo-Saxon churches of contacts with British

christians and British churches. The advance of the Anglo-Saxons
into British territory during the seventh century was always
backed by military power which had sometimes to be used, but
much of it was evidently a process of peaceful treaty and colonization. When the Northumbrians moved over the Pennines in the
mid-seventh century, we know that their arms caused the British
clergy in the region of the Ribble to flee, but their absorption of
the British kingdom of Rheged around Carlisle and in South-West
Scotland later in the century may well have been more peaceful.[6]
Oswy himself had been married to a princess of Rheged before
he married Eanfled. The victories of Ethelfrith over the British had
brought the Northumbrians to the Tweed around 600, but there is
reason to believe that their colonization of the territory between
the Tweed and the Forth was achieved by more pacific means.[7]
Although the Mercians took their Christianity from the Irish and
Northumbrians, the history of relations between the Mercians and
the Welsh was on the whole one of firm alliance and friendship
until shortly before 700, as Professor H. P. R. Finberg has shown.[8]
Of the border sub-kingdoms of the Mercians, the Hwicce
(occupying roughly Gloucestershire and Worcestershire) were
planted by King Penda, not directly at the expense of the Welsh
but at that of the West Saxons whom he drove out of the region
in 628; the Magonsaetan (occupying roughly Shropshire and
Herefordshire most of which was Welsh-speaking), were in all
likelihood planted as the result of a treaty between Penda and
Cadwallon of Gwyned. Of the West Saxon advance into
Somerset and Devon in the late sixth and early seventh centuries,
Professor W. G. Hoskins has pointed out that in regions where
there was ample room for colonization, not every Saxon farmstead
had to be established at the point of the sword.[9]

To the extent that they existed, the friendly relations between
Britons and Anglo-Saxons bore fruit in the development of
Christian life. When the Northumbrian bishoprics of Whithorn,
in the south-western tip of Scotland, and Abercorn, on the Forth,
were established, the traditions of British Christianity in these
regions were absorbed into Northumbrian ecclesiastical organization.[10] From Mercia we have the evidence of Mildburg, first
abbess of Much Wenlock (Salop), being held in great reverence by
the Welsh on her monastery's property just north-east of Brecon at
Llanfillo, which she visited frequently and in which the church
came to be dedicated to her: an English patron saint of a Welsh

church.[11] It was not quite the same thing with the Welsh of South-West Wales, St. David's country. Some time in the 680s, Aldhelm, a relation of the Wessex royal family and at that time abbot of Malmesbury, wrote a letter to Geraint, King of Dumnonia, and his clergy, to try and persuade them to observe the Roman Easter and tonsure. In the course of it he complained that there were Welsh priests beyond the Severn in Demetia who, 'glorying in their own cleanness of life, abominate our communion to such an extent, that they deign neither to offer prayers in church with us, nor to eat with us at our tables for the sake of charity.'[12] This was the region where the hard core of implacable hostility to the Anglo-Saxons and the Roman missionaries survived. But Aldhelm's observations have another significance. In a letter written to a king whose power was mainly in Devon and Cornwall, this reference to South-West Wales implies that the situation was better between the West Saxons and the Britons of South-West England. And so it would seem from the fact that when Chad was consecrated bishop by Wine, the simoniacal bishop of the West Saxons, Wine associated with himself in the ceremony two British bishops, doubtless from this region.[13] There is also the grant by King Geraint of land west of the Tamar estuary to the West Saxon monastery of Sherborne; and there is the British church with British inscriptions from about 700 at Wareham (Dorset), which suggests that the British were left unmolested to worship side by side with the Saxons.[14]

EXTERNAL

As Christianity came gradually to take root in Anglo-Saxon courts, the English Church began to open itself increasingly to a great variety of influences from abroad, and, out of the interplay arises the achievement of the first period of Anglo-Saxon Christianity. The flood-gates were opened in particular as the foundation of monasteries got under way, where the life of Christian prayer and letters, essential to the health and continued existence of the Church, could be developed. The most obvious of all external influences were Rome, and—what is not quite the same thing—the papacy. The first known journey made by Englishmen to the city in which the Apostles Peter and Paul were buried and from which Gregory had sent Augustine was that of Wilfrid and Benedict Biscop in 653. From then on there is varied evidence for an inexhaustible stream of pilgrims, who took every kind of route through Gaul or the Rhineland. Benedict Biscop himself made several more journeys to collect books and artefacts, and in one of these journeys Ceolfrid, his successor at Jarrow, accompanied him; the priest Nothelm went to work in the Lateran archives to gather evidence of the Gregorian mission; abbots went to secure the special privileges of protection which the papacy began to issue for monasteries in the seventh century; kings went to pray at the tombs of the apostles and to die; we know of a party of nuns because the abbess Aelffled of Whitby wrote to a colleague near Trier about them, and of a lady called Wethberga because her solicitous brother feared that she had been imprisoned in the Holy City.[15]

It is possible that Anglo-Saxons journeyed to Italy with the greater will on account of a long-remembered association with the Lombards in their continental homelands of Northern Europe.[16] Be that as it may, Italy must have meant a lot more to these travellers than just Rome or the papacy. We shall see that Naples and Capua left their mark on Biscop's book collecting. Moreover, although the Byzantine (or Eastern imperial) and Western worlds were falling apart in certain ways during the seventh century, the papacy learnt much from the Byzantine imperial court which it put to use in this period, and many of its occupants were themselves Easterners. The Exarchate of Ravenna was still nominally responsible for the rule of all Byzantine possessions in Italy from Venetia to Sicily; so late as 653, the year in which Biscop and Wilfrid set out from Kent, the Emperor Constans II, in an attempt at direct control of the papacy, had used the exarch to capture and exile Pope Martin. The friction was caused by the Monothelite heresy in the East, but normally the popes still recognized Constantinople as the political capital of the Roman Empire and the emperors recognized Rome as the religious capital. And something of Byzantine civilization was still left in the Italy which Biscop saw.[17]

So far as the papacy itself was concerned, the most important single thing which the early English Church owed to it, in the period after Gregory's pontificate, was the appointment of Theodore to be Archbishop of Canterbury. In 667 the Anglo-Saxon archbishop-elect died in Rome while he was there to be consecrated and to receive his pallium. The pope at the time was Vitalian (657–72), who of all seventh-century popes had the longest pontificate and was amongst the most instrumental in exposing Rome to Eastern influences. Now he exposed the Anglo-Saxons to a 67-year old monk from Tarsus in Cilicia (Asia Minor), who knew both Greek and Latin and who arrived amongst them in 669. He began an episcopate of 21 years by lifting Chad bodily on to the horse which he thought the latter ought to ride as becoming a bishop's dignity. He went on to conduct a fundamental and shrewd organization of dioceses and monasteries, to establish a school at Canterbury which was of the first educational importance, and to acquire a reputation as a guide in matters of Christian morality and penance which is reflected in his Penitential. In all this he managed to make use of his eastern experience, to remain loyal to Rome and the papacy, and to gear the traditions of the Irish church to his work in a way symbolized by his dedication of the church at Lindisfarne. Bede says of him that he was the first archbishop whom the whole English church willingly obeyed (which was an important factor in the adumbration of Anglo-Saxon political unity):[18]

> Nor were there ever happier times since the English first came to Britain, for they had strong and Christian kings who were a terror to barbarian peoples; the desires of all were bent on the joys of the heavenly kingdom about which they had recently heard; and whoever wanted to study sacred learning had masters ready to teach him.

Theodore's time as archbishop was considered by Bede to be the climax of the Golden Age to which he looked back.

The importance of the Synod of Whitby in the so-called triumph of Roman authority in England can easily be exaggerated. The synod was primarily an affair of the Northumbrian church and it occurred at just the time when Northumbrian political power was beginning to ebb. Wilfrid's clarion assertion of papal authority was doubtless important and influential in itself — not the mere fact of such an assertion, for everyone accepted that the pope had some sort of authority over the whole Church, but the scope which he allowed to this authority and the suggestion that the Roman Easter was not only a matter of discipline but also one of faith. The most unequivocal enunciation of papalism in seventh-century England, however, came not from Wilfrid but from his friend, Aldhelm, abbot of Malmesbury, in the letter to King Geraint of Dumnonia which we have already mentioned.

Aldhelm here cites the most famous of all the petrine texts in the Bible and then expresses a doubt whether those who do not observe the Roman Easter, who spurn the principal decrees and doctrinal mandates of Peter (the bearer of the heavenly keys) and of his Church, can enter the kingdom of heaven. But perhaps, he says, some griping reader of books (*quilibet strofosus librorum lector*) will excuse himself by saying that he believes in the Holy Trinity, the mystery of the Incarnation, the Passion and Resurrection, and so forth. To these Aldhelm can only say that if they hope thus to conceal themselves under the bulwarks of this excuse, (Aldhelm is not a succinct writer), he will shatter them with the projectiles of apostolic castigation; he will say to them that the catholic faith is in vain and the glorying in it an inanity for the man who does not follow the doctrine and rule of St. Peter.[19]

Not everyone, however, was as impressed as this by the doctrine and rule of St. Peter. One has only to think how loosely English bishops and kings sat to the papal decrees about Wilfrid's diocese and monasteries. Furthermore, most of the early Anglo-Saxons who went to Rome thought less about the papacy than about the tombs of the apostles or the collection of books and relics. And as Dr. Wallace-Hadrill has pointed out, the English were less devoted to the papacy as an institution than to the person of Pope Gregory. Throughout the Whitby *Life* of this pope, 'the stress is upon Gregory's personal apostolic relationship with England rather than upon his papal relationship'.[20]

We have already indicated the wealth of contacts between England and Ireland in the seventh century. Those between England and Frisia were already developing on the basis of trade and were to issue in the missionary work of Wilfrid and Willibrord late in the century; while those between England and Gaul were also multifarious, as they had been earlier. The geographical pattern here is dominated, naturally enough, by the great rivers of Gaul which provided the seafaring Anglo-Saxons with their ingress to the continent. Aldhelm corresponded about his writings with Abbot Cellanus of Péronne (on the Somme), a monastery where Fursey was finally buried after leaving East Anglia.[21] The *Life* of Bertila, abbess of Chelles, tells us in general terms that at the request of Saxon kings she sent her disciples to help them establish monasteries for monks and nuns.[22] Chelles was on the Marne, close to where that river flows into the Seine. We can-

not help thinking of Chelles when we learn that a Frankish nun
called Liobsynde came to Much Wenlock to help Mildburg,
daughter of King Merewalh of the Magonsaetan, found her
monastery there about 680, during Bertila's rule.[23] St. Philibert,
abbot of the island monastery of Noirmoutier near the mouth of
the Loire, did business with Irish ships in the mid-seventh century,
but ships from Britain also came to Noirmoutier, as two separate
miraculous narratives in the saint's *Life* show.[24] When a Frankish
writer speaks of 'British' ships he could mean either British or
Saxon, for the term would be associated with the whole island.
In this connection it is worth remembering that Professor
W. G. Hoskins has argued convincingly that the West Saxons
pushed along the Dorset coast and across the Axe into what is
now Devon early in the seventh century. After the battle of Bindon
in 614 they must already have controlled the old Roman port of
Axmouth.[25] This early south-western orientation of the Saxons
would have enhanced the line of communication with the Gaulish
Atlantic seaboard and the Loire. In any case the advance brought
the West Saxons into closer association with the British of
Dumnonia who looked naturally in this direction.

Anglo-Saxon pilgrims to Rome must have helped to foster links
with Gaul on their way, and it may sometimes have happened that
these links came to assume an importance as great as that of the
ultimate goal of their journey. We shall see it happen to Wilfrid
whose first journey to Rome was chiefly significant for what he
learned at Lyon which lay on his route. And there is some reason
to believe that Lyon and the basin of the Rhône may have remained
particularly important to English book collectors.[26]

Beyond Gaul and Italy, Anglo-Saxon communications extended
to the East Mediterranean. Archbishop Theodore had come from
this region and, as we shall see, gave his Anglo-Saxon pupils
some idea of what it was like. For the most part, however, contact was probably indirect, but it was not necessarily insignificant
or uninfluential for that. Bede, for instance, knew quite a lot
about Egypt and the Holy Land from books. His library had a
copy of the *De Locis Sanctis* of Adamnan of Iona, a book recording
the travels to the holy places of a Frank called Arculf, with whom
Adamnan had himself spoken. Again, when Bede wrote on the
Song of Songs, he explained how he had learnt about the trees and
aromatic herbs which it mentioned from 'books of the ancients';
by this he meant chiefly Pliny's *Natural History*. For how could

he (he added), born and brought up as he was at the far end of the earth, know about things at its centre in Arabia or India or Judea or Egypt, except from books?[27] Educated Anglo-Saxons knew that they were on the periphery of the world and instinctively felt that the Mediterranean was its centre. There could be no more striking testimony to their absorption of Mediterranean culture. Bede constantly showed his awareness of the Mediterranean world in small ways, like his reference to the resin of the cedar tree and its properties as a preservative for bookbindings,[28] or his mention of the way in which dark Ethiopians were represented in wall paintings.[29]

Archaeological objects and works of art are important evidence for the influence of the East Mediterranean. In Kent and East Anglia several Coptic bronze bowls, made to be hung for ornament, have been found in seventh-century burials; three Byzantine buckles have been found in Kent, and there are the Byzantine silver dishes and spoons of the Sutton Hoo ship-burial.[30] Art historians have seen various East Mediterranean symptoms in the Anglo-Saxon culture of the period. The ornament of vine scrolls so much to the taste of those who carved memorial crosses in eighth-century Northumbria is considered to afford the closest known parallels to Coptic stone decoration.[31] The scenes of Christ's life and of his standing triumphant on two beasts, carved on the eighth-century Ruthwell cross, are all common in Mediterranean iconography, particularly in Egypt and Syria; and one scene, the Flight into Egypt, is known at this time from only one other representation—on a golden amulet or pendant which is probably Egyptian.[32] When St. Cuthbert's coffin was translated to a place of honour in Lindisfarne church (698), several treasures were placed in it, amongst them some precious East Mediterranean fabric and an ivory comb. This comb, vertical in shape, has teeth on two sides and a large hole in the middle. The hole is a decorative feature deriving its effect from a geometrical relation to the whole design, and it corresponds to the circular inlays on a number of Coptic combs. In fact it is a type of comb to be found in Coptic Egypt.[33]

It is unlikely that the explanation of most of these phenomena, and more besides, was travel between Britain and the East Mediterranean or any other kind of direct contact. There is, it is true, a remarkable story in the contemporary biography of the Patriarch John of Alexandria, who died in 616, relating to the journey of a boat from Alexandria to Britain with a cargo of grain, half of which the *protos* of a British town purchased for gold and the other half of which he exchanged for tin.[34] It is not certain that 'Britain' in this context means our island rather than Brittany or even somewhere in the north-west of Spain, although what is said fits the circumstances of South-West Britain at the time quite well. Whatever the case, the story at least shows that a voyage across the Mediterranean and up the Atlantic seaboard was something to be contemplated. This, however, was before 616, and a century later the journey across the Mediterranean would not, for a variety of reasons, have been so much a matter of course.

Many of the precious objects imported into Anglo-Saxon England could have been presents. Presents were given on an enormous scale and on every conceivable occasion in this period; present-giving was a major form of patronage, of political and diplomatic activity, of personal relations, and of religious proselytism.[35] When we think, for instance, of the ivory comb which Pope Boniface V sent to Ethelburga, wife of King Edwin, about 619,[36] and of relations between Rome and the East, there is no difficulty in imagining what an ivory comb of Coptic type, perhaps actually made in Egypt, should be doing in Northumbria in 698. We do not have to imagine travels between Britain and Egypt. Some of the Coptic bronze bowls may represent trade or purchases abroad, but as they were common amongst the Lombards in Italy, there is no need to suppose that they were acquired from further afield. Many may not have been manufactured in Egypt at all, but may simply represent European manufactures in the 'Egyptian taste', which was a feature of seventh-century civilization. As to the vine scroll ornament in stone sculpture, there can be no supposition of travellers with sketch books, and still less of the actual transport of stone, although not everyone travelled light in this age.* The inspiration, or models, for this type of ornament must have come from light Egyptian commodities which were all over the Mediterranean and Atlantic worlds, in particular carved ivories and the famous textiles. Aldhelm had a chasuble which he had brought from Rome and which was still preserved at Malmesbury in the twelfth century, when William of Malmesbury, the historian and anti-

---

* Aldhelm was said to have returned from Rome with a marble altar, which not surprisingly broke while crossing the Alps.

11. The Lindisfarne Gospels, Carpet Page on f. 94. *c.* 698 (see pp. 160–61)

12. (*right*) Binding of the Stonyhurst Gospel of St. John, seventh to eighth century (see p. 156)

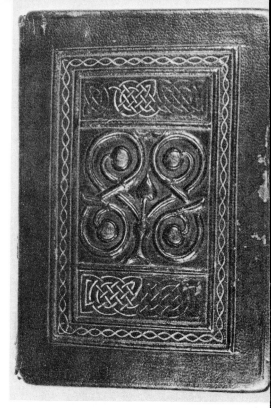

13. (*below*) The Franks Casket: panel with Wayland the Smith and the Adoration of the Magi, seventh to eighth century (see pp. 222–23)

quarian who knew it well, described it. It was of finely woven scarlet fabric, decorated in black with scrolls, and inside the scrolls were representations of peacocks.[37] Birds were not uncommon in vine scroll ornament, and that is probably what this vestment had. There is, of course, nothing to prove that it was Egyptian fabric; William of Malmesbury was not even certain where Aldhelm had acquired it. But it gives a clear insight into the sort of means by which ornamental patterns travelled.

Much stress has recently been laid on the role of Visigothic Spain as a direct mediator of East Mediterranean culture to Ireland and thence to England.[38] There was undoubtedly much coming and going between Spain and the East Mediterranean, at least until the mid-seventh century. There was also a strong Spanish influence at work on Irish prayers and liturgical practices, and the writings of the great Spanish scholar of the early seventh century, Isidore of Seville, were certainly known early in Ireland. But it is possible to exaggerate the strength of Hispano-Irish links in this period. First of all, one may search the text and voluminous notes of the learned articles of Professor J. N. Hillgarth, who seeks to establish such links, without finding a single piece of evidence of travel or written correspondence or direct communication of any kind between Spain and Ireland in the seventh century.[39] This is the more remarkable as the evidence for contacts of both countries with practically everywhere else in the civilized world is traced by the same author with great verve and much success. In the second place, leaving aside the liturgical aspect of the matter— liturgy is not the simplest of geographical evidence—the brunt of the argument is the early dissemination of the writings of Isidore of Seville. Without Isidore, the case for Spanish intellectual and cultural influence on Europe in his time would look altogether rather thin. Sometimes when one might really expect it to show, as between the treatise of Hildephonsus of Toledo (657–67) on Mary's virginity and Aldhelm's treatise on virginity, it is completely absent. Now if we speak of Isidore, the truth is that he quickly became known *everywhere* in the seventh century and no particular significance in the way of direct contact attaches to this being demonstrable in the case of Ireland. There are good reasons for the existence of more evidence of early Irish manu- scripts than of others, but these are to do with the chances of survival.[40] Likewise the doxology from the acts of the Fourth Council of Toledo (633), which was engraved on the late seventh-century cross at Fahan Mura in Donegal, is not necessarily a sign of direct Spanish influence on Ireland, (as suggested by Professor Hillgarth), because this doxology might be found anywhere by that time.[41]

The line of communications from Spain up the Atlantic seaboard to Southern Ireland and South-West Britain was deeply engraved on Prehistory. In Megalithic times, indeed, it was 'the stalwart, dark, broad-headed people', spreading from the Eastern Mediterranean and along this route, who helped to people the west of the British Isles. But if one looks, for instance, at the distribution maps of late Bronze Age articles like the double-looped palstaves, one sees that even where there is a centre of diffusion from the Spanish coast, these articles are to be found in the basins of the Garonne or the Loire as well as in the British Isles. Gaul is the intermediary.[42] Isidore's writings may have been diffused up the Atlantic, but the more likely chief route would be by way of Saragossa (whose bishop Braulio 'published' the *Etymologies*), along the old Roman road to Septimania. This rich, important and civilized province, situated round the Mediterranean coast from modern Catalonia to the mouth of the Rhône, had remained in Visigothic hands. In Isidore's time the contacts between Franks and Visigoths were relatively easy and there is no difficulty in imagining his works being carried up the Rhône and copied at cities like Vienne and Lyon which had remained centres of classical study.[43] On this basis it will be apparent that the Irish were not indispensable to introduce the Anglo-Saxons to Isidore's writings.

The Mediterranean world, then, could mean many different things to the Anglo-Saxons. Placed as they were on the edge of the known world, they nonetheless had the advantage of benefiting from the experience of Germanic peoples who had settled within the Roman Empire and had already adapted Mediterranean culture and religion to themselves and been adapted to it, most of all the Franks. They were able to absorb this culture and religion in various ways and in various blends.

9 Wilfrid

If there were popularity stakes for the story of the Anglo-Saxon conversion to Christianity, they would not be won by Wilfrid. The discreet silences of Bede, and the protestations of his own monk and biographer, Eddius, have both, in their different ways, helped to detract from the saint's reputation. In the *Realencyclopädie* for Protestant Theology and Church (1908), not perhaps the obvious place or date to find a favourable verdict, Böhmer wrote that in truth Wilfrid did not fight for Right, nor for Rome, *'sondern für sich selber.'* Meissner pursued him with a relentless hatred through the pages of an acute book on the Celtic Church, which reads rather like the fears of a paranoiac Irish abbot. Even dispassionate historians, however, find the apparently self-centred litigiousness, the pomp and circumstance, and the crusading energy of the man unattractive. There are perhaps other sides to the story, but we write this chapter less to present these for their own sake than to show a leading figure of the English Church as an admirable example of some of the chief influences operative in his period.

We can follow Wilfrid's career from the *Life* written by Eddius, a highly partisan document but the work of a contemporary who knew his subject well. Eddius was a Kentish singing master, who was called North by Wilfrid and became a monk at Ripon.[1]

After the Synod of Whitby, Colman withdrew from Northumbria and was succeeded as bishop of the Northumbrians by Tuda, who had been educated amongst the Southern Irish and accepted the Roman Easter. But Tuda died of the plague in the same year, and Wilfrid was chosen bishop. Wilfrid went to Gaul for his consecration to avoid any question of the validity of his orders; for in Britain at the time he could not have found three bishops to perform the ceremony, whom he would have regarded as free both of simony and schism. What he was actually made bishop of is a controversial matter, into which we do not intend to enter, except to say that the weight of evidence seems to suggest that both Oswy and Alfrith originally appointed him, intending him to be bishop of all the Northumbrians like his predecessors, but with his see at York.[2] Wilfrid himself, with his experience of Lyon, would think in terms of a diocese with a fixed see, and York, which had been Paulinus's see, was an obvious centre. That, anyhow, was the position which Archbishop Theodore allowed him in 669/70, and which he retained until his expulsion from Northumbria by King Egfrith in 678. The rest of his story, as given in Eddius, until his death at a ripe old age in 709, turns around the attacks made on his position as a diocesan and on the control of the numerous monasteries which he had founded all over England. We are told that towards the end of his life, as he was riding with his priest Tatbert, Wilfrid told him his life-story.[3] That story—of a man who had probably spoken with Aidan, who numbered almost every Anglo-Saxon king of his day amongst his friends, who had nearly been martyred in Gaul, who had refused the bishopric of Strassbourg, and who was well known in Rome, must have been one of the most fascinating chronicles ever to have escaped into thin air.

WILFRID, THEODORE AND THE SYNOD OF HERTFORD

A much more serious issue for the English Church than that of the celebration of Easter was brewing up for some time before it came to the boil at the Synod of Hertford in 672; the issue of whether dioceses should be large or small, or whether there should be one diocese or many for each Anglo-Saxon kingdom. The strategy of further missionary effort, the method of pastoral care for the faithful, turned to a considerable extent on this principle of organization. When Archbishop Theodore arrived in England in 669 he found an uncertainty about whether Wilfrid or Chad should be bishop of the Northumbrians; he found one bishop for the East Angles, one at Rochester, none in Mercia, and only the simoniac, Wine, in Wessex. That was the meagre total. He made Chad bishop of the Mercians with a see at Lichfield, and Chad was succeeded on his death soon afterwards by Wynfrith; he consecrated the Gaulish Eleutherius to be bishop of the West Saxons with his see now in the *civitas* of Winchester. He himself, however, favoured the division of these large dioceses and put the question on the agenda of the Synod of Hertford. It was evidently the item which took up the time, but the discussion got nowhere. 'About this matter we have for the present remained silent,' says the ninth canon.[4]

Theodore had met with opposition; we might ask ourselves where that opposition came from. Besides Theodore, four bishops were present at Hertford, and Wilfrid, though absent, was represented by proctors. Of these five we may first rule out Bishop Putta of Rochester, a mild old music master. Nobody would contemplate a campaign to divide the diocese of Rochester. The problematical Wynfrith, bishop of the Mercians, probably was, and the other three must certainly have been, opposed to Theodore on this point. The wily old archbishop bided his time and took his opportunities. When Bishop Bisi of the East Angles became too ill and feeble to object, he divided his diocese into two.[5] When Wilfrid was exiled from Northumbria in 678 he promptly divided his diocese at first into three, and then, in 681, into five.[6] If Eleutherius of Wessex had given a chance, he would have doubtless moved in there too, knowing that the diocese had previously been split. By the same token Eleutherius would have been the last person to agree to the division of his diocese. He had come to a diocese of all Wessex and was the nephew of the Frankish Agilbert, who had returned to Gaul and become bishop of Paris precisely because King Coenwalh of Wessex had tired of his foreign lingo and had split his West Saxon diocese.[7]

It is worth saying, while we are about it, that these moves of Theodore amounted to something new and fundamental in the history of Anglo-Saxon dioceses. His policy was to combine the virtues of both Roman and Irish organization. On the one hand he established bishoprics with specific sees, not necessarily in important places which had a history going back to Roman times, for he regarded accessibility to populated areas as more important; but each bishop had a definite seat. If bishoprics were to be multiplied without chaos, this was essential. On the other hand he arranged the bishoprics territorially with a scrupulous regard for political or tribal divisions. East Anglia was divided into Norfolk and Suffolk (Elmham and Dunwich); in Mercia, where Theodore must have been responsible for the division of the diocese, although Bede says nothing of it, Lichfield remained, while the Magonsaetan, the Hwicce and the Middle Angles all got their own bishoprics (Hereford, Worcester and Leicester); in Northumbria episcopal authority was carefully balanced between Bernicia, Deira and Lindsey (Lindisfarne, York and presumably Lincoln). Added to this, several clauses of the Synod of Hertford gave definition to the general relations of bishops with each other and with monasteries. In fact, Theodore established a working principle of diocesan organization in England, however vicissitudinous the subsequent history of some of the sees. He showed a grasp of the kind perhaps only possible to the complete outsider.

One might practically speak of Theodore's opponents at Hertford as forming a Gaulish party in that their notions of the bishop's office were those of Gaulish episcopal might. It would be well to see their attitude against the general background of Gaulish influence on the English Church about which Mr. Wallace-Hadrill has written.[8] Eleutherius had come from Gaul; Wilfrid's long stay in Lyon had, as Eddius tells us, been decisive for his education in ecclesiastical matters;[9] and although nothing is known of Bishop Bisi personally, East Anglia was evidently in many ways a centre of Gaulish influence, and one of Bisi's predecessors was Felix, a Burgundian and bishop for 17 years.[10]

The force of Wilfrid's personality makes it natural to see him as the leader of this party. Episcopal might recurs as an obvious motif through Eddius's *Life* of him—his splendid building programmes at York, Ripon and Hexham, his large retinues, the retinue which he provided for the Frankish Dagobert when he restored him to the throne of Austrasia, his treasure at Ripon, his lavish generosity, his bold speeches, his friendships and adept conversations with kings, the hatred he inspired in queens. It is all to be found in Eddius and Eddius knew Wilfrid well enough and long enough, if not always to be accurate, at least to reflect generally his master's concepts. Most significant of all in this respect was Wilfrid's triumphalist episcopal consecration by Agilbert at Compiègne, at which 12 bishops participated, and the new bishop was carried into the sanctuary on a golden chair. A newly consecrated bishop surrounded by 12 colleagues: the symbolism was clearly that of Christ and His Apostles. The Gaulish Church pitched the interpretation of the bishop's office high on these occasions. It is interesting that the tomb of Agilbert himself survives in the Merovingian crypt of Jouarre in present-day Normandy, and that on it were carved representations of Christ seated in majesty and the 12 apostles.[11]

The position of the Gaulish bishops, public officers and servants of their cities in imperial times, was enhanced by the barbarian invasions. They increasingly became great proprietors with grants of immunity. Since it was Lyon which Wilfrid had visited, it might be worth glancing at some of the surviving fragments of information on the bishops of Lyon during the two centuries up to Wilfrid's time.[12] In these bishops we can see Gaulish episcopal might in action as Wilfrid would have experienced it. A certain scale and grandeur is apparent in their public activities together with a certain monastic simplicity in their personal lives. Nobody who visited Lyon in the seventh century could fail to learn something about Patiens, the Gallo-Roman aristocrat, who had been bishop two centuries earlier under the Burgundian rulers. His monument was the brilliant church of St. Just, in which one could read the inscriptions of Sidonius Apollinaris, celebrating Patiens's 'aedis celsa' with its light glimmering on the gilded ceiling, its marble of various tints, its multi-coloured glass windows and its surrounding colonnades.[13] Patiens was the bishop of whom it was said that the king praised his feasts and the queen his fasts, the bishop of whom it was remembered that during a famine in the 470's he had distributed free supplies of corn throughout the Auvergne at his private expense.[14]

Early in the sixth century there was a bishop called Stephen, another example of a bishop involved in high-level politics. He granted some of his possessions in the Auvergne to the bishop of Rodez.[15] The two appear to have been in an intrigue together against the Arian Visigoths in favour of the Franks.

One of the mid-sixth century bishops, Nicetus, was a great-uncle of Gregory of Tours, and a notable builder, improver of the bishop's house and planter out of vineyards.[16] He is seen visiting the domains of his see in Provence during the winter; but nothing was allowed to come before his attendance at divine office. If he were called out of church on business he would quote irrelevantly, as though he were a simpleton, something from the psalms he had just been chanting, chanting in the antiphonal style which was said so to interest him.[17]

Around 600, in the time of Pope Gregory the Great, Bishop Aetherius had a bitter dispute with the bishop of Vienne over the right to wear the pallium.[18] Finally we come to Bishop

Annemundus, Wilfrid's friend and patron. A promising young man appears on the scene, impresses by his way of life and his talk, and the bishop is in the position promptly to offer him a province ('*bonam partem*' of Gaul) to administer. Professor E. Ewig, discussing the downfall of Annemundus along with several other bishops in the time of Ebroin, Mayor of the Neustrian Palace, has shown that the bishop's brother was count of Lyon and that Annemundus seems altogether to have exercised a kind of policy best described as '*Territorialpolitik*', the building up of an aristocratic republic with a bishop at its head.[19] Frankish history is full of majestic appearances of bishops—their consecrations, their building up of city walls, their processions, their speeches. Who can forget the brilliant interview in which Gregory of Tours protected his citizens from the king's tax collectors?[20] The power of these bishops depended on the sense of what Ewig calls '*Das Tremendum*'.

The emphasis on external splendour, political influence and prowess, and on material resources, this emphasis by truly religious men had a pastoral rationale behind it—the fostering of the true faith, the correction of wrongdoers of all classes, the relief of the poor, the endowment and supervision of monasteries, the education and encouragement of young men, the general good order and protection of the community.[21] For the sake of their flocks, it could be argued, bishops were compelled to cut an impressive figure beyond their own dioceses, to be dignitaries of more than local importance. It was in the interest of their flocks that kings should be instructed in their duties by persons whom they respected, that bishops should be able to stand up to kings, and that as the chief officers of government in the cities they should exercise a commanding presence when surrounded by the agencies of otherwise unrestrained commotion. Gaulish episcopal might, doubtless sometimes abused, was the potential means of realizing a genuinely pastoral ideal, as Wilfrid must have seen at Lyon.

The size of a diocese was itself rarely an issue of trouble or dispute in Gaul, for by the seventh century the pattern of dioceses on the basis of Roman cities had long since crystallized.[22] But it is not hard to see how in seventh-century England, men familiar with the Gaulish traditions and ideals should have translated these into the issue of the size of dioceses. In Gaul cities counted for much, with their history, their buildings, their fortifications, and (even in this age) their education; in Anglo-Saxon England at this time they meant on the whole rather little. Political prestige for an Anglo-Saxon bishop, therefore, lay rather in identification with a whole tribe or kingdom; there was little enough basis for it otherwise. That is why the bishops at the Synod of Hertford wished to retain the principle of one bishop for one kingdom.

Furthermore, on the size of a diocese depended the scale of a bishop's revenues. In his famous letter to Archbishop Egbert of York, Bede makes it quite clear that this was one important reason why bishops did not want their dioceses divided.[23] Besides the landed endowments of their sees, these revenues were probably of three main kinds. First, Ine's Laws enforce the payment of 'church-scot', and this was a payment in kind, due from every household on November 11, after the harvest had been brought in.[24] Secondly, there were offerings of money at the altar during mass and fees paid for burials, as well as tithes which were at this time voluntary. These would normally go to the monastic or minster church which served the particular area, as they did in Gaul by this time; but they could have been important to Anglo-Saxon bishops to the extent that they still relied on their own travels to minister to their flocks. Thirdly, there was the tax which every church paid to the bishop for its chrism, which was by this time the chief source of revenue for Gaulish bishops (apart from the revenue of their own estates and those of their sees), and was doubtless significant in England, too.[25] These dues would not be an unimportant consideration to bishops in their pastoral work, and in the building or rebuilding of cathedral churches such as Wilfrid undertook at York. The building of Wilfrid's churches at Ripon and Hexham may have been largely paid for out of the endowments of those monasteries; but how was an expensive operation like the repair of York Minster and the re-leading of its roof financed?

As against all this, Theodore's ideas of the episcopal office fit precisely with those of Pope Gregory the Great. If we speak of Gregory it will be possible to see a rationale behind Theodore's actions. There was no intrinsic conflict between Gregory's ideals and those of the Gaulish bishops, but there was certainly the possibility of an important divergence of emphasis. To Gregory the problem presented itself like this. On the one hand a pastor must take care of external matters otherwise he neglects his flock; he must uphold a certain external appearance and not be too humble

or depreciate himself too much, otherwise he loses the authority
to restrain and discipline those under him. On the other hand he
must not indulge in outward show to gratify his self-importance;
he must not grow cold amidst external works for want of
internal humility or the fire of contemplation.[26] This is also how
the problem presented itself to Theodore. To his mind, the bishops
trained in the Irish tradition had failed to strike a balance. Where
St. Martin of Tours refused to ride anything better than an ass,
these bishops even insisted on going round on foot; they neglected
their external dignity; they had to be made to ride horses.[27]

Theodore's actions fit neatly with a letter of Gregory the Great
in which he expresses to his rector in Sicily discontent at being
sent only one sorry nag and five asses. He cannot ride the nag
because it is too sorry; nor can he ride the asses because they are
asses. He trusts to being sent something suitable. And there is
another letter of this pope in which he shows again his views on
the proper appearance and deportment for a bishop. Here he
refers with displeasure to a bishop of Naples who was obsessed
with ship-building and was reported to go down to the sea daily
in such dirty old clothes that he was totally lacking the character
or venerableness of a bishop.[28]

Gregory had been more inclined still, however, to emphasize the
dangers of worldly rule and vain glorying in position. The
Pastoral Care is full of it. If pastors were excessively entangled in
secular business the stones of the sanctuary would be scattered in
the streets. If pastors coveted their office in order to say, as the
king of Babylon had said, 'Is not this the great Babylon, which I
have built to be the seat of the kingdom, by the strength of my
power and in the glory of my excellence?', would they not slay
themselves with the sword of ambition?[29] The greater the external
manifestation of power, the more need to keep humility in the
heart; Gregory's letters constantly show his unease about external
manifestations of power. When he reproved a fellow bishop he
preferred to play down the papal position and rather emphasize the
bond of brotherly love between them.[30] With regard to the
display of pallia, whereas Gaulish church councils insisted on
metropolitans wearing them for mass,[31] Gregory barely tolerated
it; and as to those metropolitans who processed through the streets
wearing them, such a thing drove the pope to a pitch of anxiety
for their souls.[32]

One point in particular about which Gregory felt uneasy, when he looked at the Gaulish church—and this was a significant reaction to episcopal grandeur—was the way in which bishops were elected. He complained frequently that he heard reports of simony, and scarcely less acceptable was the way in which laymen would be elected, and by a 'sudden leap' would be raised to the episcopal office.[33] That was all he said; but there may have been some more deep-seated unease behind it. For when we compare the kind of elections which were actually made in Gaul with the kind which Gregory liked to see, the result is a rather good touchstone of the tension which existed between the two ideas of the bishop's position. In Gaul the bishop was frequently the Great Man brought in from outside—Gregory of Tours came from a family of Lyonaise aristocrats and grew up in the Auvergne; Agilbert had been bishop of the West Saxons before he became bishop of Paris. Examples could be multiplied. The Great Man might be an aristocrat, or an administrator, or a saint, or a combination of these things. Whereas Gregory liked to see a worthy cleric, known for his gravity—there was nothing Gregory liked to see more than a grave man—who had worked his way up in his own church, elected bishop of it. So it was at Salona and at Syracuse, while the Neapolitians were told that it would be a serious disgrace to their clergy if they had nobody fit to be elected.[34]

Not that Gregory actually wrote anything in favour of small dioceses (except by implication in his diocesan scheme for Britain); not that the external power connected with a large diocese necessarily could not be balanced by the humility of the bishop's heart. But it is easy to see the grounds on which a large diocese might be mistrusted. Moreover, Gregory had said that a pastor should be a neighbour in compassion to everyone.[35] Theodore might well have asked himself whether one bishop for the whole of Northumbria could possibly have been a neighbour of *any* kind to everyone. At a later date the point was trenchantly made by Bede in his letter to Archbishop Egbert.[36] In recent years it has been made by the Council of Clergy in the Roman Catholic archdiocese of Liverpool and been accepted by Archbishop Beck.[37] We also read in Gregory much about the motherly quality which a pastor should have and which implies a closeness of personal contact with his whole flock. The little ones, he says, enduring the waves of temptation will have recourse to the pastor's understanding 'as to a mother's bosom'.[38] But could the spiritual needs of the whole of Northumbria be satisfied by only one mother's bosom, however commodious?

We have said that Gregory's ideas of the Pastoral Office enable us to see a rationale behind Theodore's attempts to create more and smaller dioceses. There is, of course, nothing to connect Theodore clearly and directly to Gregory. One thing which must obviously have influenced Theodore is that in Asia Minor cities, and therefore as a general rule bishoprics, were far more numerous than for the equivalent area in Gaul. A glance at the map of *civitates* in the fifth-century empire reveals it. But in this point the experience of Gregory the Great would be similar. It is certain that from an early period bishoprics were thick on the ground in Central and Southern Italy.[39] Dioceses had varied in size (for different reasons) from the earliest times of which we know anything about the subject. Professor S. F. Greenslade has recently written of the differences of practice and of opinion in the fourth century, for instance; these led the Council of Sardica in 343 to forbid the consecration of bishops for villages or small cities, which needed no more than a priest, '*ne vilescat nomen episcopi*'. But on the other hand he has also drawn attention to the *Didascalia*, a third century Syrian document which speaks of the pastoral office in terms similar to those of Gregory the Great. Of the *Didascalia*, Professor Greenslade writes, 'the ideal here portrayed of the pastoral bishop is one which could only become actual in a small diocese'.[40]

To both Theodore and Gregory, then, a diocese would mean a fairly small administrative unit within the empire; both could easily have been heirs to the same line of pastoral thinking, as expressed, for instance, in the *Didascalia*, although they would not have known this document itself. It is not unreasonable to suppose that a sketch of Gregory's ideas represents roughly what would have been Theodore's. In addition, Theodore had the company of Abbot Hadrian to keep him in 'true doctrine' on his way to England, and when he arrived at Canterbury he would have found it full of the writings of Pope Gregory, writings much venerated. They were the obvious literature to focus his attention on the pastoral duties which lay ahead of him.

In the ninth canon of the Synod of Hertford, therefore, and in subsequent events related to it, we see the clash of two pastoral concepts. At one level this conflict was occasioned by the difference between the numerous city-bishoprics of the Eastern

Mediterranean world, and the world of the Anglo-Saxons where cities meant little and the generally accepted unit for a diocese looked like becoming the kingdom. At a deeper level it was between two pastoral concepts which we might call (within our context) Gregorian and Gaulish. The two protagonists in the debate in England were Theodore on the one side and (albeit he was not personally present at the synod itself) Wilfrid on the other.

ASCETICISM

Having considered Wilfrid's Gaulish interpretation of the episcopal office, we turn to another feature of Eddius's presentation of his subject. Eddius bristles with allusions to the Old Testament. Samuel and David, Baal and Jezebel are all there in force, with many others besides, a fertile supply of similes. As Balak summoned Balaam, so the king and queen of Northumbria summoned Archbishop Theodore with bribes to come and divide Wilfrid's diocese. King Egfrith, while he lived in obedience to Wilfrid, triumphed over his enemies, as had Joash, king of Judah, while Jehoiada the high priest was still alive. As Rehoboam, the son of Solomon, had humiliated his people with tribute, so a Frankish bishop accused King Dagobert of wasting the Austrasian cities.[41]

Psychologists sometimes speak of a person's 'characteristic situation'. One might say that Wilfrid's was well illustrated during his return from his magnificent episcopal consecration in Gaul when his boat was washed up onto the shores of Sussex.[42] And here, in Eddius's narrative, the guns of the Old Testament flash and pound. The South Saxons were still pagans; a glance at Wilfrid's boat was enough to convince them that it was worth a little trouble. Wilfrid's powers of conversation having for once failed him, the pagan chief priest stood up on a mound and attempted like Balaam to curse the people of God. But one of the bishop's companions hurled a stone from a sling in the manner of David, which found its mark on the Wizard's forehead. Death took him unawares as it did Goliath and he fell on the sand. The pagans then prepared for battle, but in vain did they draw up their array, for the Lord fought with the few, even as Gideon with his 300 warriors slew the 120,000 Midianites. Against the pagan hordes the holy bishop could pit only 120 warriors—120, the number of years in Moses' age. We may pass over the fact

that 120 was quite a nice little army for the period, picked
warriors, doubtless, from the booming North-East, ranged against
the ill-prepared, ill-armed, uncouth locals of Sussex. The position
of Wilfrid was not so parlous as that of Gideon. The battle
began. Wilfrid and his clergy bent their knees and raised their
hands to heaven, as Moses had called continually upon the Lord
for help, Hur and Aaron raising his hands, while Joshua fought
against Amalek. The untamed heathens were overthrown, the tide
was brought back before its time, and the holy bishop finally put
in at Sandwich.

Eddius was not, of course, by any means original to use the
Old Testament in writing a saint's life; Old Testament examples
feature quite prominently, for instance, in Gregory the Great's
influential account of St. Benedict in the *Dialogues*.[43] But it is
not easy to find a hagiography with direct allusions on the
scale of the life of Wilfrid. There may well be something of the
influence of Gildas's History and his extensive use of the Old
Testament to show how men could be saved or damned. The
immediate clue to Eddius's method, however, seems to lie in
Bishop Acca, Wilfrid's priest who succeeded him at Hexham.[44] It
was for Acca that Eddius wrote Wilfrid's *Life*, in the second
decade of the eighth century, and it was for Acca at just the same
time that Bede was writing his commentaries on the Old Testament
books. Bede's commentaries on the Old Testament are largely
allegorical and one can go through them finding interpretations
of many of Eddius's allusions. In his book on Esras he explains the
meaning of the bases of the altar, to which Eddius alludes when
he speaks of the altar at Ripon.[45] In his book on Samuel, Bede
writes of the significance of the stones in David's scrip, and
explains how suitable it was that he should have struck the
Philistine on the forehead, for so the stupidity of those who nurture
false dogmas was exposed.[46] Then follows still more about the
Philistine's forehead! In the book on Solomon's Temple Bede
comments on the significance of Moses' Age. Moses was the
lawgiver, so 120 represented lawful doctrine; 120 was the number
of the primitive church who received the grace of the Holy Spirit
and lived upright lives according to the law.[47] The story of the
Sussex beach makes very good allegorical sense in the light of all
this.

It would be a worthless exercise to enumerate systematically
those allusions of Eddius which can be found in the books written

by Bede for Acca. The point is that Acca was a focus of interest and helped to inspire the work being done by various scholars, not least by Eddius. In the Old Testament one could find 'types' of Christ, the Faith, the Church. Eddius used it to find 'types' of Wilfrid. He created for England a fusion between two key spheres of intellectual activity — biblical interpretation and hagiography.

A rather important point for the understanding of Wilfrid arises out of Eddius's use of the Old Testament. M. Fontaine has recently argued most interestingly that Sulpicius Severus cast St. Martin much more in the mould of the prophets than in that of Christ.[48] The dramatization and physiological detail of Martin's miracles are much closer to those of Elias and Eliseus than to those of the New Testament. Martin's fight against paganism in Gaul, with his challenges to pagan priests, the danger to his life, the popular awe at the divine manifestation, reads not unlike Elias's defiance of the prophets of Baal on Mount Carmel. His relations with the Emperor Maximus bear a relation to the prophets' attacks on the weaknesses of unbelieving kings. Once indeed, in the *Dialogues*, Sulpicius Severus actually likens Martin to the prophets.

M. Fontaine goes on to argue with equal conviction that this is most unlikely to be a mere literary device of Sulpicius Severus, but that Martin himself wished to give his acts a prophetic colour. For the prophets, especially Elias and Eliseus, were the standard traditional models of the Eastern ascetics, with whom Martin had contacts.

The same kind of thing, though in a thinner strain, is found in Eddius's Life of Wilfrid. Wilfrid is said to suffer the persecutions of queens as the prophets suffered them. Like the prophet Ezechiel he was elected (to his bishopric, Eddius means) at the age of 30. His miracles are explicitly compared to those of Elias and Eliseus.[49] If we apply M. Fontaine's principles to Eddius's Life of Wilfrid — and there is no reason to doubt that Eddius cast Wilfrid in the same general mould as Wilfrid would have have cast himself — then two conclusions follow. First, that Wilfrid's own life was based on the Old Testament, and here we note the interest of the Old Testament also to the epic poets of early Anglo-Saxon England. Secondly, that in a certain sense Wilfrid saw himself in the tradition of the desert fathers who modelled themselves on the prophets both in their retreats and in their public actions. This leads us into a subject which seems not to have received so much as a short paragraph's treatment in print, namely Wilfrid's asceticism.

Dr. Wallace-Hadrill has spoken of the fusion in the Gallo-Roman episcopate of the missionary zeal of Martin of Tours and Lérins on the one hand, and the old episcopal tradition of service to the *civitas* on the other. He adds, 'one overlooks the element of the former in the circle of Sidonius Apollinaris, which had its links with the monks.'[50] These comments are very relevant to Wilfrid, for they lead us to reflect on the way in which asceticism sat together with his other qualities as bishop. In a general way Eddius leaves no doubt about Wilfrid's ascetisicm. When, as a young man, he was about to go to Rome for the first time, he spent a year in Kent where he impressed King Erconbert with his continual prayers, fastings, readings and vigils.[51] Again Eddius tells us that, summer and winter, he bathed in cold water at night, and when he explains that Wilfrid was neither drowned by waves of feasting nor thrown into the pride of abstinence,[52] we are reminded of how the devil tried to tempt Anthony the Hermit to eat too infrequently and of how Saint Guthlac would eat every day for fear of giving an opening to the devil.[53] Moreover, Wilfrid attracted hermits to his spiritual leadership. When he was dying there came to him 'his abbots and anchorites',[54] and when he had appointed Tatbert, his kinsman, to succeed him as abbot of Ripon, he allowed Caelin, who had been looking after the monastery, 'to return to desert places and to practise the contemplative life as he had done before.'[55]

Considering that the bishops of Lyon and other Gaulish bishops were well versed in monastic and ascetic traditions, there would be no possibility nor point in trying to decide what Wilfrid had learnt in Gaul and what in England. The idea of pilgrimage, for instance, so familiar in Irish asceticism, was equally a familiar notion at Lérins from its earliest days.[56] Nevertheless it is easy to underrate the influence on Wilfrid of the four happy years which he spent at Lindisfarne; and much too easy to imagine that the Synod of Whitby broke his love and admiration for the place. At Whitby he was like a lawyer with a brief, and through con-viction as well as a taste for public performance, he pressed his brief for all it was worth. His brief concerned the date of Easter. There is no reason at all why the spiritual ideals of Lindisfarne should have lost their meaning to a man who acted in this frame of mind.[57]

With regard to the idea of pilgrimage, almost as soon as Wilfrid had arrived at Lyon for the first time at the age of 19 or 20, the bishop offered that he should administer a province and marry his niece. Wilfrid refused and the words which Eddius put into his mouth are of special interest. 'My vows have been rendered to the Lord and I will fulfil them, leaving my kin and my father's house as Abraham did, to visit the Apostolic See, and to learn the rules of ecclesiastical discipline, so that our nation may grow in the service of God.'[58] Abraham was the standard model for Irish pilgrims and Rome was a not unusual objective for Irish pilgrims in the seventh century. The peculiar twist here—and the argument was immediately recognized as a good one by Bishop Annemundus —is the idea that pilgrimage equipped one for service to the nation (gens). It was the fusion of the ideas of pilgrimage and public service to the city.

One might think it an accident of Eddius's writing that Wilfrid's argument came out like this were it not that Wilfrid is reported as using exactly the same argument on a later occasion when Eddius himself would almost certainly have been present. When Wilfrid was returning from Rome in 680 he was met by a Frankish bishop with a threatening manner and an army. He accused Wilfrid of having restored to the Austrasian throne, in the person of Dagobert, a waster of their cities and despiser of their counsels. To this Wilfrid replied with one of the supreme speeches of his career. What he is reported as saying—and again it was accepted as a good argument by the Frankish bishop—was that he had helped this man in exile and pilgrimage (*exulantem et in pere-grinatione degentem*) and he had exalted him to be a builder of cities and a consoler of citizens (*aedificator urbium, consolator civium*).[59]

Another side of Wilfrid's spiritual experience is touched on by Eddius when he writes of how King Egfrith of Northumbria put him into prison after his return from Rome in 680. He was placed under a close guard in a dark dungeon where no sunlight penetrated by day and no lamps were lit at night. But in the dark of night the guards heard the man of God singing psalms and were awestruck to see light, daylight it seemed, coming out of the dungeon. Then Eddius breaks into a prayer, beginning '*O lumen aeternum*'. 'Now,' he says, 'Thou didst deign to bring the light of an angelic visitation into the deep obscurity of the dungeon as he prayed,' just as Peter had been chained in prison when the angel of the Lord stood by him and a light shone in his cell.[60] The whole narrative is not dissimilar to that occasion described by Adamnan, when Columba retired to a wild island near Iona and shut himself up in a hut for three days without eating and drinking, and at night an extraordinary light was seen escaping through the key-hole and the chinks in the door as the meaning of Holy Scripture was made clear 'to the eyes of his most pure heart.'[61] Wilfrid was bathed in one of those great floods of light which were the outward sign of the exquisite consolations received by Irish saints in their life of hardship for Christ.

As to the way in which Eddius speaks of Wilfrid's experience as an angelic visitation, that is reminiscent of the Irish familiarity with the ministrations of angels. The prayers in the Book of Cerne, which has a strong Irish base to it and which as a collection seems to have Lindisfarne connections, are full of the joys of angels, the praises of angels and the food of angels, and of invocations to the archangels. We shall see that one must look to Coptic inspiration for the place which the archangels occupied in Irish prayer and art.[62] Another of Columba's angelic experiences finds a parallel in Eddius. When the holy angels who had been sent to conduct his soul from the flesh were already in sight, Columba had a sudden vision that four years had been added to his life.[63] Exactly the same thing happened to Wilfrid when he was old and sick.[64] It was the archangel Michael who appeared to him in a white robe and said, *'Ego sum Michael, summi Dei nuntius'*, almost as if Eddius were thinking of something like the later prayer to Michael, which invokes him as *'summi tonantis nuntius'*.[65]

ROMANISM

What of Wilfrid's famous (or notorious) Romanism? It would be easy to exaggerate the significance of his appeals to the papacy over the division of his diocese and the attacks on his monastic empire. They hardly did much to advance papal authority in England because papal authority was that far advanced in any case, without needing Wilfrid to help it. Dr. Kathleen Hughes has shown that appeal to the pope in important ecclesiastical matters was regarded as a normal course of action even in seventh-century Ireland.[66] Papal protection for monasteries, such as Wilfrid secured for Ripon and Hexham from Pope Agatho in 679, was

quite common by that time. When Wilfrid returned to
Northumbria in 680 it was suggested by some that his papal
privileges were secured by bribery and by others that they had
been forged, but nobody suggested that in principle they should
not have been obtained.[67] It was generally accepted, furthermore,
that bishops who felt that they had suffered infringement of
their rights should appeal to the pope. In the mid-sixth century
the notorious Gaulish bishops Salonius and Sagittarius of Gap
and Embrun appealed to John III against their deposition by a
council at Lyon,[68] and had the documents in their case been
preserved by a partisan institution and been written up by a
partisan biographer, such as Wilfrid had in Ripon and Eddius, they
could have been made to look like champions in the advance of
papal authority in Gaul—which would be nonsense. So much, in
these things, depends on the chance survival of evidence. If we
knew more about others we might see that Wilfrid's attitude to
the papacy was quite commonplace amongst Anglo-Saxons, only it
happened to be he whose difficulties necessitated appeal to the
pope and he who had his Eddius to record them.

In one point, however, Wilfrid was significantly Roman, or
perhaps rather Gregorian, namely in his missionary methods as
seen particularly amongst the Frisians and South Saxons. There
were two different kinds of approach to missionizing in the early
Middle Ages. Of one kind Martin of Tours, as reported by Sulpicius
Severus, was the classic exponent. This approach was frontal and
dramatic. It was based broadly on the destruction of pagan
temples, the smashing of idols, challenges to pagan priests, and the
missionary's placing himself in grave danger so that his provi-
dential extrication from it might cause the benighted infidels to
gasp with wonder. These were the methods employed by the
Irish saints, whom Wilfrid did not at all in this particular resemble.
Adamnan's Life of Columba, describing the saint's work among
the Picts, is full of contests with the magicians of King Brude—
over dead bodies, over contaminated wells, and even one plain
shouting match. It is also full of Columba's extricating himself
from dangers to the awe of the pagans, and these include his being
chased by some mysterious monster in Loch Ness![69] Columbanus
was much the same. At Bregenz he had come upon a pagan
festival at which a great pot of beer was to be offered to Woden,
prior to its consumption. He breathed on it and it exploded with
a loud report.[70]

Gregory the Great was the classic exponent of the other approach, which, it is no surprise to learn, was based on the attempt to strike a balance. Gregory's methods, eschewing all drama and all suggestion of Old Testament prophetic style, fit against an imperial background. For Jews he believed in mildness and persuasion, together with a little 'blandishment' in the form of rent remission. For pagans, however, he generally considered sterner measures more appropriate. The pagan slaves of Corsica were to be chastized by beating and torture so that they might be 'brought to amendment'; the pagan peasants of Sardinia were to be burdened with a rent which should make them 'hasten to righteousness.' During the course of the English mission Gregory changed from a policy of stern measures and compulsion to one of mildness by which the Anglo-Saxons should be led to Christianity step by step.[71] The old temples were now to be kept for Christian worship; Christian festivals were to be accompanied with the old feasts of cattle. This was not necessarily a dramatic change in his whole notion of missionary method; it may have been just a shift from one side to the other of an accepted balance.

In the early eighth century Boniface, in his mission to the continental Saxons, inclined to the dramatic missionary methods of the school of Martin of Tours. Bishop Daniel of Winchester, on the other hand, trying to persuade him that reasoned arguments should be put to pagans 'not in an offensive and irritating way but calmly and with great moderation', showed himself to be more in harmony with Gregory's milder methods.[72] Wilfrid's missionary enterprises occurred over 40 years before Bishop Daniel wrote to Boniface. What Wilfrid may have learnt of Gregory's missionary policy in general, or of his letters concerning the English mission in particular, during his lengthy visits to Rome and to Kent, must remain an open question. Moreover there is no evidence of what his policy was on the precise points about which Gregory had written to Mellitus—pagan temples and pagan festivals. What is clear, however, is that Wilfrid's whole attitude to missionizing approximated more closely in spirit to Gregory's mixture of step-by-step mildness, compulsion and material inducement than to anything else. Thus, no matter how fearsome Wilfrid might have appeared to the pagans who had attacked him on the beaches of Sussex, when he returned some 15 years later to convert them he was all gentle persuasion and milk without guile, all 'suaviloquia eloquentia' as

Eddius says. But it may be noted that for all that, some of the
South Saxons were converted willingly while others were converted at the king's command. When Wilfrid preached to the
Frisians in 678 he was helped by a particularly plentiful catch of
fish that season.[73] May be the 'blandishment' of his fishing
expertise, another of his gifts amongst the galaxy, lay behind this.
Certain it is that he taught the South Saxons how to fish and that
thereafter, hearing his preaching, 'they began to hope for
heavenly goods.'[74]

The formative years of Wilfrid's teens and early twenties, therefore, were dominated by Lindisfarne, Rome and Lyon; and the
result was that some of the great traditions which moulded English
Christianity coalesced in a remarkable way within this one man.

10 The Northumbrian Monasteries

Monasticism lay at the heart of early English Christianity, but the word 'monastery' might mean anything from the famous royal foundations or episcopal sees to the communities of perhaps three or four in the churches which served the pastoral needs of a scattered area. Indeed it was not unknown for individuals to live under personal monastic vows. Such was Cuthbert's foster-mother, Kenswith, who lived in a village probably somewhere in the Lammermuir Hills, and was described as a nun and a widow.[1] One source of ambiguity in the term 'monastery' was that there was no universal, prescribed rule of monastic life. The Rule of St. Benedict was well known in the seventh century and was regarded by many as particularly authoritative, but it was not to reach its exclusive eminence in the West until the ninth or tenth century. In Rome itself at an earlier date the rule in any monastery was the rule of its abbot, and it was based on his own monastic experience and his knowledge of other rules in existence.[2] The rule followed by Augustine's monks at Canterbury, for instance, was his own rule.

It is clear that by 700 a large number of monasteries of one kind or another was in existence amongst the Anglo-Saxons. They owed their foundation to royal or aristocratic endowment. The sproutings of the next 50 years became, to Bede at least, positively alarming. We shall consider this problem in a later chapter, but we confine ourselves for the moment to the great Northumbrian monasteries of the late seventh century. There were, of course, many monasteries in other parts of England at this period which were just as celebrated in their time. About 669 Ceolfrid left Ripon in order to visit and learn from the monasteries of Kent and the famous foundation of St. Botulph at Icanhoe in East Anglia.[3] Northumbria owed much altogether to Kentish monasticism; Biscop had been abbot of SS Peter and Paul, Canterbury, for two years before founding Wearmouth and Jarrow, Oftfor had left the monastery at Whitby to continue his education at Canterbury, and Eddius had come from Kent to teach the chant at Ripon. As to Icanhoe, it was under the auspices of this house that Mildburg's monastery at Much Wenlock was founded.[4] Again, Sir Frank Stenton uncovered from documentary sources the importance of *Medeshamstede*, later Peterborough, in the mid and late seventh century. From this monastery a whole string of dependencies stretched through the length and breadth of Mercia.[5] Yet notwithstanding all this, we concentrate on the Northumbrian monasteries at present for two reasons. First, thanks to contemporary writers (above all Bede), to surviving works of art, and to the excavations of archaeologists, it is these monasteries of whose quality of life we can form the clearest picture. Our knowledge of others, except for centres of learning like Canterbury or Malmesbury, are mainly based on charters or glimpses from letters. And second, the greatest Northumbrian monasteries represent something quintessential in the Anglo-Saxon civilization of their time, which is worth studying for its own sake.

All the most famous of them were on the East Coast or on the rivers flowing into it, placed where there were fine harbours, easily accessible from the South, from the continent, and from each other. To travel up the beautiful coastline of North-East England and to pass through the dismal urban agglomerations bearing names with the richest early Christian associations— Hartlepool, Wearmouth, Jarrow—is a moving experience. Anyone doing this journey by boat, let us say around 690, must have been struck by one thing in particular—the radical diversity encountered within a mere hundred miles, diversity of monastic culture and way of life, diversity in the whole physical appearance of the monasteries. This diversity was due to the many different traditions in Mediterranean lands on which it was possible to draw, to the different way in which each house had adapted Mediterranean culture and religion to Northumbrian traditions and society, and to the different aspects of Northumbrian aristocratic society—for these monasteries were predominantly aristocratic institutions—which each house represented.

WHITBY

The hypothetical traveller might begin from the South at Whitby, with its commanding site on the cliffs, its view out to sea in one direction and to the rolling North Yorkshire moors in the other, and its superb harbour below. The monastery, as it seems from its partial excavation, was laid out in the Irish manner.[6] It consisted of separate little buildings for the churches, workshops and cells, all surrounded by a rampart. It was all like the *domunculae*, the little houses of which Bede writes when he was describing the appearance of the similar monastery of Coldingham further North, and it is reminiscent of the huts in which the monks of Iona lived. During the Whitby excavations three rectangular buildings with thick stone walls were discovered; two measured 18 x 11 feet and the other 23 x 12 feet. Each had a stone hearth, a lavatory partition and an external drain. There was also an L-shaped building with a large stone hearth, possibly a smithy. Amongst the other finds were a stone inscription to the abbess Aelffled who died in 713 or 714, fine bookcovers, book marks and styli, in fact the equipment of the monastic scriptorium, glass beads and fragments of drinking glass, though no window glass, and—for it appears we are dealing here with persons having Gaulish contacts—nail-cleaners and ear-picks in the Frankish fashion.

The small rectangular buildings were perhaps cells for one or two inmates, yet it is worthy of note that a dependent monastery built a few miles away at Hackness around 680, shortly before Abbess Hilda died, did not have this Irish layout but something more like the regular plan which we shall see at Jarrow and Wearmouth, for Bede refers to a nun who had a vision there in 680 'in the dormitory of the sisters' (*in dormitorio sororum*).[7] Here were no individual cells. The difference of plan between Whitby and its dependency reflects a characteristic ambiguity in the whole ethos of the mother-house at this time. Hilda, the foundress, had learnt the monastic life from Aidan, but Whitby was also the house of the great ladies of the Northumbrian court. Eanfled, daughter of Edwin and wife of Oswy, who had had a childhood in Kent during which she had imbibed the Roman tradition, retired here with her daughter Aelffled, and these two succeeded Hilda in turn to the rule of the house. It was under the rule of Aelffled that the Whitby Life of Pope Gregory, with its probable drawing on Canterbury traditions, was composed, and Aelffled herself was a staunch supporter of Wilfrid.[8] On the other hand she was also a close friend of Cuthbert of Lindisfarne and the two met frequently to talk about spiritual matters.[9] In the Whitby of about 690, therefore, Roman and Irish traditions were mingled in a quite distinctive way. But it was to Gaul that the monastery owed the nature of its constitution.

Whitby was a double monastery. The institution of monks and nuns living in corporate and liturgical unity and in geographical proximity was the most important monastic importation from Gaul to Anglo-Saxon England. It used to be thought that double monasteries represented the Irish influence, until Dom Stefan Hilpisch showed that the much discussed example of St. Brigit's church at Kildare was the only known Irish example and that on closer inspection Kildare proved to be no such example at all.[10] Double monasteries originated amongst the Eastern monks, generally as a means of satisfying the ascetic yearnings of their sisters. Everyday life in these institutions was marked by the strictest rules of segregation except for the purposes of worship, and in the nature of their origins they were generally, though not invariably, ruled by abbots. One such abbot was a stylite whose pillar gave him a particularly favourable vantage point. In Gaul the situation was somewhat different. The founding of double monasteries there represented the female response to the inspiration of St. Columbanus in the early seventh century. High-born women founded nunneries on their own estates and communities of men became associated with them in order to offer mass, give the sacraments, and to assist in the administrative and manual tasks which it was difficult for women to perform alone. In the nature of the case, therefore, such Gaulish monasteries were usually, though not invariably, ruled by abbesses.[11]

In England the superior was—where the fact is ascertainable—without exception an abbess. It was in East Anglia, with its Gaulish contacts, that English women first showed an interest in the monastic life. A daughter and a grand-daughter of King Anna of the East Angles were amongst the earliest Anglo-Saxons to become nuns in Gaul. Hilda, who was sister-in-law of King Ethelhere of the East Angles, was staying in East Anglia (she was of a Northumbrian family, being a great-niece of King Edwin) with the intention of becoming a nun in Chelles when she was recalled to Northumbria by Aidan.[12]

The position of abbess was an ideal one for royal widows or virgins in a barbarian society where men died younger than women. Cuthburga, foundress of Wimbourne in Dorset, was sister to King Ine of Wessex; Ethelfryth, foundress of Ely was daughter of King Anna of the East Angles. Ethelfryth did not wait to become a widow. Married to Egfrith of Northumbria, she preserved her virginity against his marital advances (with the encouragement, it would seem, of Wilfrid) for 12 years, until around 672 he agreed, in despair, to her taking the veil. The judicious Plummer observed that 'this matter may have had much to do with alienating Egfrith from Wilfrid.'[13]

These abbesses were formidable ladies. The royal Tetta, abbess of Wimbourne, who ruled a community of some 50 nuns and gave her commands to the monks through a window, adhered so strictly to the principles of segregation that she denied entrance 'not merely to laymen and clerics but even to bishops.'[14] Not all of them, however, took so firm a line with bishops. Nor were all of royal birth, for double monasteries clearly became extremely popular. We come across them everywhere and it is striking that only at Coldingham do we hear of any scandal. Sometimes, indeed, we catch poignant glimpses of their life, as at Barking, where a little boy of three years called Esica was being brought up by the nuns when he caught the plague and died:[15]

When he was at the last gasp, he called three times upon one of the virgins consecrated to God, directing his words to her by her own name, as if she had been present, Eadgith! Eadgith! Eadgith! and thus ending his temporal life, entered into that which is eternal. The virgin whom he called was immediately seized, where she was, with the same distemper, and departing this life the same day on which she had been called, followed him that called her into the heavenly country.

It may seem as if we are removing ourselves rather far from Whitby in all this, but the influence of Hilda and Whitby in the spread of double monasteries must have been considerable, not least since Whitby gave five bishops to the English Church, one of them Bosa, who supplanted Wilfrid at York in 678.

WEARMOUTH AND JARROW

Leaving Whitby, the hypothetical traveller would pass Hartlepool, the first double monastery in Northumbria, where Hilda herself had been abbess for a while before the foundation of Whitby, and he would come to the monasteries of Wearmouth and Jarrow.

Benedict Biscop founded these two monasteries, the former at the mouth of the Wear and the latter a few miles away near the mouth of the Tyne, as one confraternity (Wearmouth in 674, Jarrow in 681). By 716 they had together some 600 monks. Biscop was a Northumbrian noble, a gesith of King Oswy, who in his twenties had decided to go abroad and became absorbed with Mediterranean culture and monasticism. His experiences, before King Egfrith endowed his foundations, included a two-year stay at the famous monastery of Lérins and several visits to Rome, on the first of which (in 653) he had been in the company of Wilfrid as far as Lyon and had parted from him, perhaps puzzled if not annoyed that anyone could be seduced by Lyon when Rome beckoned.

During his travels in Italy, Biscop would have been able to observe the effect of Byzantine imperial patronage on the beautification of churches, the policy of *kosmesis*.[16] For a new church or for one which needed refurbishing the imperial *ateliers* in Constantinople would produce gospel-books de luxe with golden letters on purple grounds, ivory episcopal chairs like that of Maximian at Ravenna, silk vestments and hangings, and mosaic workers to fit mosaics on the spot. Biscop carried out precisely a policy of *kosmesis* for his two monasteries. His activities are well known, his procuring of masons from Gaul to build churches 'in the Roman manner,' and glaziers also from Gaul to glaze the windows of his churches and monasteries as well as to teach the skill to the Anglo-Saxons who were ignorant of it; his collecting of relics, vestments, chalices and icons; his borrowing of John, the archchanter of St. Peter's, to teach the chant and manner of reading aloud used in the Roman basilican monasteries; and above all his accumulating (mainly from Italy and Gaul) a celebrated library.[17] In his later years his travels intensified to such a degree that he placed an abbot under him in each monastery —Eosterwine in Wearmouth and Ceolfrid in Jarrow. The icons which he brought back for Jarrow after his last journey must have been particularly interesting. They pointed the connection between the Old and New Testament. Thus two icons representing Isaac carrying the wood for his sacrifice and Christ carrying the Cross were placed side by side, and likewise two more representing the brazen serpent raised by Moses and Christ exalted on the Cross. This idea of parallel demonstrations was common in Byzantine art of the sixth century, though more usually in the form of a New Testament scene flanked by Old Testament prophets rolling out appropriate prophetic texts on scrolls. So it is done in a fine gospel-book written on purple sheets, the famous Sinope Codex.[18]

Wearmouth and Jarrow were not Benedictine monasteries in the sense that they exclusively followed St. Benedict's Rule. Indeed, this is what Biscop said to his monks during his last illness:[19]

> You cannot suppose that it was my untaught heart which dictated this rule to you (i.e. the rule he had composed for them). I learnt it from 17 monasteries, which I saw during my travels, and most approved of, and I copied these institutions thence for your benefit.

Nevertheless on some points at least he regarded the Rule of St. Benedict as having special authority.[20] Moreover, his general pattern of monastic offices would probably have approximated to that of St. Benedict, so apparently did his idea of manual labour. For we are told that Eosterwine, who had been a gesith of King Egfrith 'was so humble and like the other brethren, that he took pleasure in threshing and winnowing, milking the ewes and cows, and employed himself in the bakehouse, the garden, the kitchen and in all other labours of the monastery.'[21] There was another important respect in which his monasteries fore-shadowed the later Benedictine monasteries of the Continent—and here our traveller would have been struck by a great contrast with Whitby and Coldingham or Lindisfarne: the lay-out.

Thanks to Professor Rosemary Cramp's excavations of Wearmouth and Jarrow, at present in progress, we are just beginning to perceive the physical shape of these monasteries. At Jarrow, Professor Cramp has uncovered a long range of seventh-century building running parallel with the church, and at Wearmouth she has found the floors to have been surfaced with pounded brick in the manner of the Roman *opus signinum* and the windows to have been glazed with coloured and plain glass. The excavations seem to point to an arrangement of church and public buildings (refectories, dormitories and the like) around a cloister. Of Wearmouth, Miss Cramp writes that it appears 'regularly planned and elaborately constructed.'[22] Biscop's plan is obviously derived in a general way from the world of Roman secular buildings, so often placed around a court of some kind.

The products of both the scriptoria and the mason's yard at Wearmouth and Jarrow draw us in many ways to the Mediterranean world. It has recently been shown quite clearly how the most famous of all their manuscripts, the *Codex Amiatinus*, was inspired by a copy of Cassiodorus's great codex of the Bible, and how the Northumbrian scribes followed with great scrupulousness the illustrations in their model from Vivarium.[23] This was the book which Abbot Ceolfrid took for the pope on his pilgrimage to Rome when he retired from the abbacy as an old man in 716. He died at Langres before he reached his goal, but the book (of which the *Anonymous Life* of Ceolfrid tells us) survived and can be definitely identified by the colophon at the front of its text. It is now in the Laurenziana Library in Florence. Its sheets (27½ inches x 20½ inches) are of vellum and it has been calculated that the skins of 1,550 calves would have been needed to make this and the two similar volumes which Ceolfrid is known to have had made for Wearmouth and Jarrow. This is perhaps some reflection on the landed wealth of these two houses. The pieces of stone sculpture found in the excavations at Jarrow, the pieces of decorative frieze and the stone panels, have a double interest. On the one hand they show a marked similarity to the vine scroll ornament on the decorative sides of the later Ruthwell cross, which is suggestive of Jarrow's artistic influence in an exciting field.[24] On the other hand they appear to derive from Mediterranean, and perhaps Coptic, vine scroll ornament.[25]

To go a little further into the Coptic symptoms of Jarrow and Wearmouth: the *Codex Amiatinus* is by no means the only surviving product of the Jarrow/Wearmouth scriptorium. Much smaller and simpler, though scarcely less remarkable, is a seventh-century manuscript of St. John's Gospel now in the possession of Stonyhurst College. Its pages measure no more than about 5¼ inches x 3½ inches. This little book may well have been Bede's own copy of St. John's Gospel, the copy from which he was struggling to finish a translation into Anglo-Saxon before his death, a book perhaps laid with him in his tomb.[26] We can tell that it was written at Jarrow or Wearmouth because the hand is very distinctive; not Italian, as is seen from the occasional tell-tale use of insular abbreviations or letter shapes, but based on Italian models.[27] It is an exquisite hand. Sir Roger Mynors has written:[28]

Great men in those days did not disdain to write books with

their own hands, and the text of this book gives one the impression that it might well be the work, not just of a monastic scribe however good at his craft, but of some highly qualified scholar.

What makes this book unique, however, is that it is the only one known with its original, seventh-century binding. Its central ornament is a double vine scroll and this, together with its method of sewing, and material of red African goatskin, all relate it to Coptic bindings.[29] (Fig. 12).

RIPON AND HEXHAM

From Jarrow it was some 30 miles up the river Tyne to Hexham, one of Wilfrid's monasteries and from the year 678 the seat of a bishopric. Hexham and Wilfrid's earliest monastery of Ripon must have had something of the same Mediterranean flavour about them as Wearmouth and Jarrow. Wilfrid, too, had glaziers, Roman chant, basilica-type churches, and gospels written in golden letters on empurpled parchment. For all we know the lay-out of his monasteries may have been similar to Biscop's. But it would be as great a mistake to have done with these two after bracketing them as Romanizing abbots, as it would to have done with Newman and Manning after bracketing them as Roman Catholic cardinals. There was a contrast in the whole ambience of their monasteries which must have been apparent to any visitor.

The contrast lay in the two men. It was not just that the one was a collector who returned from Rome fondling his treasures, while the other returned fondling legal decisions and rules of ecclesiastical discipline (in fact, Wilfrid was also something of a connoisseur); nor was it just that their deathbed scenes were so different, the one exhorting his monks to keep his library intact and anxious to overcome the physical difficulty of kissing a brother abbot, while the other was dividing up his treasure so that his abbots might 'be able to purchase the friendship of kings and bishops.' The real point is that Biscop had lived the life of an ordinary Northumbrian noble, a warrior companion of the king, until he was 25. For all his travels he remained at heart a Northumbrian nobleman. He got his estates from the king, as other seasoned campaigners did; he made them into monasteries as other Northumbrian gesiths were coming to do. His monasteries owed their success to his ability to acclimatize Mediterranean culture to Northumbria. And for all their Mediterranean culture Wearmouth and Jarrow were thoroughly Northumbrian monasteries, perfectly integrated into Northumbrian society. Biscop's counsel was said to be indispensible to King Egfrith, who himself marked out the position of the altar at Jarrow. Ceolfrid, Biscop's successor, announced his decision to retire from the abbacy only three days before he set off for Rome lest he should be embarrassed by gifts of money from Northumbrian noblemen.[30]

With Wilfrid it was quite another thing. He too was a Northumbrian aristocrat by birth, but from the age of 14 to 25, surely an impressionable period, the age during which Biscop was a gesith of King Oswy, Wilfrid was dominated by his experiences at Lindisfarne, Lyon and Rome. His instincts were those of a cosmopolitan churchman. True, he got on well with Northumbrian kings for periods, but always better with the Mercians. True, King Egfrith was present at the consecration of Ripon church and made grants of land to the monastery, but these were lands across the Pennines in the Ribble valley, deserted by the British priests when they fled before the Northumbrian advance,[31] while he endowed Wearmouth from his own property (*de suo largitus*).[32] Hexham, Wilfrid's other chief monastery, was founded on an estate of Queen Ethelfryth, who was hardly a pillar of the Northumbrian establishment.[33] And whereas there appears no question of Biscop's founding or controlling monasteries elsewhere, Ripon and Hexham, as Wilfrid's special monasteries, were the focal houses of a whole monastic empire. This empire had been built up partly through Wilfrid's friendships with kings, particularly the Mercians, which issued in royal grants for monastic foundations, and partly by the fact that abbots and abbesses all over England submitted themselves and their property to his rule. As a basis of uniformity throughout his confederation of monasteries he used the Rule of St. Benedict. It was not that Wilfrid was a megalomaniac. From Columbanus onwards, if not from earlier, every monastic reformer ruled such an empire with the specific object of safeguarding the purity of the monastic life in as many instances as possible from interference, particularly the interference of laymen or bishops.[34]

The details of which actual monasteries composed this empire are particularly obscure. The evidence allows us to name only a few, but there appears a possibility that the architecture of seventh-century Anglo-Saxon churches might shed further light on the matter. First, let it be said that of Wilfrid's church at Hexham, at least, we can form quite a good picture.[35] During some 30 years while work was in progress on the new nave of Hexham before its completion in 1908, the resident architect, C. C. Hodges, kept a careful record on the plan of every piece of Saxon stonework which he observed under the foundations. Our knowledge of the church is based on these records and Eddius's description. It was about 100 feet long and 65 feet wide. The nave (25 feet wide) was divided into four bays by three massive rectangular piers on each side. From these piers, walls across the aisles divided them into *porticus* or side-chapels, and these were flanked on the outside by passages running the length of the church. At the West end of the passages, spiral stairways led to upper chapels in the West wall and perhaps above the aisles. The main altar would have been raised above the crypt, while the bishop's stone frith-stool, which survives at Hexham to this day, would have stood with its back to the East wall of the sanctuary and the seats of the clergy on either side according to the Mediterranean fashion. The sanctuary was divided from the body of the church by a low stone screen as in Roman churches. Two fragments of the sculptured panels of this screen survive, and there would have been other sculptured panels set into the walls, not to speak of the decoration of pictures, hangings and lamps.

Now as to the point about Wilfrid's monastic empire, there is a certain peculiarity in this Hexham plan which is shared by Ripon, Brixworth (Northamptonshire) and Wing (Buckinghamshire), but not by several others of the known seventh-century English churches, for instance Bradford-on-Avon (Wiltshire), Deerhurst (Gloucestershire), Reculver (Kent), Escomb and Wearmouth (Co. Durham). These latter are essentially plain rectangular churches of nave and chancel (sometimes ending in an apse) whose *porticus*, if they have any, project from the rectangles. The former are essentially basilicas with nave and aisles divided by piers, but they sometimes look like the churches with *porticus* because the aisles are divided by cross walls. The basilican plan is obviously not a cast-iron criterion for membership of Wilfrid's monastic confederation, for the plan of Jarrow church was of this kind, but it is suggestive in the case of Brixworth and Wing. And where one can particularize so little about this confederation (whose existence is known from Eddius) — besides Ripon and Hexham we can name only Oundle

14. (*right*) Engraving on St. Cuthbert's Coffin, *c.* 698 (see pp. 189–190)

15. (*left*) Book of Kells, early ninth century (see pp. 189–90)

16. (*right*) Wall-painting from Saqqara, Egypt, sixth century (see pp. 189–90)

17. (*left*) Coptic Ivory, seventh to ninth centuries (see pp. 189–90)

and Selsey with certainty—it is worth having such suggestions.[36]
One may well ask how it was possible for Wilfrid to combine
the supervision of his flourishing monastic empire in other bishops'
dioceses with his emphasis upon his own diocesan authority. How,
in such a situation, did he reconcile the twin expressions of his
pastoral zeal in the roles of bishop and of monastic reformer? Was
it, as some would believe, that he always considered himself to
be right, whatever the role in which he was currently acting?
There is a simpler and less strained explanation. If one looks at
the letters of Gregory the Great or at the actual situation in
Gaul in the seventh century one sees that even monasteries which
were not under the special protection of the papacy expected to
have a certain independence of their bishops.[37] They expected to
elect their own abbots or abbesses and administer their own
property without interference. Only when there were faults to be
remedied, deviations from a true way of monastic life to be
corrected, would the local bishop normally be expected to step
in. It was just such faults and deviations that Wilfrid hoped to
eliminate by his monastic confederation and thereby render the
interference of bishops unnecessary. So far as authority over the
monasteries and the disposition of their property was concerned, he had every right to expect the freedom in other dioceses
which he apparently extended to Wearmouth and Jarrow in his
own.

LINDISFARNE

Returning down the Tyne from Hexham, the traveller might
continue to sail up the north coast until he reached the island of
Lindisfarne. After the Synod of Whitby, when Colman and his
Irish followers withdrew from Lindisfarne, the abbacy was taken
over by Eata who, though he had been one of the English boys
trained by Aidan, accepted the Roman Easter. Nonetheless, the
monastery would still have had its Irish lay-out in 690. An early
ninth-century poem, by a poet called Aethelwulf, tells the history
during the previous century of a small and unidentified monastery
subject to Lindisfarne, and gives several insights into the life of
the numerous separate cells which characterized this lay-out. In
one place, for instance, Aethelwulf describes how as a boy he
himself had for six years shared a cell with an older monk. 'For
six years,' he says, 'we enjoyed the peace of one house' (*unius*

domus requiem), thereby implying the individually built cell and referring to the régime of nocturnal psalms and hymnody which obtained in that of Wulfsige.[38] In such a way boys were initiated into the spiritual life.

Around 690 Bishop Eadbert of Lindisfarne was pulling the thatched roof off the wooden church (the Irish did not often build in stone where wood was available) and was replacing it with lead.[39] It was all very different from the grandiose schemes of architecture at Wearmouth or Hexham. We need not assume, however, that the church looked poor and mean inside. The chances are that it was hung with cloths, lit by hanging-bowls with finely enamelled escutcheons, and enriched by some handsome pieces of silver in the service of the altar. For Lindisfarne had a first-rate jeweller's shop. In fact it was the skills of Anglo-Saxon pagan jewellery, the continuance of the Irish tradition, and the influx of Mediterranean influence, which together produced that remarkable synthesis of culture, seen primarily in the Lindisfarne Gospels.

It is certain that almost every pen stroke in this book must have been the work of the monk, Eadfrith, and probable that he completed it just before becoming bishop of Lindisfarne in 698.[40] In the first place Eadfrith was a master of Irish calligraphy (so different from the Italian style of Wearmouth and Jarrow). The small initials of his book are decorated with spirals and trumpet patterns like the earlier Cathach of St. Columba. The great initials at the beginning of each gospel are decorated with the whole grand repertory of Celtic curvilinear ornament, which stretches back in a tradition of Irish metal-work to the La Tène civilization of the first century.[41] In these initials the whorls, spirals, *peltae* and hair-spring coils, drawn free-hand with verve and confidence, spontaneously and joyously follow the shape of the letter.

The Mediterranean element in the book blends with Eadfrith's grasp of Irish art. His portraits of the evangelists were seemingly modelled on a sixth-century Bible from Southern Italy, but they were executed with a freedom which might suggest that Eadfrith also had some crisp Italian ivories in front of him.[42] Perhaps from the same Italian Bible came those arches with processions of birds (over the canon tables), which are reminiscent of the Syrian gospel books.

Each of the four gospels is preceded by a page of abstract ornament, a so-called carpet page. If we look at one of these pages, compositions of the utmost harmony, the impression of the artistic resources available to Eadfrith becomes even richer. The general design of the page itself supposes the likelihood that he had to hand a Coptic book-binding. The central circle with its stepped compartments suggests the cloisonné brooches of Kent or crosses of East Anglia; the panels round it with their writhing animal patterns and fine birds' heads suggest something like the Sutton Hoo buckle or the decorative mounts in the Taplow burial; the four square panels of curvilinear ornament strikingly resemble the enamelled escutcheons of Irish hanging-bowls. One may make this last comparison by examining a page of the Lindisfarne Gospels on the ground floor of the British Museum and then walking upstairs to see the hanging-bowl amongst the Sutton Hoo finds. Some would even relate the lovely projections at the corners and on the sides of the pages to those in Armenian manuscripts.[43] Fig. 11).

No book could have been made with more love and care as well as technical accomplishment. To speak only of the little red dots which surround the initial letters, large and small—a decorative feature derived by Irish scribes from Egypt: the great initial letter on folio 139r, for instance, is surrounded by 10,600 dots, which could scarcely have been applied in under six hours.[44]

All this was done for St. Cuthbert. The book was probably made to stand near the shrine of the saint which was set up in the sanctuary at Lindisfarne in 698. Cuthbert was an Englishman, easily moved both to laughter and tears, and seemingly forthcoming about his spiritual experiences. Born about 634, he was brought up at Melrose by Eata in the Irish monastic tradition. As a young man he would walk or ride in the Cheviots or Lammermuir Hills and the valleys of the rivers which flow from them into the Tweed, preaching and ministering in remote villages like the earlier itinerant Irish saints. At 30 he became prior of Lindisfarne (after the Synod of Whitby), at 40 he was already leading the life of a hermit on Farne Island, at 50 he was elected bishop of Lindisfarne, and three years later (in 687), he died a death described by Bede in fine hagiographical style.

Cuthbert was the acme of Lindisfarne in its post-Whitby days. While the scriptorium was developing the 45 colour tones used in the Gospels, Cuthbert in the solitude of Farne Island and then for a brief period as bishop, was fashioning within himself a brilliant spiritual synthesis not unlike that of the Lindisfarne

Gospels in the realm of culture. The biographies of him by the anonymous monk of Lindisfarne and by Bede, written within 35 years of his death are completely different from the other early English hagiographies. There is much of St. Martin of Tours about their picture of Cuthbert—similar sorts of miracles, many of them fitted into the accounts of his missionary journeys, similar descriptions of his virtues, similar glorying in his association with the common people. At the same time they have a more distinctly Irish flavour about them. For one thing Cuthbert had a way with animals. On one occasion, it was said, he was visiting Coldingham from Melrose and at night he stole down to the sea, unaware that he had been tracked by a brother who was hiding in the cliffs. He stood all night in the water chanting psalms, and at daybreak, when he emerged to kneel on the sands, two little sea otters came out of the water, rubbed his feet with their fur, blew on them to make them warm, and returned to their abode.[45] How different from Wilfrid's seaside experiences!

Particularly impressive are the accounts of Cuthbert's life as a solitary on Farne Island, several miles out from Lindisfarne in a windswept part of the North Sea. There he grew his own barley, established a *modus vivendi* with the ravens, and built a little house near the landing stage for the Lindisfarne brethren who would visit him.[46] For himself he established a lavatory on a driftwood plank set across a sea-washed chasm in the rocks (still known as St. Cuthbert's Gut), and a cell and oratory surrounded by a circular wall of turf and uncut stone, a type of arrangement favoured by Egyptian hermits:[47]

> The wall itself on the outside was higher than a man standing upright; but inside he made it much higher by cutting away the living rock, so that the pious inhabitant could see nothing except the sky from his dwelling, thus restraining both the lust of his eyes and of the thoughts, and lifting the whole bent of his mind to higher things.

There was, however, another side to Cuthbert, or at least Bede certainly tried to present one. What he says about Cuthbert's clothes, for instance, that 'he wore ordinary garments and, keeping the middle path, he was not noteworthy either for their elegance or for their slovenliness' (although he did show a singular unwillingness to change his shoes), brings to mind St. Benedict's chapter on clothes in the *Rule*.[48] And, like the Irish themselves at this period,

he had a more Roman image of episcopal dignity than his predecessors. He often went on foot, but he had not the same passion
as Aidan or Chad to avoid horseback.[49] Above all his pectoral
cross, placed on his breast when he was buried, is eloquent
testimony to the fact that he (or at least the Lindisfarne monks
who laid it on his body) did not neglect the external appearance of
authority. It is a superb piece of jewellery, subtly built up in
registers of beading, dog-tooth ornament and effective cloisonné,
so that it acquires an extraordinary glint and shimmer from its
'architecture', and its central embellishment is a shell from the
Indian Ocean.[50] (Fig. 2).

DIVERSITY AND UNITY

Each of these great monasteries, then had its own traditions and
culture, its own *genius loci*. And the hypothetical traveller would
have been able to stop, in this journey of perhaps a hundred miles,
at many smaller and less distinguished houses in which this
diversity would have been reflected.

Some of the differences to which attention has been drawn are
of more consequence than may first appear. The arrangement of
separate cells or huts within a compound, for instance, harks back
to the Egyptian desert and implies a way of life quite different
from (more individualist than) that of the regular plan. Some
traces of that difference still survive around 700 in Lindisfarne
and the monasteries of its tradition. Daily mass in community is
an example. During the seventh century daily mass became the
rule in Roman monasteries.[51] It was clearly the rule in Wearmouth
and Jarrow; community mass was offered, apparently as a matter
of course, on the day of Ceolfrid's departure for Rome—a Thursday.
And Ceolfrid celebrated every day, while he was able, on his
journey.[52] At the same period it is equally clear that Lindisfarne
had mass only on Sundays and festivals.[53]

Mass was celebrated only on Sundays in the Egyptian
monasteries, where Saturday, being the vigil, was kept with
solemnity in the monastic office. Whether this was the case at
Lindisfarne is unknown, but it is not impossible. It was the
practice at the monastery of Bangor in Northern Ireland, from
which there happens to be evidence in the form of a book which
gives the collects to be recited and the antiphons to be sung
between the groups of psalms. Here Saturdays, as well as Sundays

and the feasts of martyrs, qualify for festal observance. In fact the purpose of the whole book was that of a companion volume to the psalter for use on these days. And the book was produced between 680 and 691.[54] Now Bangor was a monastery which had Romanized itself in point of the Easter observance nearly a century earlier and yet this office book is composed almost entirely of non-Roman, of Eastern and Gallican elements. It shows that where we are ignorant about the religious practices of the Irish monasteries in Northumbria it is not to be assumed that they were in every way busy Romanizing themselves after the Synod of Whitby.

No service books like the Antiphonary of Bangor have survived from Lindisfarne, but there is one useful glimpse of the arrangements for divine office—no more than the opening and shutting of a door—in Aethelwulf's poem about the small Lindisfarne dependency. He is setting the scene (with regrettable succinctness) for a miraculous narrative, and he says that at night, 'the brothers, following their usual custom, were at pains to enter [the church, of which the poet has just spoken] after their hymns, to complete their solemnities of spirit'.[55] Now the Roman liturgy was not rich in hymns; indeed hymns often lacked the grave and sober language necessary even to escape suspicion in Rome; but they flourished in Spain and Gaul. It is poets from these countries, like Prudentius and Venantius Fortunatus, who have given the Church some of its finest Latin hymns.[56] They flourished also in Ireland, and indeed in England, where Aldhelm and Bede were both practitioners. Aethelwulf's words remind us more particularly of 'a book of hymns for the week, written in the hand of St. Columba', which forms the subject of one of Adamnan's miraculous narratives.[57] Both in Iona and in Aethelwulf's monastery there were apparently prescribed hymns, and to judge from Aethelwulf these hymns were sung by the monks before they came to church for the night office, obviously in private in their cells as many offices had been recited in Egyptian monasteries.

Amidst the diversity among Northumbrian monasteries, the essential point is the wealth of contacts, almost universally friendly and constructive, which existed between them all.

Between Jarrow and Lindisfarne, for instance, it would seem probable that loans of books were freely made. The text for the Lindisfarne Gospels is most likely to have been derived from an old Neapolitan gospel book lent by Wearmouth or Jarrow. While the text of the Psalms in the Codex Amiatinus (Wearmouth/Jarrow) has the rubrics preceding each psalm as they are found in the Cathach of St. Columba, which suggests that the traffic might also have moved the other way.[58] Again, in her excavations at Jarrow, Miss Cramp has found a stone ornament of a bird's head, possibly seventh-century and very much in the style of the Lindisfarne Gospel ornaments.[59] A stray remark of Bede shows us that a monk, Sigfrith, of Melrose (a monastery with strong Lindisfarne affiliations) had moved to Jarrow.[60]

All these are just floating scraps of information, often the only sort of material which the historian of so remote a period has to hand. The best illustration, however, of the quality of the relationship which had been built up between Lindisfarne and Jarrow is Bede's *Life of Cuthbert*. Bede wrote his *Life* around 721 and his main source was the very beautiful *Life* by an anonymous monk of Lindisfarne, written between 699 and 705 after the translation of St. Cuthbert's body to its shrine. To the Lindisfarne monk Cuthbert was the great saint of his own house; to Bede he was something rather different, a model from whom to draw lessons about how to be a perfect bishop and monk. Bede was always the schoolmaster of Jarrow. With Cuthbert, it was he who explained how Cuthbert's obedience to God's commands enabled him to work miracles, how his clothes were what those of a monk should be, how as bishop he visited the out of the way places as Bede's own letter to Archbishop Egbert of York later said a bishop should. To the modern reader, these moral thoughts are not always an improvement on the plain narrative of the Lindisfarne monk, but so far as the Lindisfarne community were concerned, it was no doubt for precisely this didactic streak that they commissioned Bede to write a further *Life*. When it was finished, he took it to his patrons:[61]

And when my little work [says Bede in the preface] had been read for two days before the elders and teachers of your congregation and carefully weighed in every detail under your examination, no word of any sort was found which had to be changed, but everything that was written was pronounced by common consent to be, without any question, worthy of being read and of being delivered to those whose pious zeal moved them to copy it.

Now, before they allowed it to be copied everywhere, there were one or two details of Bede's work which the elders and teachers must have had to weigh very carefully indeed. The Lindisfarne monk had mentioned that Cuthbert arranged (or re-arranged) the Lindisfarne rule, but he had not explained, as Bede did, how within the monastery a party of opposition to this rule had caused the saint a lot of trouble.[62] Equally, the Lindisfarne monk had mentioned Cuthbert's successor, Eadbert, but he had not referred, as Bede did, to the storms and disturbances during the year after Cuthbert's death before he succeeded, disturbances so great that many of the monks chose to depart.[63] It speaks much for both sides that Bede was able to write of these things in perfect charity, and that they were accepted in the same spirit. Bede's name was entered in the register of the Lindisfarne congregation so that he would always be remembered in their prayers.

Some very interesting things emerge about the relations of Wilfrid's and Biscop's monasteries. After 709, Biscop Acca, whom Wilfrid had appointed to succeed him at Hexham, and Bede had a close scholarly relationship. But what of earlier days? It is often said that Bede felt a certain coolness towards Wilfrid, perhaps because of the latter's opposition to Archbishop Theodore and to the policy of dividing dioceses. Be that as it may, the same could hardly have been true of Biscop or Abbot Ceolfrid. Ceolfrid had originally joined his brother's monastery at Gilling, but when the plague hit Gilling, Wilfrid invited him and others to Ripon. Wilfrid ordained him priest in 669 at the age of 27, and immediately allowed him leave to visit monasteries in Kent and East Anglia, including the famous establishment of Saint Botolph at Icanhoe, to study their way of life.[64] When Biscop founded Wearmouth, Wilfrid agreed to release Ceolfrid to him as prior. Envy and touchiness were no part of Wilfrid's character. At first, however, Ceolfrid quickly tired of his new job, and of its responsibilities, particularly as he was unable to cope with some recalcitrant aristocrats, very likely Bernicians who resented the rule of a Deiran over them. So he returned to Ripon, until Biscop once again conquered him 'with the prayers of charity.'[65] It is obvious that Wilfrid must have had a lasting influence on Ceolfrid's life as a monk, and obvious that there can have been no ill feeling about Ceolfrid's departure from Ripon if he could return so promptly when things went wrong.

The relations of Lindisfarne and Whitby must always have been close. Cuthbert and the abbess Aelffled, as we have seen, were in the habit of meeting frequently to talk about spiritual matters. On relations between Wilfrid and Whitby, notwithstanding the hostility of Hilda, we have evidence of Aelffled's support for Wilfrid at the Synod of Nidd (703). There is more to say about Wilfrid and Lindisfarne. This is the area where one would have expected relations to break down if at all. When Theodore divided Wilfrid's diocese in 678, the Bernician province went to Eata who had his see at Lindisfarne and a possible alternative at Hexham. Eata was not perhaps Wilfrid's favourite. It was all the more tactless an appointment as it was Eata whom Wilfrid had originally displaced as abbot of Ripon in 661.[66] But why suppose that Wilfrid would carry his feelings towards Eata over to Lindisfarne? Some would answer because of his hatred of 'the Celts'. It was argued in the last chapter that there is no reason to think that he did hate 'the Celts'.

During the year after Cuthbert's death Wilfrid administered the bishopric (though not the monastery) of Lindisfarne until Eadbert was elected.[67] At the same time a monk called Ethilwald took over Cuthbert's hermitage on Farne Island. Ethilwald had received the priesthood and had lived the monastic life for many years at Wilfrid's monastery of Ripon.[68] The Lindisfarne monks honoured him, and they visited him in the way that they had visited Cuthbert. As for Wilfrid, he wholeheartedly approved of such recluses.

But whatever Wilfrid's feelings towards Lindisfarne, he clearly learned one lesson while he lived there happily as a teenager, which was to become of supreme importance to him during the course of his life—the value and efficacy of a monastic confederation. He learned it from the confederation of which Lindisfarne was a member, the confederation which was ruled from Iona.

Here, therefore, was a group of monasteries to which personal frictions and jealousies were not perhaps unknown, but in which diversity was no obstacle to Christian unity. On the contrary, they freely accepted the movement of personnel between each other, they shared each others' library facilities, and they profited from each others' scholarly, artistic and spiritual experiences. This was at the basis of their remarkable culture, which rightly causes Northumbria to be regarded as a crucible of European monasticism.

11 Prayer and Worship

In seventh-century Rome on the great festivals of the year, on
certain Sundays between Christmas and Pentecost, and on every
day in Lent except Thursdays, the pope went in procession from
the Lateran Palace in order to celebrate mass at one of the
basilicas in the city together with the Roman clergy and people.
This was the most solemn act of worship in Rome. The basilica
whose turn it was for this service was known as the 'station' for
that day.

These stational churches were mostly built on the sites of private
houses where the Christian communities had originally met for
mass in the times of persecution. At first they were known by
the names of their householders, but by the 590's they had been
renamed after patron saints. Some of them remain to this day
very much as they would have appeared to a sixth- or seventh-
century pontiff officiating there. They convey wonderfully the
ethos of Roman worship. The church of Santa Sabina, for instance,
where the stational mass was celebrated on Ash Wednesday, is a
fine example of antique dignity and repose.[1] On each side of the
spacious nave stand 12 Corinthian columns, fluted and cabled,
and carved from the purest Greek marble. 'The delicacy of the
concave and convex mouldings of the base,' M. Mâle says of
these columns, 'recall the subtle cadence of the lyric poet's short
and long syllables.' The height of the columns is nine and a half
times, and the space between them five times their diameter, the
textbook proportions of Hellenistic building. In the lofty walls
above the nave arcade are 26 large rounded windows which flood
the nave with light. (Fig. 5). At the Western entrance of the
church there still hang the original fifth-century doors, superbly
carved in cedarwood, probably the work of Syrian sculptors. Here
are panels showing Elias's ascent to heaven, witnessed in

accordance with Palestinian legend by young woodcutters; a church with twin towers like those of Syria; and Moses before the burning bush being addressed by God through the mouth of an angel. These doors remind us of the manifold contacts which existed between Rome and the East—with the emperor politically, through numerous pilgrimages to the Holy Land, through interest in Eastern asceticism, and through the movements of individuals. Above the entrance on the inside is a fifth-century mosaic representing two females who symbolize the two components of the early church—Jew and Gentile. But they are also perfect examples of Roman Christian ladies, pious, austere and grave.

The Roman Mass in 597 was much the same as we knew it until recently, the same arrangement of chants, variable prayers and readings, followed by the same canon, or Eucharistic Prayer. The main differences were that the Nicene Creed was not recited and there were as yet no offertory prayers, although offerings of bread and wine before the Eucharist were made by the faithful. As to the accompanying ceremonial, there survives in a so-called *ordo* a description of the ritual at a papal stational mass, which would appear in substance to refer to the early seventh century.[2] The only high points of external drama in this ritual were the entrance of the pope processing to the chants of the clergy, the solemn chant given out by the deacon on the step of the *ambo* (or pulpit) after the first reading, i.e. the gradual, and the procession for the reading of the gospel. Altogether it was a ceremony of notable simplicity and sobriety.

During the seventh century and after Gregory the Great's time there was an important change at Rome. In 597 there was just one Roman rite, common to the pope, the urban clergy and monasteries. During the next hundred years the popes developed their own distinct liturgy for mass at the stations. It was not that they altered the days of festivals or the structure of the Roman mass, or the character of the Roman prayers; but they took a leaf out of the Byzantine book and began to copy the elaborate and awe-inspiring ceremonial of the imperial court. A special body of papal chanters was set up, singing new and dramatic Byzantine chants, the processions to the stational churches were drawn up in careful detail, with the officers of the papal court, the *primicerius*, the *vicedominus*, the *vestiarius* and the rest of them, all in their fixed places; the vessels used by the pope became sacred cult objects, so that the wine offerings of the faithful had to be poured first into the archdeacon's *ampullas* and only from there might they be poured into the pope's chalice, *the scyphum;* and—here is a characteristic piece of Byzantine court tyranny—immediately before the pope entered the church the names of those who were to sing and read had to be announced to him, on pain of immediate excommunication for the *archiparafonista* if they were subsequently changed.[3]

This Byzantinizing of the papacy in the seventh century was an important step in its history, and it greatly impressed Charlemagne. But if there is any danger of thinking that this was the kind of thing which Rome might have given to Anglo-Saxon England, we must emphasize that it was not. It was a development of ceremonial and so left the framework of the mass and the character of Roman prayer untouched, and as ceremonial it was peculiar to the popes. What came to England from Rome would have been the simpler ceremony which we have described.

When the pope's mass at the station was over the Roman clergy who had attended would disperse to their own churches. There it was that they would celebrate on days when they did not attend the pope's mass or on the days when there was no public papal liturgy.[4] The clergy were responsible for the mass and the sacraments in their churches, as well as for the administration of the basilica's patrimony. But the monastic offices (prime, vespers, etc.) in these basilicas were very often recited by the monks from a nearby monastery, and the greatest of the basilicas were served by several monasteries for this purpose. The singing expert whom Benedict Biscop brought from Rome, for instance, was abbot of St. Martin's, one of four monasteries which performed the monastic office in St. Peter's of the Vatican. He was the Archchanter of St. Peter's, evidently responsible for co-ordinating the efforts of the various monasteries.[5] What he taught at Wearmouth and Jarrow, therefore, was the Roman monastic office.

One distinctive feature of Roman worship is clearly suggested by a famous letter of Pope Gregory the Great, written in 598. There were people in Sicily who had been asking how the pope could expect to keep the church of Constantinople in its place if he copied all their customs at Rome. Here he was, for example, introducing the *Kyrie Eleison* at mass, just as the 'Greeks' did it. Now, as we saw, Gregory had not been pleased at the patriarch of Constantinople's attempt to assume for himself the title of 'universal bishop', and the charge that he was positively apeing Constantinople, positively following its lead, stuck in his gullet. This *Kyrie Eleison* was originally a substantial litany of which the present Roman *Kyrie* is but the simplified remnant, and had the ignorant Sicilians known it, it had been introduced much earlier into the Roman Mass; but Gregory left that unsaid. What he hastened to point out in his reply was the difference between Rome and Constantinople;

> We have neither said, nor do we say, *Kyrie eleison* as it is said by the Greeks. For among them, all the people sing it together; but with us it is sung by the clerks, and the people answer.

Of this, the great liturgical scholar, Edmund Bishop, wrote: 'It will be observed that, as compared with the Greek practice, the initiative in prayer is taken from the people and transferred to officials, the singers, subdeacons and inferior clerics.'[6]

The purest emanations of the Roman spirit of worship are the collects written for the mass by Gregory the Great. Gregory was by no means the first pope to compose prayers, but he was both prolific and characteristically Roman in this field. These prayers, varying from day to day, had their rules of harmony and proportion, of short and long syllables, of rhythms and cadences, of 'concave and convex mouldings', as had the basilicas in which they were recited. Many of them survive in the Roman Missal and in the superb translations of Cranmer for the 1549 Book of Common Prayer. Here is the collect for the Feast of the Epiphany:

> *Deus, qui hoderna die unigenitum tuum gentibus stella duce revelasti, concede propitius ut qui iam te ex fide cognovimus, usque ad contemplandam speciem tue celsitudinis perducamur.*
> O, God, whiche by the leadying of a starre didest manyfeste thy onely begotten sonne to the Gentiles: mercifully grant that we which know thee nowe by faythe, maye after this lyfe have the fruicion of thy glorious Godhead.

There can be hardly a shadow of doubt that this collect was one of those written by Gregory himself. It echoes the ideas (not quite usual ideas) and even the very words used time and again by Gregory in his theological writings. By visible signs, and above all by His own incarnation, God has enabled man in his fallen state to achieve faith, to be carried away to love of things invisible, so that he may come hereafter to the very sight, the *species*, or as Cranmer so beautifully has it, the 'fruicion' of the Godhead. 'In the perception of Almighty God,' says Gregory in his *Homilies on Ezechiel*, 'our first door is faith (*fides*), and our second the sight (*species*) of Him, to which we come by walking in faith. In this life we are initiated into the former so that we may be led (*perducamur*) hereafter to the latter.' Both in the homily and in the collect there is the same transition from *fides* in this life to *species* in the next.[7]

This collect for the Epiphany, a mere 26 words, packed with the profoundest thought, formulated with absolute clarity, is a masterpiece of conciseness singularly appropriate for recitation by men who prided themseves on the fewness of their words, by men of gravity.

When Pope Gregory assumed his pontificate there were probably no official mass-books in Rome. This does not mean that pope and clergy were still making up fresh prayers each week, though that would once have been the situation. The canon of the mass, the central Eucharistic prayer itself, was already fixed in its final form; and for the prayers like the collects which varied from day to aay, there would have been some kind of filing system in which prayers would have been kept, often on individual papyri, or *libelli* as liturgists call them. This is not fantasy, but the careful deduction of scholars from the way in which this material was eventually decanted into the earliest mass-books.[8] The *scrinium* of the pope's palace at the Lateran would have had files of prayers, so would other basilicas. Into these files went the prayers which men composed themselves and which they collected from other sources. Any celebrant of a mass could say precisely what prayers he liked; there were no authoritatively prescribed formulae for the variable prayers. A celebrant might take some prayers out of the files, make his own additions, omissions, improved rhythms and other embellishments, and then replace both the original and his own rewording for the benefit of future celebrants. It is likely that there was a stage when these *libelli* were organized into small collections of mass formulae before the comprehensive mass-books, or sacramentaries, began to appear in the late sixth or seventh centuries. These sacramentaries contained only the prayers recited by the celebrant at mass and other ceremonies; the readings and texts of the chants were in different books. The missal, combining all these things, comes in (with few exceptions) only in the tenth and eleventh centuries.

As Augustine came to England during the very period in which the first Roman mass-books were being evolved, it is impossible to know whether or not he could have brought one to England. By 650 there were two kinds of sacramentary in use at Rome, one (the so-called Gregorian) which was used by the popes for their masses at the stations, and the other (the so-called Gelasian) which was used by the priests in the urban basilicas and monasteries. Some scholars would argue that Gregory the Great's pontificate saw the emergence of the papal book, in which the Sunday masses, festivals and saints' days were arranged in order and specific prayers were selected for each. This may be so, although there is no surviving manuscript from the 590's; it is a question of deducing from ninth-century manuscripts that within their matter an earlier book is embedded.[9] Even if Augustine could have brought this book to England it would have been of limited use to him because it contained masses only for the days on which the pope celebrated in public. There were many Sundays and festivals in the year for which it had nothing. From this point of view the presbyteral, or Gelasian, book would have been more useful, but it is practically certain that this was not in existence before 600.[10] Nor is there any good reason to believe—although it was argued by the author of a fine study on the Gelasian book—that there was an actual mass-book in Rome, now lost, which preceded both the papal and presbyteral books, and from which both took material.[11]

It is best, therefore, to keep an open mind about what liturgical books, if any, Augustine brought with him to England. Even if he brought the Gregorian mass-book, however, he would have needed supplementary material; and he would have been entirely free to use other prayers instead of or in addition to those in the book, drawn from whatever sources he thought appropriate. It is perhaps most likely that he did what a clerk of Verona seems to have done about the same time—ransacked the collections of prayers in Rome and transcribed bundles of them into a book, not a book which could actually be used at mass, but a kind of source book or file in book form.[12] The Verona manuscript (the so-called *Leonianum*) happens to have survived; nothing of the sort has come down to us from Canterbury, but in the circumstances of the time it would have been an eminently sensible way

for Augustine to have brought Roman mass prayers to
Canterbury.

We leave further consideration of the complicated subject of
mass-books to an appendix. The main points are that Augustine
would have brought prayers of a Roman character to England,
and that considering his close relation with the pope and the
thorough-going loyalty of himself and his monks to Gregory's
spiritual ideals,[13] Gregory's own prayers must have bulked large
amongst them. These prayers, then, many of which came to be
incorportated into the Roman mass-books, had been heard in
English churches for nearly a thousand years before Cranmer.

Heard, of course, in Latin: Latin was the language of the
Catholic clergy throughout the western world; it had been the
language of the Roman liturgy since it displaced Greek in the
fourth century;[14] it symbolized communion with the see of
Rome; to celebrate mass in any other language was unthinkable;
only heretics like the Arians celebrated their liturgy in the
vernacular. It was a very restricted audience, then, that would
have appreciated Gregory's prayers, but an influential and a
growing one. Ordinands were put through the mill, and at their
best they came out writing the limpid and unaffected Latin of
Bede.

DIVERSITY

Liturgical books tend to get thrown away. Nobody is interested in
the old books when new ones are introduced. This would be
particularly true of the early sacramentaries. The books used for
scriptural readings had a better chance of survival, because they
contained the eternal texts of Holy Writ which would always
be useful, and they were often fine works of art in their own
right. The sixth-century Italian illustrated gospel book, which
probably came to Canterbury with the Gregorian missionaries, is
a case in point. But with sacramentaries it was different. These
books reflect, in the eighth century, the same freedom to select
and devise for the individual institutions to which they belonged
as had existed for individual celebrants earlier. Once a cathedral
or monastery had changed its mass prayers—and many were doing
so all over the West, particularly after Charlemagne's liturgical
reforms—there was no use for its obsolete sacramentaries, except
for their parchment sheets. That is why so few sacramentaries

survive from before 800.[15] Either the matter on their sheets was erased and they were used again—it is significant that of the fragments of early sacramentaries which do survive a high proportion are palimpsests—or these sheets might be put to good use under loaves in the monastic bakery. A new discovery of a pre-800 sacramentary anywhere in Europe would be a thrilling event. For England from that time there survive only a few leaves from such books. One cannot be certain, therefore, how widely the Roman liturgy was used in the early period of Anglo-Saxon Christianity; probably very widely, for the seventh century marked its triumphant advance everywhere.

By the time of the Synod of Cloveshoe (747) English bishops, like their contemporaries in Gaul, were requiring uniformity, based on the Roman observance. But earlier, even within the general framework of the Roman mass and liturgy, there was ample scope for variations which could give a quite characteristic flavour to the worship in one church as distinct from another. One cannot assume that English churches, particularly in the seventh century and even amongst those which are often labelled as romanizing, had anything like a uniformly Roman liturgy.

It is, for instance, an interesting fact that one can learn more about the liturgy of Naples in the early Middle Ages from the Lindisfarne Gospels than from any other source.[16] Lists of gospel readings and of festivals precede the text of each gospel. The lists of festivals give a complete picture of the Neapolitan liturgical year, as can be shown by comparison with a ninth-century calendar on marble discovered in 1742 at the church of St. John in Naples. Amongst their Neapolitan peculiarities are the celebration of the vigil and day of St. Januarius (famed for the liquifying of his blood) and the dedication of St. Stephen's basilica, the cathedral of Naples named after Bishop Stephen I (501–13). In fact, the text of the Lindisfarne Gospels was taken from a sixth-century Neapolitan gospel-book. Whether Lindisfarne actually used the lists in their worship is far from clear, but it is certain that Jarrow, which probably lent the Neapolitan book to Lindisfarne, did so. For Bede's 50 homilies, preached on the gospel passages of various days, used passages which in several cases differed from those used at Rome, almost invariably to coincide with those of Naples. One of the homilies is for the Beheading of John the Baptist, a festival found in the Lindisfarne/Naples lists but not in the Roman calendar. In other words, Jarrow, where

Bede's homilies were preached, and where the worship was doubtless predominantly Roman, used not the Roman but the Neapolitan system of gospel readings.[17]

Side by side with the Neapolitan is another South Italian strain of influence—from Capua. This is most clearly seen in an Old English Martyrology, a book of potted lives of saints for reading aloud in monasteries on their festivals. The ninth-century vernacular version is based on a Latin original almost certainly dating from 740–55. This martyrology was a mine of information about all kinds of saints, but there were some who stumped the compiler. All he could say of these was that their masses were in the 'old mass-book' or the 'new mass-book'. The three saints of the 'new mass-book' (Nicomedes, Agapitus and Sabina) are all to be found in the Roman sacramentaries related to the papal books. The seven saints of the 'old mass-book' were all Campanians and five of them (Priscus, Lupulus, Sinotus, Rufus and Quintus) were actually represented on an early sixth-century mosaic in the church of St. Priscus at Old Capua, a mosaic destroyed in 1766.[18] Here, then, was an Anglo-Saxon in the mid-eighth-century, who was using the up-to-date Roman mass-books but still had to hand, in the 'old mass-book', something probably of the seventh century from Capua.

There must have been a period in the late seventh and early eighth centuries when this Capuan mass-book had quite a vogue, at least in Northumbria and perhaps in Mercia. The names of these Campanian saints were written into the early eighth-century Calendar kept by the Anglo-Saxon missionary, St Willibrord, in Frisia.[19] And they appear yet again in the surviving fragment of a calendar written (c. 750–85) in a Northumbrian hand which was kept at Regensburg, doubtless a connection with the English mission.[20] Considering the paucity of evidence for this sort of thing at this time, three surfacings in Anglo-Saxon contexts by such supremely obscure saints are certainly significant.

Since the abbot Hadrian, who accompanied Archbishop Theodore to England in 667, came from a monastery near Naples, he is generally assumed to have brought all this South Italian literature with him. But the grounds for this view are not better than those for the opinion of Abbot Chapman (1908) that it came to England as a result of Benedict Biscop's book-collecting in Italy. Nor should we assume that what it amounted to was the introduction of a few saints who had strange names, and some lore about the blood of Januarius. We do not know what the Capuan mass-book contained, (apart from certain saints' festivals), but we do know that at this period Southern Italy was at least as susceptible to eastern liturgical influence as Rome was.

It is clear that Gaul, too, exercised some influence on early Anglo-Saxon worship. The term 'Gallican Rite' is a misleading one in that the features which characterized it were to be found in Gaulish, Spanish and even Italian churches, though by no means necessarily in all the churches of these countries: doubtless in fewer and fewer between 600 and 800. In so far as its arrangement of mass differed in various ways from that of Rome, this mass was probably the retention of an older Roman rite which had been modified at Rome itself in the interests of greater simplicity.[21] But the actual prayers, also, were often of a quite different character—rhetorical and effusive, or at worst long-winded and bombastic in a way which contrasted strongly with Roman sobriety. Such prayers were compounds of Eastern fervour and either Spanish poetry or Gaulish rhetoric and linguistic conceit.[22] A classic example of the contrast was given by Edmund Bishop, namely the preface for Pentecost from the Roman missal, and its Spanish counterpart, ten times the length, from the so-called 'Mozarabic' missal. To quote only the closing phrases from each, those of the Roman preface run:

Wherefore with joy that knows no bounds the whole universe exults; the Powers, too, above and the Angelic Hosts together hymn Thy glory, saying evermore: Holy, Holy, Holy.

And those of the 'Mozarabic':

O flame that in burning confers fruitfulness, whom every intellectual creature, vivified by it, confesses to be the Lord Omnipotent; participating in whose fire in more abundant measure the Cherubim and Seraphim, magnifying the equality of the Holiness Divine and the Omnipotence of the Trinity, never resting and never wearying in their office, amidst the song of choirs of the celestial host, of crying aloud with ever-lasting jubilation, adore and glorify, saying: Holy, Holy, Holy.

There is practically no evidence of how far Gallican-type prayers cut any ice with English taste, but certain points within and outside the context of the mass suggest themselves. Pope Gregory encouraged Augustine to select what he would from the customs 'of many churches' for the benefit of the English Church, including those of Gaul which he had encountered on his journey; 'since things are not to be loved on account of places, but places on account of their good things.'[23] Perhaps Augustine had been impressed in Gaul by some of those beautiful and dramatic ceremonies which had originated in the East and were unknown at Rome. Perhaps, for instance, he had witnessed the blessing of the fire and heard the singing of the triumphant and brilliant *Exultet iam angelica turba* on the night of Easter.[24] Here, surely, was something for the votaries of Thor.

One Gallican feature in particular, which was probably adopted at mass in some English churches, was the episcopal benediction. The celebrant at a Roman mass often recited, after communion, a brief and sober blessing, which almost certainly derived from the blessing for the penitents during Lent in preparation for their Easter communion.[25] Such a prayer might run:[26]

Protect your people, O Lord, and mercifully clean them of all sins, for no adversity will harm them if no wickedness has hold of them.

In Gaul, by contrast, there were special blessings for recitation by bishops, and they were given *before* communion. They are rarely less than five or six times the length of the Roman prayer. They wind on, with heightened language, or piling phrase upon phrase, through ardent supplications and sometimes opaque theology. The following is the first quarter of such a blessing for the feas' of the Circumcision:[27]

May Almighty God bless you and strengthen your heart through the abundance of his mercy. Amen.
May He sanctify your mind, give breadth to your life, beautify your chastity, and always build up your dispositions in good works. Amen.

And again, in a quite distinctive Latin, the first quarter of a blessing for the feast of St. Saturnin, a typically Gallican celebration:[28]

Deus qui triumphalem palmarum meritis regia caelesti fulgente dextera pandis, quique pro te dimicantes sic decoquis in aerumnis, ut velut aurum rutilans excipias in supernis. Amen
O God, who extend with your right hand the triumphal palm to those deserving of it in the brilliance of the heavenly

kingdom, and who plunge into adversity those who fight for you that you may receive them above like shining gold. Amen.

Now the real significance of these benedictions is that they were the perfect expressions in worship of Gaulish episcopal might. It was believed in seventh-century Gaul that the Book of Numbers justified a bishop's giving out a longer and more pompous blessing than that of an ordinary priest where it spoke of Aaron and his sons blessing the people with a specified form of words. Was not Aaron's blessing that of a bishop, and his sons' that of a priest?[29] Nothing was actually said (here, perhaps, was an unfortunate oversight in the Book of Numbers) of a longer or in any way different formula for Aaron. But it could not be doubted that Aaron's blessing had been altogether more significant than that of his sons. And so 'in order to preserve the dignity of a bishop, the sacred canons have laid down that the bishop should give out the longer blessing, a priest the shorter.' The priest was to say no more than, 'the peace, the faith, the love and the communion of the body and blood of the Lord be always with you.'

The length of the episcopal benedictions, their pompous language, their place before communion, and their constant ringing with *Amens* all helped to point their importance. So, even, did the deacon's call to prayer. The Roman blessing (which still survives in the prayer after the postcommunion during Lent) was introduced with '*Humiliate capita vestra Deo*' (bow down your heads to God). In Gaul the deacon turned to the congregation and cried, '*Humiliate vos ad benedictionem*' (bow down for the blessing). A subtle distinction: Rome placed the emphasis on God, Gaul on the blessing itself.

The popes themselves disliked these exhibitions of episcopal magnificence in the liturgy. Pope Zachary wrote to St. Boniface in 751 telling him to have nothing to do with them:[30] 'With regard to the blessings which the Gauls give, as you know, brother, they are embroidered with much that is vicious. For they are motivated not by apostolic tradition (i.e. by what the popes did), but by vainglory.'

An Eleutherius or particularly a Wilfrid, on the other hand, would clearly have thought such blessings appropriate to and eloquent of their notion of the bishop's office. Wilfrid may have followed the Roman liturgy, but a collection of Gaulish blessings

would sit as happily by the side of that as a Neapolitan evangeliary
could at Jarrow.[31] It would seem that the province of Lyon was
a particularly keen centre for the collection and composition of
these blessings, so he could hardly have missed them during his
stay in Gaul.[32] In fact at the Bibliothèque Nationale, Paris, there
survive just two leaves from an early eighth-century sacramentary
written in an Irish or a Northern English hand. They had been used
for the binding of some later manuscript, and by chance they contain portions of benedictions in the Gaulish style.[33] They may have
had nothing to do with Wilfrid himself, but it would nonetheless
be surprising if he had never risen from his frith-stool at Hexham
to recite what was the counterpart in prayer to the rest of his
external life.

That Wilfrid himself used Gallican episcopal benedictions is,
when all is said and done, a matter of speculation; although it may
be pleaded that speculation is not entirely out of place when it
causes us to reflect on the liturgical influences to which England
would naturally have been exposed. What is absolutely certain,
however, is that he used the Gallican and not the Roman dedication rite for the dedication of Ripon church. Eddius describes
how the kings Egfrith and Aelfwine, together with many
ecclesiastical and secular dignitaries, came to Ripon for the
ceremony, and how 'they dedicated to the Lord the altar with its
bases (*altare cum bassibus suis domino dedicantes*) and vested it
in purple woven with gold.'[34] There was no consecration of the
altar in the Roman rite, only in the Gallican. The Roman
consecration of a church, if there was a rite apart from the
celebration of the first mass in the building, depended on the
deposition of relics in the altar. There was a procession of the
relics, the preparation of the cavity, the deposition, the sealing
of the cavity with a stone and the anointing of the stone. It was
a funerary ritual: 'The tomb of the saint is prepared for him;
he is brought thither, enclosed within it, and the interior and
exterior of the sepulchre is anointed with a fragrant unguent.'
Eddius has much to say about the church at Ripon when it was
consecrated, its columns, its altar coverings, its gospel book, etc.
But he has no mention of relics. Ripon had relics; the crypt was
built for them. That, however, is another matter. The more
dramatic Gallican rite, in contrast with the Roman, turned on the
consecration of the altar. The altar was sprinkled with wine and
water and blessed with chrism while antiphons were sung. Only

when this was done might relics be fetched from their previous resting-place and deposited. The Gallican rite was not a funerary rite, but a rite of initiation: 'Just as the Christian is dedicated by water and oil, by baptism and confirmation, so the altar in the first place, and the church in the second, are consecrated by ablutions and anointing.'[35]

To say, as Eddius says, that the altar was dedicated is not entirely unambiguous. Gregory the Great, who naturally followed the Roman rite, spoke of the dedication of altars when he meant precisely the placing of relics in them.[36] If Eddius had said no more than this, one might think he meant that relics were solemnly placed in the altar; although it would be a little odd that he made no mention of the relics. But he says the altar *with its bases* was dedicated, a phrase which would mean nothing in connection with the Roman rite but is perfectly intelligible in connection with the Gallican. We have already had occasion to notice these bases in one context; now they are of even greater interest to us in another. For the direction to the celebrant during the first part of the consecration of the altar in the Gallican rite, as we find it in the *Missale Francorum* or the *Sacramentary of Angoulême*, for instance, reads, 'Place on the corners of the altar with your finger the wine mixed with water, and sprinkle the altar seven times; *and pour the rest on the base.*'[37] The so-called champion of Rome and Roman ways appears to have been no partisan when it came to the liturgy.

Irish influences played an important part in early Anglo-Saxon worship. This is most clearly seen from the books of private prayer which we shall consider in the next section of the chapter. Quite apart from these, however, there is at least one suggestive instance of the kind of relation which existed between Irish worship and that of some English churches in the practice of singing of the Nicene Creed at mass. The history of this practice was brilliantly illuminated by the great liturgical scholar, Dom Bernard Capelle.[38] It was introduced at Constantinople around 515 by the patriarch, Timothy, in his fight against the Monophysites. It was adopted by the fathers of the Spanish Church assembled at Toledo in 589, a case of direct Byzantine influence. From Spain it spread, probably quite soon, to Ireland; the contacts between Spain and Ireland in the seventh century, whether direct or indirect, being close and varied. The text of the Nicene Creed is found in its place after the Gospel in the Stowe Missal, an

Irish mass-book of the early ninth century, most of whose matter
is acknowledged to be far older.

The next thing we find is Alcuin, the famous scholar from
York at the court of Charlemagne, attempting to persuade the
emperor to have the Nicene Creed sung throughout his empire
(c. 798). Dom Capelle proved that Alcuin's text had some verbal
peculiarities in common with the Stowe version; and that though
the Stowe text was written down a few years later than Alcuin's,
it was in fact Alcuin who was copying from or remembering
the Irish tradition of the text as represented by the Stowe Missal.
'It was at York,' he says, 'that Alcuin learnt the Irish text which
one sees long afterwards returning spontaneously to his pen.'
Here is a case in which, without direct evidence from England,
we are suddenly given a glimpse of how an Irish custom had
penetrated English worship.

Rome gave much to the rest of Europe in the early Middle
Ages, but she also received much. The Roman liturgy is a mixture
of many spiritual traditions and one of the great centres of their
mingling, before they were finally passed back to Rome, was early
Anglo-Saxon England.

PRIVATE PRAYER

The world of private prayer can be very different from that of
the public liturgy, yet it is as essential a part of the Christian life.
The eminent Jesuit, Professor Josef Jungmann, has written: 'The
idea that the life of the primitive Christians revolved exclusively
around the liturgy is not correct. And it cannot be correct,
simply because it would be unnatural and in contradiction to
the rules laid down in the Gospels. How could the Christian life
exclude private and personal prayer?'[39] Early Anglo-Saxon England
produced no Tertullian to write a treatise on prayer, nor a
Theresa of Avila to expound the most wrapt and intimate
moments of her spiritual life. But it has left a few collections of
Latin prayers for private use, the most interesting of which are
the Books of Nunnaminster and Cerne. These cannot be treated as
conspectuses of the whole range of private devotions; their prayers
are prods, aids to memory,[40] equipment for the recovery of a
wandering mind during those long and often arid periods when
men fulfilled the Gospel precept—'go into thy inner room and
shut the door upon thyself.'

The Book of Cerne derives its name from the fact that at one stage it belonged to the monastery of Cerne Abbas in Dorset. The manuscript itself was written in Mercia early in the ninth century, but no scholar doubts that most of its prayers are much earlier, and the work of Bishop and Levison has strongly suggested that as a collection of prayers the book evolved at Lindisfarne or in the orbit of Lindisfarne influence during the seventh and eighth centuries, although the possibility that it was a Mercian compilation cannot be ruled out.[41] There is nothing homogeneous about the collection; it is very much a scrap book or a 'work of marquetry' as Dom F. Cabrol called it.[42] In the style of the prayers one can detect Roman strains in some places and borrowings from Spain in others. But the basis of the mixture is certainly Irish.

Various Irish traits stand out quite markedly in the Book of Cerne, the most obvious being the preoccupation with penance. Whereas the majority of the Nunnaminster prayers are focused on the life and person of Christ, many of the Cerne prayers pay close attention to the frame of mind, the state of virtue or vice, and the general psychological condition of the person praying. In the latter book confessions of one kind or another abound:[43]

> I confess to you, my Lord God, that I have sinned in heaven (sic) and on earth, before you and your angels, and before the face of all your saints. I have sinned through neglect of your commandments, I have sinned through pride and envy, I have sinned through detraction and greed, I have sinned through gluttony and fornication.... I have sinned through blasphemy and desire of the flesh....

and in short there appears to be practically no way in which the extremely comprehensive sinner of this prayer has not sinned. The truth is that it is not so much a genuine confession as a means of examining the conscience; it was a prayer to be gone through slowly by one who would carefully consider the implications of his own thoughts and actions under each item.

The importance of this kind of prayer becomes clear when we remember that the early monasteries of Ireland were great centres of penance, both for monks and for laymen. Laymen would take a priest as a private confessor, or spiritual director, or soulfriend (anmchara), and would live a penitential life attached to a monastery. This also happened in the Irish-type monasteries of

England. It was what the saintly Adamnan was doing at
Coldingham in Northumbria during the late seventh century.
Horrified by some sin which he had committed, he had put
himself under the direction of an Irish priest who admonished
him to eat only on Sundays and Thursdays for a year, after which
he would review the situation. Meanwhile the priest returned to
Ireland, nothing more was ever heard of him, and Adamnan
continued for the rest of his life in his ascetic course at
Coldingham.[44] This system of penance as a continuous way of
life, rather than formal confession and formal enjoinment of
penances by a bishop, was developed in the West by the Irish.
Sixth-century Ireland saw the beginning of books known as
penitentials, books containing lists of sins with appropriate
penances for the guidance of confessors. Every conceivable sort
of sin, and many sorts which were scarcely conceivable, found a
place in these lists.[45] It was not that the Irish were more exotic
sinners than anyone else, but their minds were a great deal more
compendious. Commutations of long penances were also given for
the occasions when something shorter and sharper was required.
Thus instead of a year's penance, for instance, a penitent might
undertake the black fast: three days without eating, drinking or
sleeping; three nights, the first spent in water, the second naked
on stinging nettles, the third on nutshells.[46]

Another Irish feature in the Book of Cerne is that of the
'breastplate' prayer, a prayer in which God was asked to protect
the various parts of the body in turn, and which perhaps harks
back to the charms of pagan days:[47]

> Guard my mouth lest I speak vain things and tell profane
> tales.... Guard my eyes lest they look upon a woman with
> lustful desire.... Guard my ears lest they listen to detraction
> or the idle words of liars.... Guard my feet lest they frequent
> the houses of leisure.... Guard my hands lest they stretch out
> often for gifts.

Sometimes these prayers appear to reach an almost lurid pitch
of self-accusation:[48]

> By your loins which were always filled with divine virtue, renew
> in my loins the spirit of holiness. By your most chaste head,
> O Christ, have mercy on my wicked head. By your blessed
> eyes, spare my polluted eyes....

In many of these prayers, it will have been observed, the elements of litanizing and categorizing are strong. The Irish were very enumerative. They had their three kinds of pilgrimage, their seven gates of heaven guarded by the seven archangels, their 365 veins of the human body. They had a method of expounding Scripture (based on Servius's Commentary on Vergil) by multiplying the questions which they put about any particular passage —its time, its place, the language, the authority; and then they would go still further, like the seventh-century commentator on Mark, expounding the four evangelists, who were as to *figura* the four elements, as to *prophetia* the vision of the four beasts by Ezechiel, and as to *demonstratio* the four mercenaries who divided Christ's clothes by lot.[49] In a similar way, to list the parts of the body which needed protection, to examine the conscience, to divide faults into categories and sub-categories, to shade off with increasing refinement one form of sinfulness from another, all this was an essential function of Irish penitence.

Not all the litanies in the Book of Cerne are 'breastplates' or confessions, and there is much which is tender and delicate, such as the invocations to the Holy Trinity, 'Thou art my living bread, Thou art my catholic unity, Thou art the guide to my homeland. . . .'[50] And if some of the litanies seem repetitive or tedious, we must remember that they were not meant to be rattled off in top gear. When a prayer goes, for instance, 'Hear me as you heard the three boys in the fiery furnace; hear me as you heard Susannah and delivered her from the hand of the two elders; hear me as you heard Peter on the sea and Paul in chains,' each of these invocations was matter on which to meditate, to linger, to bring associations flooding into the mind.[51]

The Irish were great users of heightened language, both in public worship and in private prayer. A good example is the form of words which they used for the consecration of the wine at mass. There are two independent testimonies to this: the Stowe Missal, where its occurrence is remarkable because the canon or central Eucharistic prayer here is essentially Roman, and an Irish palimpsest mass-book of the seventh century, an extremely rare and interesting compilation of an almost entirely Gallican character, whose leaves were used in the ninth century for a Latin glossary.[52] The formula of consecration in both these books added only a single word to that which was normal, but it was a word loaded with significance, a word which carries us far from the cool light of Rome to the hottest regions of Spanish prayer. Instead of saying 'hic est enim calix sanguinis mei' the priest said, 'hic est enim calix *sancti* sanguinis mei' (this is the chalice of my *holy* blood).[53] There was a world of difference in the early Middle Ages between blood and holy blood. The climate of Irish prayer and that of Spain, from which Ireland derived much, was peculiarly favourable to the use of such heightened, almost melodramatic, phrases. So the Spanish and Irish spoke not simply of paradise, but of the loveliness of paradise (*amoenitas paradisii*), not simply of the day of judgment, but of the day of fearful judgment (*dies tremendi judicii*), not simply of Christ's blood, but of his holy blood. Every one of these phrases can be found in the Book of Cerne.[54] And if there were such a thing as a Time Machine which could only be used for five seconds, it would be well worth turning it on to the consecration of wine during mass at Lindisfarne.

The Spanish element in the Book of Cerne is altogether important. Many eminent liturgists have found the book a happy hunting ground for 'Spanish Symptoms', beginning with Edmund Bishop, followed up by Dom Cabrol, who picked out amongst other things the description of Christ as Alpha and Omega, and by Cardinal Mercati who published a paper entitled 'More Spanish Symptoms', all of them echoing Traube's original 'Spanische Symptome'.[55] Bishop spoke of the 'Hispano-Hibernian' character of the book. The term is appropriate, for so important were the correspondences between Spain and Ireland in matters of worship, that it is often difficult to know whether something should be described as Spanish or Irish. A particularly clear case of Spanish influence is the most remarkable of Cerne's prayers to the Blessed Virgin. Spain was an advanced centre for devotion to the Virgin in the seventh century. Her feasts, introduced into Rome by the Syrian, Pope Sergius (687–701), were established much earlier in Spain through its direct Syrian contacts. Here the devotion was taken up with ardour. Hildephonsus, bishop of Toledo (657–67), wrote a treatise on Mary's virginity, the *Liber de Virginitate Perpetua Sanctae Mariae*. This treatise, written at white heat, constantly erupted into fervent prayers to the Virgin.[56] The expressions by Hildephonsus of confidence in the Virgin's power, his urgent repetitions, and his piling on of adjectives are echoed in the Cerne prayer in question:[57]

Holy Mother of God, ever Virgin, beautiful, blessed, glorious
and generous, chaste and pure, inviolate and undefiled, Mary
immaculate, chosen and beloved of God, endowed with
singular sanctity and worthy of all praise, who are mediator
for the sins of the whole world, hear, hear, o hear us, holy
Mary. Pray and intercede for us and do not disdain to help
us. For we have confidence and we know that you can obtain
everything you wish from your son. . . .

On this prayer, the remark of Bishop cannot be bettered. 'It
may read to some,' he wrote, 'as betraying a mind overstrung, to
others only as if evidencing a desire to outdo a forerunner.' Its
style is in marked contrast to that of Alchfrith's prayer to the
Virgin which follows it in Cerne. Alchfrith was almost certainly
an eighth-century Northumbrian hermit, living within the orbit
of Lindisfarne.[58] His relatively sober prayer opens, 'Holy Mary,
glorious mother of God and ever virgin, who deserved to bear a
saviour for the world, hear me and have mercy on me now and
everywhere, on account of the honour and glory of your most
excellent virginity.' Another prayer in Cerne, on the subject of the
Cross, is interesting because one portion of it is identical with the
prayer said by the priest after the veneration of the Cross on Good
Friday in the Spanish liturgy, and this in its turn takes us back
to the Holy Week celebrations in Jerusalem itself. It also carries
us into that world of Anglo-Saxon devotion to the Cross, expressed
in the icon of Christ exalted on the Cross which Biscop brought
home to Jarrow from his travels, and most sublimely in the old
English poem on the *Dream of the Rood*.[59]

The Book of Nunnaminster derives its name from the fact that
it belonged to a Winchester nunnery probably founded by King
Alfred's queen, Ealswith, on her own property. Its leaves measure
$8\frac{1}{2}$ inches x $6\frac{1}{4}$ inches, and it would appear to have been written
in the ninth century, but by a scribe who was trying to copy an
older hand and doubtless had an older manuscript before him.[60]
The prayers are certainly earlier than the ninth century, though
we cannot say where or by whom any of them were originally
composed. There are some prayers of a distinctly Irish character,[61]
and others for the great liturgical feasts written by someone who
had the phrases of the Roman mass-prayers ringing in his
ears,[62] but the core of the collection is a homogeneous group of
some 20 prayers on Christ's Passion.[63] Some of these prayers are

long and effusive, others have an almost Roman conciseness, all are marked by open if restrained fervour.

To take the theme of the Passion for daily prayer was in accordance with some of the oldest traditions of the fathers. In the *Apostolic Tradition*, for instance, Hippolytus of Rome says, 'If thou art at home, pray at the third hour and praise God; but if thou art elsewhere and that time comes, pray in thy heart to God.' At this hour he recommended the Christian to think of Christ nailed to the Cross. 'Pray likewise at the sixth hour,' he wrote, 'for at that hour when Christ had been hanged upon the wood of the cross the daylight was divided and it became darkness.' At the ninth hour prayer should be protracted, 'for in that hour Christ was pierced in his side and shed forth blood and water.'[64] The passion on the cross, the darkness, the piercing of Christ's side—each is also the subject of one of the Nunnaminster prayers.

The piercing of Christ's side, the blood and water which had flowed out as a healing medicine for man in his fallen condition, were themes to which the Byzantine prayer books, in particular, constantly returned.[65] In fact from the fifth century onwards, reflection on the physical sufferings of Christ was a marked feature of Byzantine and Syrian devotion. The finely illustrated sixth-century Syrian gospel-book of Rabula shows Christ on the cross in a tunic, his arms naked, his hands and feet fastened by nails, his face eloquent of suffering. The good thief inclines his head towards Christ and casts down his eyes, the other lifts his head arrogantly. Beneath the cross the mercenaries sit in heated argument. To one side stand the weeping women of Jerusalem, to the other side Mary and John, the former hunched with grief and drawing a cloth to her face. It is a scene of realism and pathos.[66] One cannot help seeing the influence of this kind of piety in the Book of Nunnaminster, mediated to it through some Spanish or Gaulish channel. It is significant of the same influence that the prayers in the Book of Nunnaminster are addressed to Christ. Prayers addressed to Christ are found in all the Eastern liturgies, at Lérins, and in many other parts of Spain and Gaul during the sixth and seventh centuries, as a gesture against the Arian heretics who denied Christ's divinity. In the *Missale Gothicum* (probably Autun *c.* 700) there are prayers recognizably addressed to Christ because they invoke the 'Saviour of the world' at the end, just as the Nunnaminster prayers all end with the invocation, 'O Lord Jesus Christ'. At Rome in this period, by contrast, prayers were addressed to the Father through Christ.[67]

The Nunnaminster prayers on the Passion all have the same method of construction. They begin with a fervent invocation, bring an image to mind, and then, often quite tersely, the image is made the basis of a request for the spiritual good of the one who prays. The concise prayer on the Crown of Thorns, for instance, runs:[68]

Thou, my merciful God and helper, who didst not disdain to bear the crown of thorns on Thy venerable head, I give you thanks and, through this, most earnestly beseech you to grant me pardon for whatever wrong I have committed through the senses of my head. For I shall be overwhelmed by the density of all my sins as if surrounded by thorns, unless I am protected by your aid, O Lord Jesus Christ.

We come finally to other spheres where English devotion appears to have been influenced, however indirectly, by the East Mediterranean world. English devotion to the Blessed Virgin, for instance, certainly took something from the Syrian pope, Sergius I (687–701). One of Aldhelm's poems shows how quickly the observance of her four festivals, introduced into the Roman liturgy by this pope, was taken up by the Anglo-Saxons.[69] These feasts were introduced, during the eighth century, into the calendar of the Lindisfarne dependency about which Aethelwulf wrote, not without some resistance from the monks.[70] Very likely the English were also influenced by Egypt in this devotion. The Madonna with her child was a favourite subject in Coptic art. Some representations between about 450 and 700 show her seated in majesty, perhaps on an imposing throne with a thick cushion and a jewelled footstool, while the child sits on her lap looking stiff and facing outwards.[71] But there were many other more humane renderings, which took their inspiration from the representations of the Egyptian goddess Isis and her son Horus, popular both with the Copts and the Greeks in Egypt. In these renderings the Madonna could be seen suckling her son in various attitudes of motherly concern, or hitching the child up to her breast on her forearm, in one such case as she casts an intimate glance up to heaven.[72] The boldest example of all is a small ivory, where the child sits on his mother's hand facing her, his little arm round her neck and his cheek rubbing against hers.[73]

When such scenes could be found on small ivories or Coptic textiles, there is no difficulty in seeing how they could have a wide influence. The early ninth-century Book of Kells, one of the summits of Irish art, has a Madonna and Child influenced directly or indirectly by this kind of representation. The child sits along his mother's knee facing her. His left hand touches her breast, his right hand is placed on hers with the tenderest of gestures. But our attention is already caught by something much earlier in Northumbria, the Madonna and Child engraved on St. Cuthbert's coffin at Lindisfarne in 698. Here the child turns to the front with his hand raised solemnly in blessing. He has a hieratic posture. Yet he sits *along* his mother's knee facing her, her arm round his shoulder, in such a way as to imply that the artist had a model of the tender, Egyptian kind before him.[74] (Fig. 14).

The models for the figures engraved on St. Cuthbert's coffin were Mediterranean, but the whole scheme for its decoration— the Madonna and Child, and the rows of apostles and archangels— comes from the world of Irish prayers and litanies. As on the coffin there is a row of archangels, so in the Book of Cerne there is a prayer invoking each of the archangels by name.[75] This interest in and devotion to the seven archangels is something which links Irish culture to Coptic papyri and Ethiopian legends not to say superstitions.[76]

The last word on private prayer should perhaps be left with Bede. It appears that to his pen we owe a small Irish type of compilation called *Libellus Precum*, which consists of some 300 verses selected from the psalms and intended probably as a source-book for meditation. A similar compilation forms part of the Book of Cerne and seems to have been made by Bishop Ethelwald of Lindisfarne, who bound the Lindisfarne Gospels.[77] In addition, Bede sometimes breaks into a prayer during his writings and he had the occasional habit, of which we have already spoken, of addressing his prayers not to the Father, nor to any saint, but to Christ. One of these prayers concludes the *Ecclesiastical History* :[78]

And I beseech Thee, good Jesus, that as Thou hast so graciously given to me a sweet share in the words of Thy knowledge, thou wilt some time bring me in thy loving kindness to the fountain of all wisdom, there to stand for ever before Thy face.

12 Books and Studies

There was no scholarship without books, and there were no books in early Anglo-Saxon England unless they were obtained from abroad, either sent by friendly monasteries or collected on personal travels. Most monasteries would have had libraries of sorts, and besides the famous collectors of books, like Biscop and Ceolfrid, there must have been many who were less well-known and were doing the same thing on a smaller scale. In one of his scriptural commentaries, for instance, where he is writing of St. Paul's receiving one less than 40 strokes, Bede mentions a Bishop Cuthwine of the East Angles:[1]

> The way in which this (i.e. St. Paul's strokes) is to be understood and was understood by the ancients (he says), is shown by a picture in that book which the most reverend and learned Cuthwine, bishop of the East Angles, coming from Rome, brought with him to England. In this book almost all the sufferings and toils of the apostle were depicted in their due place.

He continues with a description, which need not concern us, of the picture of St. Paul's flogging, which makes it clear that he had seen the book himself. No such book has ever been found, although it was suggested by the great Munich palaeographer, Traube, that it might have been an illustrated copy of Arator's *History of the Apostles*. Bishop Cuthwine is known also to have possessed an Italian illustrated manuscript of another Christian poet, Sedulius, a copy of which is now in Antwerp.[2] The main point about Cuthwine is that if he had not been mentioned by Bede, we would hardly know of his existence; he would be merely a name in a list of East Anglian bishops (which shows that he occupied the see sometime between 716 and 731).[3] If it is only by the merest chance and quite incidentally that we catch a glimpse of important acquisitions of books by a bishop collector, much of this kind of activity must now be entirely hidden from the historian's view.

There is little to be said, however, of studies at a place like Dunwich; one could perhaps say somewhat more of houses like Whitby and Breedon (Leicestershire), which must have had distinctly good libraries.[4] Our chief focus, in terms of available evidence, is bound to be on three centres, all of which had outstanding libraries and outstanding scholars to use them. The three were Canterbury, with its manifold Continental connections; Malmesbury, which had Aldhelm, with his Irish, Gaulish and Roman contacts, as abbot; and Wearmouth/Jarrow, which had Biscop's library and Bede.

ALDHELM

Although the name of the Venerable Bede is almost synonymous, to some minds, with Anglo-Saxon studies, the first Anglo-Saxon author who showed profound learning and extensive reading amongst the Christian Fathers was Aldhelm. Aldhelm was born probably in 639, a kinsman of the West Saxon royal family, but of uncertain relationship. During the 660s he was being educated at the most important educational institution of the time in Wessex or perhaps in the whole of Britain, the monastery of Malmesbury, which was ruled by the Irish abbot Maildubh. After Theodore and Hadrian had arrived at Canterbury in 669 he studied under them for some time there. About 675 he succeeded Maildubh as abbot of Malmesbury, and during his 30 years in the abbacy established himself as one of the leading Anglo-Saxon churchmen. In 705 he became first bishop of Sherborne, a see whose creation marked the successful absorption of Dorset into the West Saxon kingdom.[5] He died in 709 at Doulting in Somerset.

Our chief biographical knowledge of Aldhelm comes from Book V of William of Malmesbury's *Gesta Pontificum*.[6] William was a monk of Malmesbury in the twelfth century, so that as a source he is very late. Moreover he had an axe to grind, since part of his purpose was to establish his abbey's property rights with reference to the actions and documents of the great abbot of its early days. Some of William's matter is obviously legend. In fact there is room for a critical study of his book, on which we do not intend to embark. But two general points can be made here. First, no scholar has doubted the authenticity of the surviving 13 letters written by or addressed to Aldhelm, a very interesting little collection, several pieces of which we owe solely to William's preserving their text. Second, William was an enthusiastic antiquary with a genuine nose for ancient objects, and he knew of several such objects associated with Aldhelm. There were the Old and New Testaments which Aldhelm was said to have bought from Gaulish sailors near Dover while he was visiting Canterbury for his episcopal consecration; there were the altar and chasuble which he was said to have brought back from Rome. These things were kept at Malmesbury in the twelfth century and were pegs on which to hang biographical traditions, probably with an authentic basis. That Aldhelm visited Rome as abbot is attested not only by the altar and chasuble, but also quite independently by the letter which an Irishman sent to him.[7] William also knew the stone crosses which were said to mark the places where Aldhelm's body had rested overnight when it was being carried back from Doulting to Malmesbury.

Aldhelm's writings are in extremely difficult Latin. Many of his sentences are of immense length and incredibly complex structure, and he was a specialist in that vocabulary of long and exotic words, which he doubtless learned from his Irish teachers and which was later to be known as *Hisperica Famina*.[8] Bede said of him that he was 'lucid in style,'[9] and at first sight no compliment could seem less well deserved. And yet once the obstacle of vocabulary is overcome, it can be seen that Aldhelm had sufficient mastery of syntax to give some of his longest sentences flow and momentum.

Apart from his letters and charters, Aldhelm's known writings consist of some ecclesiastical poems, a treatise on virginity of which he wrote both a prose and a metric version, and the so-called Letter to Acircius, which is a treatise on poetic metre incorporating his famous hundred riddles. Of the ecclesiastical poems the most interesting is that written about 690 to celebrate the church of Bugga, abbess of Withington in the kingdom of the Hwicce, and daughter of King Centwine of Wessex. This poem is quite informative about the church, as a building, for it speaks of the sun shining through its glass windows (this was the period when Biscop was importing Gaulish glaziers, and perhaps the same thing was done at Withington), and of the light being diffused through the four-square temple, of its brilliant jewelled chalice, and of the splendour of its cross whose plates of gold and silver were set with gems (another instance of early English veneration of the Cross).[10]

The treatise on virginity was written in a prose and a metric version for Cuthburga, sister of King Ine of Wessex, and the other nuns at Barking, around 686.[11] It begins with an elaborate comparison between virginity and athletic or scholarly exercises, the Latin of which, like the rest of the treatise, must have been more than exercise for the minds of most of the ladies to whom it was directed. In the first part of this work, a general discussion of virginity, Aldhelm used Ambrose, the *Conferences* of Cassian, and above all the great African fathers, Cyprian, Tertullian and Augustine. The second part, consisting of specific examples of male and female 'virgins' in history, is based largely on the Bible, Eusebius's Church History in Rufinus's translation, and various individual and collected lives of saints.[12] In the first part Aldhelm quotes often from the Bible, but he has a special penchant for making his points by piling on metaphors and similes. He wishes to say, for instance, that virginity is preferable to marriage, although he does not spurn the married state (which would have been unwise considering the likely number of aristocratic widows in his audience); off he goes on how gold is to be preferred to silver, the brilliantly coloured peacock to the dark gull, the bubbling of a pure fountain and the continuous flow of aqueducts to the cool water from a well or cistern which has to be drawn up by a bucket and wheel.[13] Through all this he moves gradually to the chief purpose of his treatise, the admonition against pride in these high-born nuns, particularly pride in the kind of clothes they wore. It was the wife, he says, taking up St. Paul's distinction between the wife and virgin, who decked herself out with necklaces and jewelled rings; the virgin should shine with modesty. The wife fashioned her hair in delicate curls; the virgin preferred to wear the crown of virginity on her unkempt head. The wife was like the gaudy woman on the beast of the Apocalypse, drinking from the golden chalice; the virgin should show forth the chaste life and good example of the heavenly citizens. He castigates 'dressed-up impudence' in nuns with a citation from Cyprian's *De Habitu Virginum* about the kind of woman who was dressed 'as if she either had a husband or were on the search for one.'[14]

The most elaborate of Aldhem's writings is the treatise on poetic metre, or the Letter to Acircius. Acircius is almost certainly identifiable with the scholarly King Alfrith of Northumbria (685–705), and the treatise was written some time after 685.[15] It opens by recalling Aldhelm's close relationship with his correspondent in the past at the time of the latter's confirmation and reception of the sevenfold gifts of the Holy Spirit. Then follows a long disquisition on the mystical significance of the number seven, which comes into the light of day, where metres are concerned, with the observation that Aldhelm will explain the 28 (7 x 4) feet, as well as the eight principal kinds of metre and the hundred which derive from them.[16] Then comes a general survey of types of hexametre, followed by the riddles, followed by the treatise on the 28 kinds of feet, each illustrated with a profusion of words which form examples. He ends by remarking with truth that nobody of the Germanic race had sweated in this kind of business before himself. The fact was that every teacher in the early Anglo-Saxon period, who wanted to introduce his pupils to Christian culture, had to teach them the universal language of that culture, its grammar, and the rules of its poetry. It was the same with Bede, and the same with Archbishop Tatwine of Canterbury.

Aldhelm must have studied the interpretation of Scripture at both Malmesbury and Canterbury, and he regarded this without question as the most important kind of scholarship. But equally, like any educated Christian of his period, he did not doubt that Scripture could be understood only with a solid grounding in Grammar and Rhetoric and the other traditional subjects of a classical education in the liberal arts. These were the essential preliminary studies to work on the Bible, as Augustine had long since made clear in his *De Doctrina Christiana*. It is to these fields that Aldhelm's writings largely related, and in them that he was perhaps largely interested. Even his prose treatise on virginity, in which he quotes and interprets passages of the Bible, really owes more to the methods of rhetoric than to those of scriptural commentary. He never set out to produce a large-scale exposition of Christian learning, as Bede did. What he committed to writing was inspired by particular needs in that circle of royal patrons and monastic founders to which he belonged.

We should reckon that Aldhelm's writings, occasional pieces as they were intended to be, do not reflect his full significance or influence in the field of learning. It was partly a matter of the time at his disposal. As abbot of Malmesbury he held, unlike Bede, an important administrative position, and in his own right he cut a political figure of consequence. Then, like his predecessor as abbot (who left no known work), he was a teacher, and several of the letters which he wrote or received show him as one who advised and encouraged all kinds of young men trying to make their way in the world of scholarship. This being so, it is particularly worth knowing something of the studies at Malmesbury and Canterbury which lay behind his reputation. At least we have evidence of a kind for the curricula at both places.

So far as the classical education in the liberal arts was concerned, which preceded the higher study of the Bible in the context of Christian education, it is known, thanks to the eminent German scholar, Professor B. Bischoff, that the Irish favoured a curriculum of studies in the early Middle Ages which was not quite usual.[17] The usual division of subjects, particularly after Isidore of Seville had popularized it in his *Etymologies*, was Grammar, Rhetoric, and Dialectic as the *trivium*, and Arithmetic, Astronomy, Geometry and Music as the *quadrivium*. But instead of the *quadrivium* the Irish often took *Physica* in seven subjects which meant the four subjects of the *quadrivium* together with Astrology, Mechanics and Medicine. This system they derived probably from Isidore, but from his *Differentiae* which was less popular than his *Etymologies*. Now Aldhelm refers on at least four occasions to these seven subjects, either as forming the sevenfold division of the *Ars Physica*, or more generally as the seven philosophical disciplines.[18] One can presume that this was the curriculum with which he became familiar under Maildubh at Malmesbury.[19]

Important as Aldhelm's studies under the Irish may have been in his formation as a scholar, he regarded them as decidedly inferior to what he was offered at Canterbury by Theodore and Hadrian. In a well-known letter to Bishop Eleutherius of the West Saxons (671), he described his work at Canterbury which was so absorbing that he excused himself from joining the brethren at Malmesbury for Christmas.[20] He was studying Roman Law, the hundred different types of metre, the rules of feet, the recondite subject of music in which there were few teachers (he clearly means the theory of music rather than just the chant), poetic figures, the seven types of *pathos*, and the principles of calculation. In this last field, which included fractions (Aldhelm was finding these difficult), calculations of times and seasons such as Bede's in his *De Temporum Ratione*, astronomy, astrology and horoscopic computation, Aldhelm felt especially that he was taking great strides forward. In later days he could not understand why the young men must be forever going off to Ireland to get their learning when there was Canterbury at hand. Shortly before Theodore's death in 690 Aldhelm wrote to one, Eahfrith, expressing pleasure at his return to his own country from Ireland after six years. With friendly irony he wrote the letter in a style to show that the Irish could be outplayed at their own game of long words and inflated language. The demonstration gave him no difficulty. Part of one sentence reads:[21]

> For just as, when the shades of night recede and Titan in his turn rises with his chariot on the smooth waters, the swarm of honey-bees, heavy with its golden burden, carries it over the burgeoning tops of the blossoming linden trees to meagre honeycombs; in the same way, if I am not mistaken, the crowd of voracious readers and all the rest of their eager crew gather thirstily from the worked-over pages of prolific and holy writers not only the arts of grammar and geometry and the twice three unmentioned subjects of the *Ars Physica*, but also the preferable fourfold secrets of allegorical and tropological learning. . . .

Why, Aldhelm wanted to know, did readers converge in fleets upon Ireland when the learned Greek and Roman teachers in Britain itself (i.e. at Canterbury) were all but ignored? In another letter, to a certain Wihtfrid, who was about to set out for Ireland in pursuit of scholarship, he warns his correspondent not to trifle with prostitutes or brothels.[22]

The influence of the Canterbury school on Aldhelm can be clearly seen in some of his later work and interests. With regard to Roman Law, for instance, William of Malmesbury transcribed in the twelfth century a Roman Law book, from Aldhelm's own copy, and his transcript is now in the Bodleian Library, Oxford.[23] It was Alaric's *Breviarium*, the code of vulgar Roman Law which this Visigothic king issued for his Roman subjects in 506. The possible connection between Aldhelm's possession of this code and the formulation of King Ine's Laws (Wessex) between 688 and 694 would perhaps make an interesting subject of study. Again,

Aldhelm had written to Eleutherius that he was studying the hundred types of metre and the rules of feet at Canterbury; his treatise on metre deals precisely with these things, making frequent reference to Greek grammatical terms (doubtless learnt in Theodore's school) and sometimes, as in the use of accents, distinguishing between Greek and Latin usage.[24] He had also written that he was studying the seven kinds of *pathos*, i.e. modifications in the metric structure of hexametres; his treatise has a section dealing with this subject, although it only mentions six kinds.[25] And there is a passage of the same treatise which perhaps preserves a fragment of Theodore's scriptural exegesis, to which we shall return in dealing with biblical studies. How much Greek Aldhelm learnt from Theodore is a moot point; there is no good evidence that he actually read Greek writers, but he seems to have learnt something of the technicalities of Greek grammar.

Behind Aldhelm's studies under the Irish at Malmesbury would have lain the new learning of Isidore of Seville, whose last and most influential work, the *Etymologies*, was released to the scholarly world by Braulio of Saragossa in 636. It is not necessary to suppose that Aldhelm could have obtained Isidore's writings only through the Irish. There exist two early manuscripts containing some of Isidore's works, which palaeographers consider to be from South-West Britain, and one of these bears traces of a direct relation to the Spanish exemplar from which it was derived.[26] This is not surprising when one considers that the Anglo-Saxons were not less in touch with Gaul and probably Spain than were the Irish, and the early spread of West Saxon power westwards along the south coast would have enhanced their contacts.[27] It may have been in this way as much as from Ireland that Isidore's works came to Malmesbury. But whatever one makes of the routes by which these works travelled, it is certain that Aldhelm was very well read in Isidore, and likely that he had studied the great Spanish author during his time at Malmesbury.

When all is said and done there is little point in trying to distinguish exactly between what Aldhelm owed to the Irish, to Theodore and Hadrian, and to his reading of Isidore. If we compare the Irish curriculum in the liberal arts with what we know of that at Canterbury, which certainly included astrology, and probably medicine to judge from Theodore's known interest in the subject,[28] the two seem very similar. It was the level of scholarship at Canterbury rather than the curriculum which impressed Aldhelm. A late classical education could well have run on the same general lines in Asia Minor, Seville, and for that matter in the Irish schools. What can be shown are some of the ways in which Aldhelm was affected by this late classical culture, of which Isidore was in many ways a very good representative. We seek, therefore, to show, with the example of Aldhelm's riddles, that he is eminently intelligible in the light of Isidore, whose writings he knew well and cited often.[29]

ALDHELM AND ISIDORE OF SEVILLE

The cultural and intellectual influence of Spain in the seventh century, and particularly of Isidore, was of great importance.[30] The Visigothic kings of Spain in the late sixth century, rulers of great ability, gained an access of political strength for two reasons. First, they were able to overcome the provincial separatism which caused whole Spanish provinces to attempt to cut themselves off from the royal government centred at Toledo, and make themselves politically independent. And secondly they were able to solve the problem of Roman-Visigothic relations. The Visigoths had been Arians when they settled in Roman and Catholic Spain, and for most of the sixth century it was the policy of the Visigothic Kings, not to persecute the Catholics, but to keep the two elements in the population distinct and to foster Arian Christianity with its Gothic liturgical language as a Gothic religion. The official conversion of King Reccared to catholicism in 589, however, marked the point at which it was realized that if the ruler was to control the process by which Visigoths were becoming Catholics and were in fact marrying Romans, he must pursue a conscious policy of bringing Goths and Romans together; if the Visigoths were to retain their political power they must pursue a policy of political Romanization. From 589 the kings enjoyed the full support of the Catholic church which was of the greatest importance in the creation of a stable and unified kingdom. This was the political background to Spanish cultural influence in the seventh century.

The most important centres of learning in Spain at this period were Saragossa, Toledo and Seville, but of these only Seville exercised an influence of international importance. In fact the influence of Spain is predominantly the influence of Isidore of Seville. Seville was the chief city of the province of Betica, for whose cultural strength various factors were responsible. First, it had remained the most Roman of all provinces. Its buildings, its education, its institutions retained more of classical antiquity than any other province of Spain or of Europe. No Spanish province had fewer Visigothic settlers. Second, the Byzantine province in Southern Spain, established by Justinian in 554 and not abolished until 629, although it was unpopular with both Visigoths and Romans, helped to keep Spain in touch with the Greek culture of Byzantium, and Betica in particular profited from this. Third, the Lombard invasions in Italy had not affected the important centre of classical, Greek and theological learning founded by Cassiodorus at Vivarium in the extreme South, and there were clearly direct contacts by sea between Southern Italy and Southern Spain. Fourth, and perhaps most important, it was mainly Betica which received the North African refugees who were fleeing the persecutions of the Arian Vandals or (after the mid-sixth century) the Moorish raids which the incompetent Byzantine government was powerless to check. This link helps to explain Isidore's grasp of the traditional classical culture and his learning in African Christian writers like Tertullian and above all Augustine of Hippo. The writings of Isidore—on History, on Biblical Exegesis, on Liturgy and Canon Law, and especially on the Liberal Arts, were a grand attempt to lay the foundation of learning and culture which would give a coherent, Roman civilization to the new, united, Gothic Spain, for which he felt a wholehearted patriotism. These writings represent the unique position of Betica in the first half of the seventh century, on account of its political stability and its geographical advantages, to salvage for the medieval world the benefits of Classical Antiquity.

Isidore's most influential work, the *Etymologies*, was so called because it took as its starting point the origins of words. But a word and its origins, once rightly understood, opened a window on the fundamental nature and essence of a thing. Words were a means to perceive reality. They were an essential part of the study of grammar, and grammar, to Isidore, was a great deal more than a means of correct expression; 'it was also an instrument of intellectual research, determining a certain form of culture.'[31] So in his encyclopaedia of useful knowledge, which this work was intended to be, Isidore devoted his first and longest book to a survey of grammar. Then, in further books, he dealt with the other subjects of the liberal arts; and these were followed by more books on the Scriptures, on God, on the Church, on man; and then yet more on those aspects of Natural History which were traditionally taught with Grammar so that a student could comment on the meaning of a text in all its various aspects. To compile the 20 books of his own encyclopaedia, Isidore ransacked the encyclopaedias current in his day, like those of Martianus Capella and Cassiodorus, and also the Bible, the Fathers and the classics. But he relied especially, as one can see from the internal criticism of the *Etymologies* by scholars, on a mass of ephemeral literature which has largely disappeared—extracts, extracts of extracts, commentaries, introductory pamphlets to particular authors, doxographic manuals which collected the opinions of various writers on various subjects. Isidore did not read Greek, and he had no real grasp of any philosophical structure, but he helped to save the fragmentary remains of Greek learning in the West by his use of translated Greek manuals and translations of Origen and John Chrysostom. All this material was sifted, extracted and digested by a team of industrious workers at Seville, carefully supervised by a bishop too involved in state and diocesan affairs to have produced such a work single-handed.[32] The *Etymologies* made its mark because it was a great salvaging operation, and because it was a lucid and systematic exposition of the basic learning considered necessary for clerical life and biblical studies.

It may be that on the crest of the Isidoran wave, much came to Aldhelm which was not specifically Spanish. His knowledge of African writers, for instance, may owe something to it. Again, besides his use of classical grammarians like Donatus and perhaps Irish ones also, he was indebted for some of his grammar to a sixth-century grammarian called Audax, a figure so obscure that to the question of who he was, Julian of Toledo could only reply *grammaticus est*. Audax first appears in the contest of grammatical studies at Seville and Toledo in the seventh century; and indeed, to keep his grammar beside one while reading Aldhelm helps to make many things clear in the latter.[33] Source clarifies derivative.

Aldhelm's hundred Latin riddles, the idea for which was taken from the hundred riddles of the obscure Symphosius, have been enigmas in more senses than one. This can be seen from the way in which a recent and excellent survey of early Anglo-Saxon studies refers baldly to 'the curious riddles, cryptograms and acrostics which are to us so strange a feature of the writings of Aldhelm.'[34] Aldhelm's riddles, though varying considerably in length (unlike those of Symphosius which are each of three lines), are all (like those of Symphosius) in verse. The following is a translated example:[35]

> Once I was water, full of scaly fish;
> But, by a new decision fate has changed
> My nature: having suffered fiery pangs,
> 'I now gleam white, like ashes or bright snow.

This is salt. With these riddles Aldhelm gave the lead in an attractive genre; it became very much to the taste of the Anglo-Saxons, whether in Latin or the vernacular. It may be that riddling had always been a popular game, and that the alliterative circumlocutions of which the Anglo-Saxons were fond, like fish-flood for sea on the inscription of the Franks Casket, are a sign of it. But Aldhelm's riddles must be understood primarily in the context of a literary culture.

The first point to notice about them is their incorporation into a treatise on poetic metre. In fact their composition probably preceded that of the treatise, but their place in it is nonetheless significant.[36] This is what Aldhelm himself said about them:[37]

> Wherefore our solicitude, fired in its exertion by the examples of these men (i.e. those who had used riddles or enigmas to illustrate their points) and stimulated by their ingenuity and invention, has striven to compose ten tens or twenty fives, that is one hundred enigmatical representations. And just as in a grammar-school the first beginnings of intelligence are exercised so that progress can be made to work of greater substance, so when there is in these modest beginnings no little grasp of the rules of metrical definition and the tripartite differentiation of verses can be correctly kept in the line of scansion, then the aforesaid collection of enigmas can be recited, beginning with those consisting of four lines of verse, and going on, as the occasion presents itself, with those of five, six or even seven and more lines. I have taken care always to place in these lines, according to the discipline of poetic tradition, colons or commas

either penthemer or hepthemer after two or three feet (i.e. after five or seven half feet). For if dactylic hexametres lack a fixed and equal balance, they totter along in slippery steps.

In short, Aldhelm intended his riddles to be illustrations of poetic metre.

The second point is the importance attached to the enigma or riddle itself in grammatical studies. It was one of the figures of speech called tropes, which helped to clothe the otherwise bald and jejune expression of what was written. Isidore devotes a substantial passage in his Etymologies to tropes, in the course of which he explains the difference between allegory and enigma. Allegory, he says, has a double meaning or force, one thing being said and another figuratively meant; whereas an enigma or riddle has only one meaning, but an obscure one adumbrated through certain images.[38]

Aldhelm had the further aim, by illustrating metres with riddles, to convey, at the same time and in an attractive manner, knowledge about creation: 'from various qualities of created things, heavenly and earthly, I have extracted matter now of a grand, now of a simple nature.'[39] The subjects of some of his riddles were the things of everyday life in Anglo-Saxon England, such as salt, bellows, bubbles, the tall lighthouse; but it is very easy to exaggerate this side of the matter. The main feature of Aldhelm's riddle subjects is the fact that more than half of them are treated in Isidore's Etymologies. And indeed, contrary to the implication of some modern authors, subjects like peacock, the Pliades, silkworm and particularly unicorn, could hardly have had much to do with Aldhelm's own observations of nature; nor is it probable that he had himself seen a salamander quench the flames amidst which it was placed. The salamander riddle is, in fact, a good example of the similarity in matter between Isidore and Aldhelm. Aldhelm's riddle goes:[40]

Living in midst of flames I feel no heat,
And laugh to scorn the dangers of my pyre.
No crackling fire nor glowing ember's spark
Consumes me, for their hot, bright flames grow cool.

Isidore, on the salamander, explains that it is a poisonous creature, which, if it creeps on to a tree infects all the fruit with a venom lethal to those who eat it, and even the water of a pool into which it has fallen becomes deadly poison. He continues, 'it fights against fire and alone amongst the animals extinguishes flames, for it lives in their midst without being harmed or consumed; and not only because it cannot be burnt but also because it extinguishes the fire.'[41] Now this notion of the salamander's resistance to heat was very common and we do not purport to prove that Aldhelm must have had it from Isidore, although there are enough other coincidences of the same kind to make it likely. Certainly some of his subjects came from Pliny's *Natural History* rather than from the *Etymologies*, such as purple-mussel and yarrow, and from somewhere other than these two sources he got the idea that a locust's heart was under its knees. The main point, however, is that whatever the source of subject matter, the riddles were an exercise in encyclopaedic learning of the kind which Isidore expounded.

Here again, as in their other purpose of illustrating poetic metres, they were solidly based on grammar. For, as we have already said, this kind of encyclopaedic knowledge was used together with grammar in order to enable a student to comment on a text in all its aspects.[42] Just as Natural History was an extension of grammar in the *Etymologies*, so were the riddles a similar extension as Aldhelm used them in his treatise on metre.

THEODORE, BEDE, AND THE BIBLE

During the early centuries of Christianity there developed two main kinds of approach to the interpretation of the Bible, by no means exclusive of each other but giving rise to different emphases; one was especially associated with Antioch, the other with Alexandria. The earliest exponents of both approaches naturally wrote in Greek. The Antiochene approach tended to be literal, that is to expound what was actually written in terms of its literal sense, its history and geography and so forth.[43] One of the most famous representatives of this school was Theodore, bishop of Mopsuestia (c. 350–420), a city in South-East Asia Minor not far from Antioch and only some 40 miles from Tarsus, the home town of Theodore, archbishop of Canterbury. The school of Alexandria, its theological tradition dominated by Origen, developed a greater interest in the allegorical approach, in which the text of the Bible was treated as a collection of signs pointing to deeper spiritual truths for those who had mastered the

techniques of interpreting them. The 'dislocation of human consciousness,' of which mankind was the victim as a result of
original sin and the Fall, had lost him the direct perception of
Divine Truth, but God had granted to those who would reflect
and meditate to see something of His mysteries through the
veil, as it were, of the Bible.[44]

The allegorical interpretation came to hold a commanding
position in biblical studies, so that examples of it can be cited
from almost anywhere. It was not only something regarded of
use and relevance to academic theologians, but also something
applicable to Christian life and society altogether. Gregory the
Great, for instance, who wrote largely allegorical commentaries on
Ezechiel and Job had occasion to reprove Bishop Natalis of
Salona for his habit of feasting, and this bishop was impertinent
enough to defend his vice from Scripture. Had not Abraham, he
said, received three angels while he was feasting? Had not Isaac
blessed his son while satiated? In his reply Gregory began by
observing that he had yet to hear that angels had visited *Natalis*
at the banquet table. He went on to explain that things done in
history had an allegorical significance. If Abraham had received
three angels that was to say that he had saluted in them the
Holy Trinity; if Isaac had blessed his son while satiated that
was to say that his senses had been extended into the power of
prophecy because he was filled with divine food.[45] It could be
objected to this method of interpretation that it was arbitrary and
subjective to the point of fancifulness. But it had quite clearly
defined rules, and the cardinal rule was that any interpretation
was correct if it contributed to 'the reign of charity'. After all,
the Bible was the chief source of meditation for monks in particular and for Christians in general, and yet the Old Testament, at
least, was full of matter which on the surface, or according to the
literal sense, was either quite useless for this purpose or even
positively disedifying. As they stood, the accounts of Noah's
drunkenness or Isaac's banqueting, not to speak of the eroticism
of the Song of Songs, were scarcely conducive to godly thoughts
or virtuous behaviour, and it was therefore necessary to look for
figurative interpretations of them until they were. But once such
interpretations were found, what did it matter if there were many
different ones for the same passage? Could not necklaces, rings
and bracelets all be made from the same gold?[46]

When we turn to early Anglo-Saxon England we find a great

representative of the Antiochene school in Archbishop Theodore. Theodore, who certainly expounded the Bible as well as the liberal arts at Canterbury started with one great advantage. He could transmit in Latin to his pupils his knowledge of Greek authors. By the seventh century there was very little reading knowledge of Greek to be found in the West.[47] Many scholars had a smattering of Greek words or grammatical terms, but after the fourth century there were few who any longer had the capacity to absorb the thought of Greek writings. The chief exceptions to this rule were the scholars of the so-called Ostrogothic Renaissance in sixth-century Italy, Boethius and Cassiodorus. But the works of Boethius were practically unknown to the early Anglo-Saxons; and as to Cassiodorus, although Biscop had obtained from somewhere his text of the Bible and Bede knew his commentary on the Psalms, neither seem to have known his *Institutiones* which would have given them a guide to the Greek literature at Vivarium.[48] Bede's grappling with the Greek text of the Acts of the Apostles, which he is known to have possessed, was an impressive feat,[49] but we must not imagine that his grasp of the true meaning of certain words in this book gave him the entrée to Greek philosophy and culture. The general ignorance of Greek, therefore, was the measure of Theodore's advantage in being fluent in it. So far as the Bible was concerned, the tradition of Alexandrian, allegorical commentary had been securely planted in the Latin world. The contribution of particular value which Theodore could have made at Canterbury was the kind of rich, literal exegesis which Theodore of Mopsuestia's commentary on the Psalms, for instance, had displayed. Theodore of Mopsuestia believed that all the psalms had been composed by David, but that David had spoken prophetically 'in the persons' of later men, like Hezekiah or even Christ himself. He had therefore applied the literal or historical interpretation not only to David's time, but also to the situations which were the subjects of prophecy, to Hezekiah and the Assyrians, or to the sufferings of Christ. And in addition he had frequently pointed the moral application of a passage.[50]

This was the kind of exegesis which Theodore could have taught at Canterbury. Fifty years ago it might well have been thought impossible to write a single sentence on Theodore's methods of scriptural commentary, except for this kind of speculation about what they could have been. Now, however, it is possible to piece together a few fragments of evidence, which show quite clearly his Antiochene bent, albeit a somewhat different Antiochenism from that of Theodore of Mopsuestia on the Psalms. The most important discovery in this field was published by Professor Bischoff in 1954. He found, in a manuscript of the eleventh century now in the Ambrosian Library at Milan, glosses on the Pentateuch and the Gospels which he could identify as fragments of Theodore's commentaries.[51] These glosses showed the kind of learned and literal exposition in which Theodore specialized, making use of his knowledge of the Near East. Where the Book of Numbers (XI,5), for instance, spoke of *pepones*, he explained that these were melons which grew to so great a size in Edessa that a camel could hardly carry two. Where the Book of Leviticus (also, by chance, XI,5) spoke of the *choerogryllus*, he explained that this was a creature like a pig, but smaller, and that it inhabited the mountain crevasses of Sinai. This knowledge was beyond the ken of Isidore.

Another scholar, Paul Lehmann, argued convincingly in 1919 that in the so-called *Liber Quaestionum*, doubtfully attributed to Bede, at least those questions which dealt with difficult points of biblical exegesis (as distinct from the doctrinal ones) were genuinely his work.[52] This gave another piece of evidence for Theodore's teaching at Canterbury, and of a particularly interesting kind. For we have here not only the same kind of learned geography as in the Milan glosses, but also the fact that a verbal report of the teaching had reached Bede. This is what Bede wrote:[53]

The same apostle (Paul) said, 'a night and a day I was in the depth of the sea' (2 Cor. XI,25). I have heard certain men assert that Theodore of blessed memory, a very learned man and once archbishop of the English people, expounded the saying thus: that there was in Cyzicus (Asia Minor) a certain very deep pit, dug for the punishment of criminals, which on account of its immense depth was called *the depth of the sea*. It was the filth and darkness of this which Paul bore, amongst other things, for Christ.

We come now to something which is a more hypothetical matter as to whether or not it is yet another piece of evidence for Theodore's scriptural teaching; but the chances of its being so seem strong enough to make it worth mentioning. It is a passage in Aldhelm's treatise on metre. When Aldhelm dealt with the 28 metrical feet, he gave for each, as we have said, many words as examples. In the middle of his list for the spondee comes *carex* (a sharp kind of rush), whose ablative, *carice*, Aldhelm was careful to distinguish from the word *carica*:[54]

> For *carica* (he says) is the name of the fruit from the fig-tree, whence the lumps of *caricae* are prepared from fresh figs. The famous hermit living a solitary life on the border between the Syrians and the Saracens according to strict laws of abstinence, who sustained and nourished his weary limbs and wasted groin with five figs (a day), is inappropriately said by some to have eaten five rushes contrary to nature. It is as much in accordance with human nature to be fed on ripened figs as it is with the nature of the brute buffaloes and chamois in those parts to be fed on rushes.

This passage is the only digression of its kind in the whole treatise and is entirely irrelevant to the illustration of what a spondee is. Aldhelm quite simply could not resist imparting a juicy morsel of information at this point. If it really is a fragment of Theodore's biblical exposition, this is the most extraordinary place in which to tumble on it; but it is hard to see what else it could be. First of all, though Aldhelm did not mention Scripture in his letter about his studies at Canterbury, it is almost inconceivable that he never came across Theodore's biblical scholarship. Second, the information in the passage is more likely to be derived from Theodore than from any other source. Aldhelm could not have learnt about the eating habits of the buffaloes and the chamois from Isidore, but they could easily have formed part of Theodore's regional knowledge. He could not have learnt about the hermit living on the border between the Syrians and the Saracens from Cassian, who might have been thought a likely source and whose writings Aldhelm knew, at least in part.[55] But again this hermit could easily have come within Theodore's knowledge. Had he lived before the Muslim conquests of the 630s the border between Syrians and Saracens would have been the Syrian desert, some distance from Tarsus and Cilicia; and yet tales of ascetic hermits were told widely in Eastern monastic circles. Third, and most important, there could have been many creatures which ate rushes in the Near East, but Aldhelm names just two, the *bubalus* (buffaloe) and the *tragelaphus* (chamois), which are mentioned in the Vulgate version of Deuteronomy XIV,5 among the animals whose meat was clean and might be eaten. We know that Theodore commented on the Pentateuch, one of whose books was Deuteronomy. If there is no comment on this passage in the Milan manuscript, that is only to say (what is obvious) that the complete lectures of Theodore were not preserved in writing. We know from his Penitential that he was interested in the question of clean and unclean meat.[56] Aldhelm's passage looks as if it had its origins in a very characteristically Theodoran gloss on the Deuteronomy animals.

It is not surprising that we have to scrape around for evidence of Theodore's scriptural teaching whereas most of Bede's commentaries, with their high proportion of allegorical content, survive in tens of manuscripts. The Antiochene school of interpretation did not remain popular, even throughout the Dark Ages. Little as we have, however, we can dimly perceive from it the figure of one of the greatest teachers in English History. His pupils wrote up parts of his commentaries, they talked about his lectures, they recorded in a penitential his judgements and his observations about the differences between Greek and Latin church discipline. Rightly did Bede emphasize his work in education. Much can and has been said about the way in which the Bible was domiciled to Anglo-Saxon society. The people of Israel could be understood as God's war-band; their kings (like those of the Anglo-Saxons) were both warriors and patrons of the Temple; the revenge of God on their enemies could be seen as a successful blood-feud. *The Dream of the Rood* is a superb example of the poetic presentation of a biblical subject in Anglo-Saxon social terms; here the relation between Christ and his Cross is depicted as that between a bold young warrior and his loyal gesith or thegn. But Theodore went one better. Albeit so little of his work survived, while he himself taught or remained a living memory he managed in a sense to domicile Anglo-Saxons to the Bible. To these people with their cows and sheep, their barley and lentils, this vigorous old man presented, at first-hand, arresting pictures of exotic animals and foods, of deserts and mountain crevasses, of cities with strange names operating unheard of punishments. Some, at least, he succeeded in transporting in their imaginations to the Near East; these were able to see that it was possible for the world of the Bible to take on a vivid reality in their minds.

*   *   *

Bede's writings range over most of the chief branches of European learning in his day. They cover grammar and rhetoric, chronology and astronomy, history and hagiography. Bede had not much to write on philosophy. He did not write works of a purely speculative and doctrinal character as, for instance, Augustine had done. With the exception of the *De Trinitate* Augustine's works of this kind were mostly polemics against heresy.[57] Bede found heresy as detestable as Augustine had done, remarkably so for a man who lived in a country at that time absolutely untroubled by it; but in his case, unlike Augustine's, this detestation did not issue in philosophical treatises. It was reserved for his scriptural commentaries. To Bede the interpretation of the Bible verse by verse was the most fundamental of all intellectual activities; the commentaries which he wrote on an astonishingly large number of Biblical books account for the greatest part of his stupendous output, almost all of which belongs to the last 30 years of his life. He considered the literal interpretation to be very important for giving substance and interest to the text, especially in the case of the New Testament, which needed less allegorical interpretation to make it conducive to 'the reign of charity'. This led him to an extensive use of works such as Isidore's *Etymologies,* Pliny's *Natural History,* and also Jerome *On Hebrew Names* and Adamnan's *De Locis Sanctis* for information about Palestinian geography.[58] But in all his commentaries, whether on the Old or New Testaments, it is the allegorical method which is dominant.

Bede made no virtue of originality, although most of his works bear his own quite distinctive stamp. His great achievement was to colonize the vast tracts of the fathers, particularly Ambrose, Jerome, Augustine and Gregory the Great, for the benefit of Anglo-Saxon monastic schools and, as it turned out, for countless readers in Carolingian Europe.[59] The commentary on Luke and the exchange of letters between himself and Bishop Acca of Hexham in connection with it provide a good example of his purpose. In his letter inviting Bede to write the commentary Acca expressed his awareness that other fathers had already written about Luke, pre-eminent amongst them Ambrose. But Ambrose, he said, was too lofty for the rude intellects of their own day to cope with; and, moreover, there were certain things which he had not troubled to discuss because he considered them too obvious. In his reply, Bede described how he had put together matter derived from Ambrose, Augustine, Gregory and Jerome and other fathers, either by direct quotation, or in his own words for the sake of brevity. And so that the reader might see what came from which author, and lest he should speak as though the sayings of greater men were his own, he had placed the first letters of the particular father's name in the margin. He adjured future scribes to observe these signs.[60] Some did, as we know from surviving manuscripts.[61]

These four great fathers of the Latin Church were by no means the limit to Bede's reading on Scripture. For his work on the Apocalypse, for instance, it has been shown that he used a stern and enthusiastic African Donatist called Tyconius, who interpreted the book in the pattern of a struggle between the true Church, the City of God, on the one hand, and the City of the Devil on the other.[62] And for his exposition of the Book of Proverbs he made extensive use of a rather rare fifth-century commentary by Bishop Salonius of Vienne.[63]

Bede differed from Theodore in standing in the full stream of the allegorical tradition; he was heir to the central Latin tradition of scriptural exegesis. But he shared Theodore's interest in science and natural history. This was reflected partly in his taste for observation, partly in his attempt to build up a coherent system of the universe in his *De Rerum Natura*. In this work he used that of Isidore with the same title, and yet Bede's stature as a scientist owed something to his perception of Isidore's limitations and to his having at least a portion of Pliny's *Natural History*.[64] What concerns us here, however, is that natural history was highly relevant to the allegorical as well as to the literal interpretation of scripture. Many animals, plants and other natural objects were mentioned in the Bible, and only with factual knowledge about them could they be made to yield their spiritual mysteries. The point was expressed by Augustine of Hippo when he mapped out that masterly programme of studies, which he regarded as preliminary to the study of the Bible, in his *De Doctrina Christiana*:[65]

An ignorance of things makes figurative expressions obscure when we are ignorant of the natures of animals, or stones, or plants, or other things which are often used in the Scriptures for purposes of constructing similitudes. Thus the well-known fact that a serpent exposes its whole body in order to protect its head from those attacking it illustrates the sense of the

Lord's admonition that we be wise like serpents. That is, for
the sake of our head, which is Christ, we should offer our
bodies to persecutors lest the Christian faith be in a manner
killed in us, and in an effort to save our bodies we deny God.
It is also said that the serpent, having forced its way through
narrow openings, sheds its skin and renews its vigour. How well
this conforms to our imitation of the wisdom of the serpent
when we shed the 'old man', as the Apostle says, and put on
the 'new'; and we shed it in narrow places, for the Lord directs
us, 'Enter ye in at the narrow gate.' Just as a knowledge of the
nature of serpents illuminates the many similitudes which
Scripture frequently makes with that animal, an ignorance of
many other animals which are also used for comparisons is a
great impediment to understanding. The same thing is true of
stones, or of herbs or of other things that take root. For a
knowledge of the carbuncle which shines in the darkness also
illuminates many obscure places in books where it is used for
similitudes, and an ignorance of beryl or of diamonds frequently
closes the doors of understanding. In the same way it is not
easy to grasp that the twig of olive which the dove brought
when it returned to the ark signifies perpetual peace unless we
know that the soft surface of oil is not readily corrupted by
an alien liquid and that the olive tree is perennially in leaf.
Moreover, there are many who because of an ignorance of
hyssop—being unaware of its power either to purify the lungs
or, as it is said, to penetrate its roots to the rocks in spite of the
fact that it is a small and humble plant—are not able at all to
understand why it is said, 'Thou shalt sprinkle me with hyssop,
and I shall be cleansed.'

Augustine was in fact calling for an encyclopaedia of just the
kind which Isidore, salvaging some of the natural history of the
ancient world, compiled for this purpose in his *Etymologies*.
Bede knew the *De Doctrina Christiana*,[66] and his commentaries
are full of natural history, much of it derived from Isidore and
used in Augustine's way. In his work on the Song of Songs, for
instance, on which he commented chapter by chapter and verse
by verse, as in his other scriptural treatises, the following is the
first part of his comment on that verse where the bride is
describing her beloved—'his belly as of ivory, set with sapphires'.
(V,14):[67]

The stomach occupies a very vulnerable position in our body, both because it is strikingly lacking in protective bones, and because the groin, to which every wound is dangerous, is contained within it. Now ivory is the bone of the elephant, which is said to be an animal of outstanding chastity and very cool blood. Whence its death is frequently brought about by the attacks of a dragon, which desires to cool its burning wounds by drinking the blood of an elephant. The sapphire is a stone whose colour is attested by Holy Writ where it says, 'And they saw the God of Israel: and under his feet was a pavement as if made of sapphires, bright as the heavens.' The stomach of the beloved, therefore, implies his human frailty, in which he is like us. The ivory shows the beauty of his chastity, by which (while remaining in the flesh) he is immune from the corruptions of sins. The sapphires express the sublimity of his heavenly virtues, by which he is radiant in the flesh.

The whole tradition of commentary on the Song of Songs before Bede, rich amongst the Greeks and poor amongst the Latins, had been to interpret it allegorically in the pattern of Christ's relations with the Church. It was obvious, therefore, that Bede would interpret the beloved here as Christ. On the whole, however, he was unusually independent in this work. He did not know Origen's commentary, which surpassed his own in subtlety;[68] he did know Aponius, his chief predecessor amongst Latin commentators. Between Bede and Aponius there are some points of contact, but the drift of their interpretations is usually very different (certainly it is at this point), and Bede is invariably the more lucid and succinct.[69] The passage which we have quoted, therefore, is almost certainly not derivative but is original. Bede's information comes mainly from Pliny rather than Isidore in this case, but there is a suggestion of Isidore in Bede's observation on the chastity of elephants. Pliny spoke only of their modesty which caused them to copulate in secret, and he also said that they could be very wild in sexual intercourse. Whereas Isidore said quite clearly that they were averse to it (aversi coeunt).[70] Bede's passage might raise a smile, with its strange lore and its apparently fanciful allegories, and yet, considering its purpose to edify, it is difficult to see how a word of it could have been bettered. It expounds certain points of natural history, probably after comparison of two sources; it then draws what are made to appear the obvious conclusions with absolute clarity and very few words; and the end product is a thought of considerable beauty.

ALDHELM AND BEDE

It will by now be apparent that, for all Bede's admiration of Aldhelm, these two great teachers of the Anglo-Saxon race had radically different ideas of their function as scholars. Bede's life work was mainly devoted to Scripture; Aldhelm's, to judge by his surviving works, turned much more on the liberal arts, especially grammar and rhetoric. On the surface it might look as if there was after all not so much difference between them. One might wonder, in the first place, how many of Aldhelm's works were lost. Then it might be pointed out that Bede, like Aldhelm, wrote a treatise on poetic metre; and conversely that for Aldhelm, as for Bede, the study of Scripture provided the only justification for the preliminary study of grammar. As to the possibility of Aldhelm's writings being lost, there is no reason to believe that any substantial part of his output suffered this fate. There are references in letters of the period to some sermons and poems written by him which have not survived, and William of Malmesbury mentions some Anglo-Saxon poems, which have also disappeared. Aldhelm refers occasionally to other works of his own which are still extant, but to nothing which is now lost. Moreover, his works circulated quite widely on the Continent after his death (although he enjoyed nothing comparable to the success of Bede), and there are several references in monastic library catalogues to manuscripts of his writings: none are to works no longer extant.[71] Here is a net of evidence, then, through which only the odd work or two, at most, would have been likely to slip.

With regard to Aldhelm's belief that the only justification for the study of grammar was as a preliminary to the study of Scripture, there is no doubt about this. While he was bishop of Sherborne (705–09) he wrote a letter to a pupil called Ethelwald, employing the clear and unaffected Latin which its author could write when he had to be understood, and this says:[72]

If you work hard at secular learning do it for this purpose: whereas the whole or almost the whole text of the divine law obeys the rules of grammar, you will only understand easily

the most profound and sacred meanings of divine eloquence in
your reading in so far as you have fully learnt those rules
beforehand.

It is proper to stress the weight which Bede gave to grammar,
and the supreme motivation for study which Aldhelm believed to
lie in Scripture although he himself never wrote a scriptural
commentary. But we cannot ignore the important difference of
emphasis between them; Bede, following Gregory the Great, was
much the stricter about the relation of grammar to theology.
First of all, when Bede wrote about metre he used the Christian
poets and avoided the pagan ones for his illustrations as a matter
of principle. Occasionally he adopted a pagan quotation if he had
found it in a Christian source like Isidore, but generally he
preferred to stick to writers like Ambrose, Sedulius, Arator and
Fortunatus. Of certain metres he said that they could be found in
Porphyry, 'but as they are pagan we may not touch them.'[73]
Aldhelm, on the other hand, was completely untroubled by such
considerations, in this being like Isidore. His pages are stiff with
quotations from Vergil.[74] Second, and still more significant, is the
stage in their careers at which Bede and Aldhelm respectively
wrote their treatises on metre. Bede wrote his as a deacon, for he
addressed his 'fellow deacon, Cuthbert' at the end of it.[75] When
he was about 30 he was ordained a priest and that clearly marked
the point at which he felt that he should graduate to scriptural
commentaries; to him a priest's business was with Holy Writ.
But Aldhelm's treatise, which was in any case a far more elaborate
affair than Bede's, was written when its author could not have been
younger than in his late forties or his fifties and when he had
been a priest for over ten years.[76]

Now this difference did not at all arise from one scholar's
having more sense of the social and religious purpose of learning
than the other. It would be entirely wrong, for instance, to imagine
that Bede was working for the salvation of souls while Aldhelm
was just an arid pedant. Both men showed a deep concern for
the needs of the society in which they lived and worked. This
concern is palpable on almost every page which Bede wrote, but
how could it be otherwise with Aldhelm, when we know that
he used to take his lyre down to a bridge over the river at
Malmesbury and sing to the passing crowds in order to win them
to church?[77] If we want to understand the difference, we must

consider the different traditions and circumstances under whose influence each worked.

Once again Aldhelm can best be understood with reference to Isidore. Visigothic Spain, during the long period of Isidore's episcopate, was a kingdom where optimism and confidence reigned. The kings had been converted to catholicism and there was a fruitful rapprochement between Goths and Romans. Isidore was a busy bishop to whom pedantic learning would have had no interest. He saw his task as the attempt to lay a broad basis of Roman culture in the Visigothic kingdom, for the sake of its Church and for the sake of its government, and he worked with the feeling that there was time to do this expansively. Naturally an important aspect of the use of this culture must have seemed to any bishop, particularly to one who knew Augustine's writings as well as Isidore did, its enabling monks and clergy to understand the Bible. But Isidore was more anxious to lay the basis properly than to move on hastily to such applications. His problem, as Professor Fontaine has said, 'was not to put pagan culture at the service of Christian knowledge, nor even to orientate this culture towards an understanding of the sacred texts; it was to reconstitute from diverse sources the unity of a truth which ... possessed in itself a validity independent of all context.'[78] Certainly a scholar who could cite Vergil, Varro, Nigidius and Christ, in that order, as authorities on the prognostication of rain, felt no great qualms about the juxtaposition of pagan and Christian learning in order to achieve his basic purpose.[79] Whether a piece of knowledge was derived from a Christian or a pagan source was irrelevant to him.

It was something of all this that Aldhelm had caught. He, too, lived in a situation of political advance and optimism, for his was the period when Wessex was fighting successful wars against the British, when it was ruled by strong kings, and when the Laws of King Ine marked an important step forward in sophisticated legislation. He, too, was a busy man of affairs both as abbot and as bishop. He, too, tried to build a useful culture on an expansive basis.

Bede, on the other hand, lived and worked in a situation of political instability. Between the death of King Alfrith in 705 and the accession of King Eadbert in 737 after Bede's death, Northumbria had five kings, some of them pious but all of them weak. The vertiginous politics of Northumbria, however, would not have been the side of the matter which most impressed itself on Bede's mind. For him, the relation of Christian culture to society presented a much deeper problem. It may seem strange to say it of an unworldly monk, working quietly away in the cell of his monastery, but Bede worked with a sense of tearing hurry. He had to act, at least until later days, as his own dictator and scribe, and could not produce his works fast enough. This haste constantly comes to the surface. In his commentary on Genesis, he interpreted the passage about the dove, which returned to Noah's ark with the olive branch in the evening, as referring to those men of love outside the Church, who are recalled to it in the last age by the reconciliation of spiritual men, or by the mouth of the dove, as if in the evening (quasi ad vesperam).[80] To Bede it already was evening. The end might come at any moment; there was no time to be lost. His commentaries speak often of those who are 'snatched' from the devil.[81] When he was writing on the book of Esras, his eye caught the description of Esras as scriba velox, a scribe quick or ready in the law of Moses.[82] Esras was called scriba velox, he says, because he rewrote not just the law but the whole of sacred scripture, and the Hebrews said he had invented easier letters which could be more quickly written— exactly a description of what insular minuscule was. Nowhere is the feeling of urgency more clearly seen than in the letter describing Bede's death, written by Cuthbert, not the Lindisfarne saint but the later abbot of Wearmouth and Jarrow.[83] On the day before he died he was still cheerfully teaching his pupils in the monastery, saying from time to time, 'Learn speedily, I know not how long I shall be with you, or whether my Maker will remove me shortly.' His last piece of work was a translation of St. John's Gospel into Anglo-Saxon; it is a clear example of the pastoral motivation which informed his whole activity. On the day of his death, the Vigil of the Ascension (735), the boy Wilbert reminded him that there was still one chapter left to dictate, but he added, 'it seems hard for thee to be questioned further.' Bede replied, 'it is easy, take thy pen, and mend it and write quickly.' At the ninth hour he wanted to distribute his few belongings to his fellow priests, and he told Cuthbert himself to run quickly and fetch them, which he did in great agitation. In the evening, after a day of joy, Wilbert said to him again, 'There is still one sentence, dear Master, which is not written down':

And he said, 'Well, then, write it.' And after a little space the boy said, 'Now it is finished.' And he answered, 'Well, thou hast spoken truth; it is finished. Take my head in thy hands, for it much delights me to sit opposite my holy place where I used to pray, that so sitting I may call upon my Father.' And thus upon the floor of his cell singing 'Glory be to the Father, and to the Son, and to the Holy Ghost' and the rest, he breathed his last breath.

Bede was influenced by many of the fathers, but he was in a special way the spiritual child of Gregory the Great. One example of this, amongst the many, is the seventh book of his commentary on the Song of Songs. Now Gregory had started a commentary on this book, but only a small fragment was extant. And so Bede, not to be denied the opportunity of sitting at his master's feet, so to speak, combed through the whole corpus of Gregory's other writings to find stray comments on the Song of Songs, and it is this collection of comments which occupies his entire seventh book.[84] Gregory had the same sense of haste that is seen in Bede, derived from the same combination of pastoral zeal and the feeling that the world was politically, morally and physically collapsing about his ears. Isidore had very easy remedies for 'unreasonable sadness', brought on by anxiety and despair; there were the consolations of friendship, the reading of Scripture, the hope of eternal reward, and so on. Gregory could but struggle on from moment to moment. As M. Delehaye has said, 'there are fewer groans and sighs with Isidore than with Gregory.'[85] It is not surprising that Gregory's main scriptural works are commentaries on Ezechiel and Job, two Biblical books in which the action of God is seen at its most cataclysmic.

What, then, was the urgent task to which Bede devoted his scholarship? It was nothing less than the establishment of the Church, and particularly its priesthood, on earth. From the books or personalities or subjects of the Bible on which he chose to comment, the scriptural basis of this task could be clearly discerned; these things, rightly understood, provided abundant food for meditation on its nature and the means of its fulfilment. The Song of Songs, for instance, was regarded as an allegory of the relations between Christ and the Church; Samuel was the great judge and priest of Israel who anointed kings; Solomon's Temple and Tabernacle were obvious allegories for the building up of the Church; the books of Esras and Nehemiah, dealing with the re-establishment of Israel and the rebuilding of the Temple after the return from the Babylonian Captivity, called, as it were, the sinful sons of the Church to repentance. Penance for those who had fallen and reconciliation with the Church were constant themes with Bede. In his commentary on St. James's Epistle he made a major contribution to the doctrinal history of the sacrament of Extreme Unction, referring as it did to reconciliation with the Church before death. And he was careful to note in his life of St. Cuthbert that the saint had received the last sacraments as he was dying. Bede's great strength was in this sphere where doctrine and the practical life of the Christian met.[86]

Penance was necessary for all, but for none more than those who were set apart by their clerical order; it was essential for priests and deacons who had fallen through drunkenness or lust or pride. Bede did not forget the laity, the mules with which the Jews had returned from Babylon to Jerusalem.[87] They, too, with their slow wits and carnal minds, were a part of the Church, who by submitting themselves to spiritual masters and humbly carrying their load, might be snatched from diabolical captivity. There was indeed still much to be done to win men to the Faith, much even in the Northumbrian countryside, as Bede's letter to Archbishop Egbert of York explained. As to the foremost layman, the king himself, he had a vital part to play in establishing the Church; just as the return from the Babylonian Captivity had been led by Zorobabel and Josue, the one a king, the other a priest; just as Christ himself was both king and priest.[88] Generally, however, Bede's emphasis was on the position and role of the clergy. The importance of the teaching of bishops and priests in the rebuilding of the Temple was obvious enough, but if people were to be called from the spell of their vices to the vision of true peace, the ministry of the word exercised by deacons was also important.[89] The ecclesiastical hierarchy down to this grade was the dynamic force in salvation.

The transition from the ancient to the medieval world was not a smooth and regular one in Europe. The pendulum swung back and forth according to the particular pressures of time and place, and it is not easy to say whether Gregory or Isidore was the more 'medieval' figure. But so far as Anglo-Saxon England was concerned, Aldhelm lived just in time and in the right place to catch the last flickerings of Classical Antiquity, if we think in terms of general purpose and motivation in study. With Bede we have moved decisively into the Middle Ages.

13 Saints and Heroes

So far we have spoken of Anglo-Saxon Christianity as though it were composed mainly of elements derived from foreign Christian cultures. Little has been said of the contribution made by the native Germanic and pagan tradition. Indeed, Christian culture did not in all respects favour the survival of its traces. Clearly, pagan temples were reconsecrated as Christian churches, pagan charms and spells were adapted for Christian prayer, and pagan smiths and jewellers' shops turned their hand to Christian ornament. Anglo-Saxon kingship itself developed into a remarkable amalgam of Christian and pagan elements. By the ninth century kings underwent a Christian ceremony of consecration and anointing, but they continued to trace their genealogies back to Woden.[1] Kings gradually assumed a Christ-like character;[2] yet Christ Himself took on some of the qualities of the old Germanic heroes, so that Christ and his apostles, for instance, could be seen as a lord and his thegns.[3] The kings of the Old Testament also, fighting against the enemies of God, fitted well into the pagan mental framework of man's fight together with the gods against the evil giants. Christian kingship came to develop a lofty sense of public duty, which is grandly expressed in the closing scenes of *Beowulf*, and finds a small but significant echo in Bede's statement that King Edwin provided brass drinking-bowls at springs for the benefit of travellers.[4] But this was partly the assimilation of a much older and pagan concept of the king's peace and justice, the king's 'truth', the *fir flathemon* of the Irish. If the king judged without favour, said an old Irish tract much influenced by pagan concepts, protected strangers, wards and widows, restrained thieves and chastized adulterers, etc., there would be peace, a calm atmosphere, a serene sea and fertility of the earth.[5]

We shall not, however, devote this chapter to the popular game of looking for 'pagan survivals'. Rather we seek to show how something of a more general character came into Anglo-Saxon Christianity from the spirit of the pagan Heroic Age. For the ability of Christianity to come to terms with the values of the Heroic Age was a primary factor in its success among the Anglo-Saxons.

HEROIC SAGAS

The great figures of legend, pre-eminently those who took their origin in Scandinavia, were the common imaginative property of the whole at least of the Northern Germanic world in the Dark Ages—of the Scandinavians themselves, of the Continental Saxons and Frisians, and of the Anglo-Saxons. The Germanic peoples had issued from Scandinavia and its legendary heroes came to be a cultural bond between them. The evidence of their place in Anglo-Saxon imaginations is naturally scanty, since the surviving written records come from religious institutions, whose official policy (whatever the real inclinations of their members) was to scorn such pagan 'garrulities'. But the recitation of their deeds in royal and aristocratic halls must have played a great part in setting the values of war and policies.

Nor was it only through such recitations that they were familiar. The famous episodes of their sagas were depicted, perhaps often, on objects of value or daily use. In 1857 Sir Augustus Franks purchased a whalebone casket (9 inches x 7½ inches) from a Paris dealer.[6] This dealer had acquired it from a Professor Mathieu of Clermont-Ferrand, who obtained it from a middle-class family near Brioude. The family had used it as a workbox. It was established by A. S. Napier from a study of its runes that the box had been made in Northumbria between 650 and 750. The inscription on the front panel refers to the whale from whose bone the casket was made: 'the fish-flood lifted the whale's bones on to the mainland; the ocean became turbid where he swam aground on the shingle'. The event must have been a great one in the lives of the north-eastern coast-dwellers. Top and sides, the panels are carved with narrative scenes of great liveliness and variety, while at their corners are spritely little animals which appear to have a direct relation to creatures on the Coptic tomb-stones of Egypt. One of the side panels represents the mourning for the most famous of all ancient Germanic heroes, Sigurd (or Siegfried). It is dominated by the figure of his horse, Grani, the grey horse who stood with drooping head at the side of his dead lord.

The front panel depicts the legend of Wayland the Smith, the most famous representative of a craft to which magical powers were often attributed amongst the ancient Germans. He it was who fashioned Beowulf's corselet so that it resisted the dagger of a giantess, whose deeds were celebrated in the early poem *Deor*, and who gave the name of his smithy to a copse of trees strewn with boulders on the top of the Berkshire downs. He was lamed by the orders of King Nidud so that the king would be able to retain his magical services for ever. On the casket Wayland is seen taking his revenge. Already he is working in his smithy on the skulls of Nidud's two sons:[7]

> The skulls where once their hair had grown
> He set in silver fine,
> And gave them both to King Nidud
> As goblets for his wine.

The king's daughter, Bodvild, whom Wayland violated, is seen entering the smithy with her maid. She has a ring to be repaired:

> He brought to her the strong brown ale,
> (His cunning was more deep)
> So that she sat in Volund's seat
> And there she fell asleep.

On the right is Aegil, the smith's brother, strangling birds in order to make a magic coat of their feathers so that Wayland might escape in flight from the king:

> Volund rose up into the sky,
> And loud, loud laughed he;
> Nidud the king remained below,
> Grieving bitterly.

The company which these panels keep is interesting. Two others on the casket represent the capture of Jerusalem by Titus and the story of Romulus and Remus, the kind of subjects which could have been found illustrated in world-chronicles of the period, or perhaps in volumes like the handsomely produced Cosmography which Abbot Ceolfrid of Jarrow sold to King

Alfrith. While on the same panel as the grisly Wayland is a rather pious representation of the Adoration of the Magi. (Fig. 13).

The Franks Casket, as it is called, must have been particularly valuable in its day; the raw material itself was a rarity. And yet even this precious object escaped oblivion or ruin by a hairs-breadth. The losses of artistic objects and historical evidence of this kind are incalculable. Occasionally, however, something is found which sheds a little extra light on the currency of these legends and heroes. An Anglo-Saxon cemetery at Burwell in Cambridgeshire, for instance, yielded a little bronze cylindrical workbox of the mid-seventh century, the lid of which appears to show Sigurd lying in the pit driving his sword into the dragon Fafnir as Fafnir crawled across it on his way to the water.[8]

Anglo-Saxon priests and monks shared the universal interest in heroic saga. The Synod of Cloveshoe (747) found it necessary to forbid priests from reciting the sacred texts in church with the tragic intonation of the secular poets. It was hardly to be expected that the deeds of ancient heroes or for that matter of more recent Northumbrian ones could leave cold the monks of Wearmouth, Northumbrian aristocrats as many of them were and strong-blooded ones at that,[9] or the monks of Hexham and Ripon whose founder's actions were remembered with more than a flavour of heroic saga about them,[10] or the monks of Lindisfarne, who lived near the royal hall of Bamburgh with its stirring memories of the early days of the Bernician dynasty. It may even be doubted whether they were foreign to the lay servants and cowherds of Whitby as they passed the lyre round at their feasts.

Bede took various opportunities to recount sagas in the *Ecclesiastical History*; not the famous ancient lays but stories of Northumbrian kings who lived within a century of his own life-time. It amounted to much the same thing, however, in the type of interest. One of these sagas concerns an incident leading to the conversion of King Edwin to Christianity:[11]

> The next year (626) there came into the province a certain assassin called Eumer, sent by the king of the West Saxons called Cuichelm, hoping to deprive King Edwin at a stroke of his kingdom and his life. He had a two-edged dagger dipped in poison to the end that if the wound were insufficient to kill the king, the poison might complete the work. Now he came to the king at the river Derwent, where there was at that time

a royal villa, on Easter Sunday. He came in as if bearing a message from his lord, and while he was in an artful manner delivering his pretended embassy, he started on a sudden, drew the dagger concealed under his cloak and rushed on the king. When Lilla, the king's most beloved minister, saw this, having no shield at hand with which to protect the king from death, he promptly interposed his own body to receive the stroke. But the wretch struck home with such force, that he even wounded the king through the body of the dead gesith. Being then attacked on all sides with swords, he also slew in the confusion another gesith, whose name was Forthhere.

The Latin language was not perhaps the ideal medium to bring out the tenseness of situation or the interplay of personalities in a story like this; Bede's narrative gives only a hint of the electric atmosphere which a *scop* in the Northumbrian royal hall might have conjured up around the incident.[12] Nonetheless it is the true stuff of heroic saga—treachery, utter personal loyalty, life and politics dramatically affected by individual actions, men innocently caught up in malevolent forces and overpowering tragedy. A notable feature of this story (and others like it in the *Ecclesiastical History*) is the profusion of proper names. The assassin, the two kings, the river, the beloved minister, even the insignificant gesith who happened to be killed in the mêlée, are all carefully named. The names were essential to the handing on of the story. The same phenomenon is found in many other cultures with an important oral element, so that the traditional stories sometimes undergo material changes while the names, pegs on which the minstrels hang the stories, stick fast. Sets of names could be passed on from one *scop* to the other as sets of cartoons were passed on in stained-glass businesses later in the Middle Ages.

A milestone of such significance in the painful journey of Edwin towards Christianity was sufficient reason for Bede to tell this saga, but the sort of thing was not generally considered fit matter to occupy the minds of monks. Even the historical books of the Old Testament were considered too exciting to be read at the evening meal although they at least were Holy Writ. In the year 797 when Alcuin was anxiously casting about in his mind as to why God had allowed the Norsemen to raid the monastery of Lindisfarne a few years previously, he concluded that the

monks' habit of listening to heathen poems at dinner had had
something to do with it. 'What has Ingeld to do with Christ?'
he asks, 'Narrow is the house; it will not be able to hold them
both.'[13] Ingeld was the handsome prince of the Heathobards who
married the Danish princess Freawaru in an attempt to settle the
long and bitter feuds between the Danes and the Heathobards. But
it had not worked. For when Prince Ingeld entered the banqueting
hall with his bride, he and all the Heathobards had been galled
to see the Danish retainers of Freawaru seated at the banquet,
swaggering in armour and flaunting swords which had been won
in the slaughter of their own people. The Beowulf poet imagined
some fierce old Heathobard spearsman stirring up feelings of
revenge and reviving the feud with some such talk to a young
warrior, 'My friend, can you recognize that weapon which your
own father last carried into battle, when these brave Danes killed
him and held the field after the death of Withergyld and the
destruction of our men? Now the son of one of his killers...'
and so on. Then the day would come when one of Freawaru's
Danish retainers, 'drenched in blood from a sword-thrust', would
forfeit his life for what his father did, oaths would be broken on
both sides, and Ingeld's hatred of the Danes and desire for revenge
would cool his love for his wife. That was the tragedy of Ingeld—
the hesitation between the love of his father and comrades and
the love of his wife, between the duty of vengeance and the
obligations to his oath of peace when he married.[14] It was not,
perhaps, the most monastic of dilemmas.

Alcuin's letter has made notorious the fabulous tastes of
Lindisfarne monks in the 790s. Less well known is the fact that
they were already evincing the same tastes more than a century
earlier. A party of monks went out one Christmas Day to visit
Cuthbert on the island of Farne and to sit down to a feast with
him. They were in a very good mood, but Cuthbert, who knew
how to be merry on occasion, was filled with a sense of foreboding. To use his own reported words: 'In the middle of the
repast, I said to them, "I beseech you, brethren, let us be cautious
and watchful, lest by recklessness and carelessness we be led into
temptation." But they answered: "We beseech you, let us be
joyful today, because it is the birthday of our Lord Jesus Christ."
And I said: "So be it." And a little time after, while we were
indulging in feasting, rejoicing and storytelling (fabulis), I again
began to warn them that we should earnestly engage in prayers

and vigils and be ready for the approach of any temptation. They said, "You give us good, yea excellent instruction, but nevertheless because the days of fastings, prayer and vigils abound, today let us rejoice in the Lord." '[15] The cause of Cuthbert's foreboding was the plague which broke out at Lindisfarne the next day, so that whether he warned against story-telling in itself or only in the circumstances is not quite clear. But the word *fabulae* implies secular rather than religious talk, even pagan tales, to judge by other occasions when Bede uses the same word.[16]

The passion of Anglo-Saxon monks for heroic saga, therefore, was a somewhat inhibited one, indulged under the cloak of religion or at Christmas. But for all that, it had a profound influence, particularly on feelings about saints and on the whole outlook towards Christian sanctity. At many a turn the world of heroic saga coloured the presentation of saints' lives, and this in its turn influenced the actions of those who aspired to sanctity.

It has been pointed out, for instance, that Willibald's *Life of St. Boniface*, written between Boniface's death in 754 and the year 768, has a striking similarity in its mourning scenes to those of *Beowulf*, not so much in significant details (except perhaps in the retainers' lament for their dear lord) as in the whole solemn and elegiac mood.[17] An even clearer parallel lies between Willibald's account of Boniface's martyrdom and the following roughly contemporaneous event in Wessex, recorded as a saga in the Anglo-Saxon chronicle under the year 757:[18]

In this year Cynewulf and the councillors of the West Saxons deprived Sigeberht of his kingdom because of his unjust acts, except for Hampshire; and he retained that until he killed the ealdorman who stood by him longest; and then Cynewulf drove him into the Weald, and he lived there until a swineherd stabbed him to death by the stream at Privett, and he was avenging Ealdorman Cumbra. And Cynewulf often fought with great battle against the Britons. And when he had held the kingdom 31 years, he wished to drive out an atheling who was called Cyneheard, who was brother of the aforesaid Sigeberht. And Cyneheard discovered that the king was at Meretun visiting his mistress with a small following, and he overtook him there and surrounded the chamber before the men who were with the king became aware of him.

Then the king perceived this and went to the doorway, and

nobly defended himself until he caught sight of the atheling
[and thereupon he rushed out against him and wounded him
severely]. Then they all fought against the king until they had
slain him. Then by the woman's outcry, the king's thegns
became aware of the disturbance and ran to the spot, each as
he got ready [and as quickly as possible]. And the atheling made
an offer to each of money and life; and not one of them would
accept it. But they continued to fight until they all lay dead
except for one British hostage, and he was severely wounded.

It is this very picture of a lord surrounded by his faithful band,
his *comitatus* who share his fate in a surprise attack, which
Willibald gave of Boniface's martyrdom. The last and most
dangerous exploit of Boniface's old age was a missionary journey
to the Frisians.[19] His helpers here are carefully named—Eoban,
the bishop; Wintrung, Walthere and Ethelhere, priests; Hamrind,
Scirbald and Bosa, deacons; Wachar, Gundaecer, Illehere and
Hathowulf, monks. He took with him for an intended ceremony
of confirmation 'a picked number of his personal followers' and
pitched a camp on the banks of the River Boorne. But at dawn
before the converts arrived, a mob of armed pagans rushed into
the camp. Boniface gathered the clergy around him, took up the
relics of saints and carried them out of his tent. There he exhorted
all to lay down their arms, to suffer martyrdom with courage,
and to endure with steadfast mind the sudden onslaught of death
so that they would reign for evermore with Christ. 'Whilst with
these words he was encouraging his disciples to accept the crown
of martyrdom, the frenzied mob of heathens rushed suddenly
upon them with swords and every kind of warlike weapon,
staining their bodies with their precious blood.'
Willibald continues with an account of how the pagans then
stole Boniface's book-chests, thinking they had acquired a hoard
of gold and silver; of how they became drunk, began to quarrel
about the division of the spoils and resorted to bloodshed; of how
the survivors broke open the chests, found to their dismay manuscripts instead of gold vessels, pages of sacred texts instead of
silver plate, and in their disgust they scattered the books over the
marshes whence they were later recovered intact. Many of the
old heroic tales were about the winning of a treasure. Treasure
fascinated their hearers for its own sake, as sex fascinates the
modern reader. Some form of this fascination often played a part

in the feelings of monks towards their saintly heroes. The first thing which the monks of Boniface's monasteries wanted to know was the fate of these valuable books, taken by the heathens for treasure. At the end of his life Wilfrid is pictured bringing out and disposing of the treasure which he had accumulated, in a certain way as Beowulf, before he died, longed to handle the treasure which he had won from the dragon's hoard.[20] The translation of St. Cuthbert's body in 698 to its shrine, when the jewelled cross, the Coptic textiles and ivory comb, and the portable altar which he had used were placed with His body in the coffin,[21] must in some ways have resembled the cremation of Beowulf, whose treasure was placed with him on the pyre, or, in real life, the scenes at the burial of the Sutton Hoo ship.

The most significantly 'heroic' feature of Willibald's narrative, however, is this relationship between a spiritual leader and his clergy, seen in terms of the relations between a secular leader and his war-band. It was by no means the first time that the lesson of this kind of loyalty had been presented to Christian clerics. During one of Wilfrid's periods of exile, Aldhelm had written to Wilfrid's clergy exhorting them to support their bishop:[22]

If laymen, ignorant of the divine knowledge, abandon the faithful lord, whom they have loved during his prosperity, when his good fortune has come to an end and adversity befallen him, and prefer the safe ease of their sweet native land to the afflictions of their exiled lord, are they not treated by everyone with hateful jeering, ridicule, loud execration? What then will be said of you if you should let the pontiff who has fostered you and raised you go into exile alone?

One important feature of Germanic society which remained immune to Christianity, indeed which Christianity to some extent absorbed, was the constant emphasis in the heroic stories on revenge, revenge for one's own wrongs, for those of one's comrades and above all for those of one's kin. Revenge in this society was not only tolerated; it was a solemn duty. It could be regarded as essential to the preservation of social order. The desire for vengeance was one of the deepest and, as it seemed, often one of the noblest yearnings of heroic warriors. In *Beowulf* we have an undoubtedly Christian audience sympathizing with the longing of Hengest to avenge his dead leader, Hnaef, on the apparently innocent and gentlemanly Finn. All winter as he lodged in Finn's hall he could think of nothing else. Professor Dorothy Whitelock has shown that the sense of moral justification for blood-feuds remained unaffected by Christianity throughout the Anglo-Saxon period, at least among laymen.[23] The position of the clerics was equivocal. Bishops sometimes arbitrated in blood-feuds to secure a money settlement, but as Dr. Wallace-Hadrill asks, 'How will you get arbitration without the sanction of bloodshed?' The clergy could not, according to their vocation, fight. But to quote Dr. Wallace-Hadrill again, writing of the attitude of Gregory of Tours towards the blood-feud:[24]

> God's vengeance is of the same nature as that of any head of a family or warband. He strikes to kill, to avenge insult—to himself, to his children or to his property. The Frankish churchmen cannot in any other way see *ultio divina* in a society dominated by the bloodfeud. We may know that Romans XII,19—'vengeance is mine, I shall repay, says the Lord'—has nothing to do with bloodfeud, but to the Franks and Gallo-Romans it was not so clear.

We may apply these words equally to Anglo-Saxon churchmen. Eddius saw the wrongs, the exile of his beloved *Hlaford*, Wilfrid, avenged when Egfrith was killed at the battle of *Nechtansmere*. And even Bede's attitude was equivocal. Because though he approved of Sigbert of the East Saxons for forgiving his enemies as a Christian should, he was happy to think that the British monks got what they deserved at the battle of Chester.[25]

GUTHLAC, BEOWULF and ANTHONY THE HERMIT

The culmination of English 'heroic' Christianity was achieved in the Fens, where, amidst bogs and swamps and 'black waters overhung by fog', the hermit Guthlac wrestled with demons. Guthlac was born probably in 674 to a father called Penwalh. This man was of the Mercian royal blood and had an estate in the region of the Middle Angles, around modern Leicestershire.[26] Penwalh was a Christian and had his son baptized. From the first the young Guthlac eschewed 'the nonsensical chatter of the matrons and the empty tales of the common people', and bringing to mind the valiant deeds of the heroes of old, he took to arms. These were times when raids were beginning across the border between the Britons and the Mercians, and before Offa's dyke was built.[27] They were disturbed times which offered scope for private enterprise. At the age of 15 Guthlac became a freebooter. He gathered together a band of followers and went around devastating enemy towns and estates, a lucrative and apparently respectable occupation. To his biographer it was a mark of incipient sanctity already in this phase of his career that he should have returned to its owners a third part of the booty which he collected. One night, however, after nine years of this, he was unable to sleep as he contemplated 'the wretched deaths and shameful ends of the ancient kings of his race, the fleeting riches of the world, and the contemptible glory of his temporal life'. In the morning he addressed his astonished companions, bidding them choose another leader, and promptly went off to receive the Roman tonsure at the double monastery of Repton. After two years at Repton, learning the monastic office and discipline, he made his way to the river Granta near Cambridge, whence a local man called Tatwine guided him in a fisherman's skiff through trackless bogs to the utterly remote and desolate island of Crowland. Here, in the side of an old burial-mound, or barrow, he made his dwelling. He was 26 and the year was probably 699 or 700.

Crowland attracted devils as sea-islands attract puffins. Guthlac's sudden presence among them constituted a threat of the first magnitude to their established order (or disorder), which it was necessary to counteract by every possible means. The means were classic but varied.[28] Now they tempted Guthlac to despair, now to excess in fasting. One night they would come to his den as ghastly, shrieking humans with wild faces, filthy beards, scabby thighs and swollen ankles; another night they would assume the shapes of hostile beasts, roaring, hissing or croaking as appropriate. Hieronymus Bosch would have felt at home in Crowland.

Guthlac died in 715 and before 749 an East-Anglian monk called Felix had written his *Life*. Orderic described the style of Felix as '*prolixus et aliquantulum obscurus*'. Nonetheless the hagiographer had access to much first-hand knowledge of his subject including that of some of the countless visitors who found their way to Crowland when Guthlac made it famous. The *Life* was a compound of this knowledge and the author's hagiographical reading. His description of Guthlac's virtues came word for word from the *Life of Fursey*, his miracle stories were like those in Bede's *Life of Cuthbert* or Gregory the Great's *Dialogues*, much of his more recherché vocabulary was lifted from Aldhelm on Virginity.

Two things influenced Felix more significantly than the rest. One was the thought-world of heroic saga and folk tale as shown to us in the poem *Beowulf*; Guthlac's struggles with the devils have a relation to Beowulf's with the monsters and the dragon. The other was Athanasius's *Life of St. Anthony*, describing this hermit's combats with devils, which was available to the West in the Latin translation of Evagrius. Thus Felix's *Life* does not present us quite simply with Guthlac, but Guthlac cast in the mould of East-Anglian culture of the first half of the eighth century. That does not mean that the *Life* is far removed from the real Guthlac, who was himself part of that culture and indeed helped to fashion it.

Beowulf is a poem in Anglo-Saxon, more than 3,000 lines long and dating probably from the eighth century. It is about a mythical hero whose story is set in the Scandinavian world of the fifth and sixth centuries. There are some indications that it was intended for recitation at three separate sittings. It relates how the Danish king Hrothgar had a magnificent hall called Heorot in which his warriors lived and feasted. But a fiendish monster called Grendel, who lived in darkness, inhabiting 'the fastnesses of moors and fens', heard the happiness and the lyre music accompanying the poet's recital of God's creation, and began to ravage the hall and to slaughter the warriors until Beowulf, a mighty prince of the Geats, a people living in the south-east of Sweden, came to Heorot, lay in wait for Grendel at night, grappled with him single-handed when he raged in with his 'horrible firelit eyes', and wrenched off one of his arms, mortally wounding him.

Grendel's mother then ravaged the hall in revenge, but Beowulf pursued this giantess to her underwater cave. In the struggle he was all but stabbed to death by her, but God saved him (the poet is not very explicit about how), and seeing on the wall a sword which no ordinary mortal could lift, with an ancient blade forged by giants, Beowulf swung it on her neck and she dropped to the ground dead.

Beowulf returned to King Hygelac of the Geats and in due course he himself became king and ruled for 50 years. In his old age, however, his kingdom ran into trouble with an enraged dragon. A chieftain, the last survivor of his race, had deposited his immense ancestral treasure in a barrow near the sea. Later the dragon, 'passing by', as Professor Smithers dryly remarks,[29] took possession of the mound and the treasure and now he was angered by the theft of a jewelled cup. At night he would fly over Beowulf's kingdom, spewing fire and creating havoc. With the help of the one of his followers who had not deserted him, the young Wiglaf, Beowulf was able to overcome the dragon and to win the treasure-hoard for his people. But he was fatally wounded in the fight and amidst the mourning of his people for whom disaster was now prophesied, he was laid on the funeral pyre and the treasure was burnt with him.

Of this plot Mr. Kenneth Sisam has written:[30]

We do not believe in these particular monsters, and are inclined to treat the main plot as childish. For an Anglo-Saxon audience, gathered in a hall as night came on, with the dark creeping into corners beyond the firelight, these monsters were real terrors. Even as they listened, a giant from the hills and fens might be prowling outside the doors, a dragon might be leaving his trail in the sky or setting sparks to the thatch.

Although *Beowulf* was without a doubt composed in England, the hero's fights with the monsters are a version of the Scandinavian folk-tale known as the Bear's Son because of the hero's great strength and propensity for hugging his opponents. Thus Bothvar Bjarki rid the Danish court of a monster which had been attacking it and on which no ordinary sword would bite. Grettir waited in the dark at Thorhall's Farm to grapple with the monster Glam, and he struggled with an ogress at Sandhaugar, lying in wait for her at night in a farmhouse and cutting off her arm as he was dragged to the brink of a nearby gorge. On this occasion Grettir subsequently dived under a waterfall and reached a cave in the ravine behind it, where he killed a giant as the giant grasped at a sword hanging on the wall. Between these stories and those of *Beowulf* there are many differences when they are examined in detail. But it is clear that they all derive ultimately if independently from a common, Scandinavian story-pattern.[31]

The same is true of the dragon and burial mound episode in *Beowulf*. At least ten Scandinavian versions of this story have been discovered—like that of Herraudr, prince of the Geats, who killed King Harekr. This king lived in a horrible lair full of gold and jewels and changed himself at will into a flying dragon. Professor G. V. Smithers has illuminated the way in which Sigurd's slaying of the dragon Fafnir bears in numerous points a similarity to the Beowulf story.[32]

A grasp of the essential features of the Scandinavian stories (which go back at least to the sixth or seventh centuries) can often make an obscure point in Beowulf clear, occasionally indeed where some critics have been disposed to see a weighty Christian moral in the obscurity. Thus when Beowulf had all but succumbed to Grendel's mother, God saved him. How? This was the point where in the Scandinavian story a light would suddenly have shone in the cave.[33] These giants and giantesses were creatures of darkness with terrible eyes, but once a light was directed on their eyes they were powerless. Having been saved, Beowulf seized the magical sword which frequently hung on the cave walls in these circumstances. Heroes had been helped out of tight squeezes before a Christian God came into the story. Again, the treasure of the dragon's hoard which Beowulf won was burned with him because it was 'as useless to men as before'. It was not useless, as some have thought, because gold ought to be no object of glee or avarice to a good Christian. It was useless because it had potentially baleful associations for men still alive, and because the grave-goods supplied to a dead man for his life in the world of the dead were by that fact of no more use to the living.[34] Another point which becomes clear from the Scandinavian background, though it was not clear to the Beowulf poet, is that the 'last survivor' who entered the mound with his treasure must actually have turned into the dragon.[35] The adversaries of heroes had the habit of turning into dragons; the worlds of heroic saga and folk-tale were not entirely separate.

It is doubtful whether Beowulf himself actually existed but his exploits are set against a Scandinavian background which has many genuine historical elements. His lord, King Hygelac of the Geats, was killed in a raid on the lower Rhineland, probably between 520 and 531.[36] That would put the rule of the Danish Hrothgar in the early sixth century and Beowulf's imagined rule of the Geats in the middle of the same century. A good case can be made for equating the village of Leire in the north of the island of Seeland with the site of Heorot.[37] Out of the allusions to and digressions about real and legendary feuds and wars of the fifth and sixth centuries, moreover, the poet has woven a dark and tragic backcloth which enhances the dignity of his main theme. Thus, while during the adventures at Heorot the talk has naturally been of Danish or Frisian heroes, during the dragon fight the theme of the revival of the old Swedish/Geatish enmity gathers like a thunder cloud on the horizon.[38]

We need not linger over the digressions in *Beowulf* because it is the monsters and dragon which chiefly bring us into contact with Guthlac. On the similarity of outlook which characterize *Beowulf* and Felix's *Life of Guthlac*, Professor Whitelock has written:[39]

It is of interest that Felix, the author of the Latin *Life of St. Guthlac*, should let the saint address his demon tormentors as the seed of Cain.... Thus in this mid-eighth century work, which shares with our poem the conviction that marshes are the abodes of monsters, one gets support for the (*Beowulf*) poet's view that evil broods are sprung from Cain. The points of contact between *Beowulf* and this Latin *Life* do not end there. There is, of course, a general similarity of theme, the poem telling how a deliverer saved human habitations from the ravaging of the monsters who haunted the 'misty moorlands' and the 'fen retreats', by physical struggle,[40] and the *Life* describing how a hermit took up his abode on a haunted island in the fens and drove away the demons by spiritual conflict. Guthlac 'girded himself with spiritual weapons against the snares of the foul enemy'; he turned into weapons for himself the shield of faith, the breastplate of hope, the helmet of chastity, the bow of patience, the arrows of psalmody; a little farther on the arrows of the devil are ,mentioned. The poet makes Hrothgar use the metaphor of spiritual armour against the devil's arrows in his warning speech to Beowulf on the dangers of pride. The devil first came to attack Guthlac as he was singing psalms and canticles; Grendel's hostility was aroused by the sound of festivity in Heorot, and the poet has given us as a sample of the entertainment a religious hymn sung by the minstrel.... Felix describes a rifled tumulus, above which Guthlac built his first hut, in words which would suggest a chamber-tomb, if such were conceivable in this part of England; the dragon in *Beowulf* guarded treasure in a chamber-tomb, which was rifled after its death.

To these points of Professor Whitelock it is possible to add a further one. Guthlac's struggles normally occurred at night; his assailants, like Beowulf's monsters, were creatures who operated in the dark. One night they carried him through clouds and mists to the black caverns and gloomy abysses of hell. They were about to thrust him in when St. Bartholomew appeared. Bartholomew was Guthlac's special protector because it was on his festival that Guthlac had arrived at Crowland. Bartholomew appeared in a sudden splendour of heavenly light, like the flame which gleamed clearly as the sun filling the cave of Grendel's mother. At this moment the demons who had Guthlac in their control began to gnash their teeth, to howl and flee, to fear and tremble.[41] They could not stand light.

At the age of 15 and the start of his military career, so Felix says, Guthlac was fired as he remembered the valiant deeds of the heroes of old. Maybe Felix remembered these heroes as he wrote. Maybe, too, Guthlac had not entirely forgotten them (in spite of his later professions of disgust) as he wrestled on Crowland. Which heroes of old? Was Beowulf amongst them? It is an open question whether the poem as we now have it had been composed when Felix wrote, let alone when Guthlac lived. But it is probable that the story would have been known, and not least in East Anglia. Beowulf was a Geatish hero. The Anglo-Saxons were interested in the heroes of many different Germanic peoples.[42] but Beowulf was from Gotland (Sweden). The Sutton Hoo ship burial has shown a general connection between Sweden and East Anglia,[43] and it has recently been argued with some force that Eastern England was a likely outlet of the Swedish fur trade after the Avar conquest of Pannonia had blocked the Danube route to the Byzantine market.[44] As we know it the poem itself is probably Mercian. But whether or not Felix knew of the poem or of the hero the similarities in outlook between the two cannot be gainsaid.

There is, however, also an important difference in outlook between the two.

Beowulf is suffused with Christian allusions, phrases and ways of thought. many of which greatly heighten its poetic effect. It was recited in a thoroughly Christianized company.[45] That is not to say that it had any specifically Christian message or deep and hidden theological content which the audience of retainers would be sure to uncover if they only dug hard enough with their warrior brains.[46] One thing, however, might naturally have suggested itself to those who reflected on the poem at a deeper level as they heard it, and this has been brought out by Professor J. R. R. Tolkien:[47] namely the way in which the fusion between pagan tradition and Christianity in *Beowulf* affected the heroic values.

In the Northern imagination, in the Northern concept of courage, man and the gods fight side by side, but not on the side which wins. They battle against Chaos and Unreason, against the forces of the hostile world, against monsters, against the offspring of darkness; they exult in the fight and they think defeat no refutation. They put up an 'absolute resistance, perfect because without hope'. Now the Christian still fights the old enemies, the old monsters; he is still an 'alien in a hostile world, engaged in a struggle which he cannot win while the world lasts.' On the other hand, for him there is not the same old prospect of ultimate defeat. Beyond Time appears the hope of eternal victory. Man now fights not together with the old gods but with the one eternal God. And when he hears the monsters, the creatures of Northern myth, described as the seeds of Cain—for it was at this point that 'New Scripture and old tradition touched and ignited'—he is 'assured that his foes are the foes also of *Dryhten*'. One might think that Christianity would have given a new optimism to the heroic world.

But—and here we come to one of the subtlest of Professor Tolkien's points—the *Beowulf* poet, though removed from the direct pressure of the old despair by his confidence in the Christian God, still *feels* it with a poetical intensity. He looks 'back into the pit'.[48] This feeling, especially discernible in the sombre relevance of the digressions to the main plot, is very important.[49] For it has been argued that, on paper, *Beowulf's* resistance had been far from hopeless. He had made easy work of a giant and a giantess and although he received a fatal wound in his third fight, he outlived his dragon antagonist whose carcase was unceremoniously shoved into the sea.[50] This does not, however, invalidate Professor Tolkien's words, 'The shadow of despair, if only as a mood, as an intense emotion of regret, is still there. The worth of defeated valour in this world is deeply felt. As the poet looks back into the past surveying the history of kings and warriors in the old traditions, he sees that all glory ends in night.'

This is just where *Guthlac* differs radically from *Beowulf*. There is no shadow of despair in Felix's *Life*; only a temptation to despair given by the devil whom Guthlac sends reeling back. There is no emotion of regret, only the absolute confidence that Guthlac, with the help of God and St. Bartholomew, will win a series of resounding victories. Nobody could have placed a lower estimate on defeated valour in this world than Guthlac after his 'conversion'. Guthlac, like the *Beowulf* poet, had looked back into the past and surveyed the history of kings and warriors in the old traditions, but when he contemplated their 'wretched deaths and shameful ends' and the 'contemptible glory of this temporal life', he decided in one night to have none of it.[51] Next morning the sun rose (apparently a rare event in Anglo-Saxon literature), the birds sang and Guthlac confidently announced that he was devoting himself to the service of God. For him the sparrow would not fly out of the firelit hall into the darkness of the unknown again, it would fly into a world which could be systematically charted and conquered.

Here the decisive influence of Athanasius's *Life of St. Anthony the Hermit* comes in.[52] Anthony was a Copt born near Alexandria probably in 251; he lived to be 105 years old. Athanasius's *Life*, written in Greek within a few years of Anthony's death and well known in the West through Evagrius's Latin translation, is perhaps the supreme masterpiece of Christian hagiography. With only a few strokes of the pen it conveyed an unforgettable picture and a model of how to achieve sanctity, which was to continue in its direct influence at least to the Curé of Ars. It would be rash to say that even now its influence was dead. Athanasius tells how as a young man Anthony espoused a life of asceticism after hearing the Gospel, 'if thou wilt be *perfect*, go and sell all that thou hast and give to the poor, and come and follow me'; how about the age of 35 he retired into complete solitude and lived in a deserted fort on the East bank of the Nile, on the 'Outer Mountain' at Pispir; how after 20 years, when he had become famous as a hermit he emerged for the first time to speak with those who had come to be his followers; how on this occasion he was neither embarrassed nor elated by the crowds who had come to him, neither obese with want of exercise nor emaciated with his fastings and struggles; how, after organizing these followers as hermits, he retired in 313 more completely into solitude, travelling with a caravan for three days until he came to a place at the foot of Mount Colzim, the 'Inner Mountain'; here were a spring, a few scraggy date-palms and a small patch of land for the cultivation of grain—and Anthony liked it.

The 'Inner Mountain' was Anthony's last retreat. He was utterly in the desert and only 20 miles from the Red Sea. These are the words of Charles Kingsley about the site:[53]

> The eastward view from Anthony's home must be one of the most glorious in the world, save for the want of verdure and of life. For Anthony, as he looked across the gulf of Akaba, across which, far above, the Israelites had crossed in old times, he could see the sacred peaks of Sinai, flaming against the blue sky with that intensity of hue which is scarcely exaggerated, it is said, by the bright scarlet colour in which Sinai is always painted in medieval illuminations.

Anthony was no escapist. On the contrary, he retreated in order to embrace the most real of all struggles, that with himself and with the powers of darkness. The main point of Athanasius's *Life* is to describe Anthony's intense wrestling with the devil. At first these combats took the form of his struggles with his inner self. Gold was placed in his path as he walked in the desert. His chastity was violently attacked and 'filthy' thoughts of women flooded his mind; Coptic sculpture afforded plenty of material for this kind of temptation.[54] Only when all human temptation had failed, when Anthony had achieved a measure of self-analysis and knowledge, when he had brought into a certain coherence the bundle of his underlying and warring inclinations, only then did the devil, or rather the devils, appear to him in more tangible form. They burst into his chamber at night in the forms of lions, bears, asps, and scorpions, etc. They would make a fearful commotion; they would create smoke and fire around him; and then they would suddenly change to the method of blandishment and praise of his asceticism. It may seem strange to say that this struggle with the devils in their more manifest form was considered the higher level of the spiritual conflict, but so it was. For now Anthony could do nothing of himself; his own efforts at spiritual advancement had become in a sense irrelevant, he was offered no opportunity to resist temptation. There was nothing but to trust completely in his Faith.[55]

One quarter of Athanasius's *Life* is taken up by an address to his hermits, put into the mouth of Anthony. It is almost all about the methods of the devils.[56] They could quote Scripture and

sing the psalms in order to deceive; if the fasting was going well
they might advise *complete* abstention from food, which was a
form of pride and indiscretion; they could send a hermit to sleep
at prayer, but rouse him from bed in order to pray. Anthony
explained how it was that the devils could seem to foretell things;
he explained how a divine visitation could be distinguished from
a diabolical one. This address, so important in the *Life*, is marked
by an absolute confidence that the methods of the devil could be
systematically analyzed, exposed and counteracted. Indeed, at
times Anthony's tone was almost that of a headmaster whose
problem was to control a gang of unruly schoolboys. That the
sanctions would be effective was a matter of course. At one time,
he says, a 'very tall demon' appeared and announced himself to be
the power of god. But 'I blew a breath at him', called on the name
of Christ, and 'big as he was', he disappeared. On another occasion
there was a polite knock at the door and a towering figure
introduced himself as Satan. "What are you doing here?" I asked
him.'

It is certain that Felix knew the *Life of St. Anthony*, and there
is no reason why Guthlac himself should not have known it. In
many particulars Guthlac's struggles are based on St. Anthony's.
We are told of Anthony that in his period of 'apprenticeship' he
observed the outstanding virtues of various ascetics in order to
imitate them—the earnestness in prayer of one, the kindness of
another, the fasting and sleeping on the ground of yet another,
and so on. Guthlac is said to use the same method at Repton.[57]
Anthony warned his hermits of the temptation to excessive fasting
and he himself normally ate once a day. Guthlac ate a piece of
barley bread every day and when the devils tempted him to
extend his fast, he began to eat under their very eyes.[58] Between
Guthlac and Anthony there is a striking similarity in the up-
heaval of animal forms and noises with which their devilish
tormentors molested them.[59] But above all it is the mood of
confidence that the powers of darkness will not prevail (the mood
which distinguishes the *Life of Guthlac* from *Beowulf*), which
the *Life of Anthony* imparts to the struggles of Guthlac.

Felix's *Life of Guthlac*, therefore, is a remarkable instance of
the absorption of Christianity into Anglo-Saxon society. It is
created out of the worlds of Germanic heroes and East
Mediterranean hermits. Without either it is inconceivable. It is a
fusion of two great and widely separated traditions.

14 Church and Laity

A hundred years and more after the arrival of Augustine, the problem of the laity for the bishops and clergy was still as much a missionary problem as it was a pastoral one; there was still as much to be done converting pagans as there was ministering to the faithful. Bede's *Life of St. Cuthbert* shows, with a story from the 650s, how resistant the pagans of the Northumbrian country-side could be to the new religion which their rulers were attempting to establish. The story tells of some monks of South Shields who were bringing wood down the river on rafts, when they were swept out to sea by a gale and all help was to no purpose:[1]

On the other bank of the river stood no small crowd of the common people, and he (Cuthbert) was standing among them. These were watching the rafts on which the monks were sadly gazing, being carried so far out to sea that they looked like five tiny birds riding on the waves, for there were five rafts. Thereupon they began to jeer at the monks' manner of life, as if they were deservedly suffering, seeing that they despised the common laws of mortals and put forth new and unknown rules of life. Cuthbert stopped the insults of the blasphemers, saying: 'Brethren, what are you doing, cursing those whom you see being carried away even now to destruction? Would it not be better and more kindly to pray to the Lord for their safety rather than to rejoice over their dangers?' But they fumed against him with boorish minds and boorish words and said, 'Let no man pray for them, and may God have no mercy on any one of them, for they have robbed men of their old ways of worship, and how the new worship is to be conducted, nobody knows.' When Cuthbert heard this reply, he knelt down to pray to God, bending his head to the ground, and immediately the violent wind turned about and bore the rafts safe and sound to land amid the rejoicings of those who were guiding them, and left them in a convenient place near the monastery itself. When the countryfolk saw this, they were ashamed of their own unbelief, but forthwith they duly praised the faith of the venerable Cuthbert and thereafter never ceased to praise it. In fact a very worthy brother of our monastery, from whose lips I heard the story declared that he himself had often heard these things related in the presence of many by one of these same people, a man of rustic simplicity and absolutely incapable of inventing an untruth.

The 650's were relatively early days, but paganism was still a sizeable problem in the eighth century. In his commentary on Samuel, Bede spoke of those who in his own day were being snatched from the devil, and of Christian churches which were being set up in places where some still worshipped idols.[2] Towards the end of Guthlac's life—he died in 716—the man who, according to the saint's prophecy, was to succeed him in his hermitage at Crowland, was still a pagan living amongst pagans.[3] The late seventh-century laws of King Wihtred of Kent contain prohibitions against the worship of idols, and the roughly contemporary laws of King Ine of Wessex set greater weight by the oaths of communicants than of others in the law courts.[4] The Penitential of Archbishop Theodore, whose evidence, as we shall see, takes us well into the eighth century, says: 'if those who are baptized are not allowed to eat with or give the kiss to catecumens, how much more should this be so with pagans.'[5] There survive no ecclesiastical laws from a time when Anglo-Saxon Christians felt themselves still to be set in the midst of a society organized on predominantly pagan lines, as there survive earlier in the case of Ireland;[6] but in this ruling, contamination from paganism or indifference to its survival were still felt to be serious dangers to a Christian soul. There was perhaps a period, a kind of second phase in the conversion, when Christianity had to face less the hostility of pagans than the feeling of both pagans and Christians that social relationships mattered more than those of religion.

At the head of the pastoral ministry, in England as everywhere, were the bishops. Bede's famous letter to Archbishop Egbert of York (734) in which he castigated the contemporary church of Northumbria for its faults with the outspokenness of a man

feeling his end draw near, urged the pastoral need to multiply
bishoprics.[7] He thus took his place in a debate of long standing.
But the advice went unheeded by Egbert, about whom there was
something of a Wilfrid. He was a prelate with a large diocese, a
flourishing school in his cathedral, and a great deal of political
prestige. In his day the Northumbrian dioceses created by
Theodore south of the Tweed still survived, with the exception of
Ripon. The disappearance of Ripon meant that Egbert was left
as the only Bishop of Deira, and no see had been established west
of the Pennines. Nowhere, in fact, did the multiplication of
bishoprics go on apace, chiefly because the endowment of a see
was expensive, and the larger monasteries, which could have
stood the expense and could themselves have become sees, were
too jealous of their independence and their endowments to allow
it. Wessex was finally divided between the sees of Winchester and
the newly created Sherborne in 705. But the best that could
generally be hoped for was that Theodore's work and ideals
would hold their ground. They did so in East Anglia and (except
for some vagaries in the history of the see of Leicester) in Mercia.
Moreover, Theodore's new sees had been admirably placed from
the point of view of communications and accessibility to areas of
population. They were fixed sees, but sited to make possible a sort
of continuation of the work of the Irish wandering bishops which
Theodore so much admired. Hereford, for example, is not known
to have been a place of any consequence before becoming a
bishopric, although there had been a Roman town (Kenchester)
only a few miles away. But there is some evidence that Hereford
was on a Roman road, and at an important crossing of that road
with the River Wye.[8] Lichfield, where Theodore fixed Chad's see,
was later said by William of Malmesbury to be a mean place. But
it was easily accessible on the one hand to the numerous dwellers
of the Derbyshire Peak district, the Pecsaetan, whose lead and
silver mining was probably already an important factor in Anglo-
Saxon economic life, and on the other hand to the people of
the Trent valley and the heartlands of Mercia.[9]

Monasteries, whose pastoral activities were doubtless under the
general control of bishops, were of supreme importance in the
spread of Christianity through the countryside and in the ministry
to the faithful. It is hard to imagine a monastery amongst the
seventh-century Anglo-Saxons which would have considered itself
so ascetic and withdrawn from the world that it took no part in

this work. The reverse was more likely to be true—the more ascetic the monastery, the more conscious was it of its mission to the laity. From Melrose, for instance, a monastery affiliated to Lindisfarne, both Cuthbert and his predecessor as prior, Boisil, went out amongst the neighbouring hills on preaching tours which lasted for weeks.[10] The church of every monastery would have been a resort for the laity, even if their services were held in a separate chapel or perhaps an upper floor. Sir Frank Stenton showed how important was the confederation of monasteries centred on *Medeshamstede* (Peterborough), and stretching right across Mercia, for the spread of Christianity in that kingdom during the second half of the seventh century. Bede mentions the foundation of *Medeshamstede* itself, but for our knowledge of its colonies we rely on memoranda of very early documents entered into a register of Peterborough Abbey only in the late twelfth century. Stenton's abstract of one of these documents, that concerning the foundation of a monastery at Breedon-on-the-Hill (Leicestershire), shows very clearly the missionary and pastoral functions for which the monastery was conceived:[11]

Friduric the most religious of king Aedilred's *principes*, for his soul's health, with the consent of bishop Saxulf and king Aedilred gave the land of twenty *manentes* called Bredun to St. Peter's *familia* dwelling at Medeshamstede, so that they should found a monastery at Bredun and appoint a priest of good repute to minister baptism and teaching to the people assigned to him. The brethren of Medeshamstede chose one of their number, a priest named Hedda, and appointed him abbot on condition that he should acknowledge himself to be one of their fraternity.

A monk of Breedon, Tatwine, was archbishop of Canterbury from 731 to 734.

One specific function of the monasteries' pastorate was to act as technological institutes, so to speak, of the ministry. They provided the ideas, the books, the translations, the actual material equipment for those working in the field. In his letter to Archbishop Egbert, for instance, Bede said that every Christian should recite the Our Father and the Apostles Creed daily;[12] the laity would have to recite them not in Latin, of course, but in their own tongue. Translations into the vernacular were an obvious need. Bede is not known to have gone out on preaching tours himself, but he was engaged on a translation of St. John's Gospel into Anglo-Saxon during his last days; nothing in the end seemed more urgent than translation to this scholar who had written so many treatises. There are surviving examples of the kinds of equipment which travelling bishops or priests would have carried with them, which imply the involvement of a monastery's artisans or smith or jeweller's shop. Amongst the treasures buried in St. Cuthbert's coffin was a portable altar, a slab of oak no more than 5¼ x 4¾ inches, with crosses at its corners and centre, and an inscription which reads IN HONOREM S. PETRU.[18] At Hexham is preserved a diminutive seventh-century bronze chalice, finely shaped and of just the kind to have been used with such an altar. (Fig. 10). The small and ancient Irish mass-book, the so-called Stowe Missal, dating from about 800, gives some idea of the kind of book which a bishop or priest would have taken on his travels for the celebration of the liturgy.[14] This book is written on vellum leaves measuring 5 x 4½ inches, and it contains extracts from the Gospel of St. John, the ordinary and canon of the mass, a few variable prayers and scriptural readings which would do for any mass, a few prayers for special masses, e.g. of the dead, and orders for the administration of baptism and extreme unction. No such book survives from Anglo-Saxon England, but at any time the full battery of liturgical books would have been an inconvenience to missionaries of the Irish tradition, and pocket books must have been produced from the liturgical material at monastic centres.[14a] The Stowe Missal was the kind of book with which Aidan must have gone out from Lindisfarne or Cuthbert from Melrose. What monasteries had to offer above all else, however, was training in a way of life which would make preachers effective, and instruction in faith and doctrine. The homilies of Bede, for instance, of which a collection of 50 survives, were preached in Latin and were very much for the benefit of his learned monastic colleagues.[15] They were not like the sermons of Caesarius of Arles (which seem to have been unknown to the early Anglo-Saxons), pastoral sermons directed to a lay audience.[16] But there was plenty of matter in them, and in the scriptural commentaries, which could be selected and processed and made pastorally useful.

The Old English word for a monastery was *mynster*. In the early centuries of Anglo-Saxon Christianity, before there is any sign of a parish system, it was the monasteries or minsters which, under the bishops, were the centres of pastoral organization. Their

clergy served an area much wider than that which would have
been served later by a parish church. To historians of the later
Anglo-Saxon period the word *minster* conveys something rather
different from a monastery. It conveys a body of secular clergy,
of priests, deacons, and clerics in minor orders. These clergy might
live a communal life for economic motives and they might keep
canonical hours in church; but they were not bound to the same
extent as monks by a rule of life nor by stability in one particular
house, they were *all*, by reason of their position, administrators
and pastors or were training to become these things, and those in
minor orders might be married men living in separate houses.
From the ninth century onwards there is evidence in plenty for
such minsters of secular clergy.[17] We have said in an earlier
chapter, however, that in the seventh century it is not easy to
distinguish them. It is not easy to point to any example of a
corporation in the early period and to say with confidence that its
members were secular clergy rather than monks. The term *mona-
sterium* itself covered so many different ways of life at this time.
The Synod of Cloveshoe (747) distinguishes, in its canons, between
clergy and monks, but not between monasteries and other kinds of
religious communities.[18] It may be that some of the secular
minsters of later times had been so from their foundation in cases
when they were founded in the seventh century; like the old
minsters of Kent—Reculver, Lyminge, Dover, etc.—which were
situated on the Roman roads, and some of which were at the
places where the administrative centres of Roman times had been.
But there seems to be no means of knowing this in the seventh
century, when their heads were called abbots just as the heads of
any ecclesiastical institution might be. It may be that some of
the cathedral establishments themselves, those which are known
to have consisted of secular clergy in the ninth century, were so
earlier. The witness list of a charter of King Coenwulf of Mercia
(799), for instance, shows us a body of priests, deacons and clerks
at Worcester who are clearly secular clergy. About the same
time Canterbury cathedral was a similar kind of corporation.[19]
But it is difficult to rule out the possibility of continental,
Carolingian influence in such late cases. It may be that Winchester
cathedral in the time of the Gaulish Bishop Eleutherius consisted
of secular clergy, as in Gaulish cathedrals.[20] It may be that some
of the *comitatus* which Bishop Hedda of Lichfield and Leicester
was said to have brought with him when he visited Guthlac were

secular clergy. It sounds almost likely in the case of his secretary or *librarius*, Wigfrith, who boasted before the visit that he had lived among the Irish and knew a true from a false hermit when he saw one.[21] But all this is in the realms of speculation. What is certain is that in the early centuries monasteries were important pastoral centres, and what is probable is that many of the later minsters of secular clergy had originally been monasteries, that is houses of monks.[22]

At a lower level, local churches were springing up everywhere during the seventh and early eighth centuries. We learn from Bede of two occasions when John of Beverley (bishop of Hexham 687–705, and of York 705–21) was called in by gesiths to consecrate churches (*ecclesias*) which they had built on their estates. These could have been the churches of small family monasteries as well as places of worship for the local people. We know of another occasion when Cuthbert, as bishop of Lindisfarne, dedicated the church of a small monastic dependency of Whitby.[23]

At other times, however, local churches may be called not *ecclesia* but *oratorium*, i.e. an oratory. When in the 690s the layman, Drythelm, was shocked by a dream into a new and penitential way of life, he made first for the oratory of a small estate (*villulae oratorium*).[24] Again, in the commentary on Mark, Bede wrote, 'when we come to any estate (*villam*) or property (*oppidum*, i.e. the Anglo-Saxon burgh) or any other place in which there is a house of prayer (*domus orationis*) consecrated to God, we first enter it. . . .'[25] The words used by Bede in this passage are not words for towns; his word for a town was *civitas*. They are words for the country property of a king or a gesith. The oratories are provided by the landlords primarily for themselves and their tenants. We must conclude from the evidence that quite apart from monastic churches, small oratories were a common feature of the English landscape at least by the early eighth century. Like all but the most important churches of the period, they would have been built of wood.

These oratories, however, were not parish churches, nor is there as yet any evidence of parish priests. It is possible that in the mid-eighth century some of the small family monasteries on noble estates were served by no more than a single priest and that here we have one of the germs of the later parochial system.[26] But for any clear evidence of that system we have to wait until the tenth

century. Local oratories and non-monastic churches would have
been little more than places of private prayer, except when they
were visited by the bishop or the clergy of a monastery or
minster which served them with mass and the sacraments. Priests
were in too short supply in these days for a system of parish
clergy to be feasible. It would have been considered the waste of
valuable men to confine their activities to small local communities,
when there were people all over Northumbria lacking the sacraments. Early Anglo-Saxon priests were more like sixteenth-century
Jesuits than thirteenth-century rectors. When Cuthbert went on
his pastoral tours from Melrose or Lindisfarne he would take
at least one of the priests of the monastery with him, and it was
in fact these men who preserved the memory of several of his
miracles. As bishop of Lindisfarne, he would be called in to
villages or estates by those gesiths with whom he was friendly;
by Hemma in one place, by Sibba in another and so on.[27] These
aristocratic contacts were the essential means by which
Christianity was spread amongst the peasantry who were their
tenants. Nowhere, however, in the course of the quite circum-
stantial narratives which surrounded these occasions, do we catch
any glimpse of a local resident priest. On the contrary, the talk
is all of the monastic priests in Cuthbert's own entourage. When
the Synod of Cloveshoe (747) laid down that priests were to
fulfil the work of preaching and baptizing in the places and
regions assigned to them by their bishops, this was still entirely
compatible with the notion of priests from monasteries making
tours of many churches in the course of their duties.[28]

And tours not only of churches: for there can be no supposition
that every eighth-century Anglo-Saxon lived near enough to a
church or oratory to meet there for his worship. In many parts
a cross marked such a meeting place. The parents of St. Willibald,
for example, offered him to God as a boy:[29]

> And this they did, not in the church but at the foot of the
> Cross, for on the estates of the nobles and good men of the
> Saxon race it is a custom to have a cross, which is dedicated to
> Our Lord and held in great reverence, erected on some prominent
> spot for the convenience of those who wish to pray daily
> before it.

A cross might be set up to commemorate a victory in battle,
or it might be a memorial to a particular person, and it might

well at the same time mark a place of prayer. At first such crosses would be made of wood, but by the eighth century free-standing crosses were being erected in stone and the fine carving of these stones came to be an artistic genre in itself. Miss Rosalind Hill has shown most interestingly that many of these crosses in Northumbria, where their sites are known or are implied in place-names like Crossthwaite of Crossdale, were placed near to harbours, or on Roman roads, or at natural meeting places for sheep farmers.[30] They enable us, in a remarkable way, to plot the lines of communication for pastoral activity.

The Church, with its life, structures and rules, had to be fitted into Anglo-Saxon society. In the previous chapter we saw something of this process through the literary culture of the eighth century. We give now some examples of the practical problems which it raised.

The most obvious instance of a social institution in question here is that of the kingship itself. From the start the Church acknowledged its helplessness without the support and protection of kings. More often than not they led their people to the baptismal font; they provided the initial endowments of land and buildings for bishoprics and monasteries; they protected church property with their sanctions; they enforced the payment of church dues by the people; they fought the Church's enemies, and might even (like Oswald) be regarded as martyrs in its cause. The churches which they built near the halls on their estates were centres of missionary and pastoral activity, and it may be that the administrative districts attached to these estates for such purposes as tax payment had an important bearing on the earliest pastoral units of the Church. In matters of justice affecting the Church, where churchmen could not look after their own affairs unaided, as with the murder of a bishop or priest, they gladly acceded to the king's judgement.[31] A distinction was made in many matters concerning the conduct of the clergy between secular and ecclesiastical justice, but in general it was very blurred. The services rendered by kings to the Church were amply reciprocated. The advice and legal knowledge of churchmen enabled kings to show forth their kingship in a new way by the issue of codes of law, which became increasingly sophisticated; churches provided honourable resting places for kings and queens, and ensured the permanence of their fame; the fortunes of individual kings could be radically affected by their association with saints, as in the case of Ethelbald of Mercia, who as an exile visited Guthlac and was encouraged by the saint's prophecy that he would be a great ruler.[32] In the long run, one of the most important of all benefits conferred on kings by the Church was the quasi-sacerdotal character given to them by the Christian ceremony of coronation and anointing, first known to have been performed in England in 786. The strength of early Anglo-Saxon Christianity was based solidly on the great partnerships between king and bishop, like those between Ethelbert and Augustine, Oswald and Aidan, Felix and Sigbert of the East Angles, Hedda and Ine, and the brothers Egbert and Eadbert of Northumbria. The breaking of such a partnership, as in the case of Wilfrid and Egfrith of Northumbria, brought untold disasters in its wake.

One of the foremost social problems which the Church had to face was that of bringing the marriage customs of the Anglo-Saxons into line with its own norms. It went without saying to those brought up in the tradition of the Latin Fathers that women were first of all a lure and temptation to men, and that married people, while they might by strenuous spiritual exertion and frequent carnal abstinence be saved, could hardly attain to Christian perfection. Moreover, women were not without uncleanness in themselves and were to be restrained (if possible) from receiving communion after giving birth and during their menstrual periods.[33] Whether Anglo-Saxon women, who were accorded a high status in society and were often formidable personalities in their own right, always submitted to the male-drafted rules and codes which constitute our evidence, we cannot say. These, however, were not the primary problems which faced churchmen attempting to regulate the institution of marriage itself. The primary problems arose from situations like the conversion of one partner but not the other to Christianity or the desire of one partner but not the other to leave the marriage and embrace the religious life, from the custom of Anglo-Saxon men to marry their deceased wife's sister or their widowed step-mother, and from the degree of kindred within which a man and woman might marry.[34]

The conversion of one partner to Christianity where the other remained a pagan was one of several grounds on which the dissolution of a marriage was allowed in Theodore's Penitential. Here, may be, part of the motive was the preservation of a Christian's life from pagan contamination. But the general character of Theodore's judgments in this field is admirably expressed by Sir Frank Stenton:[35]

> The whole tenor of his canons shows his anxiety that a moral life should not be made impossible for those whose marriages were broken by disaster. He had the humanity of a man who had known many countries and the customs of many churches.

The Church's struggle against men marrying widowed step-mothers, or sisters of deceased wives, was probably more severe than the surviving sources now allow us to realize. To churchmen this kind of marriage appeared to be condemned by Scripture, that is, by the Divine Law itself. For if Scripture said that nobody should uncover the nakedness of his kindred and, further, that a husband and wife were as one flesh, what were marriages to a father's wife or a wife's sister but a form of incest? The difficulty in a warrior society like that of the Anglo-Saxons, however, was that, in its aristocratic ranks at least, men died earlier than women; women were left widowed or unmarried. This was the social pressure which lay behind such marriages in pagan days. It has recently been suggested that they were even contracted polygynously on occasions.[36] One cannot help seeing the double monastery, ruled by an abbess, as in part the answer of churchmen to this problem, although it would be absurd to see in it the main motive for the development of that institution.

The Church came up against the problem of kinship and the Anglo-Saxon kindred group in various ways. Recent work done on this subject has suggested that the kindred group as a social force has been overrated. First, the terms, or rather the lack of Anglo-Saxon terms for all but the closest relationships suggest that for the most important purposes, the operative circle of kindred was a small one.[37] Secondly, kinship was not agnatic, as it was amongst the Irish, where the important factor was descent in the male line; it was bilateral, which meant that a person had the option of tracing his kindred either through male or female relatives. These two things together suggest that it would have been difficult for the structure of any kindred group to persist over many generations.[38] If anything, the fact that there was a term for the relationship between nephew and father's brother (*suhter-ge-faederan*), but none for that between a nephew and mother's brother, suggests a slight leaning towards agnatic kinship, which is what one would expect in a warrior society where kindred group and lord's *comitatus* were not necessarily such different institutions.[39] We might be inclined, therefore, to over-state the general functions of the kindred group in the nexus of social relationships. It had at least one important aspect, however, probably its most important—namely the duty of revenge for the murder of a relative. In such a case the kindred had the right to extract the *wergild*, the monetary value set on a man's life according to his social status, in compensation. We have already seen (p. 229) that the Church was neither able nor willing to oppose this institution, necessary for the preservation of order, although it is certain that Archbishop Theodore strove, both in his actions and in his Penitential, always to effect monetary settlements and prevent the actual shedding of blood.[40] Our question now is: How did the clergy and monks fit into this system? How were they protected from murder?

There is light on this subject in the *Dialogue* of Archbishop Egbert of York (732–66). This brief work is so called because its method of exposition is that of question and answer. We can best understand its function with the help of the very first of King Ine's Laws, which reads, 'First we enjoin that the servants of God rightly observe their proper rule.'[41] Ine's Law laid down very little about the clergy, therefore, since it was assumed that other codes —of canon law—would regulate their lives. Egbert's *Dialogue* was a code of this kind. It deals with such matters as priests moving from one diocese to another, monks involved in crime, the status of priests and deacons as witnesses to people's last words about their property, the value of bishops', priests' and deacons' oaths in court, impediments to holy orders and conditions for deposition from them. In fact it lays down rules for the conduct of the clergy and has much to say about their legal place in society. One of its questions concerns the eventuality of a layman killing a cleric or monk.[42] He must do penance, says Egbert, and pay a *wergild* to the Church. For a bishop the sum must be decided by consultation, presumably of the king and his *witan*. For the other grades of the clerical order the sums are named—800 silver shillings for a priest, 600 for a deacon, 400 for an ordinary monk. All these figures lie between the 1,200 shilling *wergild* payable for a nobleman and the 200 shilling *wergild* payable for a peasant. But Egbert further laid down that if the person killed was of noble birth he was to have the full noble *wergild*; he was not to suffer any loss of *wergild* by being in orders. Thus the clergy gained on the swings and the roundabouts. It is inconceivable that the *Dialogue* could have been put into effect or even issued without royal approval, and it reflects the ascendancy which bishops gained over kings where social institutions were concerned.

Another problem connected with the absorption of the clergy into society was that of the endowment of monasteries with land and the legal position of their tenure. Many of a king's aristocratic warrior retainers would have no lands and would live in the king's hall and sleep there, as in a communal dormitory at night. But at a certain point in their careers, early in some cases and late in others, they would be granted lands. This is perhaps the significance of the distinction in Ine's Laws between land-owning and non-landowning gesiths.[43] Beowulf is a case in point: after he had returned to King Hygelac of the Geats with his triumphs against Grendel and Grendel's mother already behind him, the king gave him a hall and 7,000 hides of land.[44] There were, it seems, stocks of lands from which the king could endow his warriors, but grants from these stocks were not in perpetuity.[45] They would revert to the king on the death (or treason or exile) of the grantee. In this way kings kept up, if they were wise, the landed resources necessary to reward their followers. The son of a gesith could not reckon to succeed to his father's estates. The peasantry may well have been in a different position from the warrior aristocracy; their plots may have been transmitted to family heirs by customary rules not specified in the laws.[46] It was estates held by gesiths from the king that were subject to precarious tenure.

Now this was obviously an unsatisfactory system for the endowment of churches and monasteries. Dr. Eric John has shown how from the late seventh century onwards the Roman Vulgar Law, the debased Roman Law of the late imperial and early barbarian period, was applied to this problem.[47] Out of this law developed Anglo-Saxon book-land and book-right. The most important features of book (or charter)-right, for our present purposes, were freedom of the land from secular (and especially military) service, and perpetual tenure and right of free disposal —in other words the *ius perpetuum* of the Roman Vulgar Law.

Book-right was developed in England by churchmen familiar with late Roman secular and canon law, and was applied to the tenure of land granted or confirmed to their institutions by the king.

Once developed, it was natural that laymen should hanker after this tenure in order to secure exemption from secular service and to retain landed property within their families. Since book-right, however, remained something exclusively for ecclesiastical property until the late eighth or ninth century, the obvious legal action of fiction for a family, wanting the retention or free disposal of its lands, was to turn itself into a monastery. The abbacy could be passed down in the family and the family members, the monks, would have shares in the endowments. The proliferation of such family institutions, so-called monasteries, was to Bede one of the major abuses in the Church, which he felt called on to attack in his letter of 734 to Archbishop Egbert.[48] They were monasteries only in name, he said, whose monks were but ignorant laymen given over to lust (i.e. they were married men), if indeed they were not renegade monks expelled from real monasteries. Gesiths were suddenly receiving the tonsure and calling themselves not monks, but straightaway abbots. No doubt Bede pinpointed real abuses here, but we must remember that many families used book-right or *ius perpetuum* for truly religious ends. This was an age in which a close con-nection existed between family pride and religious devotion. Some of the pagan shrines of the Anglo-Saxons seem to have been family affairs, and some of the greatest of their monasteries were likewise so. The abbacy of Gilling was passed from one relative to another in its early history, and it was Cedd's brother who completed the initial fast on the site of Lastingham when Cedd himself was called away. Iona itself had afforded a signal example of a family abbacy. And when Benedict Biscop warned his monks not to elect his brother as his successor, the warning was necessary because it would have been natural for the monks to think of a relative as successor, and in this case Biscop regarded his brother as unsuitable for the position.[49] Many establishments of less importance than Wearmouth or Lastingham were founded to be 'a home for royal and noble widows and a place of education for their children, with a number of resident priests ministering to them'.[50] A holy Englishman who founded a monastery near Namur in the eighth century had been educated at an Anglo-Saxon monastery which was described as his hereditary possession.[51] These were not unworthy institutions.

LAY SOCIETY AND THE MONASTIC IDEAL

The lack of a developed system of parishes and parish priests in the seventh and eighth centuries meant that laymen were brought directly and closely in touch with the monastic ideal. Monastic bishops and clergy were responsible for much of their pastoral ministrations. What made monasticism so dynamic a social force? First of all, after the Peace of Constantine and the subsequent establishment of the Christian Church in the Roman Empire, the monks had been a primary influence in keeping alive the sense of man's sinfulness and need of moral regeneration through an ascetic life; they preserved an acute awareness that it was only too easy for him to become immersed in the affairs of the world and to adopt the current values of worldly society. The lives and deeds of ascetics had an interest even to those who did not follow them, because they were a standing criticism of the Church as a whole. Thus lay society in a certain way took its lead from monks. Secondly, monks looked at lay society. Within the monastic movement itself the community life had come to be more and more emphasized, until it was felt that even those who had the call to live as hermits should first of all learn the discipline of living in a community. Guthlac's two-year stay at Repton shows the influence of this idea. It is already to be seen in many of the Egyptians, in Basil, in Cassian and in Honoratus of Lérins. The battle against egotism and towards perfection in the love of God, it seemed, could not be achieved if the arena of brotherly love and brotherly good deeds was entirely bypassed. Long before St. Benedict, therefore, monasticism was far from being something unsocial. And to this was added the development of the idea in monastic circles, an idea which we have already seen expressed by Gregory the Great, that the active life, the life of pastoral administration could profit from monastic contemplation. Monks could benefit their fellow men not just in monastic communities, but also outside these, and their life of prayer was a positive advantage in this, because it gave them love of God, zeal for souls, and clear ideals about men's lives, which equipped them to be preachers and guides. Thus, from an early stage, monasticism had naturally been much involved with human society, and also had had the tendency to ignore the values and structures of this society in its concentration on perfection. In this sense it was a revolutionary social force.[52]

The actual extent to which monastic ideals made an impact on Anglo-Saxon lay society is not easy to discuss. There are no sources whose purpose or effect is to give us a detailed picture of what lay society was like. Sources such as the writings of Bede, the penitentials, the carved crosses, all emanate from monastic circles; they show what monks wanted society to be, rather than what it was. But this in itself is worth knowing.

There is a clear example of monastic idealism in Bede's attitude to the leader of lay society himself—the king. Bede was glad that kings should fight, particularly if they fought the enemies of Christ; but nobody can read the *Ecclesiastical History* without seeing that he also tried, by the selection and highlighting of his material, to superimpose another image of kingship on the minds of his readers, not least on the mind of King Ceolwulf of Northumbria to whom he dedicated his work. The king was a kind of Christ, and his life should show forth the virtues of his prototype as they were cultivated in monastic circles. Oswald demonstrated his generosity and charity when he ordered a silver dish filled with dainties, which had been brought to his table, to be given to the poor. Sigbert of the East Saxons demonstrated his meekness when he was murdered by his kinsmen because he followed the Gospel and forgave his enemies. Oswin of Deira demonstrated his humility when he prostrated himself at Aidan's feet and begged pardon for criticizing the bishop about the horse which the latter had given to a beggar.[53] It was as if Bede had in mind the way in which Anthony the Hermit, the most famous of all monks, had become acquainted with a number of ascetics and imitated each in the practice of the virtue for which that ascetic was outstanding.[54] Just so, the *Ecclesiastical History* presents a gallery of exemplary kings, each of whom had many virtues, but each of whom is brought forward in a narrative of great care and skill to illustrate the particular virtue in which Bede regarded him as a pre-eminent.

In some of these instances Bede was hitting at the accepted social norms of his day. The fact that Sigbert of the East Saxons was murdered by kinsmen, suggests, among other things, that he had failed to pursue a blood-feud or to avenge his kindred for wrongs done. Warfare between kingdoms was very much tied up

with blood-feuds between royal kindreds at this time; and revenge
was regarded as not only a permissible, but even (as we have seen)
as a right and necessary consideration in warfare. The Old English
poem on Genesis represented God himself as avenging his grief
on Lucifer and his fellow rebels.[55] Now over this matter of Sigbert
Bede was in a difficulty, since it was axiomatic with him that the
observance of true Christianity brought worldly success in its
train; that, after all, was how the old pagan gods had been
judged, and paganism was not so far shaken off that Bede could
be absolved from showing how Christianity measured up to the
old standards. Yet here was a king who was not merely killed in
spite of being a good Christian—so much was true of Edwin
and Oswald—but whose death appeared actually to be caused by
his obeying the Gospel. This was unthinkable! Hence the
necessity for Bede to show, with an elaborate narrative, what was
the *real* cause of his death.

Humility was a scarcely less dangerous virtue in a barbarian
king than forgiveness. According to Bede, Aidan was astonished
at the humility of Oswin, and was led to exclaim that he had
never before seen a humble king, and to weep because such a king
could not last. Aidan had, in fact, seen a humble king before,
because he had seen Oswald humbly acting as interpreter from
Irish into Anglo-Saxon for himself.[56] But Bede, to whom a sense
of drama and rhetoric was by no means alien, wanted to give
his words a quality of starkness. As to the reason why a king as
humble as Oswin could not last, Bede piously observes that his
people were not worthy of him. The truth, perhaps, was that
Heroic Age politics were too cut-throat a game to give place to
any but the best-regulated humility. Humility, however, was the
virtue, which above all others Bede tried to impart to his concept
of kingship.[57] What was his purpose? It was the purpose of a man
who had devoted his life to spiritual reflection and to scriptural
commentary, and had never lost an opportunity in the course of
his work to write about this characteristically monastic virtue.
He had pointed out how meditation on Christ's Passion induced
humility, he had spoken of the pride of a man who had gloried in
his riches and despised the poor, he had emphasized the humility
of the Blessed Virgin.[58] And in commenting (in *The Acts*) on
how the apostles began to speak in various tongues, he referred
to, 'the unity of tongues which the pride of Babel dispersed and
the humility of the Church gathered together again'.[59]

There are several passages, both in the *Ecclesiastical History* and in the *Life of St. Cuthbert*, where Bede speaks of the concern of monks for lay people and of the attitude of the laity towards monks. In connection with the departure of Colman from Lindisfarne after the Synod of Whitby, he says that if the Lindisfarne monks at that time received any money they immediately gave it to the poor, and even the king had to expect a plain meal when he visited them. In fact so impressive was their way of life that the religious habit was held in great reverence, and wherever the monks went—and they went nowhere except to preach, baptize and visit the sick—the inhabitants flocked to them.[60] Of Cuthbert, Bede says that he would visit villages far away in steep and rugged mountains, where others dreaded to go because the people were so poor and ignorant; and when he celebrated mass at Lindisfarne on Sundays, he would weep and urge the people who stood by—many of them certainly laymen—to lift up their hearts and give thanks to the Lord. Likewise, when he was hearing confessions, he would sometimes burst into tears and so set an example to the sinner of remorse for his sins. Most revealing of all, we learn from a purely incidental remark that on Fridays most of the faithful were in the habit of fasting until the ninth hour out of reverence for Our Lord's passion.[61] The laity were freely taking up the penitential practices of the monasteries.

It was in this field of penance that we see most clearly the attempt to project an ideal of monastic life on to society as a whole. Penance in the early Church consisted mainly of fasts for certain periods and the regular recitation of prayers or psalms.[62] If the sin merited it the penance was publicly enjoined, and the reconciliation of penitents to the Church on Maundy Thursday was also a public ceremony. In the Irish Church, which was the important influence on Anglo-Saxon practice here, the essential nature of penance as an institution remained—the sacramental character of reconciliation, which could be performed only by a bishop or priest; the type of penance, based on fasting and recitation of the psalms; the refusal of communion to penitents until they had been reconciled. But there was also an important change, the effect of monastic influence. It was the custom in Irish monasteries, as it had been in those of Gaul and Egypt, for monks to put themselves under the spiritual direction of their seniors. A monk would confess his faults, not just those serious enough to merit public penance, but his faults, large and small, of thought as well as word and deed, to his confessor. The business of a priestly confessor in these circumstances became much more than just to decide whether a sin was matter for public penance or not. He was a physician to the soul under his care, feeling for its hidden cankers, and applying to them the most extended courses of healing treatment. It was for this reason that the Irish placed that emphasis on sins of thought and their cure, which we have already observed in connection with the early prayer books. The whole literature of penitentials developed in the British and Irish churches as a guide to confessors in this work. Penitentials listed large numbers of sins and suggested appropriate penances. At first they were only concerned with the sins of monks, but they came to have further sections dealing with the sins of the laity.[63] In other words, it was from monasteries, and their preoccupation with man's sinfulness and the combat against the subtle and varied methods of the devil, that the practice of penance was extended to the laity. The essential contribution of the Irish Church to lay penance, therefore, was not so much its private rather than its public character; the publicity of penance in the early Church and its privacy amongst the Irish are liable to be exaggerated.[64] It was the making of penance into an occasion whereby men put themselves under priests, sometimes actually living in or near monasteries,[65] for the direction of their whole spiritual and penitential lives.

The influence of all this is clearly seen in early Anglo-Saxon prayers and in the lives of such men as Adamnan of Coldingham (see p. 184); and also in the Penitential of Archbishop Theodore. Theodore's Penitential was not compiled by Theodore himself; as a compilation it dates probably from a half century after his death. It represents the scattered judgments and traditions of Theodore's teaching, brought together by a Northumbrian (discipulus Umbrensium), at the core of whose work was an earlier collection by an otherwise unknown Anglo-Saxon priest called Eoda. The penitential is in two parts. The second is a record of Theodore's decisions about points of ecclesiastical life and discipline in general, inspired (as the preface explains) by the enthusiasm with which men and women flocked to him for advice on account of his great knowledge.[66] The first part alone is properly speaking a penitential, consisting mainly of suggested penances for various sins, although even here there are items in which such matters as the differences between Greek and Roman penitential practices are more generally discussed. The actual manuscript transmission of the compilation has been confused and corrupted by contact with Irish penitentials on the Continent. For all its problems of text and transmission, however, there is no doubt that it represents for the most part genuine traditions of Theodore's teaching.[67] Its form owes much to Irish influence. So also does some of its matter, for Theodore approved of the Irish penitential system. We are told, for example, that he praised the commutation of penances, namely the provision by which penances lasting for years might be satisfied by shorter and sharper ones.[68] At the same time, it is—together with the somewhat later compilations attributed to Archbishop Egbert and Bede—a mine of relatively untapped information for social history. In fact, one of the reasons why the Anglo-Saxons took to this form of literature was because it fitted with an important feature of their own social organization. They calculated in their laws the compensations to be paid to a man for the various personal wrongs which he might suffer, in much the same way as the penitentials calculated the lengths of penance owing to God for various sins.[69]

For our present purposes, however, the main interest of Theodore's Penitential lies in the whole system of penance which it implies. Laymen, it is assumed, will be doing penance on a big scale, and sometimes for sins which we would not consider very serious nowadays. If they so much as enjoyed themselves too well in the mead-hall they might fetch up with a fortnight's penance; for a lustful thought, the penance would last well over a month; for indulging homosexual proclivities, seven years.[70] Their penitential life was strictly under the direction of priests, as with the Irish. No deacon might give a penance.[71] Those who had often committed theft, said Theodore, should do seven years' penance, or whatever a priest should judge in the light of the penitent's possibility of making restitution to those whom he had harmed.[72] And in another place the dominating factor of priestly discretion emerges even more clearly:[73]

> If a man has eaten food sacrificed [to pagan gods] and then confesses it, the priest shall consider the individual, in what period and in what way he was brought up, and how it

happened; and so sacerdotal authority shall be moderated for the sake of the weak. And this rule must be observed in the case of every penance and every confession, in so far as God deigns to give his help.

Bede was equally insistent that priests should direct the penance of laymen. Admittedly he suggested, with some originality, that laymen might confess sins to each other, but only small sins like idle chatter, immoderate laughter, or little carelessnesses. For graver sins—and we are already in that category with the lascivious dancing of a girl or the celebration of one's birthday— there was no way round sacerdotal authority.[74]

The practice of confession and penance seems to have become deeply rooted in the life of the Anglo-Saxon Church. This is what Archbishop Egbert of York said about one aspect of it in his *Dialogue*:[75]

> The English people have been accustomed to practise fasts, vigils, prayers, and the giving of alms both to monasteries and to the common people, for the full twelve days before Christmas, and not just on the Wednesday, Friday and Saturday but on every day of the week, as if a fast were pre- scribed by law. Now this custom, thanks be to God, developed in the English Church during the times of Pope Vitalian and Archbishop Theodore of Canterbury, and was kept as if by law, so that not only the clergy in the monasteries, but also the laity with their wives and families, would resort to their confessors, and would wash themselves of carnal concupiscence by tears, community life and alms in these twelve days; and so purified, they would receive the Lord's communion on his Nativity.

As we read what churchmen wrote about lay penance, we become gradually aware of a fundamental ambiguity in the whole attitude of the clergy towards the laity. On the one hand it was doubtful whether married people could ever achieve that level of Christian perfection to which monks aspired; they had to be content with keeping the commandments. On the other hand, if they were willing to abstain from sexual intercourse, confess their sins, fast, and receive Holy Communion frequently (as Bede recommended), then perfection was perhaps attainable after all. Indeed it was this standard of perfection which the Church, galvanized precisely by its low estimation of the married state, constantly placed before the laity as an ideal.

Nowhere were all men, clergy and laity alike, called to a life of penance more strikingly than with the carvings of the Ruthwell Cross (Dumfriesshire). This great monument of eighth-century Northumbrian sculpture, which probably continues Romano-British traditions in its figures, appears to betray in its ornamental work the influence of the mason's yard at Jarrow.[76] That is not surprising, for the pastoral influence of monasteries seems often to be reflected in art. Several carved crosses on the west side of the Pennines, such as those at Lancaster, Halton and Heysham, suggest the style of Hexham as we know it from the carved ornament on the memorial cross to Bishop Acca (c. 740).[77] The sundial on the south wall of the ancient stone church of Escomb (Co. Durham), probably the oldest sundial in England, has a serpent carved round it, which is reminiscent of the ornaments in the Lindisfarne Gospels. The Ruthwell Cross is in reality a stone shaft, two sides of which are carved with vinescroll ornament and two sides with representational scenes. And several of these scenes clearly present the ideal of penance.[78] In one, Christ stands majestically on two beasts, who lift their heads and paws towards him as if in adoration and acknowledgment. They recognize Him as their Lord. These are the beasts whose company He kept during his fast of 40 days in the wilderness. They signify the obedience, which, as Bede had carefully explained in his *Life of Cuthbert*, the animals would show towards those men who obeyed Christ's commands and emulated his penance. Another scene represents the hermits Paul and Anthony breaking bread together in the desert; while the Flight into Egypt brings to mind the same arena of penance in another way. John the Baptist, again, was a penitential figure who lived in the desert. The cross is shot through with this desert theme. Finally, the sculptor presents us with Mary Magdalen, whom commentators regarded as the same person as Mary, the sister of Martha. Here was the very type of the contemplative and the penitent. The Ruthwell Cross is not hard to put together with the prayers in the Book of Cerne; it was (amongst other things) a great litany of penance for those who prayed before it.

Epilogue

In the last years of the eighth century a wholly new threat to Anglo-Saxon life suddenly appeared; the lightning sea-raids of the Vikings. In 793 Lindisfarne was attacked and plundered, in 794 Jarrow. These monasteries never recovered their former importance. Much of English history in the ninth century is taken up with the fight against the Danes. Moreover, the abuse of which Bede wrote in 734, the control of monasteries by local aristocratic families, came to have an eviscerating effect on English religious institutions.[1] The tenth-century movement of revival and reform, conducted under the stimulus of Continental influence, presents in many ways a quite different picture from the monasticism of Bede's day. Yet the Christian culture of which we have written was by no means submerged without trace; in particular it was firmly planted on the Continent by the Anglo-Saxon missionaries and scholars of the eighth century. It was, for instance, St. Boniface and his followers who established the European reputation of Bede. When the latter died he was a comparatively obscure figure, but the Anglo-Saxon missionaries became aware of him, perhaps through Bishop Daniel of Winchester, who knew both Boniface and Bede, and within a few years of Bede's death, Boniface was writing to Wearmouth and York asking for copies of his works. Bede's success as an author in Carolingian Europe was staggering; many of his scriptural commentaries survive in tens of manuscripts from that period. He had hit exactly the right level to make the subtleties and intricacies of patristic theology accessible to a wide audience. The works of Aldhelm were transmitted to the Continent by the same means, if not with the same degree of success.[2]

The most distinguished Englishman who made his career on the Continent after Boniface's time was Alcuin. Alcuin had been a pupil of the school at York, which under Archbishop Egbert (732–66) came to take the lead amongst Anglo-Saxon educational institutions. From York Alcuin could observe, first of all, one of the great partnerships between king and bishop, namely that between Egbert and his brother King Eadbert of Northumbria (737–58)—'they were happy times for the people when king and bishop ruled in true concord'.[3] This must have been an important experience behind his own collaboration with Charlemagne. Moreover, Alcuin appears to have been familiar with a notion of kingship which comes very close to that of the seventh-century Irish tract, *The Twelve Abuses of the World*, with its echoes of pagan times, and its description of the benefits of the 'prince's truth' (*fir flathemon*). For writing about the sack of Lindisfarne, he expressed the view that among the evils which had caused God to allow such a disaster were court luxury, splendid clothes and the rifeness of fornication in Northumbria. And he added, 'We read that the goodness of the king is the prosperity of his nation, the victory of his army, the calmness of the atmosphere, the fertility of the earth, the blessing of sons, the health of the people.'[4] Under Egbert, York felt the various influences of liturgy and devotion which had been at work amongst the Anglo-Saxons. From its library Alcuin obtained good texts of the Roman sacramentaries while he was at Charlemagne's court, but his compilation of private prayers shows that he was also familiar with the Irish type of confession;[5] and we have seen that he had the text of the Nicene Creed in a peculiarly Irish form. From somewhere in the North of England, episcopal blessings of the Gaulish style, which were to retain their importance in the liturgy, seem to have passed to the Continent.[6] The York library was evidently a very rich one; Alcuin described it in a poem in praise of the archbishops of York, and it lay behind his own many sided interests. Amongst these was the characteristically Anglo-Saxon interest in science and natural history. 'My master often used to say to me,' he wrote to Charlemagne, 'it was the wisest of men who discovered these arts concerning the nature of things. . . . But many are now so pusillanimous as not to care about knowing the reasons for the things which the Creator has established in nature.'[7] Boniface and Alcuin were only the most famous of countless Englishmen, who helped to spread their religion, their culture, and their books on the Continent. And so that wonderful fusion and development of Christian cultures, which had taken place in England, passed into Carolingian Christianity, and thence into the main stream of the Western Christian tradition.

Appendix I

SOME POINTS ABOUT THE SOURCES FOR THE GREGORIAN MISSION

In a book published during the war and in an article read to the Spoleto conference on early Medieval History in 1966 Archabbot Suso Brechter has analysed the sources for the Gregorian mission in an original, critical and stimulating way.[1] This note will not go over the whole ground of his work and the subsequent discussion of it, but only over some of the issues raised in our chapter on the Gregorian Mission.

1. *Where was Augustine's see?*

Dom Brechter's arguments, already adumbrated in the book and fully elaborated at Spoleto, are fivefold.[2] Bede, he says, assumes Canterbury to have been the hierarchial as well as the monastic centre of the Gregorian mission, i.e. assumes it to have been Augustine's see. But first, Bede's evidence is never to be preferred to that of a papal letter and nowhere does Gregory call Augustine bishop (or archbishop of Canterbury); he only ever calls him bishop of the English (*episcopus Anglorum*). Second, Gregory's letter of 22 June 601 outlining his scheme for the diocesan organization of Britain makes London the southern metropolitan; Gregory intended London for Augustine's see. Third, only shortly before his death did Augustine consecrate Mellitus, whom Brechter believes to have been his intended successor in that see, and Justus as bishop of Rochester and Laurentius as bishop of Canterbury. Fourth, Bertha's episcopal chaplain, Liudhard, sat in Canterbury during Augustine's time. Fifth, Canterbury was indeed the monastic centre of the mission, although its missionary base was London. That is why Augustine was buried in Canterbury, just as Boniface, who was archbishop of Mainz, was to be buried in the abbey of Fulda.

Dom Brechter's arguments are perhaps compatible with the view that Augustine was a missionary bishop without a fixed, or at least a permanent see at Canterbury,[3] and it is certain that Gregory intended him to have a metropolitan see at London. But he goes farther. He has no doubt that Augustine was the first bishop of London (*ich habe keinen Zweifel, dass er der erster Bischof von London war*),[4] and he believes that Mellitus was consecrated in 604 to be his successor here, at the same time as Justus was consecrated to Rochester and Laurentius to Canterbury. To take Dom Brechter's last point first, there was a good reason why Augustine should be buried at Canterbury even if he were bishop of London. But the question is, was he bishop of London? There is no evidence for it, i.e. no evidence that Gregory's diocesan scheme was implemented. The scheme was not at all practical in Augustine's time. So far as London was concerned, as Mr. Bruce Mitford pointed out in the discussion of Dom Brechter's paper,[5] it would have been a very precarious missionary base in the seventh century, insecure politically and not the centre of any kingdom; nor could its dependence on Kent be guaranteed, as Professor Buchner pointed out,[6] and the support of Ethelbert and the security of East Kent were essential to the mission. Gregory himself understood the difference between an ideal world and the limitations imposed by present reality—at least to the extent that his scheme cannot be taken as evidence of the real situation. The fact that Gregory calls Augustine only 'episcopus Anglorum' does not show that he had no seat at Canterbury; still less does it show that he had one at London. As to Bishop Liudhard's sitting at Canterbury, it is hard to see the relevance of this. Is it proposed that Canterbury was in some sense *his* see? Finally, the argument that Augustine consecrated Mellitus to succeed him at London and Justus for Rochester and Laurentius for Canterbury all in 604, all his first consecrations, begs the question. If Augustine were bishop of London, Mellitus would have been consecrated to succeed him there; if he were bishop of Canterbury, Laurentius would have been consecrated to succeed him *there*.

The archabbot values the *Aussagekraft* of a papal letter,[7] but he seems to take his arguments further than this warrants.

2. *When was Ethelbert converted?*

Bede assumed that Ethelbert was baptized in 597 amongst Augustine's earliest converts. Dom Brechter doubts it.[8] Bede knew little about the Gregorian mission except what he learned from the papal letters, and these (according to Dom Brechter) give no warrant for such a conclusion—rather the contrary. First, when Gregory wrote news of the English mission to the patriarch of Alexandria in 598 and mentioned the ten thousand converts he said nothing about their king, surely a significant omission. Second, in his letter of 601 to King Ethelbert there is no sign that Ethelbert had yet been baptized. True, he spoke of the grace which Ethelbert had received, but he also admonished him to listen to Augustine, to draw closer to him in the fervour of the Faith and to foster the Faith amongst the kings and people subject to him, all of which suggested to Dom Brechter that he was not yet baptized. As to the passage about grace, we are told to remember that Gregory wrote as a diplomat, drafting his letters to potentates with great care and tact and courtesy (all this takes us far from the *Aussagekraft* of the letter), and that the reference to grace need not mean the grace of baptism, but only the grace of the Faith which the missionaries were offering him. Third, Gregory's letter to Bertha, Ethelbert's queen, written at the same time, seems to show even more clearly that Ethelbert was not yet baptized in 601. The queen was told that she should have converted her husband earlier, that so she would have reaped the reward of heavenly joy, but now she should set to work to 'make good in greater measure what has been neglected' and should strengthen the mind of her husband in the love of the Christian faith. In fact so ill did this letter seem to Dom Brechter to accord with Bede's picture of the eager convert of 597, that he believed that Bede, perceiving this, let it quietly drop under the table. He must have known the letter, thinks Dom Brechter; it must have been one of the papal letters brought from Rome by the priest Nothelm, because from nowhere else could he have had the information that Augustine dispatched Laurentius the priest and Peter the monk to Rome. But he omitted it from the *Ecclesiastical History*. The point was that Bede received the bundle of letters from the papal archives when he had practically finished his work (this Dom Brechter shows) and was in too much of a hurry to adjust his story to the evidence which did not fit it.

All this has been disputed by Dr. R. A. Markus,[9] and it is a great pity that in 1966 Dom Brechter reasserted his points without showing any knowledge of the powerful criticisms of them which the former had made. Briefly, Dr. Markus argued that the conversion of the king with his people might have been assumed by

Gregory in his letter to the patriarch of Alexandria, who in any case would not be interested in the peculiar name of this ruler of an insignificant people in the far corner of the world; that only by a very forced interpretation could the pope's letter to Ethelbert be construed to mean that the latter was not yet a Christian; and that even the letter to Bertha need not be seen, and need not have been seen by Bede, as being incompatible with Ethelbert's already being baptized.

On these points nothing can be positively proved on either side of the case. Personally I prefer Dr. Markus's interpretation of the letters to Ethelbert and Bertha; in particular it seems an extraordinary injunction to tell a man to foster Christianity among the kings subject to him when he is not a Christian himself. These letters would suggest to me that Ethelbert was a Christian by 601, although they are not clear evidence.[10] Dom Brechter's interpretation may be the right one. I should be inclined to give more weight than Dr. Markus, however, to the objection about the letter of 598 to the patriarch of Alexandria. It would surely have sounded better if Gregory could have said that the king, too, had been baptized. The situation where a king tolerated Christianity without himself being baptized was a perfectly possible one; it was the situation under Penda of Mercia. On the other hand it is possible that Ethelbert's baptism might have been assumed and might have been merely not of interest in the context. Incidentally, Bede does not say in H.E. 1, 26 that Ethelbert was converted in 597, but merely that 'when among the others' he was baptized ... ; he does, however, imply his early conversion when he says that Ethelbert's death occurred in his twenty-first year as a Christian (which as it stands is faulty because it would take us back to 596). In the date of Ethelbert's baptism, then, Dom Brechter has raised a genuine doubt. There is no proof that Ethelbert was baptized in 597 or that he was a Christian even in 601 (though there is no proof to the contrary). It would be quite plausible to think that Ethelbert had delayed for some time. All we know for certain is that he was converted some time before his death in 616.

On the matter of Bede's integrity, however, and his dropping Gregory's letter to Queen Bertha 'under the table', Dr. Markus has decisively shown that Dom Brechter went too far, and it is a pity that Dom Brechter had not realized this when he reiterated his point in 1966.[11] He showed quite simply that Bede could have had the information about Laurentius and Peter going to Rome from the preface to the *Responsa* of Gregory (whether genuine or not) and that it was indeed very unlikely that he had it from the precisely dated letter to Bertha, otherwise his own chronology at this point would have been less haywire. Mistakes Bede made, but we need better evidence than Dom Brechter's, and more convincing arguments, to bring into doubt his integrity.

3. *Are Gregory's Responsiones genuine?*

Dom Brechter argued that the purported answers of Gregory the Great to questions put to him by Augustine were all in fact forged about the time that Nothelm sent the text of them to Bede in 731. As has been pointed out,[12] Dom Brechter did not know that Bede had quoted from this work in his life of St. Cuthbert (721) and the argument cannot stand as he put it. We do not wish to anticipate the work of Dom Paul Meyvaert on the *Responsiones* here. But Brechter's argument was partly based on the view that these answers fitted the circumstances of Canterbury in 731 and would be anachronistic for Gregory's time. We may perhaps make a few observations about these detailed arguments, several of which seem scarcely tenable. On *Responsio II*,[13] in which Gregory expresses his willingness that Augustine should not be confined to the Roman liturgy but might be eclectic, might for instance choose Gallican elements, for the liturgy of the English church, Dom Brechter maintains that such thoughts are suspect in a pope honoured for his part in creating the unity of the Roman liturgy. Since Dom Brechter wrote much work has been done on the liturgy in this period, all very much tending to show that authoritarianism and uniformity in the liturgy of the Roman church begins only at a later date than this.[14] Moreover, in discussing the famous letters of Gregory to Bishop Leander of Seville about the administration of baptism, Dom Brechter pays more attention to Gregory's conclusion (that a single immersion was preferable as was the custom of the Roman church) than to his argument (that it was really not a matter of much consequence either way, but in this particular case threefold immersion might be externally identified with past heresies).

On *Responsio III*,[15] in which Gregory says that the church should receive no augmentation from the restitution of stolen property, Dom Brechter points out that in Ethelbert's laws, drafted with the help of Augustine, the increase was to be twelvefold. In Theodore's Penitential later, influenced by Irish practice, restitution was to be fourfold. In neither case was Gregory's *responsio* known. This does not seem to be a much better argument for 731 than for 601. And, Dom Brechter's arguments about Gregory's diocesan scheme, it appears to take no account of the possibility that Gregory's injunctions might be ignored in the exigencies of particular circumstances. Augustine and his monks had valuable objects for their worship and it may be that at the beginning stringent measures of protection were thought to be needed for the newcomers, surrounded as they were by pagans.

Responsio VI,[16] explains to Augustine that for the present he could only consecrate bishops alone as he was the only bishop in the English Church, but that in due course more bishoprics should be established near enough to each other to enable three or four bishops to be present at an episcopal consecration. On this Dom Brechter argues that it came from a time after that in which consecration by British bishops had been regarded as invalid and in which there were nonetheless so few validly consecrated bishops among the Anglo-Saxons that there could not be three or four bishops at an episcopal consecration; it envisages a time when bishops are near enough to each other in Anglo-Saxon England for a journey to the Continent to be no longer necessary and when several English bishops could be called together. Tatwine, he says, was the first archbishop of Canterbury whose consecration (actually in 731) fits the terms of *Responsio VI* perfectly. He was consecrated by Bishop Daniel of Winchester with three assistant bishops. But to show that this *responsio* could fit the circumstances of 731 is not to show that it could not fit those of 601. Why must this be *after* the time of Wilfrid and Theodore with their suspicion of the British orders and their individual consecrations? Why not before? The British bishops, whatever view Augustine might have taken of their orders, *were* far away. Augustine's own journey to confer with the leaders of the British church took him to the River Severn and could only be arranged because of Ethelbert's overlordship. Moreover, Gregory's diocesan scheme itself *did* envisage a time when bishops would be numerous and close to each other in Anglo-Saxon England.

The case against some of the other answers is perhaps stronger. Until a better case is made for the authenticity of the preface to the *Responsiones* it may well be right to think in terms of judging the authenticity of each answer (or letter) on its own merits and of reckoning the whole to have been assembled and edited (by Nothelm) from largely genuine Gregorian material at Canterbury.[17] Total forgery is surely out of the question.

Appendix II

There were broadly two types of sacramentary in Rome, both of them probably coming into being as a result of developments in our period or just before. There was the type known as the *Gelasianum* from a mistaken attribution to Pope Gelasius I. The earliest manuscript form of this book is the mid-eighth century manuscript (*Vatican Reginensis* 316) probably from Chelles. The book contains much Gallican matter and it has been argued that it was first assembled in France from Roman and Gallican material, previously only loosely organized. But it seems certain that behind this manuscript must lie a Roman book, at latest of the mid-seventh century. This book must have represented basically a form of the liturgy used in the basilicas and title churches by the Roman clergy, a so-called presbyteral book.[1] The other type is known as Gregorian from the attribution of the book to Pope Gregory I, a much more plausible attribution than that of the Gelasian books. This book was basically a form of the liturgy used by the popes at the stational masses. The earliest manuscript of this type is an Aachen MS of the early ninth century considered to be a direct copy of the sacramentary sent by Pope Hadrian I to Charlemagne (784–92). But as we have mentioned it is practically certain that a slightly later manuscript of this type, Padua D.47, has embedded in it a Roman book of 683.[2]

Much of the material in these two types of books overlapped (for it was drawn from a common earlier stock), but equally, many of the prayers and feasts in them were different. The arrangement of the books was different, too. The Gelasian books were in three divisions, the first containing the masses for the chief liturgical feasts of the year and the Sundays from Advent to Pentecost (the temporale), the second containing the feasts of saints throughout the year (the sanctorale), the third containing a selection of masses which could be used *ad libitum* for Sundays after Epiphany and Pentecost and various miscellaneous masses and rites. The Gregorian books, on the other hand, had the temporale and the sanctorale interlaced so that everything came together in chronological order, and being stational books they only had masses for the days when the pope celebrated at a station, which excluded, for instance, all Sundays after the Epiphany and Pentecost. And they named the station. *Paduensis* had masses for the Sundays after Epiphany and Pentecost and much else besides, but these are additions made probably between 683, when a forerunner book left Rome, and the early ninth century, the date of the manuscript.

During the second half of the eighth century there develops a type of fusion of these two sacramentaries, known to liturgists as the 'eighth-century Gelasian'. This is a North French production and has a basically Gregorian arrangement, but incorporates many Gelasian prayers, masses for the Sundays after Epiphany and Pentecost, and a choice of two prayers for the collects as in the Gelasian books and against the one given in the Gregorian books.[3] And then under Charlemagne *c.* 800 a type of sacramentary was issued by the emperor, which was basically Gregorian, but with a large supplement of Gelasian prayers and masses in a separate section. This book has done much to determine the content of the Roman missal as we know it.[4]

We have mentioned that an Old English Martyrology of the mid-eighth century whose compiler had knowledge of an old Capuan mass-book, also had to hand a new mass-book, probably of the Gregorian type. There is much evidence that in the mid-eighth century in England such Roman mass-books were gaining ground, particularly the injunction of the Synod of Cloveshoe (747) that they were to be used by the whole English Church.[5] Archbishop Egbert (*c.* 735) believed that these Roman books were based on the mass-book which Pope Gregory had given to Augustine.[6] This may have been correct or it may have been the Roman tradition of authorship which Englishmen who visited Rome in the late seventh and eighth centuries learned.[7] It seems impossible to know. What is clear is that in the mid-eighth century there were Gregorian books in England which were regarded as in a sense authoritative.

The case with regard to the Gelasian books in England is more difficult. First, it could be observed that the Gregorian books needed some such supplement of masses for the Sundays after Epiphany and Pentecost as could be had from the Gelasian books if they were to be used in the English situation or anywhere but for the pope's stations. Second, it could be mentioned that there would appear to be at least an affinity between the Gelasian books and the Capuan mass-book which circulated in England in late seventh and early eighth centuries.[8] Third, there is an interesting argument derived by Dom H. Frank from a letter of St. Boniface.[9] In a letter to Archbishop Cuthbert of Canterbury (747) Boniface quotes exactly the words of a collect, the second collect for one of the extra Sunday masses in the *Gelasianum*. This prayer is to be found in no Gregorian book, only in the Gelasian (and eighth-century Gelasian, but the quotation is too early to be explained by that). The quotation—or rather it is more like the involuntary flowing out of the words than a quotation—is very significant. It can hardly be explained except against a background of familiarity year-in year-out with this prayer as it occurred in the liturgy. To Dom Frank it would seem likely on these grounds that Boniface had brought a form of the *Gelasianum* from England. It is possible; too that he picked it up in France long before 747. The former seems more likely for a reason which will become apparent.

The paper of Dom H. Frank sits in the *Bonifatius Gedenkgabe* volume next to one by Mr. C. Hohler, which appears at first sight to contain an opposing argument.[10] This is that there was a type of sacramentary, in some ways analogous to the eighth-century Gelasian, but different in many details; Gregorian in arrangement, and having some Gregorian prayers, some Gelasian, and some which were neither. This type is called the Saint-Amand group from the provenance of its oldest (ninth century) manuscript. Largely because the divergences from Gregorian and Gelasian in these books are in many cases the very divergences of the Sarum Rite (English late medieval) and because their distribution bore a striking relation to the sphere of Boniface's missionary influence, Mr. Hohler believes this to be the type of sacramentary brought by Boniface from England to the Continent. Mr. Hohler argues that the archetype of this sacramentary must have come to England in the sixth or seventh centuries rather than at a later time: 'The eleventh century is apparently excluded since no trace of Sarum peculiarities has been found in Normandy and the two English Benedictine missals which certainly depend on the book approved at Canterbury by the first 'Norman' archbishop, Lanfranc, do not show them either. The tenth century is excluded since we have five sacramentaries earlier than c. 1050 connected with the reformed monasteries and none shows Sarum peculiarities. The archetype should therefore have reached England in the Dark Ages.'

Mr. Hohler seems to sweep aside too readily the possibility that the St. Amand type of sacramentary developed on the Continent in the Bonifacian sphere and was *later* brought to England. But even if he is right to do so, there seems no reason to suppose that the archetype was received in a developed state into England, rather than being developed here. After all, Mr. Hohler says that the St. Amand group differ considerably amongst themselves. The point would seem to be that it comes from a situation in which both Gregorian and Gelasian books were in circulation and both were used and adapted quite freely. Thus Dom H. Frank's prayer is not to be found in any St. Amand sacramentary that I have been able to check,[11] but it might nonetheless have been used in the context of this sort of compilation—if one assumes that the Gelasian as well as the Gregorian books were to hand and that things were fairly flexible.

The general situation in England, therefore, seems to be as follows. Augustine may or may not have brought a Gregorian sacramentary with him in 597 (or his followers a few years later). Its fate if he did is not known. In the late seventh and early eighth centuries (when we next have any evidence) there is a Capuan massbook in circulation, especially in the North, displaced by Gregorian books. It is possible that these Gregorian books went back to Augustine, but more likely that they were obtained from Rome in the late seventh and eighth centuries. The agreement between the Old English Martyrology and the sanctorale of the forerunner of *Paduensis* which left Rome in 683 is in certain vital points striking.[12] It may be that *Paduensis* originally left Rome in the hands of Benedict Biscop or some other Englishman. The fact that we have clear evidence of Gregorian books in the eighth century, however, does not exclude that in some places (Crediton, say) Gelasian books were used. Nor does it mean that the Gregorian and Gelasian books were not often combined (and even used with other sources) to the taste of the individual cathedrals and monasteries.

References

ABBREVIATIONS

Aldhelmi Opera   *Aldhelmi Opera*, ed. R. Ehwald, *Monumenta Germania Historica, Auctorum Antiquissimorum* Tomus XV (Berlin, 1919).

Bedae Opera Historica   *Venerabilis Bedae Opera Historica*, ed. C. Plummer (1896), 2 vols., including the *Historia Ecclesiastica Gentis Anglorum, Historia Abbatum auctore Baeda, Historia Abbatum auctore Anonymo, Epistola Bede ad Ecgbertum Episcopum.*

Book of Cerne   *The Prayer Book of Aedeluald the Bishop commonly called The Book of Cerne*, ed. A. B. Kuypers (1902).

C.C.   *Corpus Christianorum, Series Latina* (Turnholt, Belgium).

C.L.A.   *Codices Latini Antiquiores: A Palaeographical Guide to Latin Manuscripts prior to the Ninth Century*, ed. E. A. Lowe (Oxford, 1934–).

C.S.E.L.   *Corpus Scriptorum Ecclesiasticorum Latinorum* (Vienna).

Eddius   *The Life of Bishop Wilfrid by Eddius Stephanus*, ed. and trans. B. Colgrave (1927).

E.H.R.   *English Historical Review.*

Ep.   *Gregorii I Papae Registrum Epistolarum*, ed. P. Ewald and L. M. Hartmann, 2 vols.

Monumenta Germaniae Historica, Epistolarum Tomus I (Berlin, 1957).

Eph. Liturg.   *Ephemerides Liturgicae* (Rome).

Etym.   *Isidori Hispalensis Episcopi Etymologiarum sive Originum, Libri XX*, ed. W. M. Lindsay, 2 vols. (Oxford, 1911).

H.E.   *Historia Ecclesiastica Gentis Anglorum,* in *Venerabilis Bedae Opera Historica,* ed. C. Plummer, 2 vols. (1896). This is the edition to which reference is made in the following notes. Also, *Bede's Ecclesiastical History of the English People,* ed. B. Colgrave and R. A. B. Mynors (Oxford 1969), with translation by B. Colgrave.

H. & S.   *Councils and Ecclesiastical Documents relating to Great Britain and Ireland,* ed. A. W. Haddan and W. Stubbs (vol. 3, Oxford, 1881).

Life of Columba   *Adomnan's Life of Columba,* ed. A. O. and M. O. Anderson (1961).

Life of Guthlac   *Felix's Life of Saint Guthlac,* ed. and trans. B. Colgrave (1956).

Mon. Germ. Hist.   *Monumenta Germania Historica.*

P.L.   J. P. Migne, *Patrologia Latina.*

Proc. Bt. Acad.   *Proceedings of the British Academy.*

T.R.H.S.   *Transactions of the Royal Historical Society.*

Two Lives of St Cuthbert   *Two Lives of Saint Cuthbert,* ed. and trans. B. Colgrave (1940).

I. THE PAGAN KINGDOMS

The Pagan Kingdoms

1. See, for instance, P. R. L. Brown, *Augustine of Hippo: a Biography* (1967), p. 191.

2. The Letters of Sidonius, ed. W. B. Anderson (*Loeb Classical Library,* 1965), ii, 430–31, Bk. VIII, 6. For Sidonius in general, see C. E. Stevens, *Sidonius Apollinaris and his Age* (1933).

3. J. N. L. Myres, *Anglo-Saxon Pottery and the Settlement of England* (1969), pp. 62–119.

4. *Beowulf,* ed. C. L. Wrenn (1958), pp. 52—53; and J. N. L. Myres, p. 96, note 2.

5. P. Hunter Blair. 'The Northumbrians and their Southern Frontier', *Archaeologia Aeliana,* 26(1948), 98–126. But for the earliest period, see also J. N. L. Myres, in R. G. Collingwood and J. N. L. Myres, *Roman Britain and the English Settlements* (1937), pp. 411–12 and reference.

6. *Felix's Life of Saint Guthlac,* ed. and trans. B. Colgrave (1955), cc. 24–25.

7. J. L. N. O'Loughlin, 'Sutton Hoo—the Evidence of the Documents', *Medieval Archaeology*, 8 (1964), esp. pp. 7–8.

8. K. Sisam, 'Anglo-Saxon Royal Genealogies', *Proc. Brit. Acad.*, 39 (1953), pp. 287–346, has given grounds for scepticism about their historical reliability; but still with some weight are the arguments of F. M. Stenton, 'Lindsey and its Kings', *Essays in History pres. to R. L. Poole*, (1927), pp. 136–50, esp. pp. 139–40, 143–44.

9. *H.E.*, II,5.

10. *The Anglo-Saxon Chronicle*, ed. and trans. Dorothy Whitelock (1961), p. 40.

11. See, Eric John, *Orbis Britanniae* (1966), esp. pp. 5–21; and Margaret Deanesly, 'Roman Traditionalist Influence among the Anglo-Saxons', *E.H.R.*, (1943), pp. 129–46.

12. T. D. Kendrick, *Anglo-Saxon Art to A.D. 900* (1938), esp. pp. 62–73; C. F. C. Hawkes, 'The Jutes in Kent' and D. B. Harden, 'Glass Vessels in Britain and Ireland, A.D. 400–1000' in *Dark-Age Britain*, ed. D. B. Harden (1956), pp. 91–111 and 137–52; and Philip Grierson, in the *Brit. Numismatic Journ.* 3rd Ser., 7 (1952), 39–51.

13. R. L. S. Bruce-Mitford, *The Sutton Hoo Ship Burial* (1968); and 'Saxon Rendlesham', *Suffolk Inst. of Archaeol.*, 24(1946–48), esp. 234–35.

14. *Beowulf*, trans. David Wright (Penguin Classics), pp. 50–51, ll. 1020–34.

15. *Life of Guthlac*, c.17.

16. *Beowulf*, ll. 1239–40.

17. *H.E.*, III, 22. That he did not pursue blood-feuds is here suggested especially by the fact that his kinsmen murdered him.

18. Eric John, p. 22.

19. *H.E.* II. 12. Translation of L. C. Jane.

Paganism

20. *Bedae Opera De Temporibus*, ed. C. W. Jones (Ithaca, 1943), pp. 212–13.

21. *H.E.*, II, 13.

22. J. N. L. Myres, *Anglo-Saxon Pottery*, pp. 123–24.

23. Joan Kirk, 'Anglo-Saxon Cremation and Inhumation in the Upper Thames Valley in Pagan Times', *Dark-Age Britain*, pp. 126–27.

24. F. M. Stenton, 'The Historical Bearing of Place-Name Studies: Anglo-Saxon Heathenism', *Trans. Roy. Hist. Soc.*, 4th Ser. 23(1941), 1–24; *The Place-Names of Surrey*, ed. J. E. B. Glover, A. Mawer, F. M. Stenton, Eng. P-N. Soc. (1934), pp. xii–xiv, 207; Margaret Gelling, 'Place-Names and Anglo-Saxon Paganism', *Univ. of Birmingham Hist. Journ.*, 8(1961–62), 7–24.

25. *Eddius's Life of Wilfrid*, ed. B. Colgrave (1927), c.13.

26. H. R. Ellis Davidson, *Gods and Myths of Northern Europe* (1964), esp. pp. 40, 48; E. O. G. Turville-Petre, *Myth and Religion of the North* (1964), esp. pp. 35–36, 50–51, 70–72, on Woden, and 75–82, 99 on Thor.

27. H. R. Ellis Davidson, pp. 50–51, 53. For the Finglesham buckle, see reference in Chapter III, note 45, below, esp. pp. 23–27.

28. *Leechdoms, Wortcunning and Starcraft of Early England*, ed. O. Cockayne, iii (Rolls Series, 1866), p. 35: G. Storms, *Anglo-Saxon Magic* (The Hague, 1948), pp. 186–91.

29. J. N. L. Myres. *Anglo-Saxon Pottery*, pp. 137–38; see also H. R. Ellis Davidson, pp. 89–91.

30. E. O. G. Turville-Petre, 'Thurstable', *English and Medieval Studies presented to J. R. R. Tolkien*, ed. N. Davis and C. L. Wrenn (1962), pp. 241–49; H. R. Ellis Davidson, pp. 77–78, 87–88.

31. Anne Ross, *Pagan Celtic Britain* (1967), pp. 255, 257–58, 280–81, 292, 308–21. On ravens, H. R. Ellis Davidson, pp. 65–66.

32. Ross, p. 327. For Tysoe, F. M. Stenton, A-S Heathenism, p. 17.

33. C. Singer, 'Early English Magic and Medicine', *Proc. Bt. Acad.*, 9(1919–20), 341–74; W. Bonser, *The Medical Background of Anglo-Saxon England* (1963), esp. pp. 34–41.

34. G. Storms, p. 77.

35. *Ibid.*, p. 51.

36. *Leechdoms*, ii (1865), 291; C. Singer, pp. 357–58, W. Bonser, pp. 158–67.

37. *H.E.*, IV, 20.

38. *H.E.*, III, 17.

39. *Two Lives of St Cuthbert*, ed. B. Colgrave, Anon. II, 7; Bede, cc.13 and 14.

Britons

40. Collingwood and Myres, pp. 427–42.

41. K. Jackson, *Language and History in Early Britain* (1953), pp. 97–117.

42. As at Withington (Gloucs.): H. P. R. Finberg, *Roman and Saxon Withington* (1955), reprinted in *Lucerna* (1964).

43. Collingwood and Myres, pp. 444–56: and the papers by K. Jackson and N. K. Chadwick in *Angles and Britons*, the *O'Donnell Lectures* (Cardiff, 1963).

44. K. Jackson, *Language and History*, pp. 241–45; and 'The British Language during the period of the English Settlements', in *Studies in Early British History*, ed. N. K. Chadwick (1954), pp. 61–82.

45. J. M. C. Toynbee, 'Christianity in Roman Britain', *Journ. of Bt. Archaeol. Assoc.*, 16(1953), 1–24; and 'A new Roman Mosaic Pavement found in Dorset', *Journ. Roman Studies*, 54(1964), 7–14. Also W. H. C. Frend, 'The Christianization of Britain', *Christianity*

in Britain 300–700, ed. M. W. Barley and R. C. P. Hanson (1968), pp. 37–49.

46. Collingwood and Myres, p. 432; and J. N. L. Myres, 'Pelagius and the End of Roman Rule in Britain', Journ. Roman Studies, 50 (1960), 21–36.

47. K. Cameron, 'Eccles in English Place-Names', Christianity in Britain, 300–700, pp. 87–92.

48. Rosalind Hill, 'The Northumbrian Church', Church Quarterly Review, 164(1963), 165–67.

49. W. H. C. Frend, 'Religion in Roman Britain in the Fourth Century', Journ. Bt. Archaeol. Ass., 18(1955), 1–17. Much of the evidence in Anne Ross's book is from this period.

50. Nora Chadwick, O'Donnell Lectures (1963), p. 143

51. 4th Edition (1959), p. 41.

52. Gildae de Excidio Britanniae, ed. H. Williams, Cymmrodorion Record Series no. 3 (1899–1901). For the unity of this work, as against the arguments of P. Grosjean, in Arch. Lat. Med. Aev., 25(1955), 155–87, see the case presented by the articles cited in the next note.

53. On the last point, Gildas c.67. In general, see the papers of W. H. Davies, 'The Church in Wales', and F. Kerlouegan, 'Le Latin du De Excidio Britanniae de Gildas' in Christianity in Britain, 300–700.

54. A. C. Thomas, 'The Evidence from North Britain', Ibid. pp. 93–122.

55. L. Alcock, 'Wales in the Fifth to Seventh Centuries A.D.: Archaeological Evidence'. Prehistoric and Early Wales, ed. I. L. Foster and G. Daniel. The quotation is on p. 207. The stone, now in Carmarthen Museum, is described in V. E. Nash-Williams, The Early Christian Monuments of Wales (1950), no. 138.

56. Gildas, c.34.

57. E. G. Bowen, The Settlements of the Celtic Saints in Wales (1956).

58. John Morris, 'Celtic Saints', Past and Present, 11(1957), 12–13.

59. E. G. Bowen, p. 91.

60. Gregorii Turonensis Opera, ed. W. Arndt and B. Krusch, pt. 2, Monumenta Germania Historica, Scriptores Rerum Meroving. i (1885), pp. 226–27, 664–65; and A. Longnon, Géographie de la Gaule au VIe Siècle (Paris, 1878), pp. 226–27.

61. Gregorii Turonensis Opera, pp. 713–14.

62. E. G. Bowen, p. 115.

63. Gregorii Turonensis Opera, pp. 703–04: A. Longnon, pp. 466–70.

64. E. G. Bowen, p. 95.

2. BEDE'S 'ECCLESIASTICAL HISTORY'

1. H.E., V, 24, where Bede gives a summary of his life and a list of his works. For editions of the Ecclesiastical History, see p. 278.

2. *Venerabilis Bedae Opera Historica* (*Historia Abbatum auctore Anonymo*), ed. C. Plummer (1896), i, 393.

3. W. Levison, 'Bede as Historian', in *Bede, His Life, Times and Writings*, ed. A. Hamilton Thompson (1935), pp. 111–51. For a recent translation and very useful introduction to the work, see *Bede, the Ecclesiastical History of the English People and other Selections*, ed., with introduction by James Cambell (New York, 1968).

4. Quoted by Sister M. T. A. Carroll, *The Venerable Bede: His Spiritual Teachings* (Washington D.C., 1946), p. 47.

5. Bede writes about this at the beginning of his third book on Samuel: also quoted by Sister Carroll, p. 48.

6. *Bedae Opera Historica*, i, p. clxi.

7. *H.E.*, III, 19. Translation of B. Colgrave, with one or two alterations.

8. Quoted from Bede's Homilies (ii, 16) by Sister Carroll, pp. 86–87.

9. Translation of L. C. Jane.

10. J. Campbell, 'Bede', in *Latin Historians*, ed. T. A. Dorey (1966). This and the following citations are pp. 168, 170–71, 175.

11. R. W. Hanning, *The Vision of History in Early Britain*, (Columbia, 1966), esp. at p. 70: J. M. Wallace-Hadrill, 'Gregory of Tours and Bede: their Views on the Personal Qualities of Kings', *Frühmittelalterlichen Studien*, ii (Berlin, 1968), esp. at pp. 37–38.

12. Bedae *Opera de Temporibus*, ed. C. W. Jones (Camb. Mass. 1943), p. 202.

13. *C.C.*, 120, ed. D. Hurst, p. 57.

14. For this and what follows, see D. P. Kirby, 'Bede's Native Sources for the *Historia Ecclesiastica*', *Bulletin of the John Rylands Library*, 48(1966), 341–71.

15. J. Campbell, p. 165.

16. *Bedae Venerabilis Expositio Actuum Apostolorum et Retractatio*, ed. M. L. W. Laistner (Camb. Mass., 1939), esp. pp. xxxix–xli : Claude Jenkins, 'Bede as Exegete and Theologian', in *Bede, His Life*, etc. esp. pp. 157–64.

17. *Bedae Opera de Temporibus*, ed. C. W. Jones (Camb. Mass., 1943), pp. 126–27 and *De Temporum Ratione*, c.29, *Ibid.* pp. 234–35.

18. See for certain aspects of this subject B. Colgrave, 'Bede's Miracle Stories', in *Bede, His Life*, etc., pp. 201–29.

18a. 1 Cor. xiv, 22; P.L. 76, col. 110c.   19. *H.E.*, III, 15.

20. *H.E.*, III, 13.

21. *Two Lives of St. Cuthbert* (Bede, c.21), p. 224.

22. David Knowles, *Saints and Scholars* (1962), p. 17.

23. *H.E.*, I, 1. Translation of B. Colgrave.

24. *Etym.*, XIV, 6, 6. The efficacy of a saint's blessing against snakes is a common hagiographical motif, and Bede may also have been

thinking here of something like *Life of Columba*, II, 28 and III, 23.
25. B. Bischoff, 'Wendepunkte in der Geschichte der Lateinischen Exegese im Frühmittelalter', *Sacris Erudiri*, 6(1954), pp. 215–17. For Aldhelm's views, see below, p. 197.

3. THE GREGORIAN MISSION

Gregory the Great

1. E. Caspar, *Geschichte des Papsttums* (Tübingen, 1933), ii, 514.
2. *Ibid.*, pp. 347–48.
3. These phrases come from Book III of the *Moralia in Job*, P.L. 75, cols. 622B, 623A–B, 623C (ad deteriora quotidie ruunt), 624B–C, 625A, 622C. The *Moralia* is translated in *A Library of the Fathers*, 4 vols. (London, 1844–50).
4. Ep. VI, 50a, for instance was not registered.
5. Ep. V, 20.
6. Ep. XIII, 30.
7. e.g. Ep. V. 49, and VI, 24.
8. Ep. II, 35.
9. Ep. I, 50.
10. E. Caspar, ii, 431–41 and letters especially in Ep.IX.
11. Ep. VII, 2. For this subject, see R. A. Markus, 'The Imperial Administration and the Church in Byzantine Africa', *Church History*, 36(1967), 3–8.
12. Ep. V, 37.
13. Ep. V, 44. *An non universi episcopi nubes sunt, qui et verbis praedicationis pluunt et bonorum operum luce coruscant?*
14. Ep. II, 50 (p. 153).
15. Ep. VI, 58. Translation of J. Barmby, in *The Nicene and Post-Nicene Fathers*, XII.
16. E. Caspar, ii, 457–58, and see p. 457, note 6.
17. In many ways Gregory was influenced by Cassian, as was the Rule of St Benedict.
18. E. Caspar, ii, 397–98.
19. *Pauli Diaconi Historia Romana*, ed. A. Crivellucci (*Fonti per la Storia d'Italia*, Rome 1914), pp. 251–52.
20. P.L. 76, col. 1072.
21. T. H. Hodgkin, *Italy and her Invaders*, vol. 5 (1895), pp. 319–21.
22. Ep. I, 70. Translation of J. Barmby, see above, note 15.
23. Ep. I, 42 (p. 66) *et sic oblivioni mandasti, ac si tibi aliquid ab extremo mancipio tuo diceretur.*
24. Ep. IV, 9.
25. Ep. V, 39; V, 36.

26. Ep. V, 6; E. Caspar, ii, 473–74; J. M. Wallace-Hadrill, *The Barbarian West 400–1000* (1967 edition), p. 53; Dial. III, 27–28, 37.

The English Mission
27. *The Whitby Life of Pope Gregory the Great*, ed. and trans. B. Colgrave (1968), c.9.
28. S. Brechter, *Die Quellen zur Angelsachsenmission Gregors des Grossen* (Münster, 1941), pp. 127–28. For discussion about access to Roman traditions which follows, see introduction of B. Colgrave.
29. S. Brechter, pp. 126–37.
30. Ep. VI, 10.
31. Ep. IX, 222. The argument of Dom Brechter on this point is not too clear. On p. 133 he seems to suggest that the pope was not yet thinking of converting the Anglo-Saxons with his letter to Candidus, his administrator in Gaul, but rather that through slaves purchased as a result he became interested to send a mission. On p. 137 he suggests that Gregory intended the mission before he became pope. There is no certainty about this matter.
32. W. Ullmann, *The Growth of Papal Government in the Middle Ages* (1955), pp. 36–38.
33. J. M. Wallace-Hadrill, 'Rome and the Early English Church: Some Questions of Transmission', *Settimano di Studio del Centro Italiano di Studi sull' alto medioevo VII* (Spoleto, 1960), p. 535.
34. c.61.
35. E. A. Thompson, 'Christianity and the Northern Barbarians', *Nottingham Medieval Studies*, 1(1957), 3–21.
36. J. M. Wallace-Hadrill, 'Rome and the Early English Church', pp. 527–28: P. Grierson, 'The Canterbury (St Martin's) Hoard and Anglo-Saxon Coin Ornaments', *Brit. Numismatic Journ.* 3rd Ser., 7(1952–54), 39–51.
37. Margaret Deanesly, *Augustine of Canterbury* (1964), pp. 4–6.
38. S. Hilpisch in *Bonifatius Gedenkgabe* (Fulda 1954), pp. 12–17.
39. Ep. VI, 50–54.
40. H.E., I, 25.
41. Ep. VIII, 29.
42. Margaret Deanesly, 'The Familia of Christ Church, Canterbury', *Essays presented to T. F. Tout* (1925), 1–13. The first real evidence after Augustine's time seems to come from the early ninth century.
43. S. Brechter, pp. 232–58. See Appendix I for further references.
44. See J. M. Wallace-Hadrill, *Early Germanic Kingship in England and on the Continent* (1971), pp. 29, 45.
45. F. M. Stenton, 'The Historical Bearing', etc., *T.R.H.S.*, 1941, p. 23; and S. C. Hawkes, H. R. Ellis Davidson, C. Hawkes, 'The Finglesham Man', *Antiquity*, 39(1965), pp. 17–32 and Plate IV.
46. H.E., I, 30 and 32. On this matter see R. A. Markus, 'Gregory

the Great and a Papal Missionary Strategy', *Studies in Church History*, vol. 6, ed. G. J. Cuming (1970), pp. 29–38.

47. *H.E.*, II, 5.

48. *H.E.*, II, 15.

49. R.L.S. Bruce-Mitford, *The Sutton Hoo Ship Burial* (British Museum, 1968), pp. 47–56. Not all leading numismologists are agreed.

50. R.L.S. Bruce-Mitford, 'Saxon Rendlesham', *Suffolk Inst. of Archaeol.*, 24(1946–48), 234–36.

51. *H.E.*, II, cc. 9–14.

52. Nora K. Chadwick, 'The Conversion of Northumbria: A Comparison of Sources', *Celt and Saxon*, ed. N. K. Chadwick (1963), p. 164. Mrs. Chadwick argues that Edwin was baptised by a British bishop, but this is not entirely convincing, and even if true, would not diminish from the interest of Paulinus's efforts.

53. D. P. Kirby, 'Bede and Northumbrian Chronology', *E.H.R.*, 78(1963), 522.

54. I renounce my earlier and crude argument on this matter in *Studies in Church History*, iv (1967), ed. G. J. Cuming.

55. Edwin's victory over Wessex was no doubt an important factor in this change. See *H.E.*, II, 9, and *Anglo-Saxon Chronicle*, ed. Dorothy Whitelock (1961), p. 17.

56. *H.E.*, II, 15.

57. *H.E.*, II, 12, and the cruder version in the *Whitby Life of Pope Gregory*, c.16.

58. *H.E.*, II, 16.

59. F. M. Stenton, *Anglo-Saxon England*, pp. 110–113.

4. THE ROMAN MISSIONARIES

1. *H.E.*, Preface.

2. e.g. Ep. I, 18; III, 46; IV, 7.

3. *The Rule of St. Benedict*, ed. Justin McCann (1952), c.22 (*cum omni tamen gravitate et modestia*), c.47 (*quod cum humilitate et gravitate et tremore fiat*), c.7 (*leniter et sine risu, humiliter cum gravitate, vel pauca verba et rationabilia loquatur*).

4. P.L. 75, col. 610C–611D (*Moralia*, Bk. III, c.13).

5. Lytton Strachey, *Eminent Victorians*, p. 184.

6. *H.E.*, II, 2. Translation of B. Colgrave.

7. Nora K. Chadwick, 'The Battle of Chester', etc., *Celt and Saxon*, p. 169.

8. *P.L.*, 77, col. 38A (Book II, c.6). The *Pastoral Care* is translated by H. Davis (*Ancient Christian Writers* XI, 1950).

9. *P.L.*, 77, col. 36A (Book II, 6).

10. *P.L.*, 77. col. 46B (Book II, 10).

11. *P.L.*, 75, col. 639A (*non ex voto ultionis, sed ex justitiae examine:* on Job, iii, 2).

12. *P.L.*, 77, cols. 20–21 (Book I, 7).

13. C. Butler, *Western Mysticism* (1926), p. 178.

14. *H.E.*, I, 26.

15. *Gregorii Magni Dialogi*, ed. U. Moricca (*Fonti per la Storia d'Italia*, Rome, 1924), I, 2, (pp. 20–22); I, 4 (pp. 30–31); I, 5 (p. 40); III, 17 (p. 182). This work is translated by O. J. Zimmerman (*The Fathers of the Church* (N.Y.), 39, 1959.

16. *H.E.*, I, 31. Translation of L. C. Jane.

17. *H.E.*, II, 2 (ed. Plummer, p. 82 *iusta necessitate conpulsus*).

18. *H.E.* II, 5–6.

19. E. Caspar, ii, 517–18, 526.

20. *Dialogi*, II, 3 (pp. 83–84).

21. *H.E.*, II, 7.

22. *Dialogi*, I, 6 (p. 42). The word for gout is in each case *podagra*.

5. IRELAND

1. In general on this subject see J. Ryan, *Irish Monasticism* (1931), a useful book but with a tendency to attach too much weight to late evidence; L. Bieler, *Ireland, Harbinger of the Middle Ages* (1963); Nora K. Chadwick, *The Age of the Saints in the Early Celtic Church* (1961); Myles Dillon and Nora Chadwick, *The Celtic Realms* (1967); Kathleen Hughes, *The Church in Early Irish Society* (1966), especially chapters 5–8.

2. *Vitae Sanctorum Hiberniae*, ed. C. Plummer (1910), i, p. clxxiii.

3. *Ibid.*, see Plummer's introduction for a classic discussion of pagan elements in Irish saints' lives.

4. D. J. Chitty, *The Desert a City* (1966), chapter 2.

5. Cassian's *Institutes*, III, 2 (C.S.E.L. 17, 34). The writings of Cassian are translated by E. C. S. Gibson (*Nicene and Post-Nicene Fathers* XI). See also O. Chadwick, *John Cassian* (1968), pp. 15, 69.

6. *Palladius: The Lausiac History*, trans. R. T. Meyer (*Ancient Christian Writers* XXXIV, 1965), c.11. See also c.47.

7. Cassian: *Conferences* XVIII, 4 (C.S.E.L. 13, 509); *Institutes* II, 3 (C.S.E.L. 17, 18–20).

8. D. J. Chitty, chapter 3. Cassian: *Conf.* XIX, 6 (C.S.E.L. 13, 539).

9. *Conf.* III, 1 (C.S.E.L. 13, 67–68—hermit of Scete).

10. O. Chadwick, p. 69.

11. *Conf.* VIII, 1 (C.S.E.L. 13, 217).

12. *Lausiac History*, c.18.

13. *Adomnan's Life of Columba*, ed. A. O. and M. O. Anderson (1961), III, 23 (p. 524, in tegorio).

14. E. R. Norman and J. K. S. St. Joseph, *The Early Development of Irish Society: The Evidence of Aerial Photography* (1969), chapter 5, and especially figures 60, 63, 65, 66.

15. *The Antiphonary of Bangor*, ed. F. E. Warren (*Bradshaw Society*, 1895), pt II, no. 11 and pp. x–xi. Also *Sancti Columbani Opera*, ed. G. S. M. Walker (1957), pp. 128–33.

16. Kathleen Hughes, 'An Irish Litany of Pilgrim Saints', *Analecta Bollandiana*, 77(1959), 321.

17. *Vitae Sanctorium Hiberniae*, ii, 98. The life is late, but the basic elements of the story are not inherently improbable, and Fintan's austerity is corroborated by the much earlier above-mentioned litany.

18. *Life of Columba*, III, 23.

19. *Ibid.*, p. 526.

20. *Life of Columba*, III. 18.

21. O. Chadwick, pp. 18–19, 37–49.

22. C. Courtois, 'L'Evolution du Monachisme en Gaule de St. Martin a St. Columban', *Settimane di Studio*, iv (Spoleto, 1957), pp. 47–72.

23. O. Chadwick, pp. 148–49. F. Prinz, *Frühes Mönchtum im Frankenreich* (Munich, 1965), p. 65; shows lack of evidence for direct influence of Lérins on Irish monasticism.

24. J. M. Wallace-Hadrill, 'The Work of Gregory of Tours in the Light of Modern Research', *The Long-Haired Kings* (1962), esp. pp. 51–55, 69–70.

25. *Mon. Germ. Hist.*, Scriptores Rerum Meroving, i, pt. 2, pp. 713–14.

26. *Ibid.*, pp. 703–04, and A. Longnon, pp. 467, 470; and see p. 39.

27. *Ibid.*, pp. 734–35, and A. Longnon, pp. 276, 292.

28. See P. Riché, *Education et Culture dans l'Occident Barbare, 6e–8e Siècle* (Paris, 1962), pp. 141–47, esp. 145–47, pp. 324–25. F. Prinz, *op. cit.*, see especially pp. 35–7, 66–7, and Map 1B.

29. *Life of Columba*, I, 28.

30. *Jonas Vitae Columbani Libri II*, ed. B. Krusch (*Mon. Germ. Hist.* in usum scholarum, 1905), I, 23 (pp. 205–06).

31. *Mon. Germ. Hist.*, Script. rer. Merov. v, 603.

32. J. W. Waterer, 'Irish Book-Satchels or Budgets', *Medieval Archaeology*, 12(1968), pp. 70, 74.

33. See Helen Waddell, *Beasts and Saints* (1934), pp. 104–06.

34. C. A. Ralegh Radford, 'Imported Pottery found at Tintagel, Cornwall', *Dark-Age Britain*, ed. D. B. Harden, pp. 59–70, and map on p. 65.

35. H. Zimmer, 'Uber direkte Handelsbeziehungen zwischen Gallien und Irland im Altertum und frühen Mittelalter', *Sitz. der Preuss. Akad. d. Wiss.*, phil-hist kl. 49(1909), pp. 367–68. Much of

this article attempts to show the influence of the wine trade on certain features of the old Irish vocabulary.
36. D. J. Chitty, pp. 31, 44.
37. P. Grosjean, 'Gloria Postuma S. Martini Turonensis apud Scottos et Britannos', *Analecta Bollandiana*, 55(1937), 300–48, esp. 306–07, 310–15.
38. Kathleen Hughes, *The Church in Early Irish Society*, esp. pp. 77–78.
39. *Inst.* XI, 16 (C.S.E.L. 17, 202).
40. *Lausiac History*, c.11.
41. *Conf.* XI, 2 (C.S.E.L. 13, 314–15). Translation of E. C. S. Gibson.
42. *Inst.* IV, 30 (C.S.E.L. 17, 68–69); *Conf.* XX, 1 (C.S.E.L. 13, 554–55). See O. Chadwick, p. 12.
43. *Life of Columba*, I, 44. Translation of A. O. and M. O. Anderson.
44. See *Ibid.*, Introduction, pp. 94, 101–02.
45. Robin Flower, *The Irish Tradition* (1947), pp. 36, 42.
46. *H.E.*, IV, 3. Translation of L. C. Jane.
47. Robin Flower, p. 17.
48. *Ibid.*, pp. 2–3.
49. *The Anglo-Saxon Chronicle*, p. 53. Translation of Dorothy Whitelock. See in general, R. Flower, pp. 19–20.
50. i.e. St. Brendan.
51. *Life of Columba*, I, 6. The passage is also interesting in its emphasis on obedience to an abbot's rule.
52. E. R. Norman and J. K. S. St. Joseph, p. 95.
53. Kathleen Hughes, 'Litany of Pilgrim Saints', p. 318.
54. Jonas, I, 4 (p. 159).
55. *Sancti Columbani Opera*, ed. G. S. M. Walker, pp. xxiv, and 122–81, for Columbanus's rule.
56. Jonas, I, 11 and 13.
57. Jonas, I, 8 (p. 167).
58. Jonas, I, 27 (p. 216).
59. It is true that on one occasion Columbanus preached the Gospel to pagans, but this was incidentally in his travels (*Ibid.*, pp. 213–14). For a different emphasis, see the recent paper of G. S. M. Walker, 'St. Columban: Monk or Missionary', in *Studies in Church History*, 6(1970), ed. G. J. Cuming, pp. 39–44.
60. Jonas, I, 27 (pp. 216–17).

6. THE IRISH MISSIONARIES

Aidan
1. *H.E.*, III, 5.
2. *H.E.*, III, 5, 17.
3. *H.E.*, III, 25 (Plummer, p. 182).

4. *Two Lives of St. Cuthbert*, pp. 206–08 (Bede, c.16). See Kathleen Hughes, *The Church in Early Irish Society*, pp. 82–83.

5. *H.E.*, III, 5. Trans. B. Colgrave.

6. *H.E.*, III, 14. Trans. B. Colgrave.

7. *H.E.*, III, 28.

8. See N. K. Chadwick, *Poetry and Letters in Early Christian Gaul* (1955), chapter 4.

9. Sulpicius Severus's *Dialogues*, I, 2, 3 (C.S.E.L. 1, 183: *statimque eum asello suo inposuimus*). The works of Sulpicius Severus are translated by A. Roberts in *Nicene and Post-Nicene Fathers*, XI.

10. Sulp. Sev. *Dialogues*, II, 3, 15, (C.S.E.L. 1, 213).

11. *H.E.*, III, 16.

12. *H.E.*, IV, 3.

13. Sulpicius Sev. *Vita Sancti Martini*, c.10 (C.S.E.L. 1, 120). Translation of E. C. S. Gibson.

14. *H.E.*, III, 5 (p. 136, Plummer).

15. *H.E.*, III, 6.

16. See D. P. Kirby, 'Bede's Native Sources', pp. 347, 351.

17. *H.E.*, III, 3.

18. *H.E.*, III, 17 (p. 159).

19. In *Studies in Church History*, ed. G. J. Cuming, iii (1966), 131.

20. *Beowulf*, ll. 1232–33.

21. *Vita*, c.20 (C.S.E.L. 1, 128–29).

22. *H.E.*, III, 5.

23. *H.E.*, III, 14, 17.

After Aidan

24. *H.E.*, III, 16.

25. *H.E.*, III, 24: Plummer, pp. 177, 178. I am indebted for this observation to Mr. A. P. Brougham.

26. *H.E.*, III, 6.

27. *H.E.*, III, 22.

28. *H.E.*, III, 21.

29. *H.E.*, III, 19.

30. *H.E.*, III, 22.

31. J. N. L. Myres, *Anglo-Saxon Pottery*, p. 78, with references to earlier archaeological work. See also on p. 77 the author's remarks about the exceptional character of Dorchester amongst Roman towns of the South. See also Collingwood and Myres, p. 395.

32. *H.E.*, III, 22.

33. e.g. apparently F. Henry, *Irish Art in the early Christian Period to A.D. 800*, (1965), plate 73.

34. A. Clapham, *English Romanesque Architecture before the Conquest* (1930), pp. 16–26, and Plate 2; F. M. Stenton, *Anglo-Saxon*

England, pp. 111, 121; P. Hunter Blair, *An Introduction to Anglo-Saxon England* (1956), pp. 150–52; F. Henry, pp. 79, 82.
35. *H.E.*, III, 23.
36. 'Christianity and Geography', pp. 128, 132.
37. Athanasius's Life of Saint Anthony (see references to Chapter XIII below,) cc. 13, 51.
38. *H.E.*, III, 25. C.C. 119a, p. 167 (*De Templo*).

7. THE SYNOD OF WHITBY

1. The classic discussion of this whole problem is the introduction by C. W. Jones to his edition of *Bedae Opera de Temporibus* (Camb. Mass., 1943), on which the following paragraphs heavily rely. There are, however, perhaps some grounds for scepticism about his view (p. 103 and *Speculum* 1934) that the Synod was called in 664 because in the following year the Victorian and Dionysiac tables, which had worked reasonably well side by side for 85 years, were to diverge in an entirely new way. Not only is nothing said of this in the contemporary accounts of the synod, but the view takes insufficient account of the known circumstances—particularly the position of Alfrith and the effect of Wilfrid on him—which led to the gathering. The observation that had the sparing of offence been at issue one would have expected the matter to be taken up on the election of Colman rather than three years later is unconvincing.
2. P. Grosjean, 'La Controverse Pascale chez les Celtes', *Analecta Bollandiana*, 64 (1946), p. 232, note 3.
3. *H.E.*, III, 25. This lengthy chapter contains Bede's accounts of the gathering.
4. By B. Hope-Taylor. Summary in *Medieval Archaeology*, 1(1957), 148–49.
5. *H.E.*, III, 14, 24 (pp. 179–80).
6. Besides Gilling's foundation through the initiative of Eanfled, Wilfrid's invitation of several of its monks to Ripon that year, after it had suffered from the plague, may be indicative. (*Historia Abbatum Anon. Bedae Opera*, ed. C. Plummer, i, 389).
7. *H.E.*, III, 24 (p. 179)
8. *Bedae Opera*, i, 389.
9. R. L. Poole, 'St. Wilfrid and the See of Ripon', *Studies in Chronology and History*, (1934), pp. 56–81, esp. pp. 64–65. For a different view, though one not (to my mind) entirely convincing on this point, see Eric John, 'The Social and Political Problems of the Early English Church', *The Agricultural History Review*, vol. 18 (1970) Supplement, *Studies in Honour of H. P. R. Finberg*, ed. Joan Thirsk, p. 41, note 2.
10. *Eddius's Life of Wilfrid*, ed. B. Colgrave (1926). There is a more recent edition with Dutch translation by H. Moonen (1946). The

present reference is in both c.2. What follows is based on the following chapters.

11. Eddius, c.7. *Videbatur enim ei, quasi angelus Dei loqueretur.*

12. *H.E.*, III, 25.

13. Eddius, c.10.

14. J. Meissner, *The Celtic Church in England after the Synod of Whitby* (1929), in his chapter on the synod, makes this point, pp. 13–14.

15. E. John, 'Social and Political Problems' etc., p. 50.

16. P. Grosjean, *'La Controverse Pascale'*, esp. pp. 231–43.

17. *Bedae Opera de Temporibus*, pp. 89–98, and esp. p. 98, note 3.

18. Françoise Henry, *Irish Art to 800*, p. 57 and Plate 15.

19. J. Ryan, 'The Early Irish Church and the See of Peter', *Settimane di Studio*, VII (Spoleto, 1960), pp. 549–74; and Kathleen Hughes, 'The Celtic Church and the Papacy', *The English Church and the Papacy in the Middle Ages*, ed. C. H. Lawrence, esp. 66. 13–18.

20. *H.E.*, III, 27.

21. *Bedae Opera de Temporibus*, pp. 105–13. For the general background of books passing from Ireland to Northumbria, see D. A. Bullough, 'Columba, Adomnan and the Achievement of Iona', *Scot. Hist. Rev.*, 43, 111–30 and 44(1964–65), 17–33, esp. pp. 122–30, 26–27.

22. (1) Only a few churches in the far corner of the world stand out against universal usage. (2) The example of John is dealt with. (3) The practice attributed to Anatolius not authentic. (4) Columba's following what he knew with simplicity in his own day was no excuse for present practice. For the letter, see *P.L.* 87, cols. 967–78.

23. *H.E.*, III, 27.

24. N. K. Chadwick, 'Bede, St. Colman and the Irish Abbey of Mayo', *Celt and Saxon*, pp. 186–205.

25. *H.E.*, V, 22.

8. BACKGROUND: POLITICS AND COMMUNICATIONS

Internal

1. P. Hunter Blair, 'The Northumbrians and their Southern Frontier', *Archaeol. Aeliana*, 26(1948), pp. 98–126.

2. *H.E.*, III, 24.

3. *H.E.*, III, 30 (for control by Ine of Wessex over the East Saxons in the early 690's, Plummer, ii, 217); *H.E.*, IV, 3 (last sentence), IV, 12.

4. P. Hunter Blair, 'The Bernicians and their Northern Frontier', *Studies in Early British History*, ed. Nora Chadwick. For the possible influence of Pictish art on the Franks Casket, see Isabel Henderson, *The Picts* (1967), p. 144.

5. The suggestion is that of D. P. Kirby, 'Bede's Native Sources', p. 353. It is made *a propos* of the episcopal consecration of Chad, but Bede's account of this (*H.E.*, III, 28) makes it clear that Chad was not consecrated in Northumbria. He was consecrated by Bishop Wine, in the South, and the two British bishops associated with Wine would have been from the South-West. Even if Edwin were baptized by a British bishop, Mrs. Chadwick's proposal is that this would have been while he was at the court of King Cadfan of Gwynned (*Celt and Saxon*, pp. 148–49).

6. K. Jackson, 'The British Language during the period of the English Settlements', *Studies in Early British History*, ed. Nora Chadwick, pp. 64–65.

7. P. Hunter Blair, 'The Bernicians and their Northern Frontier', p. 162.

8. H. P. R. Finberg, 'Mercians and Welsh', *Lucerna*, esp. pp. 69–73.

9. W. G. Hoskins, *The Westward Expansion of Wessex*, pp. 6, 13.

10. A. C. Thomas in *Christianity in Britain*, 300–700, p. 116.

11. H. P. R. Finberg, pp. 73–75.

12. *Aldhelmi Opera*, ed. R. Ehwald, *Mon. Germ. Hist.*, Auct. Antiq. XV (1919), p. 484.

13. *H.E.*, III, 28.

14. H. P. R. Finberg, 'Sherborne, Glastonbury, and the Expansion of Wessex', *Lucerna*, p. 100: W. G. Hoskins, pp. 20–21.

External

15. W. J. Moore, *The Saxon Pilgrims to Rome and the Schola Saxonum* (Fribourg, 1937). For some of the less well-known pilgrimages see pp. 46–54; for details of some routes, pp. 56, 59, 87.

16. The relation between Kent and the Lombards is emphasized, perhaps too much, by N. Aberg, *The Anglo-Saxons in England* (Uppsala, 1926).

17. See on these matters, for instance, L. Brehier, *La Civilisation Byzantine* (1950), pp. 183–90; P. Lemerle, 'Les Repercussions de la Crise de l'Empire d'Orient au VIIᵉ Siècle sur les Pays d'Occident', *Settimane di Studio*, 5 (Spoleto, 1958), 713–31.

18. *H.E.*, IV, 2.

19. *Aldhelmi Opera*, pp. 485–86.

20. *E.H.R.*, 84(1969), 377.

21. *Aldhelmi Opera*, p. 498; *H.E.*, III, 19.

22. *Mon. Germ. Hist.* SS Rer. Merov. VI, 106–07. The life dates from the ninth century and Bertila's dates as abbess were c.658/59–705 (p. 96). see also, W. Levison, *England and the Continent in the Eighth Century*, p. 132, note 2.

23. H. P. R. Finberg, 'Mercians and Welsh', p. 74.

24. *Mon. Germ. Hist.* SS Rer. Merov. V, 602–03.

25. *The Westward Expansion of Wessex*, pp. 7–10.

26. J. M. Wallace-Hadrill, 'Rome and the Early English Church', pp. 537–45. For hospices in Gaul in the early eighth century, see W. J. Moore, pp. 87–88.

27. *P.L.*, 91, col. 1077B.

28. See Claude Jenkins in *Bede, His Life, Times and Writings*, p. 188. The fact that this information is in Isidore, *Etym.*, XVII, 7, 33, does not invalidate the point.

29. P. Lehmann, 'Wert und Echtheit einer Beda abgesprochenen Schrift', *Sitz. der Bayerischen Ak. d. Wiss.*, Phil-Hist Kl: (Munich, 1919), no. 4, p. 6. And *P.L.* 93, col. 459B.

30. N. Aberg, 'The Anglo-Saxons', esp. pp. 102–06; R. L. S. Bruce-Mitford, 'Saxon Rendlesham', pp. 234–35; Sir Martin Conway, 'Burgundian Buckles and Coptic Influences', *Proc. of Soc. of Antiquaries of London*, 30(1918), esp. pp. 80–83.

31. E. Kitzinger, 'Anglo-Saxon Vine-Scroll Ornament', *Antiquity*, 10(1936), 61–72.

32. F. Saxl, 'The Ruthwell Cross', *Journal of the Warburg and Courtauld Institutes*, 6(1943), 1–19, esp. p. 14.

33. P. Lasko, 'The Comb of St Cuthbert', *The Relics of Saint Cuthbert*, ed. C. F. Battiscombe (1956).

34. See R. Lopez, 'Le Problème des Relations Anglo-Byzantines du VII au X Siècle', *Byzantion*, 18(1948), 145–47.

35. See, P. Grierson, 'Commerce in the Dark Ages', *T.R.H.S.*, (1959), pp. 137–39.

36. *H.E.*, II, 11.

37. *Gesta Pontificum*, ed. N. E. S. A. Hamilton (Rolls Series, 1870, no. 52), p. 365.

38. J. N. Hillgarth, 'The East, Visigothic Spain and the Irish', *Studia Patristica*, IV (Berlin, 1961), pp. 442–56: 'Visigothic Spain and Early Christian Ireland', *Proc. Roy. Irish Acad.*, 62(1962), 167–94.

39. For this difficulty see especially *Proc. Roy. Ir. Acad.* vol. 62, p. 179.

40. If there is relatively little evidence for early knowledge of Isidore in Gaul, the reason may be that Gaulish monasteries were busy refurbishing their libraries in the Carolingian Renaissance; Isidore had been so well thumbed that by 800 he was being everywhere recopied. Professor Hillgarth stresses the evidence of early manuscripts of Isidore at the Continental Irish centres of St. Gall and Bobbio (*Ibid.*, pp. 182–85). The fact that this evidence comes from sheets which are either palimpsests or were used to strengthen bindings of later manuscripts shows how liable these early manuscripts were to be replaced. These two libraries put their old sheets of parchments to good use, and historians have been lucky to find them amidst particularly well preserved libraries.

41. Françoise Henry, *Irish Art before 800*, pp. 126–27.

42. Sir Cyril Fox, *The Personality of Britain* (4th ed. 1959), pp. 21–24, and Figures 8 and 9.

43. J. Fontaine, *Isidore de Seville et la Culture Classique dans l'Espagne Wisigothique* (Paris, 1959), pp. 835–41; J. Fontaine, *Isidore de Seville, Traité de la Nature*, (Bordeaux, 1960), pp. 71, 75–78.

9. WILFRID

I am indebted to Dr. J. M. Wallace-Hadrill for several helpful comments on an earlier draft of this chapter and to Dr. Eric John for some stimulating discussion.

1. *The Life of Bishop Wilfrid by Eddius Stephanus*, ed. B. Colgrave (Cambridge, 1927). Other editions are: W. Levison in *Mon. Germ. Hist.* SS Rer. Merov. VI (1913), pp. 163–263; H. Moonen, *Het Leven van Sint Wilfred* (1946).

2. The views on this matter of J. Campbell, 'Bede', pp. 177–79 and note 76 and of Eric John, 'The Social and Political Problems of the Early English Church', *Agric. Hist. Rev.*, 18(1970) Supplement pp. 46–50, appear by and large to carry conviction against R. L. Poole, 'Saint Wilfrid and the See of Ripon', in *Studies in Chronology and History*, pp. 56–81, esp. p. 65.

3. Eddius, c.65.

Wilfrid, Theodore, and the Synod of Hertford.

4. *H.E.*, IV, 5.

5. *Ibid.*, for Felixstowe rather than Dunwich, see S. E. Rigold, *J. Bt. Archaeol. A.*, 24(1961), pp. 55–59.

6. *H.E.*, IV, 12. The division of 678 was Lindisfarne, York, and the province of Lindsey. In 681, when Lindsey had finally come under Mercian dominion, Theodore created new sees at Ripon and Hexham, and also at Abercorn on the Forth for the Picts. The last collapsed after the Pictish victory over Egfrith in 685.

7. *H.E.*, III, 7.

8. J. M. Wallace-Hadrill, 'Rome and the Early English Church', esp. pp. 533–44. On pp. 540–41 are some remarks about episcopal might.

9. Eddius, c.6: *a doctoribus valde eruditis multa didicit.*

10. *H.E.*, II, 15; III, 8; III, 19. There are also the Merovingian coins found at Sutton Hoo.

11. Eddius, c.12; and for Agilbert's tomb, see, Peter Lasko, 'Prelude to Empire: the Frankish kingdom from the Merovingians to Pepin', in *The Dark Ages*, ed. David Talbot Rice (1965), p. 217 and plates 48, 49.

12. For these bishops in general, see A. Coville, *Récherches sur l'Histoire de Lyon 450–800* (Paris, 1928), esp. pp. 299–391.

13. *Sidonius, Letters,* ed. W. B. Anderson, Bk. II, 10.

14. *Ibid.* VI, 12.

15. *Gregorii Turonensis Historia Francorum,* ed. B. Krusch and W. Levison (*Mon. Ger. Hist. SS Rer. Merov.* I), II, 36. For translation, see below, note 22.

16. *Ibid.* IV, 36.

17. *Vita Sancti Nicetii* (SS. Rer. Merov. III), cc.7 and 5, p. 522.

18. Coville, pp. 348–52.

19. E. Ewig, '*Milo et eiusmodi similes*', *Sankt Bonifatius Gedenkgabe,* (Fulda, 1954), pp. 432–33. For difficulties earlier between bishops and counts, see E. Lesne, *Histoire de la Propriété Ecclesiastique en France* (Lille, 1910), i, 275–80.

20. *Hist. Franc.* IX, 30.

21. For a general discussion, see H. G. J. Beck, *The Pastoral Care of Souls in South-East France during the Sixth Century* (Rome, 1950).

22. Disputes about dioceses did occur sometimes, however, when political frontiers were redrawn in Merovingian Gaul (*The History of the Franks by Gregory of Tours,* trans. and intr. O. M. Dalton, 1927, i, 260–61).

23. *Bedae Opera Historica,* ed. C. Plummer, i, 410 (*quorum tamen ne unus quidem a tributis antistiti reddendis esse possit immunis*), and 411–12 (*Cum enim antistes, dictante amore pecuniae, maiorem populi partem, quam ulla ratione per totum anni spatium peragrare . . . valuerit*).

24. The Laws of Ine, cc. 4, 61. W. A. Chaney, 'Anglo-Saxon Church Dues: a Study in Historical Continuity', *Church History,* 32(1963) is useful, especially at p.268, but rather strains to give the date November 11 a pagan significance at pp. 271–72.

25. E. Lesne, *Histoire de la Propriété Ecclésiatique,* vol. i. For burials, offerings and tithes, pp. 177, 180, 186–90; for chrism money, p. 67; for the expenses of Gaulish bishops in relation to their cathedrals and households, see, for instance, pp. 338–39, 345–46.

26. *Regula Pastoralis,* P.L. 77, cols. 17–18 (Bk. I, 4), cols. 36C–37A (Bk. II, 6).

27. *H.E.,* III, 28; IV, 3.

28. Ep. II, 38 (p. 139); XIII, 29 (*despectus ad mare descendere*).

29. *Reg. Past.,* P.L. 77, col. 18A–B (Bk. I, 4); cols. 40–41 (Bk. II, 7); col. 41C (*se mucrone ambitionis occidant*).

30. Ep. II, 50 (p. 153, ll. 3–15).

31. *Mansi Concilia* ix, col. 933 (Council of Macon, 581, c.6).

32. See, for instance, the correspondence over the rights of the bishops of Ravenna to wear the pallium, e.g. Ep. III, 54; V, 15; V, 61.

33. e.g. Ep. V, 58; IX, 213, 215, 218.

34. Ep. III, 46; V, 20; X, 19 (*Nam grave cleri illius erit opprobrium, ut, si hic fortasse adprobatus non fuerit, alium se dicant, qui eligi debeat, non habere*).
35. *Reg. Past.*, P.L. 77, col. 32B (Bk. II, 5).
36. *Bedae Opera Historica*, i, 410–13.
37. The Catholic Herald, 21 February 1969.
38. *Reg. Past.*, P.L. 77, col. 33C (Bk. II, 5).
39. A. H. M. Jones, *The Later Roman Empire 284–602* (1964), ii, 876–78. For the contrast between the density of *civitates* in Asia Minor and their relative sparsity in Gaul, see *Ibid.*, Map V.
40. S. F. Greenslade, 'The Unit of Pastoral Care in the Early Church', *Studies in Church History*, vol. 2, ed. G. J. Cuming, esp. pp. 109–17.

Asceticism
41. Eddius, cc.19, 24, 33.
42. Eddius, c.13.
43. Also in Jonas's Life of Columbanus.
44. For Acca, see *H.E.*, V, 20.
45. *C.C.*, 119A, pp. 265–66.
46. *C.C.*, 119, p. 160.
47. *C.C.*, 119A, p. 157.
48. J. Fontaine, 'Une Clé Littéraire de la *Vita Martini* de Sulpice Sévère : La Typologie Prophétique', *Mélanges offerts a Mlle. Christine Mohrmann*, (Utrecht, 1963), pp. 84–95. I owe my knowledge of this article to Dr. Eric John.
49. Eddius, cc.18, 23.
50. J. M. Wallace-Hadrill, 'Gothia and Romania' in *The Long-Haired Kings*, pp. 35–36.
51. Eddius, c.3.
52. Eddius, c.21.
53. *Felix's Life of St. Guthlac*, ed. B. Colgrave, c.30.
54. Eddius, c.62.
55. Eddius, c.64.
56. Hilary of Arles's Sermon on the Life of St. Honoratus. P.L. 50, col. 1255. Translated in *The Western Fathers*, ed. F. R. Hoare (1954), see esp. pp. 256–57.
57. *H.E.*, III, 13 by chance shows Wilfred, Acca and Willibrord all having a conversation of an apparently favourable kind about Ireland, when Wilfrid and Acca visited Willibrord in Frisia.
58. Eddius, c.4. Translation of B. Colgrave.
59. Eddius, c.33.
60. Eddius, c.36.
61. *Adomnan's Life of Columba*, III, 18 (p. 502).

62. E. Kitzinger, 'The Coffin-Reliquary' in *The Relics of St. Cuthbert*, ed. C. F. Battiscombe, pp. 276–77.
63. *Life of Columba*, III, 22 (pp. 514–16).
64. Eddius, c.56.
65. See A. Wilmart, *Auteurs Spirituels du Moyen Age*, p. 212. The cult of Michael himself was strong in seventh-century Italy.

Romanism
66. In *The English Church and the Papacy in the Middle Ages*, ed. C. H. Lawrence, pp. 15–20.
67. Eddius, c.34.
68. *Hist Franc*. V, 20.
69. *Life of Columba*, I, 37; II, 11, 27, 32.
70. Jonas, *Vita Columbani*, I, 27 (*Mon. Germ. Hist. in usum schol.*), p. 213.
71. See R. A. Markus, 'Gregory the Great and a Papal Missionary Strategy' in *Studies in Church History*, 6, ed. G. J. Cuming (1970), pp. 29–38.
72. *S. Bonifatii et Lulli Epistolae*, ed. M. Tangl (*Mon. Germ. Hist.* Berlin, 1916), no. 23. Translated in C. H. Talbot, *The Anglo-Saxon Missionaries in Germany* (1954), pp. 75–78. For Boniface's missionary methods, see F. Flaskamp, *Die Missionsmethode des h. Bonifatius* (Hildesheim, 1929), pp. 30–37.
73. Eddius, cc.26, 41.
74. *H.E.*, IV, 13.

10. THE NORTHUMBRIAN MONASTERIES

1. *Two lives of St Cuthbert*, ed. B. Colgrave, Anon. II, 7: Bede, c.14.
2. G. Ferrari, *Early Roman Monasteries* (Rome, 1957), pp. 379–407.
3. *Historia Abbatum auctore Anonymo* in *Bedae Opera Historica*, ed. C. Plummer, i, 389.
4. H. P. R. Finberg in *Lucerna*, p. 76.
5. F. M. Stenton, 'Medeshamstede and its Colonies' in *Essays in honour of James Tait* (1933), pp. 313–26.

Whitby
6. C. Peers and C. A. Ralegh Radford, 'The Saxon Monastery of Whitby', *Archaeologia*, 89(1943), 27–88.
7. *H.E.*, IV, 21 (p. 257).
8. See *The Whitby Life of Pope Gregory the Great*, ed. B. Colgrave, pp. 39–42, 53: and Eddius, c.60.
9. *Two Lives of St. Cuthbert*, Anon. III, 6; IV, 10; Bede, cc. 23, 24.
10. S. Hilpisch, *Die Doppelklöster, Entstehung und Organisation* (Münster, 1928), pp. 29–31.
11. S. Hilpisch, pp. 1–44.

12. *H.E.*, III, 8; IV, 21 (p. 253), and S. Hilspisch, pp. 44–50, who also shows that double monasteries were developing in Spain at about the same time as they were in Anglo-Saxon England (pp. 52–55).

13. *Bedae Opera Historica*, ii, 235–36.

14. *Vita Leobae*, c.2 in *Mon. Germ. Hist.* Scriptores XV, i, 123.

15. *H.E.*, IV, 8. Translation of L. C. Jane.

Wearmouth and Jarrow

16. See Gervase Mathew, *Byzantine Aesthetics* (1963), pp. 84–93.

17. Accounts of Biscop's activities are contained both in Bede's and in the anonymous *Historia Abbatum*, in *Bedae Opera Historica*, i, 364–77, and 389–94.

18. *Ibid.*, p. 373; Gervase Mathew, p. 84; A. Grabar, *Les Peintures de l'Evangeliaire de Sinope* (*Bibl. Nat. Suppl. gr. 1286*) (Paris, 1948), esp. pp. 9–10.

19. *Bedae Opera Historica*, pp. 374–75. Translation L. C. Jane, p. 356.

20. e.g. *Ibid.*, pp. 375, 393, 396.

21. *Ibid.*, p. 371. Translation L. C Jane

22. Reports in *Medieval Archaeology*, 8(1964), p. 232; 9(1965), p. 171; 10(1966,) p. 170.

23. R. L. S. Bruce-Mitford, 'The Art of the Codex Amiatinus', *Journal of the Archaeological Association*, 3rd Ser., 32(1969), pp. 1–25.

24. Rosemary Cramp, *Early Northumbrian Sculpture* (Jarrow Lecture, 1965), pp. 10–12.

25. E. Kitzinger, see above, Chapter VIII, note 31.

26. G. Baldwin Brown, *The Arts in Early England*, vi. pt. 1 (1930), pp. 1–10 For the possibility, however, that the MS might have been placed in Cuthbert's coffin in 698, see the rather hypothetical passage in *The Stonyhurst Gospel of Saint John*, ed. T. J. Brown, (1969), pp. 28–29.

27. E. A. Lowe, 'A Key to Bede's Scriptorium', *Scriptorium*, 12(1958), esp. pp. 184–86, 189. See also E. A. Lowe, *English Uncial*, (1960), pp. 8–13.

28. R. A. B. Mynors, 'The Stonyhurst Gospel', *The Relics of Saint Cuthbert*, ed. C. F. Battiscombe, p. 357.

29. *Ibid.*, Roger Powell on the binding, pp. 363–74. See also more recently *The Stonyhurst Gospel of Saint John*, ed. T. J. Brown, pp. 17–18.

Ripon and Hexham

30. *Bedae Opera Historica*, pp. 392, 381.

31. Eddius, c.17.

32. *Bedae Opera Historica*, p. 367.
33. Eddius, c.22.
34. See especially Eddius, cc.14, 21, 47, 62, for evidence of Wilfrid's monastic empire. It is discussed by E. John, *'Saecularium Prioratus and the rule of St. Benedict'*, *Revue Bénédictine*, 75(1965), pp. 219–21.
35. H. M. and Joan Taylor, *Anglo-Saxon Architecture*, (1965), i, 297–312.
36. Sir Eric Fletcher, 'Anglo-Saxon Architecture in the Seventh Century', *Trans. of the London and Middx. Archaeol. Soc.*, 21, pt. 2 (1965), pp. 89–97: also on Brixworth, E. D. C. Jackson and Sir Eric Fletcher, *Journ. Bt. Archaeol. Assoc.*, 24(1961), 1–15; and on Wing, *Ibid.* 25(1962), 1–20.
37. e.g. Ep. V, 49; VII, 12. See also, E. Lesne, *Histoire de la Propriete Ecclésiastique*, i, 67.

Lindisfarne
38. *Aethelwulf De Abbatibus*, ed. and trans. A. Campbell (1967), II, 550–51.
39. *H.E.*, III, 25 (p. 181).
40. For this and the following paragraphs I rely mainly on *Evangeliorum Quattuor Codex Lindisfarnensis*, ed. T. D. Kendrick, T. J. Brown, R. L. S. Bruce-Mitford etc. (Lausanne etc., 1956, 1960), especially the contributions on the art of the Lindisfarne Gospels by R. L. S. Bruce-Mitford in volume 2, esp. pp. 5–16, 109–259.
41. See Françoise Henry, *Irish Art to 800*, pp. 10–16.
42. *Codex Lindisfarnensis*, ii, 170–71.
43. J. Strzygowski, *The Origin of Christian Church Art* (1923), p. 241.
44. *Codex Lindisfarnensis*, ii, 219.
45. *Two Lives of St. Cuthbert*, Anon. II, 3; Bede, c.10. For the colour tones of the Lindisfarne Gospels, see *Codex Lindisfarnensis*, ii, 121.
46. *Ibid.*, esp. Bede, cc. 17, 19–21.
47. *Ibid.*, Anon. III, 1; Bede, c.17; and see note by B. Colgrave, p. 326. Translation, *Ibid.*
48. *Ibid.*, Bede, c.16 (p. 212); *Rule of St. Benedict*, c.55. On Cuthbert's shoes, Bede, c.18.
49. *Ibid.*, Bede, c.9 (p. 186).
50. R. L. S. Bruce-Mitford, 'The Pectoral Cross', *The Relics of St. Cuthbert*, pp. 308–25.

Diversity and Unity
51. U. Berlière, *L'Ascèse Bénédictine des Origines à la Fin due XIIe Siècle*, (Paris, 1927), pp. 40–41, 156–157.
52. *Bedae Opera Historica*, i, 381–82, 386. The latter reference is

cited by G. G. Willis, *Further Essays in Early Roman Liturgy* (1968), p. 204.

53. *Two Lives of St. Cuthbert*, Anon. IV, 16; c.44 (p. 296); note by B. Colgrave, p. 359. *Adomnan's Life of Columba*, I, 44 and III, 12. carries the clear implication that at Iona in the saint's time mass was normally celebrated only on Sundays and solemn festivals.

54. *The Antiphonary of Bangor*, ed. F. E. Warren, pt. 2 (*Bradshaw Society*, 1895), esp. pp. viii–xi, xxiii–xxiv, and no. 11.

55. *Aethelwulf De Abbatibus*, ll. 659–61.

56. See F. J. E. Raby, *A History of Christian-Latin Poetry* (1953), pp. 44–140. Also Ruth E. Messenger, 'Mozarabic Hymns in relation to Contemporary Culture in Spain', *Traditio*, 4(1946), pp. 149–77. The Second Council of Braga (563), under the influence of Rome, forbade the use of all poetical writings except the psalms in church. The Fourth Council of Toledo (633), however, restored the old usage in legislation: *Sicut igitur orationes, ita et hymnos in laudem Dei compositos, nullus vestrum ulterius improbet sed pari modo Gallia, Hispaniaque celebret: excommunicatione plectendi qui hymnos rejicere fuerint ausi* (Canon 13, Mansi *Concilia* X, 622–23).

57. *Life of Columba*, II, 9.

58. *Codex Lindisfarnensis*, ii.

59. *Medieval Archaeology*, 10(1966), 170.

60. *Two Lives of St. Cuthbert*, Bede, c.6.

61. *Ibid.*, Preface, p. 145. Trans. of B. Colgrave.

62. *Ibid.*, Anon. III, 1; Bede, c.16 (p. 210).

63. *Ibid.*, Anon. IV, 14; Bede, c.40.

64. *Bedae Opera Historica*, i, 389. At this time Benedict Biscop would have been abbot of the monastery of SS. Peter and Paul at Canterbury, and Ceolfrid's visit perhaps marks the beginning of their monastic partnership.

65. *Ibid.*, i, 389, 391.

66. *Two Lives of St. Cuthbert*, Bede, seventh century.

67. *H.E.*, IV, 27 (p. 275). It is suggested by B. Colgrave (*Two Lives*, pp. 9, 357) that the troubles at Lidisfarne after Cuthbert's death of which Bede speaks, were due to Wilfrid's administration. As Bede is explicit to say, however, that Wilfrid administered the bishopric, and says nothing of the monastery (and he is the only source for this knowledge), there are no grounds whatsoever for this assertion.

68. *H.E.*, V, 1.

11. PRAYER AND WORSHIP

I am indebted to the late Revd. L. J. Crampton for some helpful discussion on this chapter, particularly when I was his client in the Radcliffe Infirmary for a few days.

Rome

1. E. Mâle, *The Early Churches of Rome* (trans. D. Buxton, 1960), chapter 3. For the possibility of Santa Sabina's being a house with a church as early as the third century, for its age as a Roman *titulus*, and for the stational liturgy there, see J. P. Kirsch, *Die Stationskirchen des Missale Romanum* (Freiburg im Breisgau, 1926), pp. 71–76.

2. Ordo XV, nos. 13, 21, 23, in M. Andrieu, *Les Ordines Romani du Haut Moyen Age*, III (Louvain, 1951). For the date, see S. J. P. Van Dijk, 'The Urban and Papal Rites in Seventh- and Eighth-Century Rome', *Sacris Erudiri*, 12(1961), pp. 454–62.

3. Ordo I, esp. nos. 8–10, 21, 38–39, 69–73, in M. Andrieu, II (Louvain, 1948). Fundamental is S. J. P. Van Dijk, art. cit. pp. 465–72, where the importance of Pope Vitalian (657–72) in this is argued. Also, S. J. P. Van Dijk, 'Recent Developments in the Study of the Old Roman Rite', *Studia Patristica*, 8, pt. 2 (Berlin, 1966), ed. F. L. Cross, pp. 299–319.

4. Doubt is cast on whether most of the Roman clergy would normally have attended the stational mass by C. Coebergh, 'Le Sacramentaire Gelasien Ancien', *Archiv für Liturgiewissenschaft* 7, pt. 1 (1961), pp. 58–60, 65.

5. G. Ferrari, *Early Roman Monasteries* (Rome, 1957), esp. pp. 366–73.

6. Edmund Bishop, 'Kyrie Eleison: A Liturgical Consultation', in *Liturgica Historica* (1918), p. 124. Gregory's letter is Ep. IX, 26. That the Kyrie in the Roman Mass is much earlier than Gregory's time is shown by B. Capelle, 'Le Kyrie de la Messe et la Pape Gélase', *Travaux Liturgiques*, II (Louvain, 1962), pp. 116–34.

7. B. Capelle, 'La Main de S. Grégoire dans le Sacramentaire Grégorien', *Revue Bénédictine*, 49(1937), 13–28; reprinted in that author's *Travaux Liturgiques* II, esp. pp. 162–65. Much of value along the same lines is in H. Ashworth, 'Gregorian Elements in the Gelasian Sacramentary', *Ephemerides Liturgicae*, 67(1953), 9–23.

8. Notably A. Stuiber, *Libelli Sacramentorum Romani* (Bonn, 1950), and H. A. P. Schmidt, 'De Lectionibus variantibus in Formulis Identicis Sacramentariorum Leoniani, Gelasiani, et Gregoriani', *Sacris Erudiri*, 4(1952), 103–73. The latter writer's view, however, that the Gelasianum was originally put together in Gaul rather than in Rome seems difficult to accept in the light of the apparently conclusive arguments of M. Andrieu, 'Les Messes de Jeudis de Carême et les anciens Sacramentaires', *Revue des Sciences Religieuses*, 9(1929), 540–74, and B. Capelle, 'Le Sacramentaire Romaine avant S. Grégoire', *Rev. Ben.*, 64(1954), 157–67. Of great value as a study of *libelli*, i.e. separately filed prayers, is J. D. Thompson. *The Contribution of Vaticanus Reginensis 316 to the*

History of Western Service Books (Oxford Unpublished D.Phil. Thesis, 1968). A useful general survey of early Roman mass-books, or sacramentaries, is in Th. Klauser, *A Short History of the Western Liturgy* (trans. J. Halliburton, 1969), pp. 54–59.

9. K. Mohlberg, in his edition of Codex Padua D47 (Paduensis), a ninth-century manuscript, believed it to have had such a forerunner from the year 595, when Pope Gregory held a synod. His argument was based on the fact that between the feasts of SS. Sixtus, etc. (6 Aug.) and St. Cyriacus (8 Aug.) came the fifth Sunday after the octave of SS. Peter and Paul (i.e. 7 Aug.). The way Sundays and saints are interlaced, therefore, implies a year in which Easter fell on 3 April. As Mohlberg showed clearly that embedded in the ninth-century MS. is an 'edition' of the Roman book of 683, the only likely or possible year before that for a forerunner (683 itself does not fit) for the date of Easter would be 595; *Die älteste erreichbare Gestalt des Liber Sacramentorum der römischen Kirche* (Münster, 1927), pp. XXXV-IX and A. Baumstrak, *Ibid*, p. 185*. The argument is neatly summarized by C. Vogel, *Introduction aux Sources de l'Histoire du Culte Chrétien au Moyen Age* (Spoleto 1966), p. 71, note 223.

This is one of the rare occasions, however, when M. Vogel does not give an entirely balanced account of the work of scholars. He does not mention K. Gamber, *Wege zur Urgregorianum* (*Texte und Arbeiten*, 46, Beuron 1956), who argues that as the date 595 is based on Sundays in August, as the *Urgregorianum* was a papal stational book, and as there was no station at that season, such Sunday masses could have been added at any time before the MS. was written in C9 (pp. 8–9). It is not, in fact, impossible that Gregory should have organized masses for such Sundays, but Mgr. Gamber's argument puts the matter sufficiently in doubt to make the date 595 quite unreliable. He then proceeds by a more thorough and sophisticated calculation (pp. 14–19) to propose that the arrangement of *Paduensis* and the *Hadrianum* (C9 Aachen MS.), which is largely the same except for the additions of *Paduensis*, can only imply the date 6 April for Easter. On this basis, he proposes 592 as the date of the original papal mass-book.

C. Coebergh, 'Les Libelli Sacramentorum de Saint Grégoire le Grand et le Sacramentaire publie sous son Nom', *Studia Patristica*, 8, pt. 2 (Berlin, 1966), ed. F. L. Cross, pp. 176–88, argues that because the year 592 would fit, this does not prove that Gregory did in fact produce a sacramentary in that year. He proposes that it would equally well fit 629 and Pope Honorius I. This may be true, but it equally does not prove that Gregory *did not* produce a sacramentary. Nor is it easy to agree with the more general points adduced against the likelihood of Gregory's composing a sacramentary by H. Ashworth, 'Did St. Gregory the Great compose a Sacramentary?', *Studia Patristica*, 2(1957), pp. 3–8; and 'Did St. Augustine bring the *Gregorianum* to England?', *Ephemerides Liturgicae*, 72(1958), 39–43. To show that Gregory was not the man to impose a sacramentary is not the same as showing that he would not have composed one.

Thus it is quite uncertain whether or not Gregory produced a sacramentary. It is not entailed necessarily in the organization of festivals or stations, if Gregory did these things. All we can say is that there was a Gregorian (i.e. papal or related to papal) book produced in 683, and that from the relation of the early Roman books with each other, it seems likely that there was an earlier version from the late sixth or early seventh century.

10. A. Chavasse, *Le Sacramentaire Gélasien*, (Paris 1957); for conclusions on the date, see esp. pp. 235, 252.

11. This was argued by Chavasse (conclusions pp. 624–25), but Dom B. Capelle, in a review, suggested that there was no need to suppose a book behind the Gregorian and Gelasian sacramentaries, but that the common material could have come from smaller collections of formulae, freely composed and copied (*Rev. d'Hist. Eccl.* 54, pt. 2, 1959, pp. 877–78). This indeed seems more likely.

12. For *Veronensis*, see the work of A. Stuiber; and *Sacramentarium Veronense*, ed. L. C. Mohlberg (Rome, 1955), esp. pp. LIX–LX; and C. Vogel, pp. 30–42. The MS. is dated to C6 and its hand ascribed possibly to Verona with certainly Veronese additions of early C7 in C.L.A. IV, no. 514, and by L. C. Mohlberg to early C7, pp. XXV–VI.

13. See above, Chapter IV.

14. See, Th. Klauser, pp. 18–24.

Diversity

15. F. L. Cross, 'Early Western Liturgical Manuscripts', *Journ. Theol. Studies*, 116(1965), 61–67, argues that sacramentaries hardly existed before 700. It is a timely reminder and based on a useful idea of liturgical development, but exaggerated. It appears to take insufficient account of the fact that sacramentaries are more likely than other kinds of liturgical manuscripts to have been destroyed. The numbers of palimpsests of sacramentary fragments show how prone these books were to become obsolete and to be destroyed; see K. Gamber, *Codices Liturgici Latini Antiquiores* (Freiburg, Schweiz, 1963), nos. 103–06, 108, 110–12, 201, 203 (Mone Masses), 204, 205, 208, 211 (Clm. 14429), 216, 221, 222. For the Canterbury gospel book, see F. Wormald, *The Miniatures in the Gospels of St. Augustine* (1954).

16. Dom G. Morin, 'La Liturgie de Naples au Temps de Saint Grégoire', *Rev. Ben.*, 8(1891), 481–93, 529–37; Edmund Bishop, *The Bosworth Psalter* (1908), pp. 152–53.

17. Dom G. Morin, 'Le Recueil Primitif des Homelies de Bede sur l'Evangile', *Rev. Ben.*, 9(1892), 312–26. See also, G. G. Willis, *Further Essays in Early Roman Liturgy*, (1968), pp. 214–15. I am not convinced by T. J. Brown in *Codex Lindisfarnensis*, ii, p. 55, note 3.

18. *An Old English Martyrology*, ed. G. Herzfeld, *Early English Text Society*, 116(1900): for date, pp. xxvii–xxxii; for the three 'new mass-book' saints, see 1 June, 18 August, 29 August; for the five 'old mass-book' ones named here, 1 June, 15 October, 7 September, 27 August, 5 September. For the mosaic, R. Garucci, *Storia dell' Arte Cristiana* (Prato, 1877), iv, 64; in general, J. Chapman, *Early History of the Vulgate Gospels* (1908), pp. 65–77. For the point about the Roman sacramentaries, see below Appendix II.

19. *The Calendar of St. Willibrord*, ed. H. A. Wilson, *Henry Bradshaw Society*, 55(1918), esp. pp. xvii–xxi and calendar. Some scepticism about the entries in this calendar, not entirely justified, is expressed by A. Chavasse, pp. 340–44. K. Gamber, 'Das kampanische Messbuch als Vorläufer des Gelasianum', *Sacris Erudiri*, 12(1961), 11–13, 109, argues the direct dependence of English liturgical books on sixth- and seventh-century Campanian mass-books, and pushes these back rather hypothetically to Paulinus of Nola.

20. *Missale Francorum*, ed. L. C. Mohlberg, with L. Eizenhofer and P. Siffrin (Rome, 1957), pp. 72–73, 83–84.

21. F. Cabrol, 'Les Origines de la Liturgie Gallicane', *Rev. d'Hist. Eccl.*, 26(1930), 951–62, esp. 957–58. Similar argument in E. Griffe, 'Aux Origines de la Liturgie Gallicane', *Bull. de Litt. Eccl.*, 52(1951), 17–43. See also W. S. Porter, *The Gallican Rite*, (1958), esp. pp. 17–46.

22. E. Bishop, 'The Genius of the Roman Rite', *Liturgica Historica*, pp. 1–19, esp. pp. 2–5 (and Bishop's translations below). W. S. Porter, pp. 48–51. For a more favourable attitude than that of Bishop towards Gallican prayers, and for a criticism of Roman prayers, see Th. Klauser, pp. 40–43.

23. *H.E.*, I, 27 (p. 49, *Responsio* 2).

24. At this period Rome had the blessing of the candle, but not the blessing of the fire or the Exultet, Chavasse, pp. 100–02, and *Liber Sacramentorium Romanae Ecclesiae* (*Vat. Reg.* 316), ed. L. C. Mohlberg (Rome, 1960), pp. 68–69. Under Gallican influence, the Exultet comes into the 'eighth-century Gelasians'.

25. This was the view of J. Jungmann, *Die Lateinischen Bussriten in ihrer geschichlichen Entwicklung*, (Innsbruck, 1932), pp. 15–20, criticized by C. Callewaert in *Eph. Liturg.*, 51(1937), 310–18, without much effect (see J. Jungmann, *Ibid.*, 52(1938), 77–96).

26. J. Jungmann, p. 19. First Friday of Lent.

27. *Missale Gothicum*, ed. L. C. Mohlberg (Rome, 1961), no. 63.

28. Text in Dom G. Morin, 'Un Recueil Gallican Inédit de *Benedictiones Episcopales* en Usage a Freising aux VII–IX Siècles', *Rev. Ben.*, 29(1912), 188. Also in another Freising collection in a mass of one martyr, ed. W. Dürig in *Archiv fur Liturgiewissenschaft*, 4, pt. 2 (1956), p. 241.

29. Book of Numbers, VI, 23. See P.L. 72, col. 94. Dom A. Wilmart showed that this treatise, attributed to St. Germain of Paris (ob. 576), was in fact written c.700, *Dict. d'Archeol. Chrét. et de Liturg.*, 6(1924), 1049–1102.

30. *Pro autem benedictionibus, quas faciunt Galli, ut nosti frater, multis vitiis variantur. Nam non ex apostolica traditione hoc faciunt, sed per vanam gloriam operantur* (Tangl. no. 371). H. A. Wilson suggested that episcopal benedictions were unusual in England in St. Boniface's time otherwise he would have been unlikely to raise the question of Gallican practice with the pope (*The Benedictional of St. Ethelwold, Bishop of Winchester 963–84*, ed. G. F. Warner and H. A Wilson, Roxburghe Club, 1910, p. xlix). Even if this were a valid argument, however, Crediton could have been one thing and Ripon or Hexham quite another c.700.

31. These collections of episcopal blessings sometimes circulated as separate compilations, later called benedictionals, and sometimes they formed a section of a sacramentary, doubtless when the sacramentary was intended for use by a bishop as well as by priests. Either way there is no difficulty in fitting them to any sort of sacramentary in use.

32. J. Deshusses, 'La Bénédictionnaire Gallican du VIIIᵉ Siècle', *Ephem. Liturgicae*, 77(1963), 169–87, esp. 179–80.

33. H. M. Bannister, 'Liturgical Fragments', *Journ. Theol. Studies*, 9(1908), 398–411, esp. 403; *C.L.A.*, V. no. 581.

34. Eddius, c.17.

35. L. Duchesne, *Origines du Culte Chretien*, (Paris, 1898), pp. 392, 399. Gregory of Tours has a narrative in his *Vitae Patrum* about the consecration of an oratory of Abbot Senoch in the region of Tours, which illustrates very clearly the secondary character of the deposition of relics in the Gallican ceremony, *Mon. Germ. Hist.* SS Rer. Merov. I, 1, p. 721. For the relevant prayers and ceremonial of the Roman rite, see A. Chavasse, *Le Sacramentaire Gélasien*, pp. 38–39, and for the Gallican, pp. 41–42.

36. Ep. VI, 48.

37. *Missale Francorum*, no. 54; *Le Sacramentaire Gélasien d' Angoulême*, ed. P. Cagin (Angoulême, 1919), no. 2024. It is doubtful whether a Gelasian sacramentary with Gallican additions would have existed as early as the 670s in Gaul. Whether it did or not,

however, hardly diminishes from the significance of Wilfrid's use of the Gallican rite here. In his time these things were all a matter of deliberate choice, as they were with the Romanizing Gallicans whose work lay behind the fusion of Roman and Gallican elements in the Gelasian Vat. Reg. 316 (mid-C8).

38. B. Capelle, 'Alcuin et l'Histoire du Symbole de la Messe', *Recherches de Théol, Anc. et Med.*, (1934), reprinted in *Travaux Liturgiques*, II, 211–21.

Private Prayer

39. Josef A. Jungmann, *The Early Liturgy to the Time of Gregory the Great* (London Paperback edition, 1960), pp. 97–98.
40. The importance of the memory in prayer, particularly in re-calling the monk's spiritual reading, is stressed by Isidore and Bede and other fathers before them. See J. Lelercq et al., *The Spirituality of the Middle Ages* (1968), pp. 65–66.
41. Edmund Bishop, *Liturgica Historica*, pp. 192–97; W. Levison. *England and the Continent in the Eighth Century*, pp. 295–302. K. Sisam, 'Canterbury, Lichfield and the Vespasian Psalter', *Review of English Studies*, N.S.7 (1956), 9–10, shows that the surviving MS is connnected with Bishop Ethelwald of Lichfield (818–30), but he does not consider the Northumbrian connection of the book (as regards its contents) to be necessarily affected by this. It makes little difference to my use of the book whether it is considered to be Northumbrian or Mercian.
42. F. Cabrol, 'Le *Book of Cerne*, les Liturgies Celtiques et Gallicanes et la Liturgie Romane', *Revue des Questions Historiques*, 76(1904), 210–22.
43. *The Book of Cerne*, ed. Dom A. B. Kuypers (1902), Prayer no. 10.
44. *H.E.*, IV, 23 (pp. 263–64).
45. *The Irish Penitentials*, ed. L. Bieler (Dublin, 1963) gives the earliest.
46. L. Bieler, 'The Irish Penitentials: their Religious and Social Background', *Studia Patristica*, VIII, pt. 2 (Berlin, 1966), ed. F. L. Cross, pp. 335–39.
47. *The Book of Cerne*, no. 6 (p. 90).
48. *Ibid.*, no. 17 (p. 109).
49. F. J. Byrne, 'Seventh-century Documents', *Irish Ecclesiastical Record*, 108(1967), 164–82, esp. 170–71; J. F. Kenney, *The Sources for the Early History of Ireland* (Columbia, 1929), vol. 1, nos. 109, 111. For the biblical commentary in particular, see B. Bischoff, 'Wendepunkte', etc. *Sacris Erudiri*, 6(1954), 209.
50. *The Book of Cerne*, p. 120.
51. *Ibid.*, pp. 118–19.

52. *The Stowe Missal*, ed. G. F. Warner, H. *Bradshaw Society*, 32(1906), II, pp. xxx–xxxvii for date and provenance, but J. F. Kenney, *Sources for . . . Ireland*, I, no. 555, p. 699, casts doubt on Warner's suggested ascription to Tallaght: For the early version of the Roman canon in this book, see K. Gamber, 'Ein Römisches Eucharistiegebiet aus dem 4–5 Jahrhundert', *Ephem. Liturg.*, 74(1960), esp. pp. 106–07; and E. Bishop, 'On the Early Texts of the Roman Canon', *Liturgica Historica*, pp. 92–94. For the early Irish palimpsest mass-book, see *Das Irische Palimpsestsakramentar in Clm 14429 der Staatsbibliothek München*, ed. A. Dold and L. Eizenhöfer, *Texte und Arbeiten* 53/54 (Beuron, 1964). For date, see Introduction pp. 30*–31*, and for relation to Gallican books, pp. 77*–96*.

53. *The Stowe Missal*, II, 13; *Das Irische Palimpsestsakramentar*, p. 16.

54. Edmund Bishop, *Liturgica Historica*, p. 84, and esp. p. 91, note 1. Also, *The Book of Cerne*, nos. 1, 10, 50.

55. E. Bishop, in *Liturgica Historica*, pp. 165–202; Cardinal Mercati, *Ibid.*, pp. 203–10; F. Cabrol, see note 42 above; for the reference to L. Traube, see Bishop, p. 165, note 2.

56. Sister A. Braegelmann, *The Life and Writings of Saint Ildefonsus of Toledo* (Washington D.C., 1942), esp. pp. 55–56. Edition by V. Blanco Garcia (Madrid, 1937); see esp. pp. 65–66 and 151 for comparison with the prayer cited below.

57. *The Book of Cerne*, no. 56 (p. 154).

58. W. Levison, *England and the Continent in the Eighth Century*, Appendix IX, pp. 295–302. The prayer is *Book of Cerne*, no. 58 (p. 155).

59. *The Book of Cerne*, no. 19, and see Edmund Bishop's Liturgical Note, *Ibid.*, pp. 253–54; A. Wilmart, 'Prières Mediévales pour l' Adoration de la Croix', *Ephem. Liturg.*, 46(1932), pp. 22–26.

60. *An Ancient Manuscript of Nunnaminster, Winchester*, ed. W. de Gray Birch, *Hampshire Record Society*, 5(1889), esp. p. 9, 17.

61. *Ibid.*, pp. 58–61, 84–88, 91–95.

62. *Ibid.*, pp. 62–66, 78–80. 1. Christmas prayer (p. 63) *Deus qui humanae* is up to *reformasti* as in the *Gelasianum*, no. 27 and the *Leonianum* no. 1239 (notes 24 and 2 above). 2. For the Epiphany prayer (p. 64), see introduction of A. B. Kuypers to Cerne, pp. xxvii–viii. 3. The Ascension prayer (pp. 79–80) relates to one of the prefaces for that feast in the *Leonianum* (*Veronensis*, no. 175). 4. The prayer *Deus qui conspicis* (p. 89) is a ferial collect in the *Gelasianum*, no. 1157.

63. *Ibid.*, pp. 67–78.

64. J. A. Jungmann, *The Early Liturgy*, pp. 101–02.

65. S. Salaville, 'Christus in Orientalium Pietate', *Ephem. Liturg.* 53(1939), 357–80; cf. *The Book of Nunnaminster*, p. 77.

66. S. Salaville, *Ibid.*, 52(1938), 224–26.

67. J. A. Jungmann, *The Place of Christ in Liturgical Prayer* (trans. A. Peeler, 1965), esp. pp. 93, 118–19, 217–22.

68. *The Book of Nunnaminster*, pp. 70–71. Contrast with the sober and patristic treatment of the same subject by Bede in his commentary on Mark XV, 16–18, in C.C. 120, p. 627.

69. *Aldhelmi Opera*, ed. R. Ehwald, *Mon. Germ. Hist.*, p. 17. On the spread of these festivals, see B. Capelle, *Travaux Liturgiques* III (Louvain, 1967), esp. pp. 276–79.

70. *Aethelwulf De Abbatibus*, ll. 460–64. The four feasts are the Assumption, the Nativity, the Purification, and the Annunciation. The poet's list is misunderstood on p. 36, note 5, of this generally excellent edition.

71. K. Wessel, *Coptic Art* (trans. J. Carroll and S. Hatton, 1965), plate 34; J. Beckwith, *Coptic Sculpture* (1963), plate 113. And for a discussion of another aspect of Constantinopolitan influence on the art of the Egyptian monasteries at this time, J. Beckwith, pp. 20–23.

72. For the latter, K. Wessel, plate 35. Examples of the suckling type are a limestone relief from Medinet-et-Faiyum (Wessel, pl. 5; Beckwith, pl. 50), and wall-paintings at Saqqara in Lower Egypt and Bawit in Upper Egypt (Wessel, pls. II, 33, 100). For discussion, see K. Wessel, pp. 120–23, and V. Lasareff, 'Studies in the Iconography of the Virgin', *Art Bulletin*, 20(1938), esp. pp. 28–29, 50.

73. K. Wessel, plate 36; J. Beckwith, plate 133. J. Beckwith dates this ivory to C8 or C9 (p. 56), but K. Wessel to C7 (p. 120.) Even if this type of representation, known as *Eleusa*, cannot be exampled before the ninth century, that is not to say that it did not exist earlier.

74. E. Kitzinger, 'The Coffin-Reliquary', *The Relics of St. Cuthbert*, ed. C. F. Battiscombe, pp. 248–64, esp. p. 261.

75. *The Book of Cerne*, no. 54 (p. 153). For a possible kind of model for the archangels on the coffin, namely a carved slab from the Hypogeum at Poitiers, see A. Clapham, *English Romanesque Architecture before the Conquest*, pp. 42–43, and fig. 14.

76. E. Kitzinger, pp. 276–77. See also *The Stonyhurst Gospel of Saint John*, ed. T. J. Brown, pp. 38–41.

77. *C.C.*, 122, pp. 452–70. See also, E. Bishop, *Liturgica Historica*, pp. 195–96, and Sister M. T. A. Carroll, *The Venerable Bede: His Spiritual Teachings*, pp. 209–11, and p. 210, note 204, for an illuminating quotation from Cassian in this connection.

78. *H.E.*, V, 24 (p. 360). Sister M. T. A. Carroll, p. 209 and esp.

p. 209, note 200, gives references to some such prayers in Bede's writings and in writings from the Lérins circle.

12. BOOKS AND STUDIES

1. P.L. 93, col. 456B–C. P. Lehmann, 'Wert und Echtheit einer Beda abgesprochenen Schrift', *Sitzungsberichte der Bayerischen Akademie der Wissenschaften, Phil-Hist. Kl.,* (Munich, 1919), no. 4, pp. 10–20.

2. L. Traube, 'Palaeographischen Anzeigen', *Neues Archiv für Deutsche Geschichtskunde,* 27(1901), 276–78.

3. W. Levison, *England and the Continent in the Eighth Century,* p. 133, note 1. For Felixstowe, see above, ch. 9, note 5.

4. The most interesting evidence of Whitby, its strengths and limitations, is the career of Bishop Oftfor of the Hwicce, who had studied there in the time of Hilda, but, *'tandem perfectiora desiderans, venit Cantiam ad archiepiscopum beatae recordationis Theodorum'* (*H.E.,* IV, 21, pp. 254–55). Breedon produced Tatwine, archbishop of Canterbury (731–34), whose *Riddles* and *Ars Grammatica* have been edited by Fr. Glorie and Maria de Marco, cc. 133, 133A.

Aldhelm

I am indebted to Mr M. B. Parkes for some helpful discussion on Aldhelm.

5. W. G. Hoskins, *The Westward Expansion of Wessex,* pp. 19–20.

6. ed. W. E. S. A. Hamilton (*Rolls Series,* 1870), pp. 330–443. A useful general survey of Aldhelm's life and writings is G. F. Browne, *St. Aldhelm: His Life and Times* (1903).

7. *Aldhelmi Opera,* ed. R. Ehwald, *Mon. Germ. Hist.,* Auct. Antiq. XV (Berlin, 1919), p. 494. For the chasuble and altar, see *Gesta Pontif.,* p. 365, for the Old and New Testaments, p. 376–78.

8. For a discussion of *Hisperica Famina,* see J. F. Kenney, *Sources for the Early History of Ireland,* i, no. 84 (pp. 255–58).

9. *H.E.,* V, 19 (p. 321): *sermone nitidus.*

10. *Aldhelmi Opera,* pp. 14–18, esp. pp. 17–18.

11. *Ibid.,* p. 229, note 1.

12. M. Manitius, 'Zu Aldhelm und Beda', *Sitzungsberichte der Kaiserlichen Akademie der Wissenschaften,* 112 (Vienna, 1886), 603–06.

13. *Aldhelmi Opera,* pp. 236–38.

14. *Ibid.,* pp. 246, 315.

15. For identification with Alfrith and for date, *Ibid.,* p. 61.

16. *Ibid.,* pp. 77–78.

17. B. Bischoff, 'Eine verschollene Einteilung der Wissenschaften', *Archives d'Histoire Doctrinale et Litteraire du Moyen Age,*

28(1958), 5–20. Aldhelm may have been familiar with Irish grammars which referred to this curriculum, like the commentary on Donatus contained in a Northumbrian manuscript of the early eighth century, now at the Benedictine monastery of St. Paul, Carinthia. (I am indebted to Dr. R. W. Hunt for drawing my attention to the discussion of this manuscript in particular within Professor Bischoff's article at p. 14.)

18. In the case of Origen, at least, the description of his studies by Aldhelm in *De Virg.* is taken from Jerome, his source (*P.L.*, 23, col. 665C).

19. Aldhelm sometimes refers to these seven subjects as the branches of *Physica*, sometimes more generally as the philosophical disciplines. The same seems to be true of Isidore, and it is not, therefore, an entirely convincing ground for questioning the authenticity of the *De Numeris* (Bischoff, p. 18, note 45) that they are described there as the seven *genera philosophiae*.

20. *Aldhelmi Opera*, pp. 475–78.

21. *Ibid., pp.* 490–91.

22. *Ibid.*, pp. 479–80.

23. M. R. James, *Two Ancient English Scholars, St. Aldhelm and William of Malmesbury* (Glasgow, 1931), pp. 13–14.

24. *Aldhelmi Opera*, p. 200.

25. *Ibid.*, p. 94.

26. C.L.A. XI, no. 1618; B. Bischoff, 'Die Europäische Verbreitung der Werke Isidors von Sevilla', *Isidoriana*, (Leon 1961), pp. 331, note 78, 334–35; W. M. Lindsay, *Early Irish Minuscule Script* (1910), pp. 10ff.

27. W. G. Hoskins, *The Westward Expansion of Wessex*, pp. 6–13.

28. *H.E.*, V, 3.

29. e.g. four times in the letter to King Geraint of Dumnonia, *Opera*, p. 483, notes 14, 16, 18, 22.

Aldhelm and Isidore of Seville

30. For what follows, see especially E. A. Thompson, *The Goths in Spain* (1969), pp. 7–180; J. M. Wallace-Hadrill, *The Barbarian West 400–1000* (Revised edition, 1967), chapter 6; J. Fontaine, *Isidore de Seville et la Culture Classique dans l'Espagne Wisigothique* (Paris, 1959), pp. 5–9, 831–861.

31. J. Fontaine, p. 29, and see the whole of the first section on Grammar.

32. *Ibid.*, p. 748–84, 849–54.

33. *Ibid.*, pp. 197–98; M. Manitius, 'Zu Aldhelm und Beda', pp. 589–91. On pp. 606–07 Manitius cites Audax on the *voces animantium*. Although Aldhelm derived his actual examples of animal noises from Suetonius (see *C. Suetonii Tranquilli, Praeter Caesarum*

Libros Reliquiae, ed. A. Reifferscheid, Leipzig, 1860, pp. 247–54), his opening exposition seems to come from Audax (contra the doubts of R. Ehwald, *Opera,* p. XX). For a passage easier to follow in Audax than in Aldhelm, compare Aldhelm on hexametres (*Opera,* pp. 81ff) with Keil, *Grammatici* VII, 336–41).

34. H. Farmer, 'The Studies of Anglo-Saxon Monks (A.D. 600–800)', *Los Monjes y los Estudios: IV Semana de Estudios Monasticos,* (Poblet, 1963), pp. 87–103; see p. 95.

35. Riddle 19. The edition of Aldhelm's riddles by Fr. Glorie in C.C., 133(1968) uses the English translation of J. H. Pitman, *The Riddles of Aldhelm,* (Yale, 1925). Translation here by same.

36. *Aldhelmi Opera,* p. XVIII.

37. *Ibid.,* p. 76.

38. *Etym.* I, 37, 26. See J. Fontaine, pp. 144–47.

39. *Aldhelmi Opera,* p. 75.

40. Riddle 15. Translation of J. H. Pitman.

41. *Etym.* XII, 4, 36.

42. The point is very well put in H. I. Marrou, *Saint Augustin et la Fin de la Culture Antique* (Paris, 1958), p. 407.

Theodore, Bede, and the Bible
   I am grateful to Dr Margaret Gibson for several helpful comments on this section.

43. For some examples of Antiochene influence in Europe, see M. L. W. Laistner, 'Antiochene Exegesis in Western Europe during the Middle Ages', *The Harvard Theological Review,* 40(1947), pp. 19–31.

44. For two highly illuminating and very different discussions of the allegorical method, see Beryl Smalley, *The Study of the Bible in the Middle Ages* (1952,) pp. 9–14, 20–26 and P. R. L. Brown, *Augustine of Hippo: A Biography,* pp. 259–63 (the phrase quoted is on p. 261). Miss Smalley discusses the Antiochenes especially on pp. 14–20.

45. *Ep.* II, 50.

46. *Ep.* III, 62.

47. On this subject see P. Courcelle, *Les Lettres Grecques en Occident de Macrobe à Cassiodore* (Paris, 1948). It is doubtful, for instance, whether the Irish would have had more than a few bits of Greek vocabulary which the possession of glosses would explain; see M. Roger, *L'Enseignement des Lettres Classiques d'Ausone à Alcuin* (Paris, 1905), pp. 268–71. On Bede, see M. L. W. Laistner, 'Bede as a Scholar' in *The Intellectual Heritage of the Early Middle Ages,* p. 113; on Aldhelm, *Aldhelmi Opera,* pp. XII–XIII. See, in general, B. Bischoff, 'Das Griechische Element in der abländischen Bildung des Mittelalters', *Byzantinische Zeitschrift,* 44(1951), esp.

pp. 27–32. On Theodore's earlier studies, see P. Riché, *Education et Culture dans l'Occident Barbare*, esp. p. 420, note 57. For the mediocrity of culture and small knowledge of Greek in seventh-century Rome, despite its being a source of manuscripts, see P. Riché, *Education et Culture dans l'Occident Barbare, 6ᵉ–8ᵉ Siècle* (Paris, 1962), pp. 393–400.

48. J. D. A. Ogilvy, *Books known to the English, 597–1066* (Cambridge, Mass., 1967), pp. 100–02, 107.

49. Claude Jenkins, 'Bede as Exegete and Theologian', in *Bede, His Life, Times and Writings*, pp. 157–64; *Bedae Venerabilis Expositio Actuum Apostolorum et Retractatio*, ed. M. L. W. Laistner (Camb., Mass., 1939), p. xiii, and at many points in the text.

50. Theodore of Mopsuestia's commentary on the Psalms was edited by R. Devreesse, *Studi e Testi*, 93(1939). A useful discussion of his methods is R. L. Ramsay, 'Theodore of Mopsuestia and St. Columban on the Psalms', *Zeitschrift für Celtische Philogie 8* (1912), although this article attributed to Columbanus a commentary which appears to be the work of Mopsuestia himself (*Sancti Columbani Opera*, ed. G. S. M. Walker, pp. lxiv–v). An interesting Anglo-Saxon Psalter with psalm headings of an Antiochene character, although surviving in a manuscript only of C11, might repay further study in this context, *The Paris Psalter*, ed. B. Colgrave (Early English Texts in Facsimile 8, 1958), also J. W. Bright and R. L. Ramsay (1907). There are some surviving fragments of Theodore of Mopsuestia's commentaries on St. Paul of C8 or C9, written probably at Anglo-Saxon Continental centres, e.g. C.L.A. I, no. 4; V, p. 42 **4.

51. B. Bischoff, 'Wendepunkte in der Geschichte der Lateinischen Exegese im Frümittelalter', *Sacris Erudiri*, 6(1954), 191–93. The arguments in favour of the identification are chiefly the combination of Greek rhetorical and Anglo-Saxon monetary terms, the relation of some of the glosses to Theodore's Penitential, and the actual mention of Theodore in a connected manuscript.

52. P. Lehmann, 'Wert und Echtheit', see above, this chapter, note 1, pp. 7–21.

53. *Ibid.*, pp. 4–5: *P.L.*, 93, cols, 456D–457A.

54. *Aldhelmi Opera*, p. 155.

55. Cassian's Conferences speak of an occasion when he himself and his companion ate a meal with the Egyptian hermit, Serenus, which included a fig each (*caricas singulas, Conlatio VIII*, 1, C.S.E.L. 13, 217). But this was in the desert of Scete on the West side of the Nile (O. Chadwick, *John Cassian*, p. 14), and only by the most erratic geography could Aldhelm be referring to this. Moreover, Serenus ate not five figs but only one in his daily meal. One might argue that Aldhelm, relying on his memory, was confusing the figs

with the five grains of vetch that Serenus ate in the same meal (*quina tantum sumpsimus grana*). Taken all in all, however, one can only suppose that Aldhelm was referring to this passage by stretching points and gratuitously assuming two muddles. I can find no other reference to any fig-eating hermit in Cassian. Even if Aldhelm's dependence on this passage of Cassian cannot be absolutely excluded, the arguments based on bubalus and tragelaphus would still seem to be particularly significant of likely influence of Theodore.

56. H&S, iii, 183, 198 (Pt. I, vii, 6; Pt. II, xi).

57. H. I. Marrou, *Saint Augustin* etc., pp. 377–79.

58. M. L. W. Laistner, *Thought and Letters in Western Europe, A.D. 500 to 900* (Reissued, Ithaca, N.Y., 1966), pp. 158–64; 'Bede as a Scholar' and 'The Library of the Venerable Bede' in *The Intellectual Heritage of the Early Middle Ages*, esp. 104–12, 124–25, 127–28, 138–39.

59. See M. L. W. Laistner, *A Hand-list of Bede Manuscripts* (Ithaca, N.Y., 1943).

60. *C.C.*, 120, pp. 5–7.

61. E. F. Sutcliffe, 'Quotations in the Venerable Bede's Commentary on St Mark', *Biblica*, 6(1927), 428–39; M. L. W. Laistner, in the *Journ. Theol. Studies*, 34(1933), 350–54.

62. G. Bonner, *Saint Bede in the Tradition of Western Apocalyptic Commentary*, (Jarrow Lecture, 1966).

63. M. L. W. Laistner, 'The Library of the Venerable Bede', pp. 136–38.

64. *Ibid.*, pp. 124–25; *Bedae Opera De Temporibus*, ed. C. W. Jones, pp. 125–26. The possibility for Biscop to have picked up a stray copy of the *Natural History* in Italy is suggested by the evidence of Italian fragments of this work, some of them palimpsests, from C5 or C6 e.g. C.L.A. IV, no. 421; V, no. 575; VI, no. 725; X, no. 1455. There is also a surviving copy, 'written apparently in North England' in C8 in Anglo-Saxon majuscule (C.L.A. X, no. 1578); this contains portions of Books II–VI.

65. *De Doctrina Christiana*, Bk II, 59–61 (C.S.E.L. 80, pp. 50–51). Translation of D. W. Robertson, Jr., *Saint Augustine On Christian Doctrine* (New York, 1958), pp. 50–51. See also, H. I. Marrou, pp. 447–49.

66. J. D. A. Ogilvy, p. 84.

67. *P.L.*, 91, cols. 1167D–1168A.

68. The Greek commentators on the Song of Songs in a general way doubtless shaped the Latin tradition of commentary, but there is no evidence that Bede himself knew their writings, certainly not where the passage under discussion is concerned. Origen's commentary was not extant down to this point in the book, or not in

the translation of Rufinus. The commentaries of Gregory of Nyssa (*Patrologiae Grecae* 44, cols. 1073–76) and of Theodoret of Cyrus (P.G. 81, cols. 161–64) on this verse are entirely different from Bede. 69. For the Latin commentary, see M. L. W. Laistner, 'Some Early Medieval Commentaries on the Old Testament' in *The Intellectual Heritage of the Early Middle Ages*, pp. 194–98. It has been shown by Dom B. Capelle (see *Ibid.*, p. 194) that the commentary attributed to Gregory the Great is, except for the passages on the first eight verses, much later. There is no point of contact between Bede and Justus of Urgell (P.L. 67, cols. 982D–983A) on this verse. Aponius's commentary is in *P.L. Supplementum* I, ed. A. Hamman (Paris, 1958). Although Bede, like Aponius, associates ivory with chastity, the general drift of their comments at this point is very different (for Aponius, cols. 943–44).
70. *Pliny: Natural History*, trans. H. Rackham (*Loeb Classical Library*), vol. 3, pp. 6–28 (Bk. VIII, 1–13) on elephants; vol. 3, p. 562 (Bk. XI, 82) on the stomach and ribs; vol. X (trans. D. E. Eichholz), p. 262 (Bk. XXXVII, 39) on sapphires. Isidore, *Etym.* XII, 2, 14–16, on elephants; *Etym.* XI, 1, 86 on bones, and XI, 1, 132 on the stomach (only the latter passage is relevant to Bede's comment); *Etym.* XVI, 9, 2, on sapphires.

Aldhelm and Bede
71. A letter of Cellanus of Péronne refers to the sermons, a letter of Lull to the poems. For these and William of Malmesbury's reference, see *Aldhelmi Opera*, p. XVII. Ehwald showed that an apparent allusion to a lost treatise on names seems so only as the result of a textual confusion (*Ibid.*, p. XVI). For references in catalogues, etc. between C7 and C11 to manuscripts of Aldhelm in monastic libraries, see e.g. E. Lesne, *Histoire de la Propriété Ecclésiastique en France*, vol. IV, pp. 76, note 1, 532, 573, 633, 642, 666, 711, 716, 731, 734, 757, 773.
72. *Aldhelmi Opera*, p. 500.
73. Quoted by M. T. A. Carroll, *The Venerable Bede: His Spiritual Teachings*, p. 40, note 205. For the background to Bede's attitude here, see M. L. W. Laistner, 'The Christian Attitude to Pagan Literature', *History*, 20(1935), 49–54; P. Riché, *Education et Culture dans l'Occident Barbare*, pp. 187–200, 438–39; Sister M. T. A. Carroll, pp. 40–43.
74. M. Manitius, 'Zu Aldhelm und Beda', pp. 547–61.
75. *De Arte Metrica*, in Keil, *Grammatici Latini*, VII, 260: *Haec tibi, dulcissime fili et conlevita Gutberte....*
76. The Letter to Acircius can be no earlier than 685, and Aldhelm became a priest at latest in 675 (William of Malmesbury, *Gesta Pontificum*, pp. 347–48).

77. *Ibid.*, p. 336.
78. J. Fontaine, *Isidore de Seville et la Culture Classique*, p. 796.
79. *Ibid.*, p. 800.
80. *C.C.*, 118A, p. 124. See also B. Capelle, 'Le Rôle Théologique de Bede le Vénérable', *Studia Anselmiana*, 6 (1936), p. 29, note 1.
81. e.g. on Samuel, *C.C.* 119, p. 47, ll. 1490–91; on Esras and Nehemiah, *C.C.*, 119A, p. 258.
82. Comment on I Esd. vii, 6, in *C.C.*, 119A, pp. 307–08.
83. *Venerabilis Bedae Opera Historica*, ed. C. Plummer, I, pp. clxii–clxiv. Translation, pp. lxxv–vii.
84. *P.L.*, 91, cols. 1223–36.
85. Ph. Delhaye, 'Les Idées morales de Saint Isidore de Seville', *Recherches de Theol. Anc. et Med.*, 26(1959), p. 30 (and see *P.L.*, 83, cols. 96–98). The quotation is also on p. 30.
86. B. Capelle, as in note 80 above.
87. *C.C.*, 119A, pp. 258, 262.
88. *Ibid.*, pp. 278–79.
89. *Ibid.*, p. 277.

13. SAINTS AND HEROES

1. K. Sisam, 'Anglo-Saxon Royal Genealogies', *Proc. Bt. Acad.*, 39(1953), pp. 287–346.
2. e.g. *The Dream of the Rood*, ed. Bruce Dickins and A. S. C. Ross (1963), p. 26, line 44. Translation in R. K. Gordon, *Anglo-Saxon Poetry*, p. 236. See also below, pp. 255–56.
3. W. A. Chaney, *The Cult of Kingship in Anglo-Saxon England* (1970), pp. 48–49.
4. *H.E.*, II, 16.
5. See M. L. W. Laistner, *Thought and Letters in Western Europe, 500–900*, pp. 144–45; D. A. Binchy, *Celtic and Anglo-Saxon Kingship* (1970), pp. 10–11. It is noticeable to what extent several of the laws of King Ine of Wessex (688–94), with their concern for agriculture, the protection of widows, foreigners and the poor, etc., fit the notion of the king's justice as described in this Irish tract, the *De Duodecim Abusivis Saeculi* (c.630–50). There may be something of the influence of Aldhelm here. For the tract, see M. L. W. Laistner, *Thought and Letters in Western Europe, 500–900*, pp. 144–45.

Heroic Sagas
6. G. Baldwin Brown, *The Arts in Early England*, VI, pt. 1 (1930), pp. 30–49. The casket is now in the British Museum.
7. *The Northmen Talk: A Choice of Tales from Iceland*, trans. Jacqueline Simpson (1965), pp. 29–36. This translation is from the

Poetic Edda of Iceland; the tale is known in earlier, less full, versions.

8. T. C. Lethbridge, *Recent Excavations in Anglo-Saxon Cemeteries in Cambridgeshire and Suffolk: A Report* (*Cambridge Antiq. Soc. Publications*, 1931), Plate III and p. 70. See also H. R. Ellis Davidson, 'Gods and Heroes in Stone', *H.M. Chadwick Memorial Studies* (1950), pp. 135–36.

9. At an early stage Ceolfrid had to suffer '*invidias quorundam nobilium, qui regularem eius disciplinam ferre nequibant*' (*Historia Abbatum auctore Anonymo, Baedae Opera Historica*, i, 390). For the Synod of Cloveshoe (c.12), see H&S, iii, 366.

10. J. Campbell, 'Bede', *Latin Historians*, ed. T. A. Dorey, p. 174.

11. *H.E.*, II, 9 (pp. 98–99). Everyman Translation.

12. See C. E. Wright, *The Cultivation of Saga in Anglo-Saxon England* (1939), pp. 80–82.

13. *Alcuini Epistolae*, ed. E. Dümmler, *Mon. Germ. Hist.*, Epist. IV (Karolini Aevi II), (Berlin, 1895), no. 124, p. 183. Cf. nos. 16–22.

14. *Beowulf*, ed. C. L. Wrenn (1958), ll.2024–69. Trans. David Wright in *Penguin Classics*. For an interpretation of this passage, see R. W. Chambers, *Beowulf, An Introduction* (3rd Edition, 1959), pp. 20–25, 282.

15. *Two Lives of St. Cuthbert*, ed. B. Colgrave, Bede, c.27, p. 246.

16. e.g. *H.E.*, IV, 20 (p. 250—*litteras solutorias, de qualibus fabulae ferunt*: see above, p. 30); *H.E.*, IV, 23 (p. 265, line 15).

17. Robert Brentano, *The Early Middle Ages, 500–1000* (1964), pp. 31–32, 230–53.

18. *The Anglo-Saxon Chronicle*, ed. and trans. Dorothy Whitelock, pp. 30–31. See also C. L. Wrenn, 'A Saga of the Anglo-Saxons', *History*, 25(1940), 208–15.

19. Willibald's Life of St Boniface, in C. H. Talbot, *The Anglo-Saxon Missionaries in Germany*, pp. 55–58.

20. Eddius, c.63; *Beowulf*, ll.2745–51.

21. *The Relics of St. Cuthbert*, ed. C. F. Battiscombe.

22. Quoted in translation by Dorothy Whitelock, 'Anglo-Saxon Poetry and the Historian', *Trans. Roy. Hist. Soc.*, (1949), p. 89. On this point there are some illuminating comments by E. John, '*Secularium Prioratus* and the Rule of St. Benedict', *Rev. Benedictine*, 75(1965), p. 216, note 2.

23. Dorothy Whitelock, *The Audience of Beowulf*, (1951), pp. 13–19.

24. J. M. Wallace-Hadrill, 'The Bloodfeud of the Franks', *The Long-Haired Kings*, esp. p. 127.

25. Eddius, c.44; *H.E.*, II, 2.

Guthlac, Beowulf and Anthony the Hermit
26. *Felix's Life of Saint Guthlac*, ed B. Colgrave, Introduction and Text. See also B. Colgrave, 'The Earliest Saints' Lives written in England', *Proc. Bt. Acad.* 44(1958), pp. 35–60; M. Schütt, 'Von heiligen Antonius zum heiligen Guthlac,' *Antike und Abendland* 5(1956), 75–91.
27. C. Fox, *Offa's Dyke* (1955), Foreword by F. M. Stenton, pp. xx–xxi.
28. *Life of Guthlac*, cc.29–36.
29. G. V. Smithers, *The Making of Beowulf*, (Durham, 1961), p. 5.
30. K. Sisam, *The Structure of Beowulf*, (1965), pp. 10–11.
31. R. W. Chambers, *Beowulf*, pp. 48–56, 62–68, 138–82: G. V. Smithers, esp. pp. 6–7.
32. G. V. Smithers, pp. 7–12, and esp. 14–16: Nora K. Chadwick, 'The Monsters and Beowulf' in *The Anglo-Saxons: Studies presented to Bruce Dickins*, ed. P. Clemoes (1959), pp. 171–203, esp. pp. 178–86.
33. R. W. Chambers, pp. 466–68; G. V. Smithers, p. 9.
34. G. V. Smithers, pp. 17–19.
35. *Ibid.*, pp. 11, 15.
36. R. W. Chambers, pp. 2–4, 381–87; Dorothy Whitelock, *The Audience of Beowulf*, pp. 39–40.
37. R. W. Chambers, pp. 16–20.
38. A. Bonjour, *The Digressions in Beowulf* (1950), pp. 36–43; *Beowulf*, ed. C. L. Wrenn, pp. 47–49, 51–53.
39. Dorothy Whitelock, *The Audience of Beowulf*, pp. 80–81.
40. Professor G. V. Smithers (p. 9) writes of the 'repeated references to Beowulf's feat in overcoming Grendel as an act of "purification" of the hall; the equivalent word *hreinsa(n)* is applied in Old Norse sagas to the act of ridding an area or an abode of trolls who haunt them. Beowulf is in fact an exorcist as well as a hero.'
41. *Life of Guthlac*, c.32.
42. R. W. Chambers, pp. 99–104.
43. R. L. S. Bruce-Mitford, *The Sutton Hoo Ship Burial, A Handbook*, (1968), pp. 69–71.
44. H. Vierck, 'Zum Fernvekehr über See im 6 Jahrhundert,' in K. Hauck, *Goldbrakteaten aus Sievern* (1970), pp. 355–95. On whether the Wuffingas of East Anglia were Swedes or Geats, see J. L. N. O'Loughlin in *Medieval Archaeology* 8(1964) pp. 1–19, and R. T. Farrell, Beowulf, Swedes and Geats,' *Saga Book of the Viking Soc.* 1972.
Other interesting studies of the relation of *Beowulf* to Sutton Hoo are: C. L. Wrenn, in R. W. Chamber's 3rd Edition, pp. 508–23; Rosemary Cramp, 'Beowulf and Archaeology', *Medieval Archaeology*, 1(1957), esp. pp. 60–63 on the helmets of *Beowulf* and Sutton Hoo.

45. Dorothy Whitelock, *The Audience of Beowulf*, c.1, and R. W. Chambers, pp. 121–28.

46. K. Sisam, pp. 19–20, 72–79.

47. J. R. R. Tolkien, 'Beowulf: The Monsters and the Critics', *Proc. Bt. Acad.*, 22(1936), esp. pp. 18–27.

48. *Ibid.*, p. 23.

49. *Ibid.*, pp. 28–29. This is the argument of Professor Bonjour's book, see above, note 38.

50. K. Sisam, pp. 25–26.

51. *Life of Guthlac*, cc.18–19.

52. *Athanasius's Life of St Anthony*, translated from Greek by R. T. Meyer, *Ancient Christians Writers* X (1950).

53. Quoted by R. T. Meyer in his introduction, p. 6.

54. e.g. K. Wessel, *Coptic Art*, plates 37–40, and p. 36.

55. L. Bouyer, *La Vie de S. Antoine* (St Wandrille, 1950), see esp. pp. 67–86. For some imaginative pages on Anthony, see also D. J. Chitty, *The Desert A City*, pp. 1–7.

56. cc.16–43.

57. *Life of Anthony*, c.4; *Life of Felix*, c.23. For a time Anthony lived in a tomb (c.8).

58. *Life of Anthony*, cc. 7, 25; *Life of Guthlac*, c.30.

59. *Life of Anthony*, cc.9, 28; *Life of Guthlac*, cc.31, 36.

14. CHURCH AND LAITY
Pastoral Organization

1. *Two Lives of St. Cuthbert*, Bede, c.3. Translation of B. Colgrave.

2. *C.C.*, 119, pp. 46–47.

3. *Life of Guthlac*, c.48.

4. H&S, iii, 216–17.

5. *Ibid.*, p. 194 (Penitential, pt. 2, IV, 11).

6. See Kathleen Hughes, *The Church in Early Irish Society*, pp. 44–7.

7. *Bedae Opera Historica*, ed. C. Plummer, i, 412–13.

8. *Historic Towns*, ed M. D. Lobel (1969), vol. 1, Hereford, p.1.

9. *Bedae Opera Historica*, ii, 208. For Wilfrid's covering of the church roof at York with lead, see Eddius, c.16. For the peak dwellers, see A. Ozanne, 'The Peak Dwellers', *Medieval Archaeology*, 6(1962), esp. p. 35. For the last reference, and for the point about Lichfield as a whole, I am indebted to the unpublished B. A. Thesis of Miss Catherine Hills (Durham, 1969).

10. *Two Lives of St. Cuthbert*, Anon. II, 5; Bede. cc. 8–9.

11. F. M. Stenton, 'Medeshamstede and its Colonies', *Historical Essays in Honour of James Tait*, (1933), pp. 313–26, esp. p. 316.

12. *Bedae Opera Historica*, i, 409.

13. C. A. Ralegh Radford, 'The Portable Altar of Saint Cuthbert', in *The Relics of St. Cuthbert*, pp. 326–35.

14. *The Stowe Missal*, see Chapter XI, note 52 above. For books of a related kind, namely the pocket gospel books, see P. McGurk, 'The Irish Pocket Gospel Book', *Sacris Erudiri*, 2(1956), pp. 249–70.

14a. Recently the magical significance which was attached to such books and their use as amulets by the clergy have been emphasized in *The Stonyhurst Gospel of Saint John*, ed. T. J. Brown, pp. 30–38.

15. *C.C.*, 122, ed. D. Hurst.

16. *C.C.*, 103, 104. ed. G. Morin (for edition). See also H. G. J. Beck, *The Pastoral Care of Souls in South-East France during the Sixth Century* (Rome, 1950), pp. 120–25. On lack of knowledge of Caesarius in England, see J. D. A. Ogilvy, *Books known to the English, 597–1066*, p. 103.

17. M. Deanesly, 'Early English and Gallic Minsters', *T.R.H.S.*, (1941), pp. 25–52. There are some useful observations on minsters and oratories in G. W. O. Addleshaw, *The Pastoral Organization of the Modern Dioceses of Durham and Newcastle in the Time of Bede* (Jarrow Lecture, 1963), esp. pp. 9–11. Also John Godfrey, *The English Parish 600–1300*, (1969), chapters 1 and 2.

18. H&S, iii, e.g. c.6, p. 364.

19. J. A. Robinson, *St. Oswald and the Church of Worcester*, British Academy Supplemental Papers V (1919), pp. 9–10. The charter is C.S.295. Margaret Deanesly, "The Familia at Christchurch, Canterbury 597–832', *Essays pres. to T. F. Tout*, (1925), esp. pp. 8–13.

20. See P. Riché, *Education at Culture dans l'Occident Barbare*, pp. 328–31.

21. *Life of Guthlac*, c.47.

22. For the example of Beverley, see *H.E.*, V, 2 and 6.

23. *H.E.*, *V. 4 and 5. Two Lives of St. Cuthbert*, Anon., IV, 10; Bede, c.34. The last reference is to Ovington which the Anonymous Life makes to appear like a parish church by saying that Cuthbert consecrated it *in parrochia eius, quae dicitur Osingadun*. But the word *parrochia* is used at this period to mean diocese or the sphere of a monastery's authority rather than parish in our sense, and the text appears to need an emendation to make this clear. Bede shows that what is in question is an estate of the monastery of Whitby, apparently with another monastery on it. This was no parish church, in the later sense.

24. *H.E.*, V, 12, (p. 304), and see *Bedae Opera Historica*, ii, 294.

25. Quoted *ibid.*, i, p. xiii. Text in *C.C.*, 120. p. 575.

26. The fifth canon of the Synod of Cloveshoe (747), *De Monasteriis Saecularium*, seems to speak of such family monasteries in laying down that, for all their undesirability, bishops shall see that they do not lack the ministry of a priest. (H&S, iii, 364).

27. *Two Lives of St. Cuthbert*, Anon., IV, 3 and 7.

28. H&S, iii, 365 (c.9).

29. C. H. Talbot, *Anglo-Saxon Missionaries in Germany*, p. 155.

30. Rosalind Hill, 'Christianity and Geography in Early North-umbria', *Studies in Church History*, vol. 3 (1966), ed. G. J. Cuming, esp. pp. 133–39. It is possible that some of these crosses were placed at the sites of early popular courts, and that the organization of such courts was used by Christian clergy. It would be an obvious missionary or pastoral method, if popular courts were already in existence in some form in the seventh century (as they might well have been). Several hundred names end with the element -cross, and it would be interesting to discover how many of these could be taken back to this period.

Some Social Institutions

31. H&S, iii, 180 (Theodore's Penitential, pt. 1, IV, 5).

32. *Life of Guthlac*, cc.49, 52.

33. *H.E.*, I, 27 (p. 56). Less compromising than Gregory the Great to Augustine is Theodore's Penitential, pt. 1, XIV, 17 (H&S, iii, 188–89).

34. Theodore's Penitential, pt. 2, XII, 12, 16, 17, 25 (H&S, iii, pp. 200–01. See Dorothy Whitelock, *The Beginnings of English Society* (1952), pp. 149–52.

35. F. M. Stenton, *Anglo-Saxon England* (1943), pp. 140–41.

36. See Eric John, 'The Social and Political Problems of the Early English Church' *Agric. Hist. Rev.*, 18(1970) Supplement, pp. 61–62, note 8.

37. Lorraine Lancaster, 'Kinship in Anglo-Saxon Society', *Journal of British Sociology*, 9(1958), esp. pp. 233–37.

38. D. A. Bullough, 'Early Medieval Social Groupings: The Terminology of Kinship', *Past and Present*, 45(1969), esp. pp. 13–15.

39. Lorraine Lancaster, p. 239.

40. Dorothy Whitelock, *The Beginnings of English Society*, pp. 42–43.

41 H&S, iii, 214–15.

42. Egbert's *Dialogue*, XII, H&S, iii, 408–09.

43. *English Historical Documents c.500–1042*, ed. Dorothy Whitelock, p. 370 (Ine, c.51).

44. *Beowulf*, ll.2195–96.

45. Eric John, *Land Tenure in Early England* (1960), pp. 50–51.

46. *Ibid.*, pp. 61–62, and esp. p. 62, note 1. This view is doubted by D. A. Bullough, 'Anglo-Saxon Institutions and Early English Society', *Annali della Fondazione Italiana per la Storia Amministrativa*, II, (Milan, 1965), p. 652, note 21.

47. Eric John, *Land Tenure in Early England*, chapters 1–4, esp. 3.

48. *Bedae Opera Historica*, i, 414–17.

49. *Ibid.*, p. 375.

50. H. P. R. Finberg, *The Early Charters of the Western Midlands* (1961), p. 161: with reference to the original foundation of St. Peter's monastery, Gloucester.

51. W. Levison, *England and the Continent in the Eighth Century*, p. 167.

Lay Society and the Monastic Ideal

52. See, for instance, Peter Munz, 'John Cassian', *Journ. Eccl. Hist.*, 11(1960), 1–22; R. E. Sullivan, 'Some Influences of Monasticism on Fourth and Fifth-Century Society', *Studies in Medieval Culture*, II, ed. J. R. Sommerfeldt (Western Michigan University, 1966), pp. 19–34.

53. *H.E.*, III, 6, 22, 14.

54. *Athanasius's Life of St. Anthony*, c.4.

55. R. K. Gordon, *Anglo-Saxon Poetry* (1954), p. 96.

56. *H.E.*, III, 3.

57. Bede's story about Oswin illustrates his humility, humility is one of the virtues which Bede explicitly ascribes to Oswald (*H.E.*, III, 6), and Sigbert of the East Saxons showed his humility by prostrating himself before Cedd and asking the bishop's pardon for entering the house of the excommunicated earl (*H.E.*, III, 22).

58. Sister M. T. A. Carroll, *The Venerable Bede: His Spiritual Teachings*, p. 148, and esp. pp. 225–27.

59. *Bedae Venerabilis Expositio Actuum Apostolorum et Retractatio*, ed. M. L. W. Laistner, p. 16.

60. *H.E.*, III, 26.

61. *Two Lives of St. Cuthbert*, Bede, cc.9, 16, 5. See also *H.E.*, III, 26 (p. 191).

62. For this and what follows, see B. Poschmann, *Die Abendländische Kirchenbusse im frühen Mittelalter* (Breslau, 1930), pp. 24–35.

63. *Ibid.*, pp. 25–28; L. Bieler, 'The Irish Penitentials: Their Religious and Social Background', *Studia Patristica*, VIII, pt. 2, ed. F. L. Cross (1966), pp. 329–39.

64. B. Poschmann, p. 35. Leo I forbade the sins of public penitents to be read out before the congregation, and Augustine of Hippo said that where the sin was secret, the correction ought also to be.

65. Those who repeated their sins of homicide, adultery or theft were required by Theodore's Penitential to enter a monastery and do penance until their death, Bk. I, VII, 1 (H&S, III, 182).

66. See preface, H&S, iii, 176–77. Also B. Poschmann, pp. 38–40, and for the dates of the penitentials attributed to Egbert and Bede, pp. 42–43: H. J. Schmitz, *Die Bussbücher und die Bussdisciplin der Kirche* (Mainz, 1883), pp. 510–24.

67. For the text and manuscript transmission, see P. W.

Finsterwalder, *Die Canones Theodori Cantuariensis und ihre Uberlieferungsformen* (Weimar, 1929), esp. pp. 22–44, 214–25.
68. Bk. I, VII, 3 (H&S, iii, 183). By 747 the payment of money had already developed as a further method of commutation (Cloveshoe, c.26, H&S, iii, 371–72) and the path to indulgences was open.
69. B. Poschmann, pp. 49–50. This point is also made by R. W. Southern. 'The Church of the Dark Ages, 600–1000' in *The Layman in Christian History*, ed. S. Neill and H-R. Weber (1963), pp. 91–92.
70. Pt. 1, 1, 5; II, 10; II, 6 (H&S, iii, 177–78).
71. Pt. 2, II, 15 (*Ibid.*, p. 192).
72. Pt. 1, III, 3 (*Ibid.*, p. 179).
73. Pt. 1, XV, 5 (*Ibid.*, p. 190).
74. Sister M. T. A. Carroll, *The Venerable Bede* etc., pp. 165, 175, note 218.
75. H&S, iii, 412–13.
76. Rosemary Cramp, *Early Northumbrian Sculpture*, pp. 10–12. For the influence of Romano-British sculpture, see R. L. S. Bruce-Mitford in *Codex Lindisfarnensis*, ii, pp. 115–16; and E. Mercer, 'The Ruthwell and Bewcastle Crosses', *Antiquity*, 38(1964), 275–76.
77. W. G. Collingwood, *Northumbrian Crosses of the Pre-Norman Age* (1927), pp. 31–33, 37–38.
78. Meyer Schapiro, 'The Religious Meaning of the Ruthwell Cross', *Art Bulletin*, 26(1944), 232–45. Françoise Henry, *Irish Art before 800*, pp. 149–50 for a comparison of the schemes of Ruthwell and Moone; she regards the relation as one of parallel development rather than of Irish influence on Northumbria.

EPILOGUE

1. See E. John, 'The King and the Monks in the Tenth-Century Reformation', *Orbis Britanniae*, esp. pp. 154–56.
2. W. Levison, *England and the Continent in the Eighth Century*, p. 140.
3. *De Sanctis Eburac. Ecclesiae*, ll. 1276–77, *Mon. Germ. Hist. Poetarum Lat. Med. Aev.* (1880–81), p. 197.
4. *Alcuini Epistolae*, ed. E. Dümmler, *Mon. Germ. Hist.*, Ep. Karolini, II, (1895), no. 18, p. 51. For the Irish tract, see M. L. W. Laistner, *Thought and Letters in Western Europe, 500–900*, p. 145.
5. Edmund Bishop, *Liturgica Historica*, p. 55, note 1. For Alcuin's private prayers, see P.L., 101, cols. 465ff., and *Dictionnaire Chrétien d' Archéol. et de Liturgie*, ed. F. Cabrol (Paris, 1907), article on Alcuin by F. Cabrol, esp. p. 1082. References to Book of Cerne, *Ibid.*, note 12; and see *Book of Cerne*, pp. XXIV–XXV, XXX, 174, 232, 233, 277.

6. H. M. Bannister, 'Liturgical Fragments', *Journ. Theol. Studies*, 9(1908), 398–411.

7. W. Levison, p. 149.

APPENDIX 1

1. S. Brechter, *Die Quellen zur Angelsachsenmission Gregors den Grossen* (Münster, 1941)); 'Zur Bekehrungsgeschichte der Angel Sachsen', *Settimane di Studio del Centro Italiano di Studi sull' Alto Medioevo*, 14(Spoleto, 1967), pp. 191–215; and discussion, pp. 497–516.

2. S. Brechter, 'Zur Bekehrungsgeschichte', see esp. pp. 205–07.

3. *Settimano di Studio*, 14 (Spoleto, 1967), p. 503.

4. *Ibid.*, p. 503.

5. *Ibid.*, pp. 500–01.

6. *Ibid.*, p. 504.

7. *Ibid.*, p. 502.

8. S. Brechter, *Die Quellen*, pp. 240–52 for this argument. The letters of Gregory are Ep. VIII, 29 to Eulogius of Alexandria, Ep. XI, 35 to Bertha, and Ep. XI, 37 to Ethelbert.

9. R. A. Markus, 'The Chronology of the Gregorian Mission to England: Bede's Narrative and Gregory's Correspondence', *Journ. of Ecclesiastical Hist.*, 14(1963), pp. 16–30.

10. I cannot attach the weight to the word *roborate* which Dr. Markus attaches to it where Gregory exhorts Bertha to *strengthen* the mind of her husband in love of the faith (p. 21). This, says Dr. Markus, would be at best odd if Ethelbert were not already a Christian. To me it would seem an equally natural word to use whether Ethelbert were a Christian who needed to show more fervour or a pagan still undecided about baptism. It is not his faith which is to be strengthened, but his mind.

11. *Settimane di Studio*, pp. 204–05, and see R. A. Markus, pp. 20–21.

12. P. Meyvaert, 'Les Responsiones de S. Grégoire le Grande a St. Augustin de Cantorbéry', *Revue d'Histoire Ecclesiastique*, 54(1959), p. 889.

13. S. Brechter, *Die Quellen*, pp. 68–72. The text of Gregory's work is *H.E.*, I, 27.

14. See, for instance, references to the writings of H. Ashworth, C. Vogel, and F. L. Cross, in Chapter XI, notes 9 and 15, above.

15. S. Brechter, *Die Quellen*, pp. 72–74.

16. *Ibid.*, pp. 81–89.

17. As do M. Deanesly and P. Grosjean, 'The Canterbury Edition of the Answers of Pope Gregory I to St. Augustine', *Journ. Eccl. Hist.*, 10(1959), 1–49. We say this in spite of confusions pointed out by

P. Meyvaert (see note 11 above) and by D. Bullough, 'The Language of Kinship', *Past and Present*, 45(1969), pp. 8–9, note 14, in their actual arguments.

APPENDIX II

1. The argument of A. Chavasse, *Le Sacramentaire Gélasien*, has been criticized in various particulars by C. Coebergh in *Archiv. für Liturgiewissenschaft*, vii, 1(1961), esp. pp. 58–65 and 71–74. But the basis of it seems to stand.
2. See Chapter XI, note 9, above.
3. For a summary of this subject, see C. Vogel, *Introduction aux Sources de l'Histoire de Culte Chrétien au Moyen Age* (Spoleto, 1966), pp. 58–67.
4. E. Bishop, 'The Earliest Roman Mass-Book' in *Liturgica Historica*, pp. 39–61. For useful observations about the liturgical reforms of the Carolingian period, some of them opposed to the traditional views, see C. Hohler in *Journ. Eccl. Hist.*, 8(1957), 222–26.
5. H&S, iii, 367.
6. *Ibid.*, p. 412.
7. For this view, see, for instance, E. Bourque, *Les Sacramentaires Romains* (Rome, 1948), i, 379–86.
8. A. Baumstark, *Untersuchungen*, in K. Mohlberg's edition of *Paduensis* (see above, Chapter XI, note 9), pp. 62*–70*.
9. H. Frank, 'Die Briefe des Heiligen Bonifatius und das von ihm benutzte Sakramentar', *Bonifatius Gedenkgabe*, (1954), pp. 60–72.
10: C. Hohler, 'The Type of Sacramentary used by St Boniface', *Ibid.*, pp. 89–93.
11. Namely that printed in P.L. 78, and B.M. Add. MS 18955. Sections (including those most likely to be relevant) are missing in Add. MSS 24075 and 30058.
12. So much is this the case if one compares *Paduensis* (see K. Mohlberg, pp. XXXV–VI, and C. Vogel, p. 71) with the OE Martyrology (see A. Baumstark, *Untersuchungen*, pp. 65*–70*) that there seems a strong possibility that the two were connected in some way, although, of course, the martyrology drew on many sources.

Index